TRAVELER

new zealand

NATIONAL GEOGRAPHIC
TRAVELER

new zealand

By Peter Turner
photography by Colin Monteath

National Geographic
Washington, D.C.

CONTENTS

Pages 2–3: Sheep graze near Moeraki Beach, Otago, South Island.
Left: Hikers enjoy South Island's Routeburn Track.

TRAVELING WITH EYES OPEN

Alert travelers go with a purpose and leave with a benefit. If you travel responsibly, you can help support wildlife conservation, historic preservation, and cultural enrichment in the places you visit. You can enrich your own travel experience as well.

To be a geo-savvy traveler:

- Recognize that your presence has an impact on the places you visit.

- Spend your time and money in ways that sustain local character. (Besides, it's more interesting that way.)

- Value the destination's natural and cultural heritage.

- Respect the local customs and traditions.

- Express appreciation to local people about things you find interesting and unique to the place: its nature and scenery, music and food, historic villages and buildings.

- Vote with your wallet: Support the people who support the place, patronizing businesses that make an effort to celebrate and protect what's special there. Seek out local shops, restaurants, and inns. Use tour operators who love their home—who love taking care of it and showing it off. Avoid businesses that detract from the character of the place.

- Enrich yourself, taking home memories and stories to tell, knowing that you have contributed to the preservation and enhancement of the destination.

That is the type of travel now called geotourism, defined as "tourism that sustains or enhances the geographical character of a place—its environment, culture, aesthetics, heritage, and the well-being of its residents." To learn more, visit National Geographic's Center for Sustainable Destinations at *travel.nationalgeographic.com/travel/geotourism.*

new zealand

ABOUT THE AUTHOR & THE PHOTOGRAPHER

Drawn by family ties and a love of New Zealand's natural splendor, **Peter Turner** has been a regular visitor to the Land of the Long White Cloud for more than two decades, traveling the length and breadth of the country numerous times on writing assignments. Australian by birth, journalist by trade, and wanderer by nature, he has worked as an editor, publisher, and journalist in Australia and for newspapers in Indonesia, Thailand, and Brunei. As a travel writer and photographer specializing in Southeast Asia and the South Pacific, he has contributed to newspapers and magazines worldwide and to more than 20 guidebooks.

Based in Christchurch, New Zealand, **Colin Monteath** is a freelance photographer, writer, and mountaineer who has traveled widely in the polar and high mountain regions of the world. In 1983, he started Hedgehog House New Zealand, a photographic library that specializes in polar, mountain, natural history, and travel imagery.

Colin has spent 28 seasons working in Antarctica (and four in the Arctic) and has taken part in 21 Himalayan expeditions. His assignments have taken him to numerous countries and to nearly every continent, and his pictures and stories have appeared in *National Geographic, Time, New Zealand Geographic,* and many other publications around the world.

Charting Your Trip

Nature has blessed the big islands of the South Pacific with many magnificent landscapes: peaks, deserts, volcanoes, seas, forests, and beaches. Here's how to make the most of your visit.

In addition to being a quite spectacular natural paradise, New Zealand is also a fascinating mix of cultures, its cities steeped in English heritage and its society shaped by Maori history. Always welcoming, easy to navigate, and with fine facilities, New Zealand offers a host of fresh-air activities, from outdoor adventures to wildlife viewing.

Admission Costs

The $–$$$$$ scale used in this guidebook delineates entry fees into attractions in New Zealand dollars:
  $ = Under $20
  $$ = $20–$30
  $$$ = $30–$40
  $$$$ = $40–$50
  $$$$$ = Over $50

How to Visit

New Zealand is neatly divided into two similarly sized islands, both wonderfully scenic in their own way and with their own character. If you are on a short visit of a week or so, it's best to concentrate on one island, but, with a little planning ahead, it's also possible to experience all the highlights of both.

A one-week highlights tour would include Auckland, Rotorua, Christchurch, Aoraki/Mount Cook, Queenstown, Milford Sound, and a return to Christchurch/Auckland. That itinerary is action-packed, and is best arranged as a package tour with internal flights and arranged bus transportation. However, if you have the time to travel at a more leisurely pace, you can easily get around independently by car; buses and flights are also readily available to the traveler.

Two or three weeks will allow you to fully appreciate the islands of New Zealand without busting a gut. In two weeks, you can savor all the highlights of the North and South Islands listed above, while three weeks or more will give you access to a host of other wonderful places.

Starting in the North

The main attractions of the North Island are Maori culture, the volcanoes, and the beaches. More intensively farmed and populated, the North Island provides more settled, rural vistas, but natural wonders also abound. A North Island one-week tour might be: Auckland, Bay of Islands, Rotorua, Lake Taupo,

Maori carving

Tongariro National Park, and Wellington. With a rental car you could also make a few side trips. Bus tours include a number of points of interest between the main sights.

The first stop for most visitors is the country's main metropolis of Auckland, lying on a wonderful harbor. This scenic Pacific Rim city holds a host of cultural attractions and the country's best restaurants, nightlife, and shopping. Maori, the indigenous peoples, always favored the warmer North Island and, for the visitor, Maori culture is at its most accessible in Rotorua, a three-hour drive south of Auckland. The country's main tourist destination, Rotorua is also famed for its geysers and bubbling mud pools.

Two other North Island standouts are also within easy reach of Auckland: The superb seascapes and rich history of the Bay of Islands await about four hours north, and the impossibly scenic volcanoes of Tongariro National Park near Lake Taupo are a five-hour drive south.

The nation's capital, Wellington, a five-hour drive south of Tongariro, is much smaller than Auckland but no less scenic, with a fine harbor of its own. At the southern tip of the North Island, Wellington is the place to get ferries to the South Island.

NOT TO BE MISSED:

Auckland, the City of Sails and hub of the South Pacific **58**

The Bay of Islands, the birthplace of modern New Zealand **84**

Rotorua—geothermal, Maori, and tourist center **124**

Volcanoes and hiking in Tongariro National Park **133**

Cultured Wellington, the nation's capital **154**

Kaikoura for whale-watching and swimming with dolphins **177**

Franz Josef and Fox Glaciers, blue-tinged rivers of ice **227**

Queenstown, one of the world's great alpine resorts **248**

Awe-inspiring Milford Sound, by boat or from the air **266**

Moving South

The main attractions of the South Island are the Southern Alps, the fjords, and the glaciers. For most visitors, the South Island encapsulates New Zealand's magnificent wilderness and, for this reason, many favor the South over the North.

Visitor Information

New Zealand's main visitor information portal is the national i-SITE network operated by Tourism New Zealand (newzealand.com). More than 80 local offices provide information and brochures, and can help you reserve accommodations, tours, and transportation.

Though helpful, these offices can be overrun in peak summer season. Also, i-SITE offices are commercial enterprises, representing local operators and taking a cut on reservations, so no differentiation is made when recommending operators.

Smaller regional tourist offices are found in almost every town. They may be run by volunteers and may not make reservations, but they provide plenty of information.

For information on national parks and walks, the Department of Conservation (DOC) has a network of offices in parks and towns. Offices sometimes list local tourist services, accommodations, etc., but in general they don't make reservations. Their website (doc.govt.nz) has an excellent rundown on New Zealand parks and recreation.

Best Times to Visit

The favored time to visit New Zealand is in the summer months from December through February, when the days are warm to mild, the beaches are at their best, and the alpine national parks are accessible. That said, from around Christmas to mid-March the main tourist areas can be jam-packed and accommodations and rental cars difficult to find.

Reservations should be made as far in advance as possible at these peak times. The shoulder seasons of October/November and April/May are slightly cooler but much less crowded and noticeably cheaper. June through September is the off-season, but ski slopes come alive in the Southern Alps and on Mount Ruapehu on the North Island.

Christchurch, the main city and gateway to the South Island, is easily accessed by air from Auckland, Rotorua, or Wellington. From here, you can head across the plains to the foothills of the mighty Southern Alps—these brooding, rugged mountains reach their peak at Aoraki/Mount Cook. Or, you can take a short plane ride or a scenic eight-hour drive southwest from Christchurch to Queenstown, a buzzing alpine resort on a superb lake ringed by mountains. In addition to wonderful scenery, this is the country's adventure capital, with outdoor activities and tours galore. Next stop, about five hours west of Queenstown by car, should be Milford Sound for a cruise on this famous fjord surrounded by vast, snow-flecked mountains. This wilderness wonderland rates as one of the most stunning sights in a country packed with beauty. (For the more adventurous, the famous five-day Milford Track walk is a must.)

The South Island's other main attractions lie on the other side of the Alps, a picturesque six-hour drive north of Queenstown. On the remote West Coast, Franz Josef and Fox Glaciers are among the world's most accessible glaciers, lying close to the sea in temperate rain forest. You can see all of the South's main highlights by rental car in a week. To save a day or two, you could consider skipping Milford or the glaciers, or even Christchurch by flying straight into Queenstown.

Tipping Tips

Tipping is always optional in New Zealand. Once tipping was considered a foreign custom, if not an outright insult, but those days have long since passed, and the practice is becoming more common. While by no means mandatory, a 10 percent tip is appreciated for good service in the country's fancier restaurants. (But don't tip if the service is subpar.) Tip taxi drivers for good service by rounding up the fare, up to 10 percent. In top hotels, it's customary to give porters NZ$1 to $2 for carrying your bags.

If You Have More Time: North Island

Northland, the "winterless north" a few hours by car above Auckland, is recommended for its fine beaches and superb seascapes along the east coast. A loop through Northland from the Bay of Islands can include the mighty kauri forests of the Kauri Coast, and those with no time limit can head past giant sand dunes to Cape Reinga, the country's most northerly point.

For a fine two-day excursion, visit the Coromandel Peninsula, an hour and a half east of Auckland, with perhaps the best beaches in the country and a fine mix of scenery. Continuing south along the east coast of the North Island, the sunny Bay of Plenty has more good beaches, while an expedition to smoking White Island about 30 miles (48 km) off the coast of Whakatane is a must for volcano hounds. The East Cape is a remote Maori area, off the main tourist circuit, which makes it a fascinating rural detour for those with a car. Traveling south down the center of the North Island, the Waitomo Caves and their glowworms are a required stop on the way to Rotorua. After absorbing the Maori culture and sulfurous geothermal activity in Rotorua, you can continue on to Lake Taupo, Tongariro National Park, and then Napier, the delightful art deco city on the east coast at the center of a prolific wine district, before heading back to Auckland.

The west coast of the North Island is a much less trammeled route, but it includes the awe-inspiring, Fujiesque volcano Mount Taranaki and the wilds of the Whanganui River.

If You Have More Time: South Island

On the South Island, the sunny northern districts of Marlborough and Nelson deserve some serious exploration. Ferries from the North Island dock in the Marlborough Sounds, the most stunning water-way in the country, while Abel Tasman National Park a few hours west has wonderful beaches and coves, which can be explored on foot, by boat, or by kayak. Other attractions include the cheerful city of Nelson, fine wineries near Blenheim, and the whale-watching and other wildlife tours that abound in Kaikoura.

Once the country's main city, southerly Dunedin, five hours south of Christchurch, has gracious reminders of grander times. On Dunedin's doorstep, the Otago Peninsula is a major destination for those interested in marine wildlife, while the Catlins farther south teem with seals, sea lions, penguins, waterfalls, and forests.

At the southernmost point of the South Island, some 450 miles (725 km) from Christchurch, Stewart Island is a remote last stop, isolated but bountiful in nature and the best place in all of New Zealand to spot a kiwi, the elusive national bird, in the wild.

Other South Island highlights include the former French town of Akaroa near Christchurch, the fine resort of Wanaka on the lake of the same name, and Doubtful Sound, a worthy rival to Milford.

Bear in mind that New Zealand's national parks hold the country's greatest attractions, offering the traveler plenty of opportunities to get out and about in magnificent wilderness. But wherever you roam in this beautiful country at the end of the Earth, little gems can be found, often more rewarding for the lack of tourist hordes. ■

How to Call Home

International calls can be made from public telephones, which take coins, credit cards, or prepaid phone cards. International phone cards available at newsstands and convenience stores offer the cheapest rates for landline calls overseas. A prepaid New Zealand SIM card for your cell phone makes a handy investment. For international calls, dial 00, then the country code, area code (minus any initial 0), and number. The country code for the U.S. is 1. (See Travelwise p. 280.)

Resident of Canterbury

History & Culture

Green-lipped mussels and Sauvignon Blanc are the local fare served on a Greenshell Mussel Cruise, which leaves from Havelock and takes sightseers out into the Marlborough Sounds.

New Zealand Today

When the first Maori arrived in canoes from Polynesia, they found a land like nothing they had seen before, a prehistoric world, isolated and unique. They called it Aotearoa, Land of the Long White Cloud, for mist would often shroud the towering volcanoes, and snow-topped peaks stretched farther than the eye could see.

View of Auckland from the Sky Tower

Teeming, ancient forests of giant conifers and temperate ferns covered much of the land, while turquoise and deep blue seas lapped the many coves and beaches of these vast, untouched islands.

Maori tribes thrived, and fought each other, in this great southern land for nearly 500 years before the English arrived and established a colony that would flourish by tapping the islands' rich natural resources. Aotearoa became New Zealand and the settlers transformed the landscape, felling timber for export and turning hills and valleys into rich farmland and rolling green pastures dotted with sheep. The newcomers clashed with the Maori, who succumbed to disease, guns, and increasing waves of land-hungry migrants, but Aotearoa would never lose its Polynesian roots.

Therein lie the seeds of modern New Zealand, a land of spectacular beauty and natural wealth, with a fascinating overlay of cultures. It is an English-speaking, developed country dominated by European culture, but Polynesian blood runs forever in its veins.

Not only is the resurgent Maori culture evident everywhere, but New Zealand is also a focus for the rest of the South Pacific, still drawing Polynesians in search of new opportunity from far-flung islands such as Samoa, the Cook Islands, Tonga, and Niue. Migrants from Asia, particularly China, are also increasingly attracted to New Zealand, while much of the large Indian community comes from the Pacific. But despite growing multiculturalism, New Zealand's population as well as its outlook remain overwhelmingly bicultural.

Two Peoples, One Country

Within a population of 4.7 million, around 15 percent identify as Maori and 70 percent European (or Pakeha, the Maori name for Europeans now widely used by both communities). This makes New Zealand a meeting ground of Maori and English cultures— an odd juxtaposition at times, but a fascinating one.

For a colonized nation, race relations began well with the Treaty of Waitangi in 1840, guaranteeing Maori rights and sovereignty over their land, but plummeted as the settler rush for land inevitably led to war. Maori were fierce fighters, but in the end no match for British military might. Colonists seized land in retribution, discarded the treaty, and consigned the tribes mostly to remote areas. The two societies lived largely separate lives until the 1950s, when Maori migrated to the cities in large numbers. Urban life delivered economic benefits, but many urban Maori lost contact with their language and culture.

In recent decades, a snowballing interest in Maoritanga (Maori culture) has seen increased participation in all things Maori and enriched New Zealand as a whole.

Best Banknote

Voted best banknote for its stunning design by the International Bank Note Society, the NZ$5 polymer note is the first in the country's new Brighter Money range. It features advanced security features and mountaineer Sir Edmund Hillary with Aoraki/Mount Cook in the background.

Governments take Maori issues very seriously and are eager to redress social and economic injustices. The greatest change in Maori–Pakeha relations came with the establishment of the Waitangi Tribunal in 1975 to rule on breaches of the Treaty of Waitangi and make compensation payments to tribes. It signaled not just a desire to redress the past, but a new era in race relations. The process continues, and biculturalism has its critics, from those calling for multiculturalism to recognize all cultures to Maori demands for a separate state, but overwhelmingly tolerance prevails. For the visitor, Maori culture, especially on the North Island, offers a colorful insight into a rich tradition. Even though many Maori are urban and urbane, they are proud to showcase their culture, at its most accessible in tourist areas such as Rotorua.

Most European New Zealanders trace their descent back to English, Scottish, or Irish settlers, and many regarded Britain as the homeland well into the 20th century. Today the country has thrown off the shackles of Britain. It is equally keen to distance itself from Australia, its bigger, brasher, patronizing cousin across the Tasman Sea, with which it shares a similar relationship to that between Canada and the United States.

Fiercely proud and independent, New Zealanders call themselves (and New Zealand culture) Kiwi, after the flightless, nocturnal national bird. National pride swells when Kiwis make a splash on the world stage, and for such a small population, the country has produced an inordinate number of high achievers. Although New Zealanders may claim to have invented everything from powered flight to jogging, nationalist indulgences are kept in check by a wry sense of humor and distrust of authority. Kiwis like to see their society as iconoclastic, egalitarian, and a world leader in social reform, beginning in the 1890s when New Zealand became the first country to give women the national vote.

Enlightened environmental, racial, and social policies continue to define the country, and with a high standard of living and relatively low crime rates, New Zealand regularly tops global livability indexes. As a small, geographically isolated country, New Zealand hasn't completely thrown off the parochialism and conformity of the past, but the

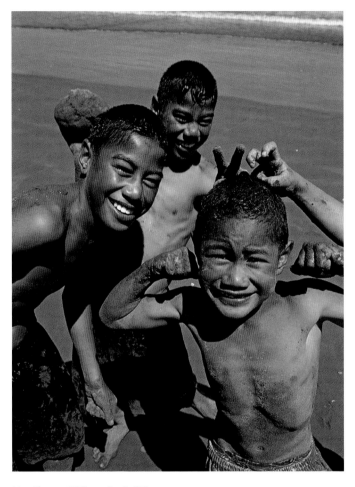

Maori boys on Waikanae Beach, Gisborne

most obvious excesses tend to be extremes of political correctness, and the Kiwi way of life is an enviable one.

European Kiwis often define their national character in terms of the early settlers. Living harsh, isolated lives, the pioneers overcame adverse conditions through hard work, determination, and adaptability. Kiwis also pride themselves on their ingenuity and self-sufficiency, and you may hear they can do anything with "No. 8 fencing wire," a reference to the popular wire gauge used on farms.

Myth as much as fact plays a part in all national identities, and while the manly values personified by rugby are lauded, alternative lifestyles are also welcome. Kiwis thrive not just in the big cities, but in small towns where artists and craftspeople abound. Women drive much of the dynamic in modern New Zealand and are prominent in leadership roles, from political leadership to the courts, bureaucracy, and business.

Despite its farming background, New Zealand is an urban society, but most visitors will end up in the countryside as they seek out the country's glorious landscapes. Even in larger towns, New Zealand has a village atmosphere where everybody knows each other or acts like it. Strangers greet each other with a smile, a quick word, a hello. On back roads, drivers wave at one another like old friends.

Off the Sheep's Back

A shifting world economy has created dramatic changes in New Zealand over the past few decades. After years enjoying one of the world's highest standards of living in a generous welfare state, New Zealand has had to make readjustments in an age of falling farm incomes. Once an efficient offshore farm for Britain, riding on the sheep's back, New Zealand has had to seek new markets and reposition its economy as Britain has looked more toward Europe for its imports and economic ties.

Agriculture, particularly dairy products, meat, and plantation timber, still dominates exports, but service industries such as tourism have assumed growing importance. As you travel around New Zealand, you will see once-booming farming towns, old-fashioned and quaint, on a downhill road. In contrast, tourist towns hum with

Travelers to New Zealand can enjoy a Middle Earth experience with a visit to a hobbit house.

development, bustling cafés, and "No Vacancy" signs, their asphalt sidewalks now replaced with creative paving, a sure sign of new money in New Zealand.

Since the 1980s, New Zealand has increasingly embraced the free market. This shift has undoubtedly brought new wealth and new opportunities. Smart entrepreneurs are finding new international opportunities for New Zealand, despite the difficulties faced by a small economy far removed from world markets. Two obvious candidates are the export-oriented wine industry and the thriving film industry. The world is increasingly savoring the fine wines from down under, and the success of the *Lord of the Rings* trilogy and *The Hobbit* attracted new overseas investment to New Zealand's world-class production houses.

Growth tends to concentrate in the metropolises such as Auckland, the only big city in New Zealand, but coastal towns are also doing well, attracting baby boomers flush with real estate winnings. Retirees, along with tourists, seek sunny climes with fine beaches and yachting harbors, with which New Zealand is well endowed.

Nature Nurtured

New Zealanders love their landscapes and the outdoors. The mountains hold a special place in their hearts—it is no accident that the first man to conquer Mount Everest, Sir Edmund Hillary (1919–2008), was a New Zealander—but the sea is equally revered. Kiwis are a fit and healthy bunch on the whole, eager to get out into nature and hike, climb, sail, swim, kayak, surf, or fish.

Despite the havoc wreaked by early settlers on the environment, or perhaps because of it, nature is worshipped in New Zealand. A superb system of national parks protects the country's national treasures. New Zealand's greatest attractions—the Southern Alps, glaciers, fjords, volcanoes, and the country's wonderful hikes—are in national parks administered by the Department of Conservation, known simply as DOC.

DOC offices in the parks and/or nearby towns are a wonderful resource with staff who can fill you in on hikes, the extensive system of huts throughout the parks, and the latest weather. New Zealand is famed for its hikes, or tramps as they are called, such as the Milford Track, Routeburn Track, and Tongariro Crossing. The nine best are designated by DOC as Great Walks: The country's premier trails through its best scenery, featuring higher-grade huts for overnighting. Most of these need to be reserved through DOC's website *(doc.govt.nz)*. Even if you don't intend to do any long hikes, bring your hiking boots, for trails are everywhere, from posted strolls through city parks to short hikes in spectacular wilderness. Walking is free, and fabulous, in New Zealand.

Though New Zealand has no native land mammals apart from bats, it has unique and prolific bird life and an abundance of marine creatures. Seals, sea lions, and penguins come ashore at many beaches and bays, where you may also see dolphins frolicking. This abundance has inspired a whole wildlife-focused tourism industry, ranging from swimming with the dolphins to whale-watching at Kaikoura on the South Island.

New Zealand's Two Personalities

New Zealand is a country of two islands, two halves, two personalities.

Dominating the country, the North Island has three-quarters of the population. Noted for its thermal activity, volcanoes, and Maori culture, the North Island also

New Zealand is famed for its hikes, or tramps as they are called, such as the Milford Track, Routeburn Track, and Tongariro Crossing.

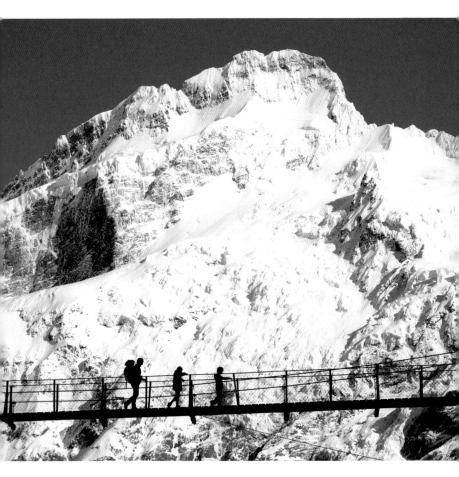

Hikers brave a swing bridge near Mount Sefton on the South Island.

has forested mountains and fine coastal scenery, though the enduring images are of pastureland and crumpled hills dotted with sheep.

The South Island is wilder, more spectacular, and the main destination for visitors. Home to mighty mountains, fjords, glaciers, and pristine lakes, wilderness is its greatest attraction. Here the Maori influence is less noticeable and its cities cling to British roots.

The North Island is dominated by Auckland, the big city of Polynesia with a population of 1.5 million, one-third of the country's total. The capital, however, is the smaller but cultured and scenic Wellington in the south of the North Island.

The North Island is also the Maori heartland, particularly in the Far North and the east where *marae* (traditional meeting places) hold strong to Maori tradition. For the visitor, the most accessible glimpse of Maori culture can be seen at Rotorua, the country's biggest tourist destination. Here the Te Arawa tribe lived long before tourists came to see the famous bubbling mud pools and geysers.

Volcanic activity defines the North Island, and the towering volcanoes of Tongariro National Park in the center are a highlight of any visit. Nearby Lake Taupo, resembling an inland sea, makes a good base. But New Zealanders often look to the sea, and the North Island is renowned for its stunning coastline. While the windswept west coast is pounded by surf, the sheltered east coast is a craggy loop of bays, beaches, and isles, at its most beautiful in the serene Bay of Islands in the Far North.

Separated by a swift and sometimes treacherous channel, the South Island is slightly larger than the North, more rugged, less populated, and even more scenic. The majestic Southern Alps run the length of the island—for a close-up view of the highest peaks, visit Aoraki/Mount Cook National Park. On the west side of the mountains, the stunning glaciers of Fox and Franz Josef are another must-see.

In the far south, ancient ice floes have carved the awe-inspiring landscapes of Fiordland. A string of spectacular fjords tatter this rugged remote coastline, a World Heritage wilderness that includes famous Milford Sound.

In the shadow of the alps, Queenstown on Lake Wakatipu is everyone's favorite resort town. It is also the adrenaline capital of New Zealand, home of the bungee jump and other thrills such as white-water rafting, jet boating (see p. 252), tandem skydiving, and parasailing.

The South Island's main city of Christchurch nestles on the Avon River, and its fine parks and neo-Gothic buildings attest to its English heritage. Second city Dunedin celebrates its Scottish roots, while the nearby Otago Peninsula is a haven for wildlife.

Blessed with unique natural wonders, it is fitting that the country counts tourism as a main industry. Where once nature was exploited, now it is treasured, and clean, green New Zealand is one of the world's most ecologically enlightened countries, keen to share its blessings with visitors.

Though the primal landscapes were forged over millions of years in isolation from the rest of the world, cultural evolution has been much more rapid. From Polynesian homeland to colonial outpost and then independent nation, New Zealand is a young but dynamic country. Though mindful of its British heritage, it has embraced its Polynesian roots to forge a unique national identity that continues to evolve as New Zealand confidently takes on the world. ■

The Kiwi Accent

No discussion of New Zealanders is complete without commenting on the accent. Similar to the Australian accent, it has diverged over the last few generations and is linked to a growing sense of nationalism and pride in Kiwi culture. Its contraction of the short vowels can confuse visitors at times, an accent most noticeable in the short *i*, such that "fish and chips" becomes "fush and chups." Other vowels are also affected: For example, "Monies lift air looks bugger then brats" is Kiwi for "Minnie's left ear looks bigger than Bret's."

History of New Zealand

The last major landmass to be inhabited, New Zealand is an isolated remnant of the continent of Gondwana, which tore apart 80 million years ago to form India, Australia, Antarctica, South America, and Africa.

Cut off from the rest of the world, New Zealand developed unique flora and a rich bird life, but no mammals walked the land. The moa, the world's largest bird at 12 feet (3.7 m) tall, roamed free of predators, except for the giant Haast's eagle. Birds came to rule a fiery world born of upheaval and eruption.

Maori Migration

Exactly why or from where the Maori originally came is uncertain, but the Maori language is most closely related to the Polynesian languages of the Cook Islands and Tahiti, so it's presumed they ventured from those regions.

Some Maori oral traditions attribute the discovery of New Zealand to the great explorer Kupe, who set sail from the Polynesian homeland of Hawaiki and called the new land Aotearoa (Land of the Long White Cloud). This story, along with theories of a later single Great Fleet migration and a separate migration by Melanesians known as Moriori, was taught as fact in New Zealand schools for many years but has since been largely debunked.

It is certain, though, that a number of *waka* (war canoes) made the journey, and Maori tribes trace their lineage to the waka their ancestors arrived in. The date of their arrival is hotly debated, some theorists claiming as early as A.D. 800, though recent opinion dates Maori settlement of New Zealand from the 13th century.

The newcomers found a land like nothing they had seen before. Stretching 1,000 miles (1,600 km), it was huge, mountainous, and fertile. The Polynesians from the tropics also found it cold. Not all of their crops would grow, and farther south the mountains were topped with *huka* (foam), as they called never-before-sighted snow.

Maori Ancestry

About 5,000 years ago, the Austronesian people of Southeast Asia developed sophisticated seafaring skills that allowed them to spread into the Pacific. By about 1000 B.C. they had reached Tonga and Samoa, becoming the ancestral Polynesians.

They stayed put in this new homeland for almost a thousand years before pushing on into the eastern Pacific. Using double-hulled canoes, they migrated east to the Marquesas, then south to Tahiti and north to Hawaii.

Maori culture became defined by adaptation, which was made easy at first by the hunting of moa. The huge, easily caught birds were found in abundance, but within perhaps as little as a hundred years they were hunted to extinction. In northern areas, seals were a major food source, but their numbers also declined.

By the 14th and 15th centuries, agriculture became more important, and the Maori less nomadic. *Kumara* (sweet potatoes) were an important crop and, unlike in the tropics, their tubers had to be kept in storage pits, which also mitigated against travel.

Maori *waka* (war canoe) at rest in Wairoa Bay, Northland

Distinct Maori styles of carving developed, as did the use of native resources such as flax for weaving and highly prized *pounamu* (greenstone or New Zealand jade) for carving.

As the population and competition for resources increased, so did conflict. Fortified villages, or *pa*, were built on hilltops and occupied at times of attack, and larger tribal groupings became more important for defense and for pooling labor for farming and fishing. Tribal war flared, but trade was also well established. A thriving greenstone trade existed between South Island Maori and the tribes of the north, and other areas similarly exported their minerals such as obsidian. By the time Europeans first visited Aotearoa in the 17th century, a Maori culture distinct from its eastern Polynesian antecedents had developed.

At the time of first European contact, it is estimated the country had a population of 100,000 Maori, the last major group of people not to have had contact with the wider world.

Kupe & Toi— The Great Explorers

Maori migration stories vary, but usually begin with Maui, the demigod who fished up the North Island from his canoe—the South Island—with Stewart Island as his anchor. Most tribes trace their ancestry to one of several *waka* (war canoes) that brought their forefathers from the ancestral homeland, called Hawaiki, but many traditions also speak of Kupe and Toitehuatahi, the great premigration explorers. Kupe features strongly in mythologies along the west coast of the North Island—some tribes say he settled in Hokianga before returning to Hawaiki and passing on directions to the new land. On the east coast of the North Island, many tribes trace their ancestry to Toitehuatahi, or Toi. In some traditions, he was an early explorer from Hawaiki; in others, he is indigenous to New Zealand and founded the tribe Te Tini o Toi (Toi's Multitudes).

European Exploration

Dutch mariner Abel Janszoon Tasman (1603–1659) was the first European to sight New Zealand. Sailing from Batavia (modern-day Jakarta) in the Dutch East Indies, he sought the great Unknown Southern Continent (Terra Australis Incognita), which geographers surmised must exist to balance the northern landmasses. Crossing the sea that now bears his name, he spied the South Island, near Punakaiki, on December 13, 1642. Five days later he anchored in Golden Bay at the top of the South Island.

Maori trumpets greeted the Dutch, who replied in kind, not knowing they had accepted a challenge to battle. Four of Tasman's men were killed in an altercation, and the Dutch ships hastily pulled anchor. Tasman continued to chart the west coast of the North Island, but dared not land. Named Nieuw Zeeland, after the Dutch province, this new world was deemed hostile and lacking in commercial interest, and no Europeans visited for another 127 years.

In 1769, British explorer James Cook (1728–1779) spent six months circumnavigating New Zealand in the *Endeavour*, coming away with a very different view of the country. Thanks largely to Tahitian chief Tupaia, who accompanied Cook and acted as a translator, Cook met with Maori on many occasions. Together with scientists such as botanist Joseph Banks (1743–1820), Cook gathered a wealth of information on the land and its inhabitants. From New Zealand he sailed on to Australia and became the first European to chart the east coast of that country. On his return to England in 1771, he was hailed as a hero by the scientific community.

Cook found the Maori "brave, noble, open and benevolent," and he visited New Zealand on each of his three Pacific voyages. Cook proved to be an enlightened leader, if a little musket-happy, and his dealings with the Maori were mostly friendly and respectful, but not without incident. On his second voyage in 1773, ten of his men were killed and eaten by Maori in Queen Charlotte Sound. To his credit, Cook showed restraint, a virtue that deserted him in Hawaii in 1779 when he was killed by villagers after a dispute over a stolen dinghy.

The Pacific also attracted French explorers, and Jean de Surville (1717–1770) arrived in New Zealand hot on Cook's heels. Marion du Fresne (1724–1772) made the Bay of Islands his base in 1772 while repairing his ships. Two months of cordial relations with the Maori soured when du Fresne and 25 of his crew were killed after a fishing expedition. In retaliation, the French sacked a village, killing 250.

Seals, Whales & Missionaries

Given the problems early Europeans experienced in New Zealand, the British decided to establish their first Pacific colony at Port Jackson (Sydney) in Australia in 1788, using convicts from Britain's overcrowded prisons to develop the colony. As the penal colony expanded, eyes looked across the Tasman for economic opportunities.

Cook had reported on New Zealand's abundance of seals, prized for their fur, and in 1792 sealers established a base in Dusky Sound at the bottom of the South Island. Despite the harsh conditions, many others followed, and hundreds of thousands of skins were taken. Within 20 years, seal populations declined dramatically, but whaling soon

The statue of Captain Cook in Victoria Square, Christchurch

became a major industry. In the Bay of Islands, the village of Kororareka (modern-day Russell) serviced dozens of British, French, and American whaling ships at any one time. This interaction signaled the first significant contact between Maori and Europeans, but taverns and prostitution flourished as well as trade. Kororareka was dubbed the "hellhole of the Pacific," but the missionaries soon brought a glimpse of their heaven. Samuel Marsden (1765–1838) set sail from Australia in 1814 to deliver the country's first sermon on Christmas Day in the Bay of Islands, and more soon followed.

The missionaries introduced more than religion. The Reverend Thomas Kendall (1778–1832), who compiled the first Maori dictionary, befriended the great Ngapuhi chief Hongi Hika (circa 1772–1828) and took him to London. On the return journey, Hika acquired up to 500 muskets that allowed the Ngapuhi tribe to settle ancient scores with devastating effect during the so-called Musket Wars (see pp. 110–111).

The signing of the Treaty of Waitangi, painted by Marcus King (1939)

British Annexation

Early European settlement was limited mostly to sealers and whalers, many of whom married local women. By 1830 the European population was only around 300, but with growing trade and increasing lawlessness in the Bay of Islands, the colony in Australia looked to bring some order to the settlement.

James Busby (1802–1871) was appointed British resident, and in 1833 he set up home at Waitangi, across the bay from Kororareka. Busby had no real power and no police force, and persistently petitioned his reluctant superiors for intervention, citing lawlessness and concern over Maori depopulation. The British finally acted, prompted by fears of annexation by the French and the private New Zealand Company, which was engaging in wholesale land grabs and sought to form its own government.

William Hobson (1792–1842) was appointed lieutenant-governor of the new colony. He arrived in the Bay of Islands in 1840 and set about convincing Maori chiefs to transfer sovereignty to Britain, a transfer that was secured by the Treaty of Waitangi.

This hastily prepared, well-intentioned treaty remains the most contentious document in New Zealand's history (see pp. 90–91). The northern chiefs met in Waitangi to debate and eventually sign the treaty on February 6, 1840. It granted sovereignty of the country to Queen Victoria, but gave Maori control of their land and the same rights as British subjects. The treaty toured the country for other chiefs to sign and on May 21, 1840, Hobson proclaimed New Zealand a British colony. The following year he shifted the capital south to Auckland.

Annexation paved the way for wholesale settlement, and as migrants flooded in, Maori disenchantment with the new order grew. Land sales were a major source of dispute, with communal Maori property often sold by those not authorized to do so.

In the South Island, fighting broke out in June 1843, when the New Zealand Company sought to establish a settlement in the Wairau Valley based on a suspect land deed. After Maori chief Te Rauparaha (circa 1760–1849) hindered attempts to survey the land, the company sent an armed party to arrest him. Twenty-two Europeans were taught a fatal lesson. In the Bay of Islands, Ngapuhi chief Hone Heke (circa 1810–1850), the first signatory of the Treaty of Waitangi, soon became disillusioned with British taxes and justice. After thrice felling the British flagpole in Kororareka, he attacked the town in 1845. Hundreds died in the following months as Heke, with his ally Kawiti, fought British troops backed by old tribal foes. After Heke and Kawiti made peace with Governor George Grey (1812–1898), war subsided, but Maori resentment simmered.

Settler Rush

From a European population of about 2,000 when the Treaty of Waitangi was signed, Pakeha numbers swelled to nearly 60,000—equal to those of the Maori—by the late 1850s. By 1881 the number of European settlers had grown to 500,000.

Early settlement was driven by the New Zealand Company, founded by Edward Gibbon Wakefield, a former convict jailed for abducting a 15-year-old heiress (she was willing; her father was not). Backed by influential patrons in London, a rehabilitated Wakefield pushed his vision of a better Britain in the Pacific, preserving British traditions, including the class system, but offering opportunities for the lower classes to advance through hard work. This approach boiled down to buying land cheaply from the Maori, selling it at a handsome profit to well-to-do capitalists, and attracting skilled labor to serve the colony and the new landed gentry.

Of all the major settlements, only Auckland grew unfettered by social or religious visions. It boomed despite losing its status as capital to more central Wellington in 1865. Half of the country's immigrants were English, followed in number by Scots, who made up one-quarter. The Irish, being mostly Catholic, were not encouraged to migrate, but their numbers swelled to nearly 20 percent of the European population during the 1860s. French settlers founded an early colony at Akaroa in 1840 and sought to claim the South Island for France, but arrived too late. By the time they reached New Zealand after months at sea, the Treaty of Waitangi had been signed.

The new migrants cleared, burned, and plowed at a ferocious rate. Sheep farming was the preferred pursuit, and by 1858 the country had 1.5 million sheep, a number that grew tenfold over the next three decades. On the South Island grasslands in particular, wool barons made fortunes, but the real economic and population boom had to wait for the discovery of gold.

New Zealand Wars

While settlement increased in the coastal areas, the hinterlands remained firmly Maori, but European agriculture soon threatened to gobble up the interior of the islands.

To counter Pakeha dominance, Maori united across tribal boundaries for the first time to stop land sales. The Kingitanga (King Movement) was formed, and its members elected a Maori king in 1856, a move seen as treasonous by most settlers. In 1860, after a Taranaki chief tried to stop the sale of land near New Plymouth, troops were sent in, sparking the Taranaki War. From their fortified *pa* (hill fort village), Maori forces inflicted heavy casualties and laid siege to New Plymouth before a truce was called in 1861.

In 1863, war broke out again and 20,000 troops were called on to crush the King Movement. Dozens of battles across the Waikato region left 1,000 Maori and 700 British troops dead; fighting spread to the Bay of Islands before the wars died down in 1864.

The King Movement was defeated and huge areas of Waikato land were seized, but guerrilla skirmishes continued for another eight years. The Hauhau, whose messianic movement combined missionary Christianity with Maori beliefs, terrorized parts of Taranaki and the east coast of the North Island before capture and exile in 1866.

This gave rise to Te Kooti (circa 1830–1893), a visionary who started his own faith

Gold

Gold was mined on the Coromandel Peninsula in the 1850s, but the gold rush took off with the discovery of the alluvial goldfields in Otago on the South Island in 1860–1861. Miners flocked from all over the world and towns sprang up overnight. Great wealth flowed through Dunedin, which became the country's largest and grandest city. Though the gold began to peter out by the 1870s, the rush had doubled New Zealand's population and rapid growth pointed to a bright future for all—except the Maori.

The Maori warrior spirit lives on in the All Blacks' prematch *haka* dance (see pp. 72–73).

and promptly led his followers to slaughter 54 people near Gisborne in 1868. Chased across the central North Island by troops and Maori forces, he battled for nearly four years before retreating into the remote King Country (see the King Movement p. 111).

Nation-building

The New Zealand Wars did much to shore up Maori prestige, but only briefly slowed the advance of settlement in the North Island. More land was seized, and businessmen-turned-politicians made huge profits.

Julius Vogel (1835–1899) provided the most effective political leadership. As premier and treasurer in a number of civilian administrations, the former journalist presided over an economic boom in the 1870s. Massive loans funded rail, road, and telegraph, and Vogel introduced assisted passage schemes to lure migrants. British women, mostly domestic workers, traveled free in an effort to redress the imbalance of the sexes. Gold, farming, and forestry had attracted hordes of single men, who often lived harsh, isolated lives, and consequently New Zealand society developed a rugged male perspective.

Fortunes waned in the 1880s as the worldwide depression hit New Zealand. Wool prices dropped dramatically, but were partly offset by frozen meat exports to England made possible by new refrigeration technology. Another major export, the kauri trees of the Coromandel and Northland, provided durable, straight-grained wood prized in ship- and housebuilding. Kauri milling was hugely profitable, but reduced the mighty forests almost to extinction by the early 20th century.

As the depression dragged on into the 1890s, poverty stalked the streets of cities in New Zealand. Cries for industrial and labor reforms brought the Liberal Party to governmental power in 1891. The Liberals introduced sweeping changes that made New Zealand the social laboratory of the world. Industrial legislation improved conditions for workers, and land reform helped break down large estates, resulting in wider land ownership. In 1893, New Zealand became the first country in the world to give women the national vote; it also introduced the aged pension in 1898 and poured money into public-health spending. Richard Seddon (1845–1906), prime minister from 1893 to 1906, acquired the moniker "King Dick" as the Liberal Party went on to dominate New Zealand politics for the next 21 years.

Political stability brought prosperity, and New Zealand's GDP per capita was the highest in the world in 1900. The North Island, no longer embroiled in conflict, overtook the South Island. Auckland grew dramatically and the country became increasingly urbanized. Maori, however, remained rural. Though improved health reversed the decline in their numbers, by 1900 they composed only 10 percent of the population.

In 1907, New Zealand went from colony to dominion status, which conferred greater independence from Britain. New Zealanders remained staunchly British, however, and were eager to follow the call of the empire to send troops to the Boer War in South

Australian and New Zealand Army Corps (ANZAC) troops in Gallipoli, Turkey, 1915

Africa in 1899. But a new sense of national identity was forming, and patriotism sprang from the rugby field when the national team (the All Blacks) defeated England in 1905.

New Zealand also went from colony to colonizer, with Britain handing over control of the Cook Islands and Niue. New Zealand wanted Samoa as well, but had to wait for World War I to wrest control of the islands from Germany.

World Wars

New Zealand again answered Britain's call to war in 1914, and 100,000 men, some 10 percent of the population, joined the Australian and New Zealand Army Corps (ANZAC) to fight in Europe and Africa. Casualties were heavy, nowhere more so than at Gallipoli in Turkey, where thousands were cut down in an ill-advised attempt to storm the heavily fortified peninsula. Almost every town across the country has a memorial honoring the dead, which nationwide totaled 17,000, a huge toll for such a small country.

The troops embodied the national self-image of ruggedness, comradeship, and resourcefulness against the odds. These quali- ties were not so well received when workers organized. The conservative Reform govern ment, which succeeded the Liberals, sent in the police when gold miners at Waihi went on strike in 1912, and a striker was killed. Socialists then began to gain popularity and the Labour Party entered mainstream politics.

Independence

In 1947, New Zealand ratified the Statute of Westminster, which gave it complete autonomy from Britain in foreign as well as domestic affairs. Despite this independence, Britain remained the homeland for many, and an adoring public turned out to welcome their new queen, Elizabeth II, when she visited in 1952–1953.

In the 1930s, the Great Depression hit hard, and New Zealand's agricultural exports to Brit- ain plummeted. Nature, too, conspired against the country when an earthquake flattened Napier and Hastings in 1931. The Labour Party grew in strength but did not gain the top post until 1935, after it had ditched its more radical socialist policies.

Under Prime Minister Michael Joseph Savage (1872–1940), Labour led the recov- ery and laid the foundations of the welfare state with increased spending on pensions, education, and health. Labour policies particularly benefited the disadvantaged Maori, though Maori and Pakeha lived largely as two separate societies.

When Britain found itself at war again in 1939, New Zealand committed 200,000 troops. Casualties were high. New Zealanders, including a Maori battalion, fought with distinction, but this time the war was closer to home. After Japan stormed British posi- tions in Asia, New Zealand looked for the first time to the United States for defense.

Boom & Bust

The end of the war brought a new dynamism to the economy, as well as greater conservatism as the Cold War intensified. New Zealand turned away from leftist Labour in 1949, and the free-enterprise National Party came to power. Fear of communism saw New Zealand send troops to Korea and form the ANZUS military pact with Australia and the United States, which would lead to New Zealand engagement in Vietnam.

Flagging Change

In 2016, after 17 months of debate, New Zealanders went to the polls to vote on changing the national flag. In a country renowned for reform, and having long ago shrugged off its colonial past to forge an independent identity, it seemed natural that the flag with a British Union Jack in the corner should be replaced. An even bigger imperative for change, it was almost identical to the Australian flag, give or take a couple of stars.

The vote for a new flag became a pet project for former Prime Minister John Key, who initiated a design competition to select an alternative, resulting in four (then five) hotly debated flags. The alternatives seemed to divide people as much as dumping the old one, but the first round of voting eventually selected a flag with the silver fern motif, and Southern Cross stars from the old flag. Then, after spending NZ$25 million, the final vote between the old and new flags was held. New Zealanders rejected the change: 57 percent to 43.

Whether it was the process that scuttled the vote, or a desire to cling to tradition, it now seems that other lingering question of becoming a republic is well off the agenda.

Refugees from war-torn Europe sought a better life in affluent New Zealand, but migration remained overwhelmingly British. Society was conformist, if not puritanical. From a country that banned Marlon Brando in *The Wild One* and forced pubs to close at 6 p.m., New Zealand writers, scientists, academics, and other elites made a beeline for more liberal London and its greater opportunities.

The 1960s and '70s ended New Zealand's isolation. Cheap air travel, satellite communication, and television helped bring in the world. Conservatism continued to dominate politics, but times were changing. Feminism challenged rugby machismo and white-oriented migration barriers fell. Demonstrations demanded troops out of Vietnam and an end to rugby games with apartheid South Africa.

Above all, the Maori challenged the Pakeha belief that New Zealand was a model of race relations. The postwar boom had witnessed mass migration of rural Maori to the cities, where unskilled jobs were plentiful. Assimilation was the norm, but by the 1970s Maori questioned not only the decline in their culture and language but also injustices past and present. Increasing radicalism, protest marches, and calls to uphold the Treaty of Waitangi unsettled many in the wider community.

Labour came to power on the winds of change in 1972, but lasted only three years as inflation spiraled along with oil prices. A National Party government under Robert Muldoon (1921–1992) tried to reverse the economic decline, rising unemployment, and social liberalism. Wage and price freezes and "Think Big" infrastructure projects only worsened New Zealand's economic woes as foreign debt skyrocketed.

New New Zealand

In 1984, voters brought in David Lange (1942–2005) and a new Labour government, which introduced sweeping reforms, including deregulation of financial markets and abolition of agricultural subsidies. Labour also forged a fiercely independent foreign policy and took a tough antinuclear stance, a popular move at home as well as in the neighboring Pacific, where France continued to test nuclear weapons. Reform of social policies—from local administration to drinking laws—was just as sweeping, and Labour set about redressing long-festering Maori grievances. The Waitangi Tribunal was given powers to assess claims dating back to the treaty of 1840, resulting in hundreds of land claims. The treaty now became a guiding agreement for race relations. The government has made multimillion-dollar settlements with most tribes, with the Ngaphui, the first signatory of the Treaty, being a notable exception.

The rapid restructuring of society unsettled many, and policy differences saw the government fragment and Lange resign in 1989. New Zealand's two-party political system began to break up as new parties tapped voter resentment at radical policies that had been introduced without electoral support. The answer, in another twist of reform fever, was to overhaul the voting system in 1993 to bring in proportional representation (known as MMP), similar to that in Germany. This system encouraged minor parties and further fragmented New Zealand politics.

However, the two party system, with minor party alliances, has held together and delivered stability through successive Labour and National governments, helped by a strengthening economy. Led by booming dairy exports to China, New Zealand's economy withstood world turmoil, but its good fortunes took a devastating turn for the worse in February 2011 when an earthquake hit central Christchurch.

Already battered by a major quake in September 2010, followed by thousands of aftershocks, a magnitude 6.3 earthquake centered just below the city hit Christchurch in the middle of the day. High-rise buildings in the city center were hardest hit, collapsing around office workers, while out in the suburbs 100,000 houses were damaged, and 10,000 totally destroyed. The country watched on in horror as emergency services combed through the rubble and the death toll mounted. The Christchurch earthquake eventually claimed 185 lives, making this one of New Zealand's worst natural disasters. While reconstruction continues unabated and the city is recovering, it may be a decade or more before Christchurch is totally rebuilt. Another big 7.8 earthquake shook remote areas of the South Island in 2016, hitting the tourist town of Kaikoura, killing two, severing the main highway, and damaging high-rise buildings some 200 miles away in the capital, Wellington.

> **New Zealand is a vastly different country than it was 40 years ago, economically and socially, as national pride looks to throw off the influence of Britain and neighboring Australia.**

Strength in adversity and adaptation to changing conditions define the country. New Zealand is a vastly different country than it was 40 years ago, economically and socially, as national pride looks to throw off the influence of Britain and neighboring Australia. The country revels in its own heroes—from sports to literature and popular music—and is eager to define its own identity. Pacific Island and Asian migrants have broadened the country's outlook, though not without some backlash. The biggest change has been growing biculturalism. Maori culture and sensibilities percolate throughout society, and MMP electoral reforms have delivered more Maori members of parliament and increased political clout.

Change has not pleased nor benefited all Kiwis, but the new New Zealand of the 21st century faces the world with a confident and independent identity. ■

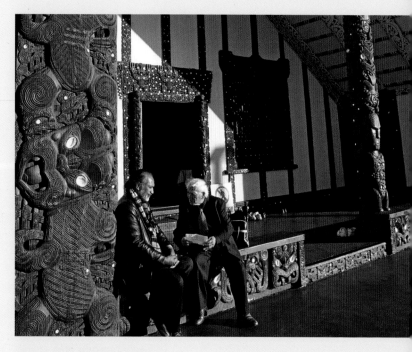

Visiting a *marae* on Lake Rotorua

Maori Culture

Maori have been in New Zealand since at least the 13th century and came from eastern Polynesia, their language being most closely related to that of Tahiti and the Cook Islands.

Some Maori oral traditions attribute the discovery of New Zealand to Kupe, who set sail from the ancestral homeland of Hawaiki. After exploring the islands he called Aotearoa (Land of the Long White Cloud), he returned to tell of his find, prompting a great fleet migration.

Scientific evidence points to a series of migrations, but Maori tribes still attribute their ancestry to one of seven canoes: Arawa, Aotea, Horouta, Mamari, Mataauta, Tainui, and Takitimu.

Social Organization

The main social grouping in Maori society is the *iwi* (tribe), usually comprising several *hapu* (subtribes). Tribal names often have the prefix *ngati* or *ngai,* meaning "the people of" or "descendants of." For example, the Ngati Pikiao (Descendants of Chief Pikiao) is a hapu living around Lake Rotorua. Together with other subtribes from the Rotorua/ Taupo region, they make up the Te Arawa iwi, which takes its name from the original canoe that brought them to Aotearoa.

In pre-European society, hapu were more important than iwi. Hapu would sometimes fight each other, though they would unite against other iwi. A hapu numbered up to several hundred members and was made of a number of *whanau* (extended family groups).

A whanau of 20 to 30 family members would occupy one or more sleeping houses and often had its own compound in a village. As a warrior society, Maori also built fortified villages, or *pa,* that they would occupy in times of war. Usually constructed on hills in strategic locations, they were terraced, with a series of concentric walls topped with stakes to repel invaders.

Whakapapa (ancestry) was an important determinant of status and tribal grouping in Maori society, and at *hui* (gatherings), speakers would often recite extensive genealogies to establish their credentials.

Power was held by the *rangatira,* or aristocratic families. The firstborn son of the senior family was the *ariki,* hereditary chief, who passed on power to his son. Below the rangatira were the *tutua* (commoners) and below them *taurekareka* (slaves) taken in battle or born into a slave family.

Another important class, the *tohunga* (priests) specialized in religious rituals and magic, but also in knowledge of agriculture, carving, genealogy, oral tradition, and tattooing.

The arrival of the Pakeha (Europeans) resulted in the dispersal of many tribes through war, appropriation of land, and missionary activity. To counter growing Pakeha influence, the tribes sought to unite in the middle of the 19th century, helping to make iwi more important than hapu.

After World War II, iwi became the dominant tribal determinant as the government set up trust boards, based on iwi, to represent Maori interests and handle compensation claims for breaches of the Treaty of Waitangi.

The urbanization in the latter half of the 20th century undermined Maori identity, and many lost contact with their tribal roots. About one-sixth now cannot name their iwi and more do not know their original hapu. However, many Maori are increasingly interested in retaining or rediscovering their tribal connections through the *marae,* the meeting place of the tribe.

EXPERIENCE: Inside a *Marae*

The *marae,* a sacred meeting place, is where Maori culture and language are promoted, tribal matters are discussed, and weddings, funerals, and ceremonies are held. A marae is usually found in the tribal homeland, and serves as a focus for members of the tribe scattered across the country. There are also intertribal city marae, university marae, and church marae. Te Papa, Wellington's national museum, has a marae (see p. 156), or you can seek out local marae *(naumaiplace .com/home/marae/search).*

Technically the marae is the gathering place in front of the meetinghouse (*wharenui* or big house), but the term commonly refers to the whole compound. Other community buildings include the *wharekai* (dining hall) for group meals. The outside area is used for welcome ceremonies and formal speeches, while the meetinghouse is the location for important meetings, cultural activities, and for entertaining and sometimes accommodating visitors.

The meetinghouse is the most important building. The house usually bears the name of an ancestor, and the building symbolically represents him with ornate carving. The *tekoteko* (carved figure) on the roof represents the ancestor's head, the *maihi* (bargeboards) angling down represent the arms, the ridgepole the spine, and the rafters the ribs. Supporting the rafters inside are *poupou,* carved representations of other ancestors.

A marae is sacred ground, not generally open to the public, but some Maori tours include marae visits. Jump at the chance if someone invites you to their marae.

Religion

Traditional Maori religion was based on nature and ancestor worship. All living things and natural elements possessed *mauri*, or life force, and a host of gods and demigods,

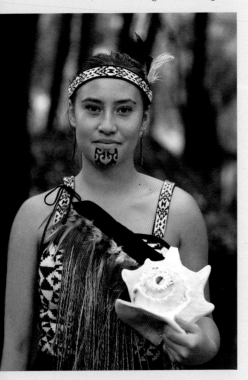

A Maori woman at a cultural show in Tanaki

usually connected to nature, required respect and propitiation through rites overseen by the priests.

Two important aspects of Maori spiritual life are *mana* and *tapu*. Mana (spiritual power or respect) could be accumulated through warfare, wisdom, oratory, inheritance, or by eating an enemy, thereby consuming his mana. Great chiefs sought and possessed great mana.

Tapu (sacred, or taboo, as Captain Cook translated it) applied to a range of restricted activities, from hunting and fishing rules to prohibitions regarding the dead or sacred places. Defying tapu could result in death, either imposed by the tribe or through sickness that would befall offenders. Some original tapu observations can still be seen in Maori funeral rites and marae protocol.

Maori underwent wholesale conversion by missionaries in the 19th century, with Christianity all but destroying their traditional religion, but the ensuing turmoil resulted in the rise of two prominent Maori Christian sects.

The Ratana movement, founded by an early 20th-century faith healer, still has a large following and considerable political influence. The smaller Ringatu or Upraised Hand faith was founded by the 19th-century guerrilla leader and prophet Te Kooti. It still claims around 16,000 followers and influences others such as the Ngati Dread, a Maori Rastafarian sect.

Mythology

Maori society brought Polynesian mythology from the homeland but adapted it to the new surroundings. The demigod Maui is a popular figure throughout Polynesia, and Maori relate many of his exploits, such as when he fished up the North Island from his canoe to the South Island (in Hawaii he fished up the Hawaiian Islands).

Maori oral tradition also places great store on genealogy and migration traditions, and tribal histories were retold via amazing feats of memory.

Myths dealing with the gods and nature explained the world and formed the basis of religion. They varied from tribe to tribe, but most had a similar creation story that began with nothingness until the earth mother Papatuanuku and the sky father Ranginui came together.

Rangi and Papa had many male children, the gods of the Maori, who lived in a parental embrace so tight no light could penetrate. The gods, tired of eternal darkness, finally decided to separate their parents. One by one they tried but failed until Tanemahuta, the god of forests, slowly applied the strength of a growing kauri tree to part the sky from the earth.

Light flooded the world, which revealed a multitude of creatures. Tane then fashioned a woman from clay, and the human race was born (see sidebar p. 92).

Maori Arts

Of the rich Maori music and dance traditions, the *haka* is the most readily identified. A war dance designed to scare the heck out of enemies, the haka is most famously performed by the national rugby team (the All Blacks, see pp. 72–73) to psych out the opposition. It is indeed a terrifying sight of stomping, body slapping, eye glaring, and tongue poking, accompanied by a booming guttural chorus guaranteed to raise the hair on your neck.

Visitors will see the haka performed at Maori concerts, where women also invariably perform the *poi* dance, a graceful performance based on the twirling of poi, (flax balls) on a string.

Maori were traditionally master carvers, unrivaled in the Pacific. Carving buildings and canoes was a privileged profession and was done with greenstone adzes before the introduction of metal tools in the early European era. Maori carving design is based primarily on human figures, such as ancestors. Spirals are also an important feature, and the *manaia* is a curious Maori motif seen variously as a bird, serpent, or human figure.

Carving included ornaments of bone and greenstone, as well as a variety of clubs for warfare. The most widely known ornament is the *tiki*, a pendant usually made of green-stone that depicts a distorted human figure with the head tilted to the side.

New Zealand's cold climate called for warm garments, and Maori women produced the best weaving in the Pacific. Plentiful flax made a fine thread woven into mats, cloaks, skirts, baskets, and other items. Most stunning are the cloaks adorned with feathers,

though they are rarely produced these days and use imported feathers on the few occasions when they are.

Maori Language

About 21 percent of the population can converse in Maori, and Maori is an official language taught in schools. *Kohanga reo* (language nests) provide total immersion

EXPERIENCE:
Learn a Few Maori Words & Phrases

Though English is spoken everywhere, Maori phrases are increasingly used in the media and everyday speech, and it is well worth learning a few words. In addition to the basic Maori listed here, geographical terms such as *awa* (river), *puke* (hill), *roto* (lake), *wai* (water), and *whanga* (harbor) are useful for understanding place-names.

kia ora: hello (also thank you)
haere mai: welcome
haere ra: good-bye
tena koa: please
ae: yes
kaore: no
marae: gathering place of the tribe
pa: a fortified village
Aotearoa: New Zealand (Land of the Long White Cloud)
tangata whenua: people of the land (often used to mean Maori)

in the language for Maori preschoolers in some areas. Maori words are increasingly used in everyday English, especially in the media, where presenters open with a *"kia ora"* ("hello"). Many New Zealanders, including Pakeha, have substantial Maori vocabularies, and government bodies have Maori and English names.

Arts & Literature

The enduring images of New Zealand are of the rugged outdoors, farming, and rugby. Against this backdrop, the arts have often been seen as a light-weight indulgence, but the search for identity and international acceptance has elevated cultural icons onto the same podium as sports stars.

Much of the turnaround can be attributed to the success of the film industry, but everywhere the arts are flourishing. The "cultural cringe," with which New Zealanders once embraced the international and disparaged anything homegrown, has long since passed. Kiwis want to read New Zealand writers, see Kiwi movies, and listen to local musicians, while theater and dance thrive in the cities. In country towns, it often seems every other person is a potter or painter.

Literature

Katherine Mansfield (1888–1923) was the first New Zealand writer to garner international acclaim. She acquired her reputation as one of the finest short-story writers in English while an émigré in Europe, but stories such as "The Doll's House" and "The Garden Party" are fine evocations of colonial New Zealand.

Outstanding Kiwi writers include John Mulgan (1911–1945), whose *Man Alone* chronicles post-WWII decline in New Zealand. Prolific novelist and Nobel nominee Janet Frame (1924–2004) is best remembered for *An Angel at My Table,* part of her autobiographical trilogy touching on her battles with the mental health system.

National treasure Maurice Gee (b. 1931) is best known for his *Plumb* trilogy. Other contemporary novelists of note include Elizabeth Knox (b. 1959; *The Vintner's Luck*), Nigel Cox (1951–2006; *Tarzan Presley*), Emily Perkins (b. 1970; *Not Her Real Name*), and Lloyd Jones (b. 1955; *Master Pip*). Booker honors would have to wait until 2013, when Elizabeth Catton (b. 1985) won the Man Booker Prize with *The Luminaries*. Maori writers provide much of the dynamism of modern New Zealand literature. *The Bone People,* Keri Hulme's (b. 1947) ambitious novel of violence, spiritualism, love, and death in the context of wider bicultural conflict, won the 1985 Booker. Witi Ihimaera's (b. 1944) novel *Tangi* (1973) was the first by a Maori writer, and his body of work includes *The Whale Rider,* made into a popular film (see sidebar p. 43). Another seminal Maori writer, Patricia Grace (b. 1937; *Potiki*) tackles relationships, displacement, mythology, and politics. Alan Duff (b. 1950) also focuses on cultural destruction, but his bleak, violent *Once Were Warriors,* later made into a hit film, offers no easy answers. His criticism of Maoridom for dwelling on past injustices at the expense of current responsibilities makes him the enfant terrible of Maori writers.

Sculptures in the Giant's House garden, Akaroa

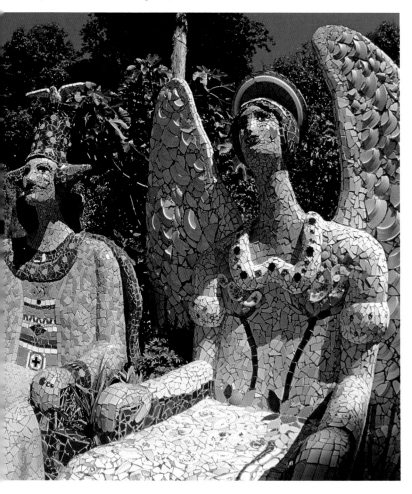

Music

A thriving popular music culture has produced a number of notable exports, most recently Lorde (Ella Yelich-O'Connor, b. 1996), who stormed the charts and Grammys in 2013 with her debut single, "Royals." The world first noticed New Zealand music in the 1970s when Split Enz enjoyed international success. Founders Neil and Tim Finn went on to lead a number of musical projects, including the widely successful band Crowded House. The local recording industry came of age in the 1980s, when the Dunedin-based record company Flying Nun launched bands such as The Chills and The Clean. More recently, popular singer-songwriter Bic Runga (b. 1976) and groups such as The Mutton Birds and The Datsuns have reached large audiences. OMC had a huge international hit, "How Bizarre," in the mid-1990s, which propelled them to brief worldwide fame. More recently divas such as Kimbra (b. 1990) and Aaradhna (b. 1983) have had success at home and abroad. Hip-hop music is popular in New Zealand, particularly among young Maori and Pacific Islanders. Important artists include Upper Hutt Posse, Che Fu, and Savage.

,New Zealand also has three symphony orchestras, including the acclaimed NZSO (New Zealand Symphony Orchestra), and is home to world-renowned opera diva Dame Kiri Te Kanawa (b. 1944).

Maori Cinema

Early movies explored Maori themes, but the first Maori written-and-directed feature was Barry Barclay's *Ngati* (1987), followed by Merata Mita's *Mauri* (1988), and Lee Tamahori's brutal *Once Were Warriors* (1994). A new Maori wave seemed imminent, but only *Whale Rider* (2002, made by a non-Maori director) received wide acclaim before the New Zealand Film Commission set about promoting Maori directors, producers, and writers. A host of Maori films followed including *The Waimate Conspiracy* (2006), *Eagle vs Shark* (2007), *The Rain of Children* (2008), and *No Petrol, No Diesel* (2009). A steady if less heady stream of Maori films continues, led by Taika Waititi's hits *Boy* (2010) and *Hunt for the Wilderpeople* (2016).

Painting

The Maori portraits of Charles Goldie (1870–1947) and Gottfried Lindauer (1839–1926) remain icons of early New Zealand art despite Goldie's work being deemed racist for many years because of his melancholic depictions of Maori elders as the last of a dying race. New Zealand's best loved painters are those who embrace the country's vistas, from the pioneering Petrus van der Velden (1837–1913) to the wonderful landscapes of Rita Angus (1908–1970), William Sutton (1917–2000), and Grahame Sydney (b. 1948). One of the country's most acclaimed artists, Frances Hodgkins (1869–1947) made her name in Britain, where she became one of the leading artists of British modernism. The New Zealand art establishment staunchly resisted modernism for decades, as seen in the conservative collections of public galleries, but artists such as the highly influential Colin McCahon (1919–1987) broke new ground. For an overview of New Zealand art, visit the Auckland City and Christchurch galleries. The country also has some good provincial galleries, such as the Govett–Brewster Art Gallery in New Plymouth. Some of the leading lights of New Zealand's contemporary art scene include Julian Dashper, Robin White, Shane Cotton, Philippa Blair, Dick Frizzell, and Michael Smither.

Dance

Ballet relies on government funding to survive, but survive it has since 1953, when the Royal New Zealand Ballet was established. The troupe's dancers typically have looked to London for careers, and returning émigrés such as Russell Kerr (b. 1930) and Rowena Jackson (b. 1926) in the 1950s provided much impetus. Jon Trimmer (b. 1929), a veteran of the Royal Ballet School and Sadler's Wells, has been a leading artist since 1962 and continues to perform character roles. Although based in Wellington, this hardworking company tours all over the country and overseas. Long wedded to classical performances, it has performed more innovative works from local choreographers in recent years. The pioneering Limbs Dance Company established modern dance here in the 1970s, working with local composers including Don McGlashan (b. 1959) and Split Enz. Though it dissolved in 1989, the group launched leading choreographers such as Douglas Wright (b. 1956) and Mark Baldwin (b. 1959). One of New Zealand's leading contemporary companies, Auckland-based Black Grace is noted for its dynamism, fusing Pacific and contemporary dance in athletic performances.

> One of New Zealand's leading contemporary companies, Auckland-based Black Grace is noted for its dynamism, fusing Pacific and contemporary dance in athletic performances.

Theater

Despite a long history of repertory theater, New Zealand had to wait until 1952 for professional theater to emerge with the New Zealand Players. Formed by Richard and Edith Campion, parents of film director Jane (b. 1954), the company lasted less than a decade but inspired a generation of thespians.

In 1964, Downstage Theatre Company in Wellington led the way, to be followed by the Mercury, Circa, and Court companies as the nascent arts scene increasingly examined New Zealand issues. Leading playwrights include British emigrant Roger Hall (b. 1939), whose social comedies were exported to the West End, and Greg McGee (b. 1950), whose landmark *Foreskin's Lament* (1980) has become a New Zealand classic. It revolves around the rugby locker rooms, questioning national identity and exploring conflict in a changing society. Though the classics and recent overseas hits continue to be a staple of New Zealand theater, since the 1980s and '90s local plays have become the norm. Maori theater has come to the forefront and demanded recognition, particularly in the works of Hone Kouka (b. 1966; *Wairoa*) and Briar Grace-Smith (b. 1966; *Flat Out Brown*). The large Auckland Theatre Company has a wide-ranging commercial program and performs in theaters around the city, while Christchurch and Dunedin also have their own professional companies. Bats Theatre and Circa are the centers of Wellington's theater scene.

Cinema

New Zealand film is dominated by *Lord of the Rings* director Peter Jackson (b. 1961), who has become the country's most influential cultural figure. Filmed in New Zealand, the *Rings* movies turned the whole country into a film set, provided a massive boost to the economy, and prompted worldwide interest in New Zealand film. The experience was later repeated with *The Hobbit* trilogy, released in 2012. Jackson's renowned Wellington-based Weta Workshop was the special effects and postproduction workshop for his *Rings* movies and *King Kong*. New Zealand not only continues to produce fine homegrown features, but the expertise and relative affordability of its production facilities make it a magnet for U.S. film and television producers.

New Zealand cinema began well before Middle Earth–inspired visions. *Sleeping Dogs* (1977), an accomplished psychological thriller, kick-started the nascent film industry and launched the international careers of actor Sam Neill (b. 1947) and director Roger Donaldson (b. 1945), whose string of Hollywood credits includes *Cocktail, Cadillac Man,* and *Dante's Peak*.

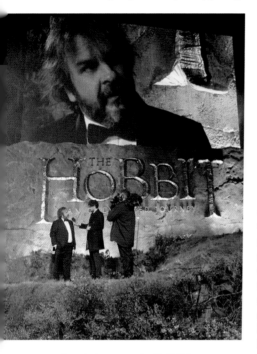

Peter Jackson promotes *The Hobbit*.

Kiwis flocked to locally made movies in the 1980s. *Goodbye Pork Pie* (1980), an exuberant road movie, was one of many hits. *Bad Blood* (1981) provided social criticism of gun-toting psychosis in macho New Zealand, while *Smash Palace* (1981), about a failed marriage and custody chase, also tackled dark themes.

Geoff Murphy's (b. 1938) *Utu* (1983) was a breakthrough Maori Western. Vincent Ward's (b. 1956) *Vigil* (1984), a brooding coming-of-age film set in the rain-drenched backcountry, moved New Zealand film into the art house and impressed at Cannes, but international acclaim had to wait for director Jane Campion, whose masterpiece, *The Piano* (1994), garnered three Oscars and put New Zealand film on the map. About a mute woman and her daughter adapting to pioneering life, it used windswept beach locations outside Auckland. Then came Lee Tamahori's (b. 1950) stunning *Once Were Warriors* (1994), a brutal tale of dysfunctional Maori family life. The international hit *Whale Rider* (2002), based on Maori legend, followed a more spiritual path.

Hit comedies include *Sione's Wedding* (2006), centered on Auckland's Samoan community, and Taika Waititi's *Boy* (2010), a Maori coming-of-age film. Waititi (b. 1975) followed up with the critically acclaimed *Hunt for the Wilderpeople* (2016), a huge hit at home. Waititi is also a longtime collaborator with Jemaine Clement and Bret McKenzie, otherwise known as Flight of the Conchords, the comedy-cum-music duo whose self-titled sitcom on HBO was an indie hit in 2007.

New Zealand Architecture

New Zealand's architecture includes no great, defining monuments, unlike Europe and America, but many buildings from its early settlement to the 20th century survive to tell the country's tale of a European society developing in isolation in the Pacific. The most notable indigenous architecture is that of the *wharenui* (meetinghouse) of the Maori. With a gabled roof and front porch, the wharenui was increasingly decorated from the mid-19th century. It became the pinnacle of the wood-carver's art, with fine carvings on the gables and inside rafters, and has also influenced modern churches, such as the chapel in Arthur's Pass Village.

The first European architects employed the early Victorian styles of the era, notably in the South Island cities of Dunedin and Christchurch, which boomed after the gold rush of the 1860s. Influential early architect Benjamin Mountford (1825–1898) specialized in the neo-Gothic style. His stone landmarks can be found all over Christchurch and include the Canterbury Provincial Council Buildings, partially destroyed in the 2011 earthquake, Canterbury Museum, and the original University of Canterbury.

Great wealth flowed through Dunedin, which still has some fine reminders of its Victorian glory days. Robert Lawson (1833–1902) was responsible for the magnificent Gothic-style First Church and imposing Larnach Castle, as well as much of Oamaru's historic precinct, while George Troup (1863–1941) acquired the nickname "Gingerbread George" for his ornate Dunedin Railway Station.

On the North Island, plentiful wood, particularly kauri, was a ready resource and proved more resistant to earthquakes than stone. Early wooden buildings showed distinctive styles, ranging from Wellington's grand Government Buildings and Auckland's Old Government House to Gothic wooden churches such as the beautiful Old St. Paul's in Wellington. Known as Selwyn churches, after New Zealand's Anglican bishop from 1842 to 1868, many of these fine wooden churches can be found in Auckland. Above all, the superb Victorian wooden villas that dot the city suburbs show a unique New Zealand style, albeit one based on existing architectural traditions.

Whale Rider

The movie *Whale Rider* (2002), based on Witi Ihimaera's novel, was an international hit filmed in Whangara on the East Cape near Gisborne. Combining legend with contemporary Maori life, it tells the story of a 12-year-old girl's battle to gain acceptance from her grandfather, the village chief and descendant of Paikea, the ancestor of the Ngati Konohi people.

According to legend, Paikea was the favorite son of Chief Uenuku from Mangaia Island. His jealous brothers plotted to kill him on a fishing trip and tell their father he had drowned. Overhearing the plan the night before, Paikea sank the canoe when they were far out to sea, drowning his brothers. Paikea drifted on a plank, waiting for death, until Tohora the whale lifted him onto his back and took him south to Whangara, where he began his new life.

Later Italianate and Edwardian baroque public buildings can also be found in abundance, and the Napier earthquake resulted in some fine art deco buildings as the town rebuilt, the best example of whole streetscapes in the country.

After World War II, architects embraced modernism, while prefab construction came to define much of suburbia, a trend that continues. Architects such as William Toomath (b. 1925) in Wellington and Christchurch's Miles Warren (b. 1929) have led the way. Recent modernistic buildings of note are the Te Papa museum and Westpac Stadium in Wellington, Sky Tower in Auckland, and Christchurch's Cardboard Cathedral (see photo p. 192) by Japanese architect Shigeru Ban (b. 1957), replacing the city's Gothic cathedral destroyed in the earthquake. ■

Food & Drink

New Zealand has a vibrant food culture, embracing a variety of cuisines and using a superb range of fresh produce, which is expanding as farmers, buoyed by the success of the kiwifruit industry, branch out into new areas. Though the country's British heritage is still evident on its tables, pan-Pacific flavors are now widely found on restaurant menus.

A visitor tries the wine at the French Festival in Akaroa.

Restaurants, wineries, cheesemakers, and a host of boutique food industries are burgeoning in a country whose culinary roots lie in British cooking—an uninspiring legacy. Though long blessed with quality lamb, beef, and seafood, for many years the staple was meat served without spice or variety, accompanied by boiled or roasted vegetables. "Meat and three veg" was the norm on the home dining table and in most restaurants. Spaghetti Bolognese was an exotic dish.

But from the 1980s on, as New Zealand increasingly turned its gaze away from Britain to embrace a wider global vision in many areas, this shift in focus fortunately included food. Modern New Zealand cuisine is usually described as Pacific Rim, borrowing across a wide region from Asia to California, but Mediterranean and Middle Eastern influences also flourish on today's restaurant menus. The visitor will not be starved of choice, and wine lists are buoyed by a wonderful range of local vintages.

Maori cooking doesn't widely permeate the dining scene, though the *kumara* (sweet potato), brought from Polynesia, is a New Zealand favorite. On visits to Maori villages, the visitor might well sample a Maori feast, traditionally cooked in a *hangi* (earth oven), where meats and vegetables are put into baskets and cooked over hot rocks in a covered pit.

If the country had a national dish, it would probably be roast leg of lamb, for even though culinary horizons have expanded, green pastures still produce the prized meat. The country's sheep numbers may have declined in recent years along with world prices, but the lamb is just as succulent, while booming beef and dairy production add to the bounty. Pork, poultry, and venison are also plentiful.

Straight From the Farm

The freshness of the produce is the key to New Zealand cuisine. Fine meats, fresh cream, and locally produced cheeses are available everywhere you turn, orchards supply a wide range of sun-ripened fruits, and the vegetables on your plate were probably grown just down the road. And though farming drives the

A traditional Maori *hangi*, or earth-oven, feast

country, the sea is equally productive, teeming not only with fish but with all manner of crustaceans.

Fresh off the Boats

The ocean provided the Maori with a ready supply of gustatory treats. They dined on such shellfish as *paua* (abalone), *pipi*, cockles, *toheroa*, and *tuatua*, treats still consumed today, though numbers are controlled or declining. In good supply are the huge green-lipped mussels farmed in the Marlborough Sounds, while the fat oysters from Bluff in the far south are not to be missed in season. Delicious crayfish and scallops are also widely available in markets and restaurants.

Whitebait is another New Zealand delicacy, at its best on the West Coast of the South Island. Netted in river mouths, the tiny young fish are typically served as whitebait fritters in an omelet mix. Commercial fishing delivers flavorsome snapper, *tarakihi*, John Dory, *hapuka*, and other varieties, while many of the country's rivers teem with trout as well as salmon, which is also farmed.

Fish-and-chip shops, found everywhere, offer inexpensive seafood. These rate as the country's favorite fast food emporiums, though New Zealand also does an excellent version of another traditional English import, the meat pie.

At the other end of the scale, fine-dining restaurants are also readily available, particularly in the big cities. Even in the remoter regions of the country, wonderful dining experiences can be found, but be aware that a lot of menus have a "me too" approach, all serving up the latest trend at similar prices, regardless of quality.

Marlborough province on the South Island is the country's best known and most productive wine region.

From the Local Vineyard

New Zealand wines rarely disappoint. Starting as an industry limited mostly to a few Dalmatian families producing cheap bulk wine, New Zealand wineries have exploded over the past 30 years. From the warm climes of Waiheke Island near Auckland to the barren extremes of Central Otago near Queenstown, New Zealand produces an exciting array of wines.

Cold winters and mild summers are particularly conducive to fine white wines, but lighter reds such as Pinot Noir and Merlot also do well. Marlborough province on the South Island is the country's best known and most productive wine region. The Wairau and other valleys here produce world-class Sauvignon Blanc, noted for its crisp floral tones, but many other varieties are grown. The same is true of the Hawke's Bay region around Napier on the North Island, noted for its excellent Chardonnay and red varietals.

Other well-known wine areas include the Kumeu region west of Auckland, the Wairarapa near Wellington, and Waipara north of Christchurch. Many wine cellars are open to visitors, and you can reserve your place on a wide variety of wine tours, including those with personalized itineraries and cycling tours. Quite a few wineries also have excellent restaurants, showcasing the best of New Zealand food and wine in delightful surroundings.

EXPERIENCE: Maori Food Tours

For international visitors, Maori cuisine is usually represented by the traditional *hangi* (earth oven) feast, a must on all Maori cultural tours from Rotorua. But the sea and forests hold a bounty of other foods and plants traditionally eaten by Maori.

Maori chef, raconteur, and television personality Charles Royal now shares his arcane knowledge of traditional foods on small group tours (*tel 07/345-3122, maorifood.com, $$$$$*). Operating out of Rotorua, these trips start with hunting for plants and herbs in the outdoors, accompanied by commentary on Maori life and folklore, and end with a feast.

Foods introduced include *pikopiko* (fern fronds), *horopito* (bush pepper),

kawakawa (bush basil), and *periperi*, a fiery seasoning. Flax, used for weaving, yields seeds that are toasted and made into a rich bread, or you may come across *huhu*, the fat grubs found in tree trunks and cooked with pikopiko to yield a traditional treat tasting like peanut butter.

Royal, who worked in some of New Zealand's top hotels and in the United States, then prepares traditional foods in a menu that may include salmon, chicken, and shellfish such as mussels, *paua* (abalone), or *kina* (sea urchin). Meals are accompanied by Maori wines and beer. Royal's food tours can also include fishing, horseback tours, and hunting for grubs. Tours are usually capped at a maximum of six people.

Land & Landscape

New Zealand is a jewel in the South Pacific, comprising large high islands, long isolated from the rest of the world and surrounded by vast stretches of ocean. Once covered in primeval forest, it is a land rich in biodiversity, and its geography is equally varied and stunning.

The country stretches more than 1,000 miles (1,600 km) from the sandy subtropical peninsula at the northern tip to the glacier-carved fjords of the far south. In between lie mighty snow-covered peaks, smoking volcanoes, vast lakes, dense forests, and fertile grasslands. Beaches, bays, and coves punctuate a convoluted, 9,400-mile (15,000 km) coastline.

Formation of New Zealand

According to the Maori, the demigod Maui, who dwelled in the ancestral homeland of Hawaiki, one day strayed far out to sea with his brothers. Using his magic fishhook, he felt a mighty tug on the line and called his brothers to help. After much straining, they hauled up the North Island, or Te Ika a Maui ("Maui's fish"). The head lies south around Wellington, while the tail stretches north to Cape Reinga.

The canoe itself became the South Island, or Te Waka a Maui ("Maui's canoe"). However, most North Island tribes referred to the South Island as Te Wai Pounamu ("the greenstone water"), for this island was the source of prized New Zealand jade.

With an area of about 104,000 square miles (270,000 sq km), New Zealand is the same size as Colorado, or about 10 percent bigger than the United Kingdom. The South Island is slightly larger than the North Island, which together make up the vast majority of the landmass, but significant smaller islands exist, most notably Stewart Island in the far south.

Lying on the boundary of the Australian and Pacific plates, New Zealand is geologically defined by the collision of these giant slabs of the Earth's crust. It is a highly active region of earthquakes, volcanoes, and geothermal activity, part of the Pacific Ring of Fire.

In the north, the Pacific plate subducts, or pushes underneath, the Australian plate, which carries the North Island. The enormous friction of this collision is responsible for the volcanoes and thermal activity of the north.

The Kermadec Trench to the east of the North Island marks the line where the plates meet, but around the center of the country the plates twist along multiple fault lines. In the South Island, the Australian plate pushes under the Pacific plate, forcing up the Southern Alps along the Alpine Fault, which runs the island's length.

North Island

Less mountainous than the South Island, the North Island makes up for it with volcanic display. All of the country's active volcanoes are found around the center

Stunning Giant Gate Falls greets visitors on the Milford Track in Fiordland National Park

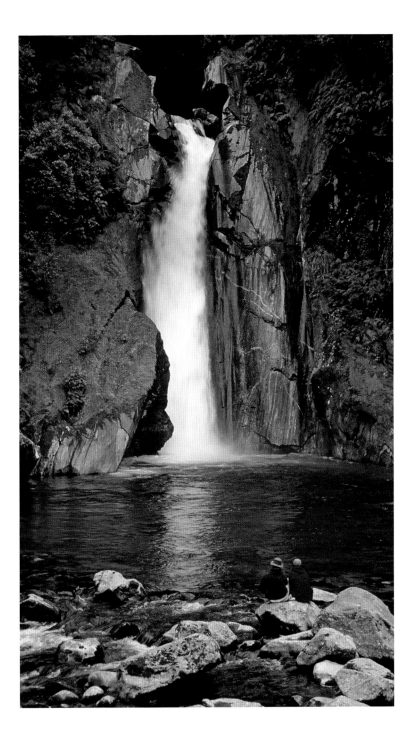

of the North Island, from smoking White Island just off the east coast, through the geothermal regions around Rotorua, to the trio of volcanoes—Tongariro, Ngauruhoe, and Ruapehu—in the high alpine desert of the Central Plateau.

Near the volcanoes, smack in the middle of the island, mighty Lake Taupo is the country's largest lake and itself the product of a massive volcanic explosion. From the lake, the Waikato River, the country's longest, surges north through fertile plains of rich volcanic soil. The farming heartland of the Waikato region is typical of the North Island, much of which is covered with lush green pasture dotted with sheep and cattle.

The Southern Alps trap the rains brought by the prevailing westerlies, making the West Coast of the South Island the wettest part of New Zealand.

Past the Waikato lies the city of Auckland, home to a third of the country's population, on a narrow isthmus that separates the Pacific Ocean and the Tasman Sea. This vibrant city sprawls for miles across old volcanic cones and is rent by harbors.

Northland, the region at the top of the North Island, is a long finger of land lashed by winds on the wild west coast, while the sheltered east coast has delightful coves and bays, such as the scenic Bay of Islands. Kauri forests once covered this area, but only a few small pockets of these massive conifers remain.

The east of the North Island extends from the attractive coastline of the Coromandel Peninsula along the Bay of Plenty, a sunny region noted for kiwifruit orchards, to the remote East Cape, a stronghold of Maori culture. Farther south, the east coast is backed by rugged forested mountains down to Hawke's Bay, a farming district noted for its wineries.

Where the west coast juts out into the Tasman Sea stands towering Mount Taranaki, a dormant volcano. The most stunning mountain in the country, Taranaki's sweeping white-tipped cone dominates the surrounding farmland for miles. Farther south along the west coast, the Whanganui District is named after New Zealand's longest navigable river, which flows from the mountains of the interior. The island tapers at the bottom, terminating at the country's capital, Wellington, which straddles fault lines that threaten earthquakes.

South Island

Scenic as the North Island is, nothing compares to the majestic landscapes of the South Island. The magnificent Southern Alps run the length of the island, flanking the highest peak of Aoraki/Mount Cook (12,316 feet/3,754 m) in the middle. They have another 18 peaks over 10,000 feet (3,048 m) permanently draped in snow and glacial ice, while most of the range is snow-covered in winter.

In the far south of the island around Fiordland, the alps are lower but no less awe-inspiring. In this region, ancient glaciers gouged out deep fjords as well as great inland lakes such as Te Anau and Manapouri. Much-visited Milford Sound is the most famous of the fjords, where sheer peaks rise from glassy waters, while low clouds threaten to drench the primeval forest.

The Southern Alps trap the rains brought by the prevailing westerlies, making the West Coast of the South Island the wettest part of New Zealand. The rain feeds a tangle of dense growth on the narrow strip of land between sea and mighty peaks, while up high, compacting snow creates the Fox and Franz Josef glaciers. These rivers of ice flow almost to the sea and are among the world's most accessible glaciers.

In complete contrast, the leeward side of the mountains is dry. Desert landscapes of craggy rock and scree are punctuated by turquoise, glacier-fed lakes. High plains of tussock grass give way to greenery lower down, but this beautiful world in the shadow of mountains is a harsh environment of freezing winters and baking summers.

Away from the alps, the east coast has rolling pasture around Southland, while the spreading Canterbury Plains around Christchurch are prime farming land. Smaller ranges and hills include the weathered volcanoes of the scenic Banks Peninsula, while in the north, the dramatic Kaikoura Ranges run next to the sea.

The far north of the island presents yet another face. Sheltered by forested mountains, Nelson and Marlborough are warm and sunny, the valleys and coastal land home to orchards and wineries. The seas are also sheltered, nowhere more so than in the stunning Marlborough Sounds, with sun-speckled waterways and forested islands just a ferry ride away from the North Island.

Climate

New Zealand has a temperate climate, and the main population centers rarely record temperatures below 32°F (0°C) or above 86°F (30°C). Climate patterns are highly variable, however, and range from subtropical in the far north to cool in the far south. The mountains experience severe alpine conditions and create a number of microclimates.

Other Islands

Stewart Island, found at the southernmost tip of the country, is New Zealand's third largest island. Despite its southerly latitude, the island has an almost tropical appearance due to surrounding waters flowing in from warmer northern climes.

Great Barrier Island is the largest island in the north, lying close to Auckland in the Hauraki Gulf. **Waiheke,** another substantial island there, is virtually a suburb of the city.

New Zealand lays claim to a number of other remote islands, the only permanently inhabited group being the **Chatham Islands,** 500 miles (800 km) east of Christchurch. Chatham and much smaller Pitt are the main islands of this rugged, isolated group. They were settled by the Morimori, a Polynesian people who developed a different culture from the Maori. It is now widely accepted they were originally Maori from the South Island and did not arrive directly from another part of Polynesia.

Other islands range from the subtropical **Kermadec Islands,** lying halfway between New Zealand and Tonga, to the sub-Antarctic **Campbell Island** and the Snares, Antipodes, Bounty, and Auckland island groups, all noted for their rich bird life.

Surrounded by sea, the islands pull in a lot of rain, between 24 inches (60 cm) and 63 inches (160 cm) per year in most places. The prevailing westerly winds bring most of the precipitation, which is heaviest on the West Coast of the South Island, while the driest area is just 60 miles (100 km) away on the other side of the Southern

Alps. Snow falls on the mountains of both islands, but is rare in coastal areas, though the south and east of the South Island may get snow in winter.

Winds are often gusty and bring sudden changes. Clouds can swirl in the sky, bringing rain, then sporadic sunshine, many times in one day. Areas sheltered from the westerlies have more sunshine; these include Nelson and Marlborough on the South Island and the Bay of Plenty and Hawke's Bay on the North Island. The lack of pollution and a thin ozone layer make for brilliant sunshine and high UV levels.

Flora & Fauna

Isolated from the rest of the world for 80 million years, New Zealand developed unique flora and fauna. Primitive forests flourished and flightless birds evolved free of warm-blooded predators, for the country had no land mammals except for two rare species of bat. Unique species include the long-beaked, flightless kiwi, the world's largest flightless parrot (kakapo), an ancient reptile species (tuatara), the heaviest insect (weta), and the world's largest tree by volume (kauri).

The sea is teeming with warm-blooded wildlife, including whales, dolphins, seals, sea lions, and many species of penguin.

Forests in New Zealand are dominated by podocarps, which are ancient Southern Hemisphere conifers, while in cooler areas, southern beeches are most common. Thick forests harbor a great array of ferns, including giant tree ferns. In subalpine areas, tussock grass and small shrubs dominate. In lowland regions, flax is common, the long leaves producing fiber used in Maori weaving.

The prolific birdlife once included the enormous moa, a flightless cousin of the kiwi that stood up to 12 feet (3.7 m) tall, but Maori hunters wiped out this ready source of food. Other flightless birds facing extinction today include the takahe, with brilliant blue and green plumage and a thick red bill, and the kakapo, a giant parrot weighing up to 6.5 pounds (3 kg).

Other, more populous parrots include the kaka and the cheeky kea, found in alpine regions and in parking lots, where they like to peck at rubber windshield seals. Native fowl include the weka and colorful pukeko, while the numerous seabirds include the royal albatross, which nests on the Otago Peninsula near Dunedin and flaunts a 10-foot (3 m) wingspan.

New Zealand amphibians feature four primitive species of frog. Reptiles include the tuatara, dating back 200 million years to the age of the dinosaurs. The country has no snakes and only one poisonous spider, the rare katipo.

The sea is teeming with warm-blooded wildlife, including whales, dolphins, seals, sea lions, and many species of penguin (see pp. 180–181).

Loss of habitat threatens many species in New Zealand, and introduced animals such as rats and the Australian possum cause widespread damage. The Department of Conservation has an active program of island restoration, clearing offshore islands of introduced pests and reintroducing native species, particularly endangered birds. ■

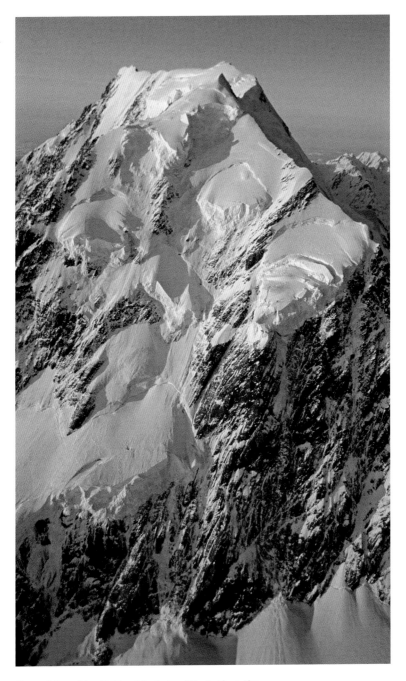

The south face of Aoraki/Mount Cook, star of the Southern Alps

The country's biggest city, sophisticated and attraction-packed, sitting on a glorious harbor near dozens of bays and beaches

Auckland & Around

Auckland skyline and harbor, looking across toward Devonport from Mount Eden

Auckland & Around

Draped over a string of volcanic cones and washed by the waters of two harbors, Auckland has been blessed by geography. The city's craggy coastline holds dozens of bays and beaches, ensuring that residents are never far from the sea, and yachts cram its marinas, earning it the moniker City of Sails.

Add to this maritime scene a mild climate, a robust economy, and all the attractions of a major city, and it is little wonder that almost one-third of all New Zealanders have chosen to live here. Though political power officially resides in Wellington, the city of Auckland is the engine that drives the economy and the country with New Zealand's greatest concentration of wealth, education, and industry.

Auckland is also the world's largest Polynesian city. In addition to Maori, Pacific Islanders from Samoa, the Cook Islands, Tonga, Niue, and elsewhere have flocked here. Add in a growing migration from Asia, and Auckland is legitimately cosmopolitan, despite its relatively small population of 1.6 million.

The city lies on an isthmus barely 1 mile (1.6 km) across at its narrowest between the Pacific Ocean and the Tasman Sea. It is here that the Maori would haul their canoes

NOT TO BE MISSED:

Downtown waterfront, the yachting, eating, and nightlife hub of the city 59

The Auckland walk, a discovery of the city's history 60–61

City panoramas from the top of Sky Tower or the Mount Eden volcanic cone 62, 68

Chic and historic Parnell 63

The Auckland Museum, a fine introduction to New Zealand and Maori culture 64

The Victorian seaside village of Devonport 66–67

A cruise in Auckland Harbour or ferry to Rangitoto or Waiheke Island 70–71

The rugged Waitakere Ranges and wild surf beaches of the west coast 74–75

overland to travel between the coasts. Briefly the colonial capital in the mid-19th century, it lost that status to Wellington in 1865, but laissez-faire growth continued.

Urban sprawl defines Auckland. It spreads over 25 miles (40 km) from the Bombay Hills in the south to Orewa in the north. Greater Auckland includes four main cities: Auckland City on the southern shores of Waitemata Harbour, North Shore City to the north over the bridge, Manukau around Manukau Harbour to the south, and Waitakere to the west. Forest and sea surround the city, providing interesting day trips west to the Waitakere Ranges and east to the islands of the Hauraki Gulf.

Most visitors pass quickly through Auckland, and soaring hotel prices are a deterrant for longer stays. But this city of water and hills has plenty of attractions. Exploration will reveal much of the soul of modern New Zealand. ∎

Auckland

On a glorious harbor with a mild climate, Auckland attracts growing numbers of residents and visitors alike. By far New Zealand's biggest city, it is also the country's cultural hub, mingling English and Polynesian influences, while offering a host of activities, diverse dining spots, and lively nightlife. Its Victorian heritage, happening inner suburbs, dormant volcanoes, and dynamic waterfront make the City of Sails one of the great Pacific Rim ports.

Yachting is a passion in the city of Auckland.

City Center & Waterfront

The Auckland central business district is a story of two cities. The traditional heart of the city is **Queen Street,** running from the ferry terminal up the hill to Karangahape Road. Dubbed the Golden Mile, Queen Street's once grand banks and finance houses may have gone, but many have undergone renovation as retail outlets. The old part of the city has other interesting pockets and shopping opportunities, particularly in the side streets such as **High Street.**

The redeveloped waterfront showcases the new face of Auckland. The City of Sails owes its initial revamp to yachting, for the Auckland waterfront underwent huge redevelopment after New Zealand won the prestigious America's Cup race in 1995, and was remodeled before the cup defense in 2000.

Viaduct Basin, on the waterfront west of the downtown ferry terminal, housed the competing superyachts and was transformed into a lively restaurant and nightlife hub. A pedestrian/cycling bridge leads from Viaduct Basin to **Wynyard Quarter,** another waterfront redevelopment completed for the 2011 Rugby World Cup, with outdoor plazas, waterfront cafés, children's playground, the Auckland Fish Market, and a tourist tram loop. To the east, the old warehouses and historic buildings of Britomart have also recently undergone a major revamp to become a bar/restaurant/shopping hub.

New Zealand Maritime Museum

The Maritime Museum *(Quay & Hobson Sts., tel 09/373-0800, maritimemuseum.co.nz, $$)* at Viaduct Basin celebrates New Zealand's sea-bound heritage, from early Polynesian explorers to America's Cup heroes. A host of galleries and vessels provide an extensive display, and you can shell out extra to cruise the harbor on the *Ted Ashby*, a traditional-style scow, or on a steam tug.

Waitemata Harbour & Queen Street

The **Ferry Building,** where Queen Street meets the water, is the gateway to Waitemata Harbour for the yachtless visitor. Cruises operate from here, though the cheapest way out onto the water

is to catch a ferry to Devonport (see p. 66), a delightful excursion for any visitor to Auckland.

Heading south up Queen Street, landmarks include **Britomart** *(12 Queen St.)*. Once the gracious chief post office, it's now the city's transportation hub, with the relocated train station underground. Shopping, dining, and bars fill the adjacent historic area along Quay Street and especially the area behind, with its promenade and Takutai Square, home to a Saturday farmers market.

Battle for Auckland

Maori legend tells of a great battle between the tribes of the Waitakere and Hunua Ranges, west and east of Auckland, respectively. A Hunua priest called on the sun to rise early, blinding the opposition, who fled. The Hunua warriors gave chase, but a Waitakere priest brought forth explosions from the earth, forming Auckland's volcanoes. The lava stopped the enemy's advance.

Halfway up Queen Street, the **Town Hall** hosts highbrow entertainment since its refurbishment and conversion to an arts venue. It imperiously guards the entrance to **Aotea Square,** a welcome city space that hosts everything from political rallies to festivals and a Friday and Saturday market. It is flanked by the modern

(continued on p. 62)

Auckland

 Map pp. 56–57

Visitor Information

✉ Arrivals hall, Auckland International Airport

☎ 09/365-9925

✉ Atrium, SkyCity, Victoria & Federal Sts.

☎ 09/365-9918

✉ 139 Quay St., Princes Wharf

☎ 09/365-9914

aucklandnz.com

Department of Conservation Information Centre

✉ 137 Quay St., Princes Wharf

☎ 09/379-6476

doc.govt.nz

A Walk Through Auckland

The best place to start a walking tour of the City of Sails is at the waterfront, heading inland to where the city's heritage unfolds. You'll finish at the Old Government House, a relic of Auckland's days as a capital city.

Start at the **Ferry Building ❶**, built in 1912, where ferries ply suburban routes to the north shore and the Hauraki Gulf islands, including Rangitoto and Waiheke. The Ferry Building also houses some excellent waterfront restaurants.

Styled after an ocean liner, the **Princes Wharf** redevelopment farther west includes exclusive apartments, the Hilton Hotel, restaurants, and bars. It is worth a wander along the wharf to see whose luxury liner or private cruiser is in town this week.

Viaduct Basin ❷ (see p. 59) is the grand-daddy of recent waterfront redevelopments. Auckland nightlife continues to thrive, with the Viaduct Basin ringed with bars, restaurants, and million-dollar waterfront views.

Continue around Viaduct Basin to **Market Square,** where the city markets once stood. Farther west, development continues, with expensive yachts moored in front of new apartments and the Wynyard Quarter area. Turn

---

After Your Walk ...

Fun stops in the evening include:

Orleans (48 Customs St. E, Britomart) Auckland's answer to Bourbon Street with jazz and blues most nights, classic cocktails, and even a few U.S. beers and wines on the drinks list.

Northern Steamship Co. (122 Quay St., Britomart, northernsteamship .co.nz) This stylish bar is located within a heritage building in Auckland's Britomart bar/dining district.

Occidental (6 Vulcan Ln., occidental bar.co.nz) After a few drinks, you might almost imagine you're in Brussels at this fine Belgian beer bar.

---

left at Customs Street West, which passes the delightfully old-fashioned **Tepid Baths,** built in 1914. Originally saltwater baths divided into male and female pools, the facility has been redeveloped and now offers freshwater pools, a spa, and a sauna.

Farther along Customs Street West, on the corner of Albert Street opposite the Downtown Shopping Centre, the French Renaissance **Old Customs House ❸** was built in 1888 and converted into shops in 1997. It once housed several government bodies, including the Native Land Court and the Office of the Sheep Inspector.

One block east, turn right up Queen Street. At No. 34–40, **Queens Arcade ❹**, an old-fashioned Victorian shopping arcade. This Auckland icon has craft, gift, and other shops to explore, including Marbecks music store, a local institution since 1934. At the next corner, Fort Street was originally Fore Street, for the shoreline once lapped here. You can picture how dinghies unloaded cargo from larger boats and Maori traded fruit and vegetables at shorefront markets.

Historic buildings on Queen Street include the neoclassical **Bank of New Zealand Building ❺** at No. 125, considered Auckland's finest building when it opened in 1867, now housing shops and an office tower.

Just off Queen Street, **Vulcan Lane** got its name from the blacksmith forges that once operated here. It is home to popular watering holes, including the wonderfully ornate Occidental Pub, dating from 1884. From Vulcan Lane, turn right onto **High Street,** lined with interesting fashion stores and other retail outlets. At No. 19, Unity Books is one of Auckland's best bookstores and always worth a browse.

Cross over High Street into Freyberg Place, named for Lord Freyberg, distinguished soldier

NOT TO BE MISSED:

Ferry Building • Viaduct Basin • Queens Arcade • Albert Park • Old Arts Building • Old Government House

and governor-general from 1946 to 1952, and head up to **Courthouse Lane,** a paved piazza reminiscent of Rome. This popular alfresco dining spot once faced Auckland's first courthouse and police station. Veer right at the cafés, take the steps up to Kitchener Street, and cross to charming **Albert Park ❻,** straddling Bowen Avenue and sandwiched between the city and the university. Despite the name, a statue of Queen Victoria stands in the center. Another statue, of Sir George Grey, honors the career administrator who served as governor of New Zealand and superintendent of Auckland.

The **Auckland Art Gallery** (see p. 62) waits on the southwest corner of the park. On the eastern side, the **Old Arts Building** (1926) is the university's most striking edifice, with a Gaudí-goes-to-Camelot clock tower. Behind this stands the **Old Government House ❼,** a stately wooden mansion with faux stone facade and lacework portico. Built in 1856, it served as the governor's residence when Auckland was the capital. George Grey planted the flame tree in the garden. The mansion continued to serve as a vice-regal summer residence after the capital moved to Wellington in 1865, and visiting English royalty stayed here. It became part of the university in 1969.

🅼 See also area map pp. 56–57
▶ Ferry Building
⟷ 1.4 miles (2.5 km)
🕐 2 hours
▶ Old Government House

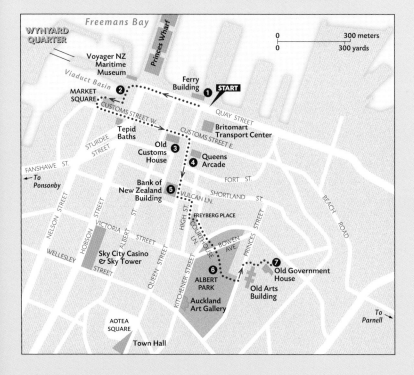

Aotea Centre *(50 Mayoral Dr., tel 09/309-2677)*, the country's main performing arts center, a modern counterpoint to the nearby **Civic Theatre** *(cnr. Queen & Wellesley Sts.)*, an ornate art deco masterpiece. The grand dame of the city's theaters, it's famous for its painted ceiling of stars representing the southern sky at 10 p.m. on an April evening.

EXPERIENCE:
Auckland Bridge Climb

For amazing views of the city and harbor, take the exhilarating climb up and over the **Auckland Harbour Bridge** along the maintenance paths.

Guides share the secrets of the bridge. Built in 1959, within a decade the bridge lacked the capacity to carry the increasing traffic to the North Shore. In 1969, extra lanes were added, thanks to the box girder clip-ons manufactured by a Japanese company: hence the nickname Nippon Clip-ons.

The climb, easily negotiated by those of all fitness levels, takes around 1.5 hours. If you find the climb too tame, you can also bungee jump off the bridge. Book the climb and jumps through **A. J. Hackett** *(Westhaven Reserve, tel 09/360-7748, bungy.co.nz)*.

It seems no Pacific city is complete without an incongruous needle-shaped tower to top all other buildings, and Auckland's version is **Sky Tower** *(Victoria & Federal Sts., tel 09/363-6000, skycityauckland.co.nz, $$)*. At 1,076 feet (328 m), it dominates the skyline by day and night, and an elevator will whisk you almost to the top for dramatic views of the city. Thrill seekers can take it a step further and plummet downward on the SkyJump, a wired adrenaline version of the bungee jump, or SkyWalk the suspended outer rim of the tower. The tower is part of SkyCity, a casino, hotel, and entertainment complex.

Culture Galore

Culture also prevails in the center city, where the **Auckland Art Gallery** *(Main Gallery: Wellesley & Kitchener Sts., New Gallery: Wellesley & Lorne Sts., tel 09/379-1349, aucklandartgallery.com)* has a diverse collection of Western art from the Renaissance and Dutch painting to cubism, with 18th- and 19th-century English painting well represented. The highlight is the Maori portraits by Auckland-born Charles Goldie and Gottfried Lindauer. The collection includes Goldie's 1898 "The Arrival of the Maoris in New Zealand," a controversial painting that promoted the myth of a single great fleet landing. The museum has undergone massive renovations, with an impressive modern addition to the original 1887 French renaissance building allowing more of the collection to be shown.

K Road & Beyond

Queen Street ends at K Road, as locals abbreviate **Karangahape Road,** which winds along the ridge above the city center. Always worth a wander, K Road's shops mix inner city grunge with history. The street has gone through many changes, from early settlement when churches vied for position, to its heyday as a Pacific enclave in the 1960s and '70s, then as an adult store and red-light strip. Asian restaurants, trendy cafés, vintage clothing, and hippy shops are now the norm.

K Road ends at **Ponsonby Road,** one of Auckland's most popular restaurant and café strips. The historic suburb of Ponsonby threw off the slum tag back in the 1970s when students and artistic types moved in. Now firmly well-to-do, Ponsonby has restored Victorian villas that cost a small fortune in a city with some of the world's highest real estate prices. The streets are a joy to wander.

Of the close-in suburbs, **Newmarket,** just beyond Parnell, is a thriving shopping area and fashion outlet center. Commuter trains run there from the Britomart center downtown. East of Newmarket, elevated **Remuera** is one of Auckland's most prestigious suburbs.

Parnell

To the east of the city center, Parnell is Auckland's oldest suburb, and its historic wooden villas are sought-after real estate. Chic restaurants, bars, and stores line the main drag, **Parnell Road,** one of Auckland's most popular dining spots. **Parnell Village,** in the middle of the strip, is a maze of boutiques, galleries, and restaurants along wooden boardwalks draped over the gorge behind.

Of the many historic buildings in Parnell, **St. Mary's Church** *(420–432 Parnell Rd.),* built in Gothic style between 1886 and 1897, is considered to be one of

The IMAX Centre, Queen Street, Auckland

the finest wooden churches in New Zealand. Its lofty interior is particularly impressive. It sits next to the Holy Trinity Cathedral.

Around Parnell

Kinder House *(2 Ayr St., noon–3 p.m., closed Mon. & Tues.)* was the home of the Church of England Grammar School's headmaster. Named after its first occupant, Dr. John Kinder, this two-story stone museum displays his watercolors and pioneering photographs. A few doors down and open on Sundays, charming **Ewelme Cottage** *(14 Ayr St., $)* is a fine example of a colonial wooden cottage. It was built in 1863 for the salaciously named vicar, Vicesimus

Auckland Museum

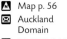

- Map p. 56
- Auckland Domain
- 09/309-0443
- $$ ($$$$ with Maori performance)

aucklandmuseum.com

Kelly Tarlton's SEA LIFE Aquarium

- Map p. 57
- 23 Tamaki Dr., Orakei
- 09/531-5065
- $$$

kellytarltons.co.nz

Lush, whose family lived there until 1968.

Off Parnell Road, Maunsell Road leads to the **Auckland Domain** *(20 Park Rd.)*, a lush 185-acre (75 ha) expanse of greenery on the edge of the city. Among

---

America's Cup Legend

In front of the New Zealand Maritime Museum (see p. 59), at the entrance to Viaduct Basin, *KZ1* is the gigantic 90-foot (27 m) sloop that challenged for the 1988 America's Cup, only to be trounced by U.S. champ Dennis Connor in a catamaran. The contest spent more time in court than on the water, but it helped to spur New Zealand on to win the cup in 1995 with *Black Magic*. The Team New Zealand syndicate successfully defended the cup in 2000, but lost it in 2003 to a Swiss challenger.

---

the gardens and cricket grounds, the **Wintergarden** comprises two domed greenhouses crammed with exotics around a Victorian formal garden. The attached fernery walk provides a wonderful introduction to the ferns of New Zealand, and in front, the Wintergarden Pavilion café is the spot to take tea.

High on the hill in the Domain, the **Auckland Museum** *(tel 09/309-0443, aucklandmuseum.com, $$)* is a major city attraction.

Although Wellington's Te Papa Museum (see p. 156) in its impressive modern space is lauded as the country's best, and is certainly better value, this museum provides a fine introduction to New Zealand. Also known as the Auckland War Memorial Museum, it is housed in a solidly neoclassical building built to honor the war dead, and one whole floor redevoted to war memorial galleries. Maori treasures, exhibits from the Pacific, and New Zealand natural history displays are some of the regular highlights. **Maori cultural performances** *(11 a.m., noon, & 1:30 p.m., also 2:30 p.m. Nov.-March, $$$)* featuring song, dance, and storytelling are a popular attraction.

Tamaki Drive

This scenic waterfront drive through some of Auckland's prime real estate shows the City of Sails at its best. The sandy beaches and calm bays facing Rangitoto Island teem with beachgoers in summer, but whenever the sun shines, yachts tack in Waitemata Harbour and kayakers, windsurfers, bicyclists, and anglers flock to the shore.

From the city center, take Quay Street, which runs in front of the ferry building, and head east. Tamaki Drive crosses Hobson Bay, lined with motorboats, before reaching exclusive Orakei. One street back from Tamaki Drive, **Paratai Drive** is millionaire's row, with fine views of some of New Zealand's most expensive houses.

Orakei is also home to **Kelly Tarlton's SEA LIFE Aquarium.**

EXPERIENCE: Nation of Sails

From the Olympics to the America's Cup, New Zealanders have earned a reputation as the world's best sailors. Auckland, with its marinas crammed with sailing craft, is known as the City of Sails, but New Zealand should be called the Nation of Sails, for sheltered harbors and bays dotted with picturesque islands offer fine sailing around the country.

If you've always wanted to experience this exhilarating sport, sailing operators offer cruises with a skipper and crew, ranging from sightseeing trips with afternoon tea to week-long ocean voyages on maxi-yachts. Alternately, you can charter a vessel to sail yourself.

Premier destinations are Auckland's Hauraki Gulf, the Bay of Islands, and the Marlborough Sounds, though you can also set your watery course from Nelson, Akaroa near Christchurch, and even Queenstown on Lake Wakatipu.

In Auckland, many operators, such as the **Explore** (tel 09/359-5987, explorenz.co.nz), offer the lucky visitor a variety of sailing trips and dinner cruises and a booking kiosk at Viaduct Basin. A highlight is hands-on experience sailing an America's Cup yacht on two-hour cruises.

For serious yachties, **Gulfwind** (tel 09/521-1564, gulfwind.co.nz) offers courses from two-day beginner lessons to longer crew and skipper classes. The **Ted Ashby** is a popular, reasonably priced option for getting out on the harbor, departing from the Maritime Museum (maritimemuseum .co.nz, see p. 59).

Bay of Islands operators include **FairWind Charters** (tel 09/402-7821, fairwind .co.nz) in Opua. This group charters 28- to 45-foot (8.5–14 m) yachts for bareboat (sail-yourself) or skippered sailing trips.

The calm waters of the Marlborough Sounds (see p. 172) are also extremely popular for bareboat or skippered cruises, lasting from a day to a week. In Picton **Compass Charters** (tel 03/573-8332, compass-charters.co.nz) has yacht charters, bareboat or skippered, on the sheltered Marlborough Sounds.

Relaxing in Waitemata Harbour

Devonport

 Map p. 57

Visitor Information

✉ 4/59 Victoria Rd., Devonport

☎ 09/445-6560

visitdevonport.co.nz

If you go to only one aquarium in New Zealand, this is it. An impressive array of big fish such as stingrays and sharks swim over you in a glass tunnel, but the pièce de résistance is the Antarctic Ice Adventure, with colonies of king and gentoo penguins, and displays that include a replica of Scott's Antarctic base. Great for children and informative for adults, Kelly Tarlton's also runs a free shuttle bus.

Tropical plants fill the Auckland Botanic Gardens.

Behind Kelly Tarlton's on the hill, **Bastion Point** was the site of a fort built in 1885 to fight off a Russian invasion that never happened. Ownership of the land, taken from the Ngati Whatua people, was always disputed. In 1977 and 1978, Maori protestors occupied the site, an event that forever changed race relations in New Zealand. The Ngati Whatua eventually won title to their land, and their *marae* stands at the southern end of the parkland.

To the north, an obelisk honors popular Labour Party prime minister Michael Joseph Savage.

Tamaki Drive continues to fashionable **Mission Bay**, with its gentle beach, seaside park, and lively restaurant strip. The road ends at smaller but even prettier **St. Helliers Bay.** Take Cliff Road from St. Helliers Bay to **Achilles Point Lookout** for dramatic views of the city, harbor, and Hauraki Gulf. Just below Achilles Point, stairs lead to delightful **Ladies Bay,** a popular nude beach.

Devonport & North Shore

A trip to Devonport, only a ten-minute ferry ride from central Auckland and a must on every itinerary, combines a cheap harbor cruise with a visit to a Victorian seaside village. Though a suburb, Devonport maintains its village atmosphere and its main-street stores and cafés are popular on weekends. Alternatively, Devonport's B&Bs make a good base to explore the city, just across the harbor.

The town's historic streets are a delight to wander and the visitor center has a good walking-tour brochure. From the ferry wharf, head up Victoria Road to browse the shops or have lunch then continue up the road to **Mount Victoria.** A ten-minute hike (or easy drive) to the top of this volcanic cone is rewarded with fabulous views of Auckland and its waters. Settled by the Kawerau people, the northern and eastern slopes show terracing and pits. Like Bastion Point, Mount Victoria once housed a fort built to defend the city of Auckland from a purported Russian attack.

Fear of the Russian threat also saw colossal fortifications built at **North Head,** 0.75 miles (1 km) farther east. The fort held three battery guns to pound any invaders entering Waitemata Harbour. On an old volcano with stunning views, North Head's military installations can be toured; informative videos play in the historic stone kitchen and the Fire Command Post theater farther up the hill.

Devonport also has small museums, the pick of which is the **Torpedo Bay Navy Museum** (64 King Edward Parade, tel 09/445-5186, navymuseum.co.nz), the museum of the Royal New Zealand Navy.

Devonport is part of North Shore City, which takes in the mostly affluent suburbs across the Harbour Bridge from Auckland. At its heart, **Takapuna** has a thriving shopping center between a small volcanic lake and a good city beach overlooking Rangitoto Island.

Farther north, the suburban sprawl pushes inexorably on. **Orewa,** 22 miles (35 km) north of Auckland where the freeway ends and Northern Gate Toll Road begins, has a pretty, shallow beach and a range of accommodations if you are traveling to or from the north and want to avoid rush-hour traffic.

Volcanoes

Auckland sprawls across 49 volcanoes, and though the Auckland volcanic field last erupted 600 years ago, it is not extinct. Most of the volcanoes are small cones less than 500 feet (150 m) high and the result of the material ejected in a single eruption. Unlike the much more active central plateau of the North Island, volcanic activity here is not caused by the collision of tectonic plates, but by an isolated hot spot or plume 60 miles (100 km) beneath the city.

Rangitoto Island (see pp. 70–71) is by far the largest volcano in the field, and the most recent one to erupt. But if Auckland does blow again, it is likely to be from a different spot in the Earth's

---

Woolen Goods

With 30 million sheep, New Zealand is a major producer of wool and sheepskin products. Sheepskin jackets and coats are good buys, and cozy sheepskin boots are an antipodean specialty.

Hand-knit sweaters are a popular cottage industry here, along with knit cloaks, vests, gloves, and scarves. High-fashion items use factory-woven woolen cloth, which is often combined with mohair or possum fur to produce a beautifully soft and warm fabric.

Local artists produce woolen weavings, and rug producers such as Dilana (dilana.co.nz) create stunning modern designs. There is a showroom at 79–81 Felton Mathew Ave., St. Johns, Auckland, and another in Christchurch.

Wallace Arts Centre

✉ The Pah
    Homestead, 72
    Hillsborough Rd.,
    Hillsborough

☎ 09/639-2010

🕐 Closed Monday

**tsbbankwallace
artscentre.org.nz**

surface, meaning a new volcano could erupt anywhere in the city.

The volcanoes provided rich soils and their steep sides natural protection for the Maori tribes who settled the region from the 14th century onward. Maori *pa* (fortified villages) dotted the cones, and extensive terracing can still be seen at Mount Eden (Maungawhau in Maori) and One Tree Hill (Maungakiekie), and across the harbor in Devonport at Mount Victoria (Takarunga) and North Head (Takapuna).

EXPERIENCE:
Cook Fish!

Auckland Fish Market is world famous for its fresh fish but few visitors realize that located just upstairs is Auckland's only dedicated seafood-cooking school, the renowned **Auckland Seafood School** (*22–32 Jellicoe St., Freemans Bay, tel 09/379-1497, aucklandseafoodschool.co.nz*). The wide range of classes on offer here include BBQ, Thai, fusion, and Mediterranean styles with some of New Zealand's best chefs. Classes typically last a couple of hours and can be booked online.

Mount Eden lies just 2 miles (3 km) south of the city center and is the highest of the mainland cones at 643 feet (196 m). Sky Tower now claims the city's highest viewpoint, but Mount Eden still provides magnificent (and free) views around Auckland. Farther south, off Manakau Road, **One Tree Hill** (600 feet/183 m) offers superb views. The largest of the Maori pa, it was named for the lone tree on top, cut down

by a white settler in 1852, but replaced by a pine, in turn attacked by Maori protestors in 1994. Dubbed None Tree Hill for many years, with just a lonely obelisk on top, a grove of native trees was replanted in 2016 in a spirit of bicultural cooperation. Eventually the trees will be culled, bar one, the survivor of the fittest.

Cornwall Park around the hill contains **Acacia Cottage** (1841), Auckland's oldest building, and **Stardome Observatory** (*tel 09/624-1246, stardome.org.nz*) planetarium. Two miles (3 km) southwest, the **Wallace Arts Centre** houses an extensive Kiwi art collection.

Auckland's Markets

Markets are scattered all around Auckland, particularly farmers markets (Saturday morning markets in Britomart and on Parnell Road are central). Alas, the main tourist market, **Victoria Park Market** (*Victoria St. W. & Union St.*), is now nearly deserted after renovations replaced stalls with upscale shops and restaurants. Nearby, close to the docks, **Auckland Fish Market** (*Jellicoe & Daldy Sts.*) has a fine selection of fresh fish and lunchtime seafood cafés, as well as a program of cooking lessons (see sidebar).

Auckland's claim as the big city of the South Pacific can be seen every Saturday morning at the **Otara Market** (*Newbury St., Otara*). Though not exclusively Polynesian, the Pacific Island influence is strong here and Pacific arts and crafts are a good buy at Auckland's biggest street market.

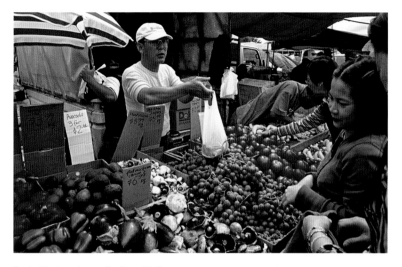

Fresh-picked produce at the Otara Market

INSIDER TIP:

Auckland Botanic Gardens offer a peaceful haven from sightseeing in the big bustling city. Don't miss the hothouses.

—COLIN MONTEATH
National Geographic photographer

More Sights

South Auckland belies New Zealand's claim to racial equality and inclusion. The suburbs of Manukau City are predominately Pacific Islander, Maori, and poor. Manukau has a few tourist attractions signposted off SH1, including **Rainbow's End,** the country's biggest amusement park with eyeball-jolting rides and more sedate attractions to amuse the kids.

At the next highway exit south, the **Auckland Botanic Gardens** *(tel 09/267-1457, aucklandbotanic gardens.co.nz),* on Hill Road, Manurewa, date only from 1973, but they have extensive plantings, with excellent native displays and a good visitor center.

Just off the western highway, 3 miles (5 km) from the city center, the **Museum of Transport & Technology** (MOTAT) is a sprawling collection of vintage vehicles from farm machinery to trains to military hardware. MOTAT has its own Victorian village re-creating early Auckland and a great collection of vintage aircraft, including a huge Solent flying boat from the bygone days of luxury air travel and a rare World War II Avro Lancaster bomber.

A tram ride around the lake from MOTAT, **Auckland Zoo** is home to the usual exotics, but the main attractions are native animal enclosures. They include the kiwi and tuatara house, New Zealand aviary, and sea lion areas. ■

Rainbow's End

✉ Great South & Wiri Station Rds., Manukau

☎ 09/262-2030

💲 $$$$$ (including all rides)

rainbowsend.co.nz

Museum of Transport & Technology

🗺 Map p. 56

✉ 805 Great North Rd., Western Springs

☎ 09/815-5800

💲 $

motat.org.nz

Auckland Zoo

🗺 Map p. 56

✉ Motions Rd., Western Springs

☎ 09/360-3800

💲 $$

aucklandzoo.co.nz

Around Auckland

Auckland's harbor opens out into the Hauraki Gulf, a sailing paradise dotted with islands reached by ferry. Rangitoto Island, a dormant volcano, makes an interesting day trip for walkers. Farther afield, Waiheke Island has fashionable B&Bs, beaches, wineries, and an artistic feel.

The Mansion House on Kawau Island is the former home of Governor Sir George Grey.

Visitors traveling farther will find remote Great Barrier Island, a scenic retreat from the bustle of the modern world. To the west, the Waitakere Ranges encompass a wilderness of regenerating forest, leading to wild, windswept beaches, rolling farmland, and wineries.

Hauraki Gulf Islands

Beyond Waitemata Harbour, more than 50 islands dot the sheltered waters of the Hauraki Gulf. The main islands can be reached by ferry from central Auckland and make an interesting day or overnight trip.

Rangitoto Island, visible from many parts of Auckland, is the youngest of the islands, born of a major eruption some 600 years ago. This symmetrical volcano rises 853 feet (260 m) from the sea, resembling a flattened Mount Fuji. From the Auckland Ferry Building, the journey takes less than half an hour. From the island's wharf, a one-hour walk leads to the top of the mountain for expansive views of Auckland and the gulf, as well as down into the forested crater. (The ferry company also runs trolley tours of the island.) Allow at least three hours including a side trip to the lava caves—rock tubes through which lava once flowed.

INSIDER TIP:

Grab a ferry to Waiheke Island for a wonderful day of café hopping and wine tasting.

—REBEKAH MAWSON
*Embassy of New Zealand,
Washington, D.C.*

Though the island is forested with pohutukawa trees, volcanic scoria covers the ground, so good footwear is recommended. A causeway connects Rangitoto to farmed Motutapu Island.

Virtually a suburb of Auckland, with 9,000 people living around its fine bays and beaches, **Waiheke Island** has long been a popular escape for city dwellers and visitors. Most of the population lives on the west end of the island, spreading out from the main settlement of increasingly chic **Oneroa**, which straddles a beautiful bay. The east half of the island is rural and picturesque. A haven for artists and craftspeople, the island abounds in galleries. Its many wineries can be visited, and a host of accommodations cater to overnight stays. Several tours run around the island, or you can rent bicycles, motor scooters, or cars from the Matiatia ferry wharf.

The largest of the islands, **Great Barrier Island** seems decades away from Auckland, despite being only two hours by ferry or 30 minutes by air. This rugged 25-mile-long (40 km) island attracts those seeking isolation. It has unpaved roads and no banks or ATMs. Electricity comes from generators and water from rain tanks. The Barrier, as locals call it, has scenic coves and beaches, fine walks, kauri forests, hot springs, and rugged mountains along its spine.

Bloody Sky

"Bloody sky" is the literal translation of Rangitoto, which seems to refer to the dramatic creation of the volcanically formed island. However, the island's name is actually taken from "Te Rangi i totongia a Tametekapua," or "the day the blood of Tametekapua was shed." Tametekapua was a Maori chief who died in battle at Islington Bay in the 14th century.

Tryphena, the main town in the south of the island, and nearby **Medlands Beach,** on a beautiful sandy bay, have most of the accommodations on the island, and they fill up in the height of summer. But at other times Great Barrier is simply serene. **Great Barrier Forest** in the center of the island has most of the popular walking

(continued on p. 74)

London, 2015: The All Blacks win another World Cup, beating "local" rivals Australia in the final.

The All-conquering All Blacks

For a small country, New Zealand has produced an inordinate number of champions in sports as diverse as cricket, golf, cycling, auto racing, rowing, squash, and yachting. But in a sports-mad nation keen to flex national muscle on a much larger world stage, rugby rules. Above all, rugby stirs national passions, and the all-conquering national team, the All Blacks, are treated as demigods (see *rugbymuseum.co.nz*).

From muddy fields in rural towns to the gladiatorial arenas of the cities, winter weekends are devoted to the national obsession. Rugby's strong link to the national identity began with the New Zealand overseas rugby tour of 1905–1906, when the upstart colonials defeated Northern Hemisphere powerhouses of the games, including England, where the game originated at Rugby School and went on to spawn variants such as American football.

Since then, the All Blacks have been the team to beat in world rugby. They have won an astonishing 75 percent of all their international games. After winning the first Rugby World Cup in 1987, the All Blacks failed to live up to their status as favorites against the main rugby-playing nations such as England, Australia, South Africa, and France. The cup eluded New Zealand for more than 20 years, a source of national mourning and recrimination, despite regular success in annual competitions against Australia and South Africa.

All was forgiven in 2011, when New Zealand again hosted the World Cup, the biggest sporting event in the nation's history, and went on to beat France in the final to claim the crown. The All Blacks defended their title in England in 2015 to again be confirmed as the world's best.

The national team takes its name from their jerseys, which traditionally are all black

INSIDER TIP:

Don't accidentally wear your new "Australia" cap if you go to a rugby match, or you may have some quick and serious explaining to do to appease the local fans.

—LARRY PORGES
National Geographic Travel Books writer

except for the silver fern logo. At the start of each match, the team famously performs the intimidating *haka,* the Maori war dance (see sidebar below).

Despite the legendary status of the All Blacks, rugby has its critics, including feminist groups and parents worried by the neck-crunching violence of the game. New Zealand rugby faced its biggest crisis in 1981, when the Springbok team from apartheid South Africa toured New Zealand despite world condemnation and massive street demonstrations by Kiwis. Public opinion

was torn and the tour was marred by violence. Despite turning a blind eye to apartheid in the past, New Zealand rugby owes much of its success to Maori and Pacific Islander players such as the great Jonah Lomu (1975–2015), born in Auckland to Tongan parents.

The All Blacks play rugby union, the dominant form of rugby in New Zealand, but that is increasingly under threat from rugby league, a breakaway variant of the game popular in England and Australia. Though rugby purists scorn league, it has grown in popularity in New Zealand with the inclusion of the Auckland Warriors in the professional Australian league, which also poaches union players for its teams. Another variant, rugby sevens, is a faster game with only seven players instead of the usual fifteen.

The national competition representing New Zealand's regions is fiercely contested and can attract big crowds. It is well worth catching a game in winter at one of the country's major arenas such as Eden Park in Auckland, AMI Stadium in Christchurch, or the Westpac Stadium in Wellington, aptly called the Cake Tin.

EXPERIENCE: Practice Your *Haka*

The Maori dance known as the *haka* is accompanied by shouting, stamping, club-wielding, and ferocious grimacing. Though not always a war dance, the haka was often performed to summon the god of war and frighten the enemy before going into battle. Today the best known haka, the Te Rauparaha haka or "Ka Mate," is performed by New Zealand's national rugby team, the All Blacks, before each match.

The Te Rauparaha haka is attributed to the legendary warrior Te Rauparaha, who when pursued by his enemies was given protection by a local chief, Te Whareangi (the "hairy man" of the verse). Te Whareangi concealed Te Rauparaha in his *kumara* (sweet potato) pit, where Te Rauparaha hid and com-

posed his celebration of life over death until he emerged into the sunlight again. Give it a go, but remember to look fierce.

Ka mate. Ka mate. Ka ora. Ka ora.
I may die. I may die. I may live. I may live.

Ka mate. Ka mate. Ka ora. Ka ora.
I may die. I may die. I may live. I may live.

Tenei te tangata puhuru huru
This is the hairy man

Nana nei i tiki mai, Whakawhiti te ra
Who causes the sun to shine again

A upane. Ka upane.
A step upward.

A upane. Ka upane.
A step upward.

Whiti te ra. Hi.
The sun shines.

Kawau Island

Map p. 79

kawauisland.org.nz

trails, including those to the **Kaitoke Hot Springs** and the historic kauri dams, built by loggers to float kauri logs downstream. The island's natural resources were ruthlessly exploited until the 1940s, but extensive reforestation since then has resulted in lush kauri and mixed forest.

EXPERIENCE:
Windsurfing

With hundreds of bays, consistent northeast sea breezes, and plenty of stores, Auckland is famed for its windsurfing. Ask longboard sailors and Olympic medalists Bruce and Barbara Kendall, who make Auckland their home. You can stop by any shop for information on where to go, lessons, and equipment. **Watersports South Pacific** (tel 09/486-7739, water sports.co.nz) in the city's north at Takapuna is a good place to start. Farther north, **Flying Forwards** (tel 09/426-6582, flyingforwards.co.nz) at Big Manly Beach, Whangaparaoa, rents beginner and pro equipment, and its more sheltered beaches make it a great place to learn. Visit wind surfingnz.org and windsurf.co.nz for more.

Long run by the Salvation Army as a rehab center, **Rotoroa Island** opened to the public in 2011 and offers sandy swimming beaches, heritage buildings, rental houses, and an exhibition center highlighting the island's history. 360 Discovery Cruises (tel 09/307-8005, fullers.co.nz) runs ferries to the island and to **Tiritiri Matangi,** an important wildlife sanctuary, home to introduced endangered birds such as the takahe and kokako, as well as tuataras.

Kawau Island

Kawau Island can also be reached by regular ferry from Sandspit (see p. 81), 50 miles (80 km) north of Auckland. Kawau has long attracted yachts seeking refuge in idyllic **Bon Accord Harbour,** which bisects this small island, some 5 miles (8 km) long. Most of the island is privately owned, and accommodations can be arranged at mainland tourist offices or via the Internet.

Kawau was home to a copper mine before one of New Zealand's founding fathers, Governor Sir George Grey, bought it in 1862. Sir George spent a fortune building the imposing **Mansion House** (tel 09/422-8882, $) and introducing a host of exotic trees and animals, including monkeys, zebras, and Australian wallabies. Until recently, the latter hopped around in abundance, but the Department of Conservation is doing its best to wipe out this non-native species. Now a museum, Mansion House and its gardens can be visited, and good short walks lead out from the house.

West of Auckland

The rugged **Waitakere Ranges,** a green haven on the city's doorstep, lie between Auckland and the windswept Tasman coast. A popular weekend day trip for residents, it can also be visited as a scenic detour skirting the city on the way to Northland. Fern-draped forest and long wild beaches give way to rolling farmland and vineyards farther north.

Access is normally through **Titirangi,** a fashionable Auckland suburb bordering Manukau Harbour and the foothills. From Titirangi, take winding **Scenic Drive** up to the impressive **Arataki Visitor Centre** (tel 09/817-0077). The spectacular views alone are worth the stop, but this is also the place for information on the **Waitakere Ranges Regional Park,** a vast area of regenerating rain forest and wild coastline, and the start of the Hillary Trail, a popular 50-mile (80 km) hike taking in some stunning coastal scenery from the ridges.

Continue along Scenic Drive to Waiatarua and turn off to **Piha,** a renowned surf beach and small resort town dominated by towering Lion Rock. The often unruly weather gives the black-sand beaches of the west coast a brooding atmosphere, beautifully captured in The Piano, the 1994 Academy Award–winning film. The opening scenes were filmed at Kare-kare just south of Piha, where you'll discover fine coastal walks.

Back at Waiatarua, take Scenic Drive north along the mountain ridge. A number of worthwhile, if poorly signposted, stops lie along this road. About a ten-minute drive from the Piha turnoff, **Parkinson Lookout** has harbor and city views, and farther on, **Pukematekeo Hill** boasts a 360-degree panorama. From Scenic Drive you can also hike 45 minutes steeply downhill to **Fairy Falls** (signposted from the road), or take an easier walk there from Mountain Road, which turns off farther north.

The main road descends to the lowlands around Kumeu, home to several good wineries. At **Kumeu,** turn left to Helensville on SH16, part of the Twin Coast Discovery tourist route to Northland. One of the region's oldest wine makers, **Kumeu River Wines** (tel 09/412-8415, humeuriver.co.nz) is on SH16 just east of Kumeu. **Coopers Creek Vineyard** (tel 09/412-8560, cooperscreek .co.nz) on SH16 at Hupaia has landscaped gardens. **Treasury Wines Estate (Matua)** (tel 09/411-5501, matua.co.nz) is north of the highway at Waimauku, near where viewing platforms at **Muriwai,** another surf-pounded beach, has close-up views of a teeming gannet colony. ■

Rainbow Warrior

On July 10, 1985, the *Rainbow Warrior*, a ship owned by Greenpeace, was bombed and sunk by a team of French intelligence agents while it was docked in Auckland's Waitemata Harbour. The environmental group had been protesting nuclear tests by France in the South Pacific. Two of the agents, disguised as husband and wife tourists, were caught by New Zealand police. Convicted of manslaughter for the death of a Portuguese crew member, they were sentenced to ten years imprisonment, but served less than three in French custody. Although the French government initially denied responsibility for the attack, it eventually accepted blame. The *Rainbow Warrior* now lies off the Cavalli Islands, near the Bay of Islands, and is a popular dive site.

A rich history, strong Maori roots, a "winterless" climate, and the most stunning coastline in the country

Northland

Cape Maria Van Dieman, Northland

Northland

The sea defines the long peninsula of Northland. It pounds the sand dunes of the west coast and caresses the sheltered bays and beaches of the east. Little wonder that the early seafarers, Maori and European, headed east. Here the Bay of Islands takes top billing for its historical import as well as its superb coastal scenery.

An angler pulls in kahawai along Ninety Mile Beach.

Many visitors to the north focus solely on the Bay of Islands, only four hours by road from Auckland, but a loop through Northland offers diverse scenery, from mighty kauri forests to the windswept splendor of Cape Reinga. Aquatic delights range from sailing and diving to swimming with dolphins. Venture off the beaten path in Northland for the best chance to find a beach all to yourself.

Northland is the birthplace of modern New Zealand. One of the first places to be settled by the Maori, Northland was home to 25 percent of all Maori by the 18th century. One-third of the population is still Maori in this rural region. Europeans also settled in Northland. Whalers and traders, followed by missionaries, arrived in the area in the early 19th century, bringing disease and muskets. Led by Hongi Hika, the Ngapuhi tribe used the new weapons to devastating effect, and a series of tribal wars erupted from 1821 until the 1830s.

Early European settlement was limited mostly to the Bay of Islands, where the inhabitants of the main town of Kororareka (Russell) soon acquired a reputation for vice and drunkenness. The British resident, James Busby, predicted decimation of the Maori population and urged Britain to intervene. The contentious Treaty of Waitangi, signed in 1840, ostensibly secured Maori rights and regulated dubious land sales, but in effect it signaled the beginning of colonization.

European focus and trade soon moved south to the new capital of Auckland, but in the latter half of the 19th century logging of Northland's kauri forests became a major industry, centered around the sawmills of Dargaville. Migrants from Croatia flocked here to dig for kauri gum. By the 1920s, most of the mighty kauri forests were gone and Northland fell into a rural slumber. Lacking industry and isolated by poor roads, it was a forgotten backwater for much of the 20th century, particularly in the far north, one of few regions that remained largely Maori-speaking until the 1970s.

Northland is often described as subtropical, perhaps wishfully, but certainly it is warmer than the rest of the country. The area can be explored by the Twin

NOT TO BE MISSED:

Coast Discovery Road, a tourist route marked
by a dolphin logo, which takes in both coasts.
If time is limited, a short loop can include
the Bay of Islands and the Kauri Coast. A
longer time frame allows exploration of the
Far North and Hokianga; the East Coast has
many opportunities for beachcombing. ■

Auckland to the Bay of Islands

Most visitors traveling north of Auckland head straight to the Bay of Islands, with little more than a lunch stop at Whangarei, the main city of Northland. Those with more time can explore the wonderful coastline east of the main highway, visiting hot springs, historic villages, fine beaches, islands, and diving spots. Past Whangarei, another coastal detour leads to the game-fishing, diving, and yachting port of Tutukaka and more beautiful beaches.

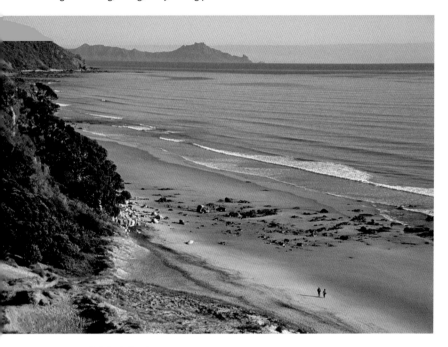

Mangawhai Heads beach

Kowhai Coast

Heading north out of Auckland on SH1, as you leave the suburbs behind, the vista opens out to the rolling hills and the ragged, convoluted coastline of the Kowhai Coast between Auckland and Whangarei.

The first stop of interest is the pretty seaside village of **Waiwera,** at the mouth of the Waiwera River. Long noted for its hot springs, the **Waiwera Thermal Resort** *(tel 09/427-8800, waiwera.co.nz, $$–$$$$$)* has thermal pools, a spa, a sauna, a fitness center, and water slides for family fun.

Picturesque **Puhoi,** just off SH1, was settled in the 1860s by Bohemian immigrants. The **Puhoi Pub** *(Ahuroa & Puhoi Rds., tel 09/422-0812)* is lined with artifacts and historical displays and is a favorite stop for a meal or a drink on the journey north.

Nestled on the Mahurangi River, 39 miles (63 km) north of Auckland, is **Warkworth,** where steamboats and scows once docked. The town clings to its river traditions, though cafés and craft shops now command river frontage. Warkworth is the gateway to a scenic coastline punctuated by coves, bays, and beaches popular in summer.

On the southern outskirts of town, the **Warkworth & District Museum** (tel 09/425-7093, warkworthmuseum.co.nz, $) has colonial exhibits, but of most interest is the kauri park opposite. The park holds the massive 800-year-old McKinney kauri, and you can take a half-hour walk through a grove of kauri trees, palms, and ferns.

INSIDER TIP:

Exploring the Abbey Caves Reserve, just west of Whangarei, is a cool and fun way to spend a warm summer afternoon.

—BRENT OPELL
National Geographic research grantee

Sheepworld (tel 09/425-7444, sheepworldfarm.co.nz, $$$), just north of Warkworth on SH1, is a theme park dedicated to New Zealand's most prolific export. Shearing and sheepdog shows (11 a.m. & 2 p.m.) are highlights.

From Warkworth, SH1 continues north through Wellsford to Whangarei, or you can turn off SH1 to visit the Kauri Coast. An alternate route to Wellsford goes via Leigh and hugs the coastline, passing small beach resorts and remote communities. This winding route is much slower, but makes a scenic excursion. This alternate route heads east of Warkworth off

SH1 to **Sandspit,** a tranquil harbor town and the departure point for ferries to Kawau Island (see p. 74). From Sandspit, the road north passes inlets, small communities, and turnoffs to fine beaches such as those in the **Tawharanui Regional Park** and at **Omaha.**

Farther on, the once sleepy town of **Matakana** buzzes on weekends when Aucklanders flock to its fashionable cafés and nearby wineries. The Saturday farmers market, open until 1 p.m., is a major draw. The fishing town of **Leigh** owes its existence to the

Abbey Caves Reserve

🗺 Map p. 79

✉ Abbey Caves Rd. 0175 Whangarei

☎ 09/430-6562

EXPERIENCE:
Pakiri Beach Rides

Horseback riding is offered all over New Zealand, but for a ride with a difference, try **Pakiri Beach Horse Rides** *(Taurere Park, Rahuikiri Rd., Pakiri Beach, tel 09/422-6275, horseride-nz.co.nz)* for exhilarating gallops on an untouched stretch of white-sand surf beach with descendants of Maori chief Te Kiri of the Ngati Wai tribe.

Rides range from one hour on the beach for beginners to two-hour, half-day, and all-day rides through the dunes and forest. Overnight and multiday rides include warrior trails and stays in a converted woolshed or on a *marae* (see sidebar p. 35).

Whangarei

🅰 Map p. 79

Visitor Information

✉ 92 Otaika Rd.

☎ 09/438-1079

✉ Town Basin

☎ **09/430-1188**

whangareinz.com

snapper that once teemed on the nearby reefs, but now caters to visitors heading to **Goat Island Marine Reserve.**

Just offshore, tiny Goat Island is surrounded by waters swarming with fish. The **Goat Island Marine Discovery Centre** *(tel*

beach is home to the rare fairy tern—observe all conservation signs. The road to Pakiri is partly gravel but is slowly being upgraded to *tarseal* (Kiwi for "asphalt").

North of Wellsford on SH1, turn off at Kaiwaka onto the Kaiwaka–Mangawhai Road for

Sheepworld allows visitors hands-on experiences.

09/923-3645, goatislandmarine .co.nz, $) has informative displays, and nearby **Glass Bottom Boat** *(tel 09/422-6334, glassbottomboat .co.nz)* has kayaks and snorkeling gear for hire as well as boat tours *($$).* **Octopus Hideaway** *(tel 09/422-6212, theoctopushideaway .nz)* offers snorkeling tours and gear, and Leigh has dive operators. Even if you don't enter the water, do explore the rocky shore at low tide, an ecosystem in itself.

Continuing over the hills from Goat Island, you'll find **Pakiri Beach,** a wild stretch of golden sand with views of the islands. The

another scenic coastal detour to **Mangawhai Heads,** a small summer resort with a few stores and accommodations. Boats moor in the estuary and a beautiful beach can be found near the point. The road then goes over the headland to **Waipu Cove,** which has a couple of RV camps on a stunning stretch of beach. Farther on, the town of Waipu lies just off SH1, from where it is 25 miles (40 km) to Whangarei.

Whangarei

A diversion rather than a must-see destination, Whangarei is

Northland's biggest city with a population of 55,000. It's at its best at the renovated **Town Wharf,** overlooking the yachts on the river in the center of town. Well worth a stop and great for lunch, it has craft shops, cafés, an information center, and art gallery.

Clapham Clocks Museum *(tel 09/438-3993, claphamsclocks.co.nz, $),* right by the big clock on Town Wharf, showcases all manner of timepieces and is best visited on the hour to hear the many weird and wonderful chimes. Four miles (6 km) west of town, **Kiwi North** *(tel 09/438-9630, kiwinorth.co.nz, $)* on SH14 has a restored homestead with colonial exhibits, a fine collection of Maori artifacts, including some wonderful feather cloaks, and a Kiwi house.

Few cities can boast a waterfall as impressive as **Whangarei Falls,** on the northern outskirts of town just off Ngunguru Road to Tutukaka. The river plunges over a basalt cliff into a deep green pool; walks lead along the river.

Whangarei also has a superb beach, accessed by Whangarei Heads Road, which wends along the harbor past the port. Pounded by the Pacific, **Ocean Beach,** 21 miles (36 km) east of town, is a sweep of pristine sand stretching north for miles. During the week, you just might have it to yourself.

Tutukaka Coast

A loop road out of Whangarei takes in the fine seascapes of the Tutukaka Coast, noted for yachting, game fishing, diving, and surfing. The road meets the sea at the beautiful aqua-and-

green estuary of Ngunguru and then winds over the headland to **Tutukaka,** with its fine harbor filled with expensive yachts from around the world. As well as being a noted game-fishing center, Tutukaka is the place to organize some of the best diving in New Zealand around **Poor Knights Islands** (see sidebar above).

Past Tutukaka, the road snakes through the hills to the peaceful estuary of **Matapouri Bay,** where a fine coastal walk *(20 min. one-way)* leads to the stunning beach at **Whale Bay.** Adjoining **Woolley's Bay** is no less beautiful, and **Sandy Bay** offers one last glorious arc of sand just before the road heads back inland to SH1. ∎

EXPERIENCE: Diving Poor Knights Islands

About 15 miles (24 km) offshore, Poor Knights Islands are part of a marine reserve washed by unusually warm sub-tropical currents that promote abundant and varied marine life, including sponges, manta rays, and tropical fish. Exceptionally clear water and a reef that plummets 328 feet (100 m) make this a world-class diver's paradise and New Zealand's top dive destination.

Underwater caves, archways, and fissures can be explored year-round with one of several dive operators in Tutukaka. **Dive! Tutukaka** *(Marina Rd., Tutukaka, tel 09/434-3867, diving.co.nz)* is one of the main operators and offers PADI courses, cruises, and more. At the Tutukaka Marina, **Ocean Blue Adventures** *(tel 274/880-459, oceanblue.co.nz)* and **Yukon Dive** *(tel 09/434-4506, yukon.co.nz)* both have dive charters, including equipment.

The Bay of Islands

Sunny and sheltered by picturesque hills, some 150 islands dot the blue-and-turquoise waters of the Bay of Islands. Of all the coastlines in a country blessed with stunning seascapes, that of the Bay of Islands is by far the most renowned. The bay's lazy resort lifestyle in one of the country's premier tourist destinations belies a more turbulent past as the cradle of modern New Zealand.

The Paihia wharf is the gateway to the Bay of Islands.

Bay of Islands
Map p. 79

History

The bay's geography is that of a drowned river system. The rising sea flooded valleys over millions of years, stranding the ridges and peaks of ancient mountains. These islands—many just clumps of rock, but others more substantial—have long provided shelter for seafarers. The first Maori canoes may have arrived around a thousand years ago, and Maori villages once thrived on the islands and coves along the picturesque coast.

Captain Cook was the first European to arrive, in 1769, and he gave the bay its name. Despite firing muskets in warning and, when that failed, letting loose cannon shot "to try what Effect a Great Gun would have," Cook found the locals friendly, and he engaged in trade and entertained chiefs. French explorer Marion du Fresne was not so lucky. In 1772, he and 25 crew members were killed here.

Europeans then stayed away until whalers began calling in

for some early 19th-century R&R. Kororareka (now Russell) became the favored village in which to fraternize with Maori "ship girls" and drink rum.

Kororareka's sordid reputation saw it dubbed the "hellhole of the Pacific." Then the missionaries arrived, to stamp out vice. Samuel Marsden delivered the country's first sermon on Christmas Day, 1814, at Rangihoua, on the northern shore of the Bay of Islands. An Anglican mission station was set up at Kerikeri, while the Catholics under Bishop Jean Baptiste François Pompallier settled at Kororareka. Some of the missionaries lapsed, however; Thomas Kendall took a Maori lover and helped the Ngapuhi chief Hongi Hika acquire muskets.

In the 1830s, James Busby was appointed British Resident to bring order to the Bay of Islands. From his home at Waitangi, in the present-day Treaty House, he pushed for greater British intervention. In 1840, Maori chiefs were convinced to transfer sovereignty to the crown by signing the Treaty of Waitangi (see pp. 90–91), and William Hobson was appointed lieutenant-governor of the new colony.

The following year, Hobson moved the administration from Kororareka to Auckland, and the Bay of Islands went from capital to backwater. Hone Heke, the first chief to sign the Treaty of Waitangi, became increasingly disenchanted with colonial rule and laid siege to Kororareka in 1845, forcing the town to be evacuated. The sacked town was rebuilt and renamed Russell.

The Bay of Islands made it onto the tourist map in 1926 when U.S. writer Zane Grey came to fish for marlin and told the world. International game-fishing competitions helped spur tourism, and the Bay of Islands is now a premier destination. The glorious bay can be explored via a host of activities, from swimming with dolphins (see p. 89) to fishing charters, but most popular are the cruises.

INSIDER TIP:

The eco-center at tiny Aroha Island is the place to go to observe wild kiwis. Call in advance to book a guided night walk (tel 09/407-5243, arohaisland.co.nz/eco -centre-2).

—CHARLOTTE BUEB
National Geographic Intelligent Travel blog contributor

Paihia

Paihia is the first port of call and overnight stop for most visitors to the Bay of Islands. Crammed with hotels, restaurants, and tour operators, Paihia has lost some charm to development, but this likeable resort town serves visitors well. It hums with vacationers in summer, and you can walk from here to the Waitangi Treaty Grounds, one of the bay's principal attractions.

At the town wharf, **Fullers GreatSights** (tel 09/402-7421, dolphincruises.co.nz) is the biggest (continued on p. 88)

Paihia
Map p. 79

Visitor Information
✉ The Wharf, Marsden Rd.
☎ 09/402-7345
northlandnz.com

NOTE: Visiting the Bay Paihia is the tourist center of the Bay of Islands and adjoins the Waitangi Treaty Grounds. At the very least, catch a ferry to the charming historic village of Russell, an excellent alternative base for exploring the bay. Kerikeri is the primary service town of the Bay of Islands region and lies inland away from the main attractions. Just outside the town, the original mission station is a major tourist area.

EXPERIENCE: Maori Culture

Traditional Maori culture is at its strongest on the *marae*, the meeting place of the tribe, usually found in the countryside. However, Maori culture also thrives in the cities, and most Maori are urban dwellers. Resurgent Maori traditions are celebrated, and the Maori influence permeates New Zealand society.

Maori artists are famed for their intricate wood carving.

Don't miss an opportunity to visit a marae if you are lucky enough to get invited, but the most accessible glimpse into Maori culture is via cultural tours out of Rotorua. Many hotels and tour operators include performances of Maori song and dance followed by a *hangi* (earth oven) feast. As you would expect, these are touristy, but the Maori involved are proud of their culture and keen to enlighten as much as to entertain. Rotorua's main Maori centers, **Te Puia** and **Whakarewarewa** (see p. 126) both offer cultural performances and hangi. **Tamaki Maori Village** *(1220 Hinemaru St., tel 07/349-2999, maoriculture.co.nz)* picks up

visitors at hotels and takes them to their re-created Maori village in the forest for evening performances. **Mitai Maori Village** *(196 Fairy Springs Rd., tel 07/343-9132, mitai.co.nz)* is another good operator. In Taupo, the equivalent can be found at **Wairakei Terraces** *(tel 07/378-0913, wairakeiterraces.co.nz)*.

Performances

The **Auckland Museum** (see p. 64) has polished Maori song and dance performances (or *kapa haka*) that are worth catching. And look out for events such as the **Pasifika Festival** *(aucklandnz.com/pasifika)*,

showcasing Pacific cultures every March in Auckland. The national kapa haka contest, **Te Matatini,** held every two years, highlights the best young Maori performers.

Immersion

For a deeper insight into Maori culture, look for rural experiences. Though limited, guides and tours can be found. Northland is a Maori stronghold.

The Waitangi Treaty Grounds in the Bay of Islands is New Zealand's most historic site. Te Whare Runanga, on the grounds, is a national meetinghouse for all Maori tribes, and its superb carvings shouldn't be missed. Guides from the Ngapuhi tribe offer insights, and local Maori tour company in the Bay of Islands **Taiamai Tours** *(tel 09/405-9990, taiamaitours.co.nz)* has a fun take, with war canoe tours (you paddle) to Haruru Falls accompanied by stories and insights into Ngapuhi culture.

At the **Te Ana Maori Rock Art Centre** *(tel 03/684-9141, 2 George St., teana.co.nz)* in Timaru (see p. 209), Ngai Tahu guides provide great insight into Maori culture and history, with tours at the center and to rock art sites outside town. **Footprints Waipoua** *(tel 09/405-8207, footprints waipoua.co.nz)* in Omapere has tours explaining the legends of **Waipoua Forest** (see pp. 99–100) and of

(see p. 209)

INSIDER TIP:

Always remove your footwear before entering a Maori *wharenui* (meeting-house), and once inside, do not eat.

—JUSTIN KAVANAGH
*National Geographic
Travel Books editor*

Hokianga Harbour, where the explorer Kupe is said to have landed. On the strongly Maori east coast of the North Island, in Whakatane (see p. 121), the Ngati Awa people offer excellent cultural experience tours *(tel 07/308-4271, mataatua.com).*

Visiting Maori Sights

Some Maori sites are *tapu* ("sacred" or "forbidden"), particularly burial grounds, and must not be entered. Before you can visit a *marae* (the tribe's compound), you must be invited and receive permission from the community or elders. Maori greet guests there with a *powhiri* (formal welcome) that begins with a chant from the women. On formal occasions, a warrior performs the *wero* (challenge), wielding a club before laying it down for guests to pick up, signifying that they come in peace. After the *hongi* greeting (traditional touching of noses), guests present a *koha* (gift) to the hosts.

Maori Arts

Maori are known for their artistry with local materials. *Pounamu* (greenstone or New Zealand jade) has been highly prized for centuries. Found only on the South Island's West Coast, greenstone was the main trade item between South and North Island tribes. The West Coast is still the center for greenstone crafts, notably at Hokitika, famed for its carving workshops, but carved jade jewelry and ornaments are sold everywhere. The most famous greenstone art form is the Maori tiki (more correctly *hei-tiki*), small pendants worn around the neck. The small humanoid figures with tilted head and protruding tongue are popular with Maori and non-Maori. Bone carving is another traditional craft with practical and ornamental uses. Bone jewelry, particularly stylized fishhook pendants, uses traditional and modern motifs.

Maori wood carvers produced some of the finest work in Polynesia, and the art form has enjoyed a recent revival. Mere (short paddlelike war clubs) are popular traditional items, though the finest examples used to be made of greenstone. Individual wood carvers and centers such as Te Puia in Rotorua produce fine works. Abalone *(paua)* shell was used as inlay in Maori carvings and today is popular in jewelry and inexpensive ornaments in souvenir shops.

Maori women weavers once made cloaks of rolled flax fibers fastened with bird feathers. Almost a lost art, cloaks are again being produced, but they are very expensive and use imported feathers or rabbit or possum fur. More common are *kete*, woven flax baskets fashioned as handbags.

Waitangi

📍 Map p. 79

Waitangi Treaty Grounds

✉ Waitangi National Reserve, 1 Tau Henare Dr., Paihia

☎ 09/402-7437

💲 $$$

waitangi.org.nz

Russell

📍 Map p. 79

Visitor Information

✉ Russell Wharf

☎ 09/403-8020

russellinfo.co.nz

operator of cruises out to the islands past the Russell peninsula. Popular tours include to the **Hole in the Rock** at Motukokako Island near Cape Brett lighthouse, with dolphin and whale experiences and a stopover at Urupukapuka Island. Fuller's Cream Trip, taking in many major sights, is based on the original 1920s service that picked up produce from isolated dairy farms and delivered mail. Tours stop and pick up in Russell. **Explore NZ** (tel 09/359-5987, explorenz.co.nz) also has cruises throughout the year, and many other companies offer water-based activities.

The Strand in the historic town of Russell

Waitangi Treaty Grounds

Across the Waitangi River, 1.2 miles (2 km) north of the Paihia wharf, the Waitangi Treaty Grounds is the birthplace of the nation of New Zealand, where the Maori chiefs signed the Treaty of Waitangi (see pp. 90–91) and William Hobson proclaimed British sovereignty.

Racial sensitivities are reflected at the treaty grounds, where Maori and Pakeha (European) styles come together. Surrounded by

English lawns, the **Treaty House,** built in 1833–1834, was the original residence of the first British administrator, James Busby. This museum re-creates a colonial house and displays a copy of the treaty. Adjoining the Treaty House, **Te Whare Runanga** meetinghouse was built in 1940 to celebrate Maori involvement in nation-building. Designed as a meetinghouse for all the Maori tribes, the intricate carvings inside depict the ancestors and artistic styles of the main tribes.

At Hobsons Beach, the mighty 114-foot-long (35 m) war canoe *Ngatokimatawhaorua* is named for the craft that legendary explorer Kupe sailed to Aotearoa. The largest Maori canoe ever built, it is launched by 80 or more rowers every few years to celebrate Waitangi Day on February 6, when the prime minister, dignitaries, and huge crowds gather at Waitangi.

Allow at least a few hours to fully explore the reserve, which includes an impressive museum, excellent café, and several pleasant walks, including to **Haruru Falls,** an invigorating 3-mile (5 km) round-trip. Guided tours and cultural performances are also offered.

Russell

When Charles Darwin visited Russell (then called Kororareka) in the *Beagle* in 1835, he described the English inhabitants as the "very refuse of society." Lawlessness, drunkenness, and prostitution were rampant.

Today the town has gone from hellhole to historic. Old wooden villas line the waterfront and the lightly trafficked streets are a

EXPERIENCE: Swim With the Dolphins

Dolphins are a common sight in New Zealand waters, where they have long interacted with humans. Two of the most famous dolphins are Pelorus Jack, who regularly escorted ships across the Cook Strait between 1888 and 1912, and Opo, who played in the shallows at Opononi with vacationers and became a national celebrity in the 1950s. It seems only natural that swimming with wild dolphins would become a commercial venture, beginning in the late 1980s. Though now common in locations around the world, New Zealand remains one of the world's most popular dolphin-swimming destinations. Operators are regulated and closely monitored and the activity is said to have minimal impact on wild dolphin behavior.

One of the best places for dolphin swimming is the Bay of Islands, where

Explore (tel 09/359-5987, exploregroup .co.nz), Fullers (tel 09/402-7421, dolphin cruises.co.nz), and Carino Sailing and Dolphin Adventures (tel 09/402-8040, sailingdolphins.co.nz) run trips out of Paihia to see and swim with bottlenose and common dolphins in a stunning natural setting.

Huge pods of dusky and other dolphins come close to shore in Kaikoura as well. Dolphin Encounter (tel 03/319-6777, dolphin.co.nz) runs the only dolphin-swimming trips there. Other places to swim with the dolphins include Auckland; Tauranga, on the east coast of the North Island; and Akaroa, near Christchurch, where rare Hector's dolphins frolic.

Book tours in advance in summer (Nov.–April) and check with operators regarding weather and other restrictions.

---

delight to wander. Russell has the feel of an island, for it is usually reached by passenger ferry from Paihia or by car ferry from Opua to Okiato, 6 miles (9 km) south of Russell. The alternative, the long and twisting Russell Road to Whangarei, is scenic but suitable only for those with time to burn.

From the ferry dock, turn left along the waterfront to the **Duke of Marlborough Hotel** (theduke.co.nz), one of the oldest inns in the country. Farther along The Strand is the historic **police station** (1870), which was once the courthouse. At the end of the road, take the track along the beach at low tide or head up Wellington Street for the 30-minute walk to **Flagstaff Hill**, also reached by car along Tapeka Road. On this hill in 1844, Nga-

puhi chief Hone Heke felled the flagstaff that flew the Union Jack, a despised symbol of oppression just four years after the signing of the Treaty of Waitangi. The flag-pole was replaced and eventually defended by a garrison after Heke axed it twice more, the last time sparking a battle for Kororareka that resulted in the town's sacking.

In the center of town, **Russell Museum** (2 York St., tel 09/403-7701, russellmuseum.org.nz, $) is well worth a look. It has a one-fifth scale model of Captain Cook's Endeavour, displays on whaling and the Battle for Kororareka, as well as colonial and Maori artifacts.

From the museum, head up Robertson Road to **Christ Church** on the corner of Church Street. Built in 1836, it is the

(continued on p. 92)

Treaty of Waitangi

For a short treaty paved with good intentions, the Treaty of Waitangi continues to be the most bitterly contested document in New Zealand's history.

Though the 19th-century treaty would signal annexation of New Zealand, Britain was at first a reluctant colonizer, following the debacle in the American colonies. But as lawlessness grew throughout New Zealand and the private New Zealand Company began a policy of wholesale settlement, even wanting to establish its own government, Britain decided that the time had come to act.

British naval officer Capt. William Hobson arrived in the Bay of Islands on January 29, 1840, to establish a colony. The Colonial Office at that time was headed by men of deep religious beliefs who had fought against slavery, and they insisted that Maori agreement be obtained. Hobson drafted a treaty in four days and set about convincing Maori tribes to transfer sovereignty to the British crown.

The Maori Question

Missionaries translated the treaty into the Maori language, and on February 5 the document was put before a gathering of northern chiefs on the lawns of the British resident's house at Waitangi. The chiefs debated the treaty into the night, and the following day 45 of them signed. The treaty then toured the North Island; by the end of the year, 500 chiefs had signed.

The Treaty of Waitangi consists of only three articles. The first grants the British monarch (then Queen Victoria) sovereignty over New Zealand. The second gives the chiefs full "exclusive and undisturbed possession of their Lands and Estates Forests Fisheries and other properties." It also says that if the Maori wish to sell land, they can do it only through the Crown. The third article grants Maoris "all the Right and Privileges of British Subjects."

Debate has raged over the differences between the English and Maori versions of the treaty, but undoubtedly the chiefs signed believing Britain would protect their interests. As settlers flooded in, however, Maori rights were pushed aside. When Maori chiefs united to restrict the sale of land in the 1860s, the New Zealand Wars ensued, and in the aftermath the settlers seized huge tracts of Maori land. In 1877, the courts declared the treaty a "simple nullity," and it was all but dead for a hundred years.

Recent Disputes

Though the terms of the treaty had been dishonored, New Zealand politicians trumpeted the agreement as an example of the equality given to Maori. In the 1970s, Maori activists put to rest the "happy native" myth. Land protests became a focus for resurgent Maoridom, and in 1975 the government set up the Waitangi Tribunal to investigate treaty breaches from that date.

In 1985, the reformist Labour government extended Waitangi Tribunal powers back to 1840, and the number of claims soon burgeoned. The first major compensation of NZ$170 million was paid to the Tainui tribe in 1995 for land seized in Waikato, and other claims included not just land but also forests, fisheries, and even FM transmission rights. Since then more than half of tribes have reached settlements totaling over NZ$1.5 billion but the claim process continues. While the country sees a need to redress past injustices, there is also a backlash against the "grievance industry," mostly from sections of the Pakeha community but also some conservative Maoris such as politician Winston Peters. Some see the financial redress as too generous, others not enough, and the process has come under attack as overly controlled by the government, or benefitting *iwi* (tribe) at the expense of *hapu* (subtribes). Overall though, the process has contributed significantly to racial tolerance and harmony, and its goal of achieving justice.

Opposite: James Ingram McDonald's 1913 portrait of Capt. William Hobson
Below: Protestors make their way to the Treaty Grounds to mark Waitangi Day.

Kerikeri

Map p. 79

oldest church in the country. Four seamen from the H.M.S. *Hazard* were killed near here during Hone Heke's 1845 attack on the town, and the original marker from their grave can be found inside the church. The graveyard outside tells the poignant tale of early settlement and includes the graves of Ngapuhi chief Tamati Waka Nene (who fought against Hone Heke), the Clendon family (James R. Clendon was the first U.S. consul), and many American whalers.

At the southern end of the waterfront, **Pompallier House** *(The Strand, tel 09/403-9015, $)* formed part of the Catholic mission founded by Bishop Jean Baptiste François Pompallier (circa 1801–1871) in 1838. This French provincial building housed printing presses to produce religious booklets in Maori. After the mission moved to Auckland, the building became a tannery.

The area's premier walk is the overnight **Cape Brett Track,** a superb ridge hike 10 miles (16 km) to the lighthouse from Rawhiti, which is 16 miles (26 km) from Russell by road or water taxi. Book permits and the Cape Brett Hut *(doc.govt.nz)*.

Near the wharf, the **Bay of Islands Swordfish Club** *(sword fish.co.nz)* on The Strand welcomes visitors wishing to view their fishing memorabilia, including a gigantic blue marlin on the wall, photos,

Maori Creation Story

In the beginning was nothingness, but then came Papatuanuku, the earth mother, and Ranginui, the sky father, who had many male children, the gods of the Maori.

Held in their parents' embrace so tight no light could penetrate, the gods tired of the continual darkness. They decided to separate their parents and break into the light. For a long time they debated the best way to part Papatuanuku and Ranginui.

The god of war, Tumatauenga, said "Let us kill our parents." But Tanemahuta, god of the forest, urged for separation, saying Ranginui should be forced up to the sky.

All the gods finally agreed except for Tawhirimatea, god of winds and storms. He held his breath as, one by one, the gods set about separating earth and sky.

Rongomatane, the god of cultivated foods, tried but failed, as did Tangaroa, god of the sea. The god of wild foods, Haumiatiketike, was also unable to part the heavens from the earth.

Tumatauenga the warrior hacked at the bonds between earth and sky, but he could not sever them.

Finally, Tanemahuta stepped up. With the strength and patience of a slowly growing kauri tree, he strained and pushed—his shoulders against his mother Papatuanuku, his feet against his father Ranginuiuntil finally they parted and light flooded the world.

Tawhirimatea fled to be with his father, and to this day vents his stormy revenge upon the world.

A multitude of creatures were revealed by the light, but humans were missing, so Tanemahuta fashioned a woman, Hineahuone, from clay.

Tanemahuta and Hineahuone had a daughter called Hinetitama, whom Tanemahuta also took as his wife. They in turn had children, ensuring that humans would flourish, but when Hinetitama found out that Tanemahuta was her father, she fled in shame to the underworld where she became Hinenuiitepo, goddess of the night.

and the 1920s catch boards that feature Zane Grey.

Urupukapuka Island

Most of the bay's islands are tiny outcrops, and only a handful were ever inhabited or farmed. The main islands are now mostly recreation areas reached by yacht or chartered water taxi. The exception is Urupukapuka Island, a stop on some of the regular cruises. Walking trails traverse grassy hills and take in archaeological sites of the Maori villages. Zane Grey camped on the island at Otehei Bay, where a fishing club resort was established in 1927. The resort, now run by **Explore NZ** *(exploregroup.co.nz /en/otehei-bay),* caters to group retreats but its bar/café is open to the public, and it also rents kayaks. Three DOC campgrounds cater to overnight campers.

Kerikeri

With a warm climate and surrounded by rich orchards and the delights of the Bay of Islands, the town of Kerikeri attracts growing numbers of residents.

Just to the north is **Kerikeri Mission Station,** one of the country's oldest settlements, established in 1819 next to the Kororiko Pa in a picturesque basin where the Kerikeri River enters the estuary. Picturesque **St. James Church** (1878) replaced the original church on the site. The imposing **Stone Store** was built in 1832–1836 as a storehouse for the mission. The Kemp family took it over after the mission's closure in 1848 and it was run as a shop for many years. Now

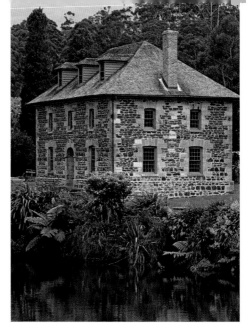

Kerikeri's Stone Store is the country's oldest stone building.

decked out as a colonial store and museum, the shop sells tours *($)* to the solidly built **Mission House** behind. New Zealand's oldest surviving European building, now a museum with some original furnishings, this elegant wooden house was built in 1821–1822 for the Reverend John Butler. The Kemp family lived here from 1831 to 1974.

A short walk beyond the wharf leads to the remains of the evocative **Kororiko Pa,** where the great Ngapuhi chief Hongi Hika assembled his war parties. Wander across the river and you'll find **Rewa's Village** *(tel 09/407-6454, $),* which replicates a Maori village with huts built by traditional means.

For a scenic and invigorating hike, take the **Kerikeri River Track,** which begins at the village parking lot and takes you to the lovely Rainbow Falls *(1 hour one-way),* passing Wharepuke Falls and the Fairy Pools on the way. ∎

Stone Store and Mission House

✉ 246 Kerikeri Rd., Kerikeri Basin

☎ 09/407-9236

💲 $

Far North

Beyond the Bay of Islands, the Far North is the warmest region of the country and home to remote bays, beaches, and Maori towns.

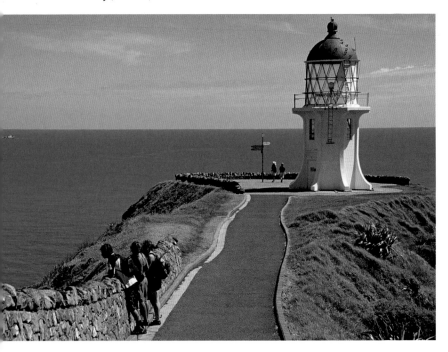

The Cape Reinga lighthouse marks New Zealand's northernmost point.

Its highlights are Doubtless Bay, which includes charming Mangonui and fine beaches, and Cape Reinga, the country's most northerly point at the end of a long peninsula of sand dunes. Exhilarating tours along Ninety Mile Beach to Cape Reinga can be arranged in Kaitaia.

Doubtless Bay

The bay's name comes from Captain Cook, who sailed past the entrance in 1769 and noted it was "doubtless a bay" in his journals. Whaling and later kauri attracted settlers. Today the sleepy fishing port of **Mangonui** offers a good heritage walk, taking in historic buildings such as the Mangonui Hotel and the courthouse. The highlight for many is the self-proclaimed world-famous **Mangonui Fish Shop** (Beach Rd.), an ideal lunch spot perched over the water with tables on a deck. **Butler Point** (butlerpoint.co.nz, tel 09/0800 687-386, $), a privately owned property at Hihi on the far side of the harbor, has a whaling museum and the 1847 house of whaler William Butler (by appt.).

INSIDER TIP:

Coopers Beach's north end is surrounded by pohutukawa trees, also called New Zealand Christmas Trees for their bright red flowers in summer.

—ANGELA GORE
*Embassy of New Zealand,
Washington, D.C.*

West of Mangonui on SH1, **Coopers Beach** is a sprawling collection of baches (New Zealandese for vacation houses) merging into **Cable Bay,** an arc of golden sand before a pretty headland, once linked to Australia by telegraph cable. The road then crosses the causeway to **Taipa,** the last part of this trio of small beach resorts, said to be the landing place of the great Polynesian explorer Kupe.

The **Karikari Peninsula,** a crooked finger of remote unspoiled beaches, forms the western flank of Doubtless Bay. Its most renowned beach, **Matai Bay,** has two perfect bays ideal for swimming. Dolphins also frolic here. Summer vacationers flock to the simple DOC campground, but at other times you may have this idyllic beach to yourself.

Cape Reinga &
Ninety Mile Beach

The country's main highway, SH1, snakes through the middle of the long Aupouri Peninsula to **Cape Reinga,** the last gasp of New Zealand at the top of the North Island. A lonely lighthouse looks out over the cliffs to the Columbia Bank where the Pacific Ocean meets the Tasman Sea, a swirling maelstrom in stormy weather. An obligatory signpost to other lands across the vast ocean only serves to confirm that this is the end of the world. The Cape Reinga Coastal Walkway, running from the lighthouse along the west coast and more sheltered east coast, can be done as a four-day hike or sampled in shorter sections. Two hours' walk from Cape Reinga, beautiful

Speed Demon

On January 26, 1932, Australian daredevil Norm "Wizard" Smith attempted to set the world land speed record on Ninety Mile Beach. His car, the *Enterprise,* was built around a massive Napier Lion airplane engine, ice-cooled and supercharged to produce 1,450 horsepower. Although hindered by the tides, Smith set a new world 10-mile speed record of 164.08 miles an hour (264.06 kph).

Tapotupuputo Bay has a basic DOC campground and accommodates motor homes.

The Maori called this windswept and remote peninsula Te Hiku o te Ika a Maui, the "tail of the fish of Maui." From his canoe (the South Island), Maui dragged a giant fish out of the sea to form the North Island. Wellington is at the head of the fish, and Te Rerenga Wairua (Cape Reinga) lies at the tip of the tail. Te Rerenga Wairua translates as "departure place of the spirit," for the spirits of the dead make the long journey here to depart Aotearoa for Hawaiki, the spiritual homeland.

Captain Cook called this the Desert Coast, for the west coast along **Ninety Mile Beach** (in fact only 60 miles/100 km long) is a desolate landscape of giant dunes and surf-pounded sand. Vehicles can drive along the hard beach sands, once the default highway before SH1 was built, but all rental car agreements ban beach use, and not without good reason.

EXPERIENCE:
Beach Bashing to Cape Reinga

By far the best way to reach Cape Reinga is to take the beach highway along the sands of Ninety Mile Beach at low tide. Given that insurance policies forbid rental vehicles traveling on the sand, a tour is the way to go. Buses and 4WD vehicles make the trip from Kaitaia and also from the Bay of Islands (a much longer day trip). Tours take in the Te Paki sand dunes, Cape Reinga lighthouse, the Ancient Kauri Kingdom woodcraft center, sand dune tobogganing, and possibly Gumdiggers Park, Rarawa Beach, and other points of interest. Kaitaia operators include **Harrisons Cape Runner** (tel 09/408-1033, harrisonscapereingatours .co.nz), **Sand Safaris** (tel 09/408-1778, sandsafaris.co.nz), and **Cape Reinga Adventures** (tel 09/409-8445, capereinga adventures.co.nz). From Paihia, **Dune-Rider** (tel 09/359-5987, exploregroup.co.nz) offers tours in a funky 4WD vehicle.

INSIDER TIP:

Even if you skip driving on Ninety Mile Beach, take the short detour to the northern access (near Te Paki) and enjoy the shifting shapes and patterns of the dunes.

—NICOLAS BARTH
National Geographic research grantee

Travel can only occur around low tide or else soft sands will swallow vehicles. Tours by 4WD and beach buggies operate out of Kaitaia (see sidebar). Beach bashing (driving) is the most exhilarating way to explore the peninsula and allow you to get up close to the giant **Te Paki sand dunes**, a spectacular sight. The dunes can also be approached along the Te Paki Stream Road, a turnoff from SH1 just before Cape Reinga.

The inland highway goes mostly through farmland, but points of interest lie off it. If you are coming from the south at the start of the peninsula, wide and wild **Waipapakauri Beach** provides the easiest access to Ninety Mile Beach. About 10 miles (16 km) farther north on SH1, a signposted road leads east to **Gumdiggers Park** (Heath Rd., tel 09/406-7166, gumdiggerspark.co.nz, $), where paths lead around the old swamp kauri forests. Gumdiggers once flocked here looking for fossilized kauri gum, the tree sap prized for varnish and linoleum. They dug

Sand tobogganing on the Te Paki sand dunes

holes all over this area and one of their huts remains. Halfway along the peninsula past Ngataki, turn off to **Rarawa Beach,** noting its white silica sands, used in glass-making. The beaches along the east coast here are also a brilliant white, culminating at the giant white sandbar at the entrance to remote **Parengarenga Harbour.**

On the northern outskirts of Awanui, the **Ancient Kauri Kingdom** *(229 SH1)* is a large shop specializing in souvenirs made from ancient kauri dug up out of the swamps, some of it 45,000 years old. Don't miss the staircase carved out of a huge kauri stump.

Kaitaia

Haere Mai, Dobro Dosli ("Welcome" in Maori and Dalmatian) greets visitors entering Kaitaia, for this largely Maori town also celebrates its Dalmatian roots. Dalmatians from Yugoslavia settled here in droves in the 19th century to

dig for kauri gum. Now primarily a place to arrange trips to Cape Reinga, the Far North's main town has all the services a visitor could want, but few reasons to stop and stay. The impressive new **Te Ahu Centre** *(teahu.org.nz)* has an information center, library, and the small **Far North Regional Museum** *(tel 09/408-9454, teahuheritage.co.nz, $).*

Just west from Kaitaia, **Ahipara** lies at the southern end of Ninety Mile Beach. This small settlement has places to stay, and not much else, but the ocean aspect makes it a pleasant alternative to Kaitaia. The giant sand dunes of the Ahipara gumfields in the hills above the beach are popular for sand tobogganing, and the beach is ideal for long walks at sunset.

Heading to Hokianga, the scenic road from Ahipara to Rawene goes through the stunted but beautiful **Herekino Forest** and continues through a delightful rural backwater of one-horse towns. ∎

Kaitaia

  Map p. 79

Visitor Information

✉ Te Ahu Center, cnr. Church & South Rds.

☎ 09/408-9450

teahu.org.nz

Kauri Coast

Mighty kauri trees grow only above the 38th parallel and once covered much of Northland. Now only a few pockets remain, most notably in the Waipoua Forest on Northland's west coast.

Matakohe's Kauri Museum is filled with beautiful golden kauri wood.

Hokianga Harbour

🗺 Map p. 79

Visitor Information

✉ 29 State Highway 12, Opononi

☎ 09/405-8869

The Kauri Coast follows SH12 from the Hokianga region, on the scenic harbor of the same name, south to the mighty trees of Waipoua Forest, then on to the smaller Trounson Kauri Park and the fascinating Kauri Museum at Matakohe.

Hokianga Harbour

Hokianga Harbour takes its name from Hokianga-nui-a-Kupe— the "departing place of Kupe"— for legend has it that after discovering and exploring New Zealand, Kupe made his last stop here and grew *kumara* (sweet potatoes) for the return voyage to Hawaiki.

French explorer Jean de Surville first sighted Hokianga in 1769, just before Captain Cook, but neither crossed the shallow sandbars into the harbor. The area relied on the kauri trade until the forests were ravaged in the early 20th century.

Today Hokianga rests in scenic slumber, its seaside towns graced with colonial homesteads and wooden churches on the backwater route between the

Kauri Coast and the Far North. Make sure to take the car ferry *(tel 09/405-2602)* that runs every hour between Rawene and the Narrows, a delightfully relaxed journey that cuts off a long drive around the harbor.

The town of **Rawene** awakens with a brief flurry of activity when the ferry docks. Otherwise the streets are quiet and a delight to wander, littered with historic buildings, including **Clendon House** *(tel 09/405-7874, clendonhouse .co.nz, $)*. You can also catch a bite at one of the town's cafés, such as the Boatshed next to the water.

Dolphin Mania

The young bottlenose dolphin Opo has been immortalized by statues, books, and folk songs (most famously Crombie Murdoch's 1956 chart topper, "Opo the Friendly Dolphin"). After she died, allegedly dynamited by an irate fisherman, the entire country mourned.

Legend lingers at **Opononi,** where a statue commemorates Opo, a wild dolphin that became a national celebrity in 1955 when it socialized with vacationers (see sidebar above). The adjoining town of **Omapere** has a quirky museum *(14 Waianga Place, ourhokianga.com, closed Sundays)* with displays on Opo and Hokianga history.

Just west of Omapere above the head of the harbor, turn off the highway and take the short

Be sure to visit Tane Mahuta (Lord of the Forest), the largest tree in New Zealand and surely one of the largest you'll see anywhere in the world.

—BRENT STEPHENSON
National Geographic research grantee

lookout point walkway from the end of Signal Station Road for a superb panorama: beautiful beaches, the pounding surf of the west coast, and the bald, ravaged hills and giant sand dunes opposite Omapere.

Waipoua Forest

The Waipoua Forest, 12 miles (20 km) from Hokianga, is the most significant kauri reserve in the country, containing three-quarters of all remaining kauri trees. Bought from the Maori in 1876, the forest escaped logging because of its remoteness. After the State Forest Service began cutting some of the trees in the 1940s, a massive petition was launched and Waipoua became a forest sanctuary in 1952.

This beautiful rain forest also contains giant tree ferns and hardwoods as impressive as the kauri in many places, but nothing compares to **Tane Mahuta** (Lord of the Forest). The first stop if coming from the north, this giant kauri towers 168 feet (51.5 m) and has a girth of 45 feet (14 m). Believed to be 2,000 years old,

Dargaville

 Map p. 79

Visitor Information

✉ 4 Murdoch St.

☎ 09/439-8360

**kauriinfocentre
.co.nz**

it is the largest living tree in New Zealand, though by no means the largest kauri ever recorded—one specimen, named the Kairaru, was three times the volume. Only a five-minute walk from the road, Tane Mahuta is the park's number one attraction.

A couple of miles south, a 20-minute walk leads from the parking lot to **Te Matua Ngahere** (Father of the Forest), the second largest tree in the forest. Just off this trail, the **Four Sisters** is a group of four graceful trees. Near the trail to the Four Sisters, another trail (40 min. one-way) branches off to the Yakas kauri, the seventh largest in the forest. The Waipoua

River Road leads to the **Waipoua Forest Visitors Centre** (tel 09/439-6455, teroroa.iwi.nz) and campground, which also has basic hut and cabin accommodations. The forest has now returned to the control of the Te Roroa people after settlement of their claims with the Waitangi Tribunal, based on breaches of the Treaty of Waitangi.

One of the best ways to explore the forest is with a Maori guide; try **Footprints Waipoua** (tel 09/405-8207, footprints waipoua.co.nz) in Omapere. Daytime and atmospheric twilight tours are available.

Waipoua to Auckland

Though much smaller than Waipoua, the 1,112-acre (450 ha) forest restoration reserve of **Trounson Kauri Park** has an impressively dense stand of kauri that can be explored by an easy half-hour loop walk. The reserve is also home to such threatened species as kukupa (pigeons), pekapeka (bats), and North Island brown kiwi. The nearby **Kauri Coast Holiday Park** (Trounson Park Rd., tel 09/439-0621, kauricoasttop10.co.nz) offers guided night walks ($$) through the forest with a good chance of spotting kiwi—a rare experience.

The northern turnoff from SH12 to Trounson is 10 miles (16 km) south of Waipoua, but this access road is mostly unpaved. From the southern turnoff, which is 25 miles (40 km) north of Dargaville, it is only 4 miles (7 km) along a paved road.

Dargaville, on Kaipara Harbour,

The giant kauri tree Tane Mahuta in the Waipoua Forest

Kauri Trees

Kauri trees have taken on an almost mystical significance for New Zealanders now that most of them have been wiped out by logging. Though the sequoia may be taller and older, for sheer wooden bulk the kauri has no equal. Growing for up to 2,000 years, the trunks can reach a diameter of 16 feet (5 m) and soar to heights of 160 feet (49 m). Moreover, the trunks don't taper inward until the first branches, sometimes over 65 feet (20 m) up, providing massive cylinders of straight-grained wood.

Kauri became the backbone of the country's timber industry and was at one stage New Zealand's greatest export.

Mills proliferated along the west coast in the 19th century and ports such as Dargaville on Kaipara Harbour boomed. The trade was so voracious that by 1900 only 10 percent of the forests remained. Now less than 4 percent are left.

A member of the Araucariaceae family, the kauri is high in resin, which the trees leak when damaged. The Maori prized this sap, or kauri gum, for burning in torches, and it was harvested in the 19th century for varnishes and linoleum. Sometimes harvesters bled the trees for the sap, but mostly it was dug up from ancient buried forests, which yielded great clumps of semifossilized gum.

---

grew up on the kauri trade. Dozens of sawmills operated around here, and in its heyday a hundred million board feet of kauri was exported every year, the equivalent of 37,000 mature kauri trees, each about a thousand years old.

Dargaville grew rich on the kauri trade, but much of that wealth has drifted away and today it is noted for kumara production. On a hill with panoramic views across the town and river, the large **Dargaville Museum** (Harding Park, tel 09/439-7555, dargavillemuseum .co.nz, $) has good exhibits on the kauri industry and a huge canoe from pre-European times, but most visitors save their energy for the more impressive Kauri Museum down the highway in Matakohe.

For a taste of the wild west coast, small **Baylys Beach**, 8 miles (13 km) west of town on Baylys Coast Road, has accommodations and a couple of good cafés on a 60-mile-long (100 km) beach.

For a complete education on all things kauri, the **Kauri Museum** (Church Rd., tel 09/431-7417, kauri-museum.com, $$) in the small town of **Matakohe** is a must-see, possibly New Zealand's best museum outside of the main cities. In addition to detailed kauri exhibits, it contains a reproduction of a sawmill, an old boardinghouse made of kauri, old machinery, and many pioneer exhibits. Pride of place goes to a huge vertical slice from the middle of a felled kauri that not only illustrates the size of the trees but the exquisite beauty of the wood.

From Matakohe, SH12 continues to Brynderwyn and joins SH1 south to Auckland. For an alternate route into Auckland, turn off at Wellsford, 17 miles (28 km) south of Brynderwyn, and follow the Kaipara Harbour on SH16 to Helensville and on to the west coast and Waitakere Ranges (see pp. 74–75). ∎

Maori culture and geysers plus volcanoes, lakes, mountains, caves, beaches, and historic towns

Central North Island

Mount Taranaki looms over the central North Island.

Central North Island

The central North Island, stretching from Auckland to the lower south around Wellington, takes in volcanoes, geysers, lakes, craggy coastlines, sweeping beaches, the Maori heartland, and green pastures that nurtured a nation.

Cutting a fiery swathe from the east coast to the center of the North Island, the Taupo Volcanic Zone holds all of New Zealand's active volcanoes, from offshore White Island to the snowy peaks of Tongariro National Park. Along this belt, geysers, mud pools, boiling ponds, and steam vent the landscape, especially around Rotorua, the biggest tourist magnet in the country.

Not only is Rotorua famous for its geothermal activity, but it also features Maori culture at its most accessible. The entire region is rich in Maori history. In the Waikato area, the tribes united to form the Maori King Movement and battle for their land. So, too, did the Maori in

Taranaki on the west coast and at the Bay of Plenty in the east, while the remote East Cape remains a Maori stronghold.

While Rotorua is the tourist destination par excellence, the visitor has many options for interesting routes and diversions. From Auckland, the main highway leads to the rich farmland of the Waikato around Hamilton, then south to the King Country and the Waitomo Caves, a magical area riddled with caverns and glowworms.

Continuing down the less traveled west coast, the Taranaki region is dominated by the towering cone of Mount Taranaki, a snowcapped dormant volcano, one of New Zealand's most awesome sights. This rural route then leads south around to Whanganui, an old river port, where jet boats have replaced paddle steamers venturing upstream into the wilderness.

Alternatively, you can head east from Auckland to the Coromandel Peninsula, which has one of the country's most scenic coastlines, as well as fine beaches and historic old gold towns.

The Coromandel leads on to the Bay of Plenty, a sunny coast with some fine beaches and the possibility of trips to see the smoking volcano at White Island. Inland of the Bay of Plenty is a scenic lake district around Rotorua, where old volcanoes have filled with waters teeming with trout.

TASMAN SEA

NEW PLYMOUTH
Egmont Village
EGMONT N.P.
Mt. Taranaki
Dawson Falls
Stratford
45

The country's biggest lake, Taupo, lies at the very center of the North Island and is so large it resembles an inland sea. To its south are the volcanoes of Tongariro, Ngauruhoe, and Ruapehu—the mighty peaks of Tongariro National Park—offering some of the best hikes in the country in the summer and good skiing in the winter.

South of Lake Taupo, Napier on the east coast is a delightful art deco city and seaside retreat. Wineries dot the countryside surrounding Hawke's Bay, and farther north, Gisborne can be the starting point for an off-the-beaten-path adventure around the East Cape or into the virgin forests and lakes of Te Urewera National Park. ■

PACIFIC OCEAN

Fletcher Bay
Port Jackson • Stony Bay
Mt. Moehau ▲ • Port Charles
Colville •
Coromandel •   Opito Bay
         (25)   Coromandel Peninsula
Whitianga •   Mercury Bay
Ferry Landing • • Hahei
Cooks Beach • • Hot Water Beach
Tairua • • Paku Summit
The Pinnacles ▲ • Pauanui
Thames • ◇ Kauaeranga Valley
COROMANDEL • Whangamata
FOREST PARK

(1)

Waihi

Ngaruawahia   (2)   Mount Maunganui
TAURANGA   Papamoa Beach
HAMILTON   Papamoa • • Te Puke
Raglan •   Bay of Plenty   Te Kaha •
Te Mata •   Matamata   Whakatane
Cambridge   (5)   Hell's   Lake   Ohope
Kawhia •   Gate   Rotoma   Ohope
                  Mokoia I.
Otorohanga •   Lake Rotorua   The Buried Village
Waitomo Caves • ROTORUA   ▲ Mt. Tarawera
Te Kuiti •   Waimangu   Lake Tarawera
           Volcanic Valley   Lake
Orakei Korako ◇   Rotoma-
                  hana
(3)   (1)   Wai-O-Tapu

Waihau Bay   East Cape
      (35)   Te Araroa
             Tikitiki •
White Island ◦   Ruatoria •
Ohiwa
Harbour   Tokomaru Bay
Opotiki •
WAIOEKA
GORGE
SCENIC   (35)
RES.
TE UREWERA   Tolaga Bay •
NATIONAL
PARK   (2)

Wairakei ◇   Aniwaniwa   GISBORNE ☆
▲TAUPO   Lake   Lake
         Waikaremoana   Waikareiti   • Whangara
Lake
Taupo   Young Nicks Head
Taumarunui •
(4) • Turangi   Tongariro
TONGARIRO   National   (5)
RaurimuSpiral ◇   Trout Centre
WHANGANUI   ▲ Mt. Tongariro   Wairoa •
N.P.   ▲ Mt. Ngauruhoe
       N.P. ☆ Whakapapa Skifield   (2)
Turoa Skifield ◇ ▲ Mt. Ruapehu   Hawke's Bay
Raetihi • Ohakune
• Pipiriki   ↟ Waiouru
• Jerusalem   Puketapu ↟ NAPIER
         Taradale
(1)   HASTINGS   Cape
WHANGANUI   Kidnappers
RIVER RD.
↟ WHANGANUI

(3)

(2)

0   80 kilometers
0   40 miles

Area of map detail

Auckland •

☆ Wellington

Christchurch •

New Zealand

Waikato

The Waikato region was once a Maori stronghold and birthplace of the King Movement, which tried to unite the tribes against the colonial land grab. Now noted for its rich agricultural land and horse farms, the Waikato is also famous for the Waitomo Caves and the Otorohanga Kiwi House. You can also take a number of interesting side trips in the region.

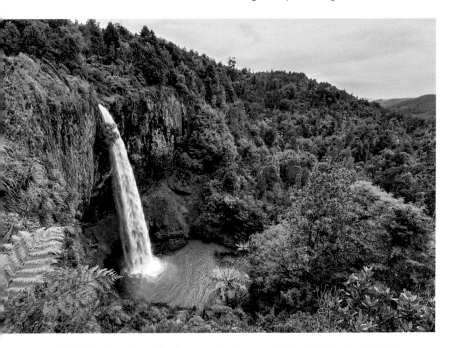

The Bridal Veil Falls (Wairēinga), near Raglan, plunges 180 feet (55 m) along the Pakoka River.

Hamilton

 Map p. 105

Visitor Information

✉ Caro & Alexandra Sts.

☎ 07/958-5960

visithamilton.co.nz

Hamilton

Hamilton (pop. 161,000) is New Zealand's fourth largest city, lying 81 miles (130 km) south of Auckland on the Waikato River, the country's longest waterway. It is the main city of the Waikato region.

Hamilton was founded on land confiscated after the New Zealand Wars, and in 1864 the gunboat *Rangiriri* established the first redoubt at Memorial Park near the town center.

The river was the town's vital link with the outside world until the railroad was built. Forested walking tracks line the river and, along with Memorial Park, form the city's green heart.

Nearby on the river, the town's main attraction is the **Waikato Museum** (*1 Grantham St., tel 07/ 838-6606, waikatomuseum.co.nz*), which has a wonderful collection of *taonga* (treasures) of the Tainui, the main Waikato tribe, including a Te Winika war canoe.

About 1 mile (1.6 km) south of the city center on SH1, avid gardeners will appreciate the **Hamilton Gardens** (Cobham Dr., tel 07/838-6782, hamiltongardens .co.nz), an expansive collection of themed plantings, including Japanese, Italian renaissance, English, and Indian. The café is a great choice for al fresco lunch.

Around Hamilton

On SH1, 12 miles (19 km) north of Hamilton, **Ngaruawahia** is the seat of the Kingitanga (Maori King Movement), formed when some of the Maori tribes united to counter British dominance. They elected the Waikato chief Te Wherowhero (circa 1800–1860)

INSIDER TIP:

A great way to explore Hamilton is on a scenic river cruise with the Waikato River Explorer (waikatoexplorer.co.nz, $$), departing daily from the Hamilton Gardens jetty.

—PETER TURNER
National Geographic writer

as the first king in 1856. He took the name Potatau and ruled from Ngaruawahia. Though the position holds no legal power, it confers great prestige, and Potatau's descendents continue to rule from here. Tuheitia Paki (b. 1955) came to the throne in 2006, after the 40-year rule of his mother Dame Te Atairangikaahu.

Riff Raff

Richard O'Brien, creator of *The Rocky Horror Picture Show*, worked in a Hamilton barbershop as a young man. It is rumored that his life of cutting hair and watching late-night double features at the local Embassy Theatre inspired the 1975 cult classic film. Today a bronze statue of Riff Raff, the hunchback, stands on Victoria Street.

On the northern side of town, the **Turangawaewae Marae** (29 River Rd.), contains the king's ancestral residence and a traditionally carved meetinghouse, but is open to the public only on the annual Regatta Day in March.

Thirty miles (48 km) west of Hamilton via SH23 is New Zealand's prime surfing destination, **Raglan**, a delightful seaside village on a sheltered inlet ideal for kayaking and swimming. The historic **Harbour View Hotel** (14 Bow St., tel 07/825-8010) dominates the main street lined with cafés. A pedestrian bridge leads to the spit and the ocean, but Raglan's famous surf beaches are farther out along the Wainui Road.

Ngarunui Beach, 3 miles (5 km) southwest of Raglan on a large bay, has a gray-sand beach and surf lifesaving club that operates in summer; surfing lessons are offered. Farther west, **Manu Bay** has a left-hand break and the **Indicators** offer world-class surf.

To reach the spectacular, gushing **Bridal Veil Falls/Wairēinga,**

Raglan

⚠ Map p. 105

Visitor Information

✉ 13 Wainui Rd.

☎ 07/825-0556

raglan.org.nz

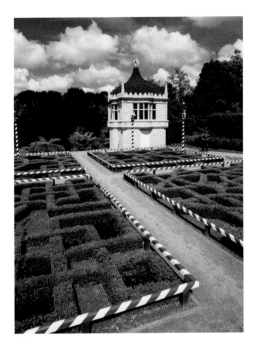

The Tudor Gardens of Hamilton Gardens

horse stud tours. Historic buildings and antique shops grace the town, while plaques in the pavement commemorate the pantheon of local equine heroes.

More recently Cambridge has become a cycling destination, with the **Great New Zealand River Ride** *(te-awa.org.nz)* heading north of town, and to the south, the 64-mile (102 km) **Waikato River Trails** *(waikatorivertrails .co.nz)*. **Sanctuary Mountain Maungatautari** *(tel 07/870-5180, sanctuarymountain.co.nz, $)* breeds endangered bird species and tuatara in a significant forest and wildlife sanctuary south of Cambridge. It has an impressive visitor center, a network of walking trails, and wildlife tours.

INSIDER TIP:

The air quality of the Waitomo Caves is monitored by a Scientific Advisory Group to determine how many people can visit the caves daily. Book early.

—JORGE I. NÚÑEZ
National Geographic research grantee

Cambridge

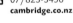 Map p. 105

Visitor Information

✉   Queen & Victoria Sts.

☎   07/823-3456
    cambridge.co.nz

Matamata

◪ Map p. 105

Visitor Information

✉   45 Broadway

☎   07/888-7260

take the turnoff 8 miles (13 km) out of Raglan on SH23 to Hamilton. Just past the tiny town of Te Mata, turn left and head 2.5 miles (4 km) to the falls. A scenic but rough, hilly road *(subject to closure; ask in Te Mata)* leads on to sleepy **Kawhia** on the impressive harbor of the same name. Kawhia is sacred to the Tainui people as the landing place of the ancestral Tainui canoe.

Fifteen miles (24 km) south of Hamilton on SH1, the green and very English town of **Cambridge** has horse racing in its veins, and its stud farms have produced many champions. New Zealand loves its racing, and Waikato thoroughbreds have excelled at home and across the Tasman Sea in Australia. Ask at the visitor center about

Another renowned horse breeding center, **Matamata,** 33 miles (53 km) east of Cambridge on SH27, has achieved fame for **Hobbiton** *(tel 07/888-6838, 501 Buckland Rd., Hinuera, hobbitontours.com, $$$$$)*, built on a nearby farm for the filming of the *Lord of the Rings* and *Hobbit* movies.

Tours of the hobbit houses start from the café or from the Matamata visitor center.

The town of **Otorohanga,** 31 miles (50 km) south of Hamilton via SH3, has long drawn tourists to its famous **Otorohanga Kiwi House** (*Alex Telfer Dr., tel 07/873-7391, kiwihouse.org.nz, $$*). Though kiwi houses, featuring New Zealand's beloved native birds, have sprung up everywhere throughout the country, this is still the most popular, largely because of its

into these rugged hills between Lake Taupo and the coast, a no-go zone for Europeans until the king laid down his arms in 1881.

The Maori camped at the Waitomo Caves, but never lived in them permanently, no doubt because of flooding. (*Waitomo* means "water cave.") A few early Europeans visited the caves, but it was not until the 1880s that the area was surveyed and the extent of the vast underground network became known. More

Otorohanga
🅰 Map p. 105
Visitor Information
✉ 27 Turingo St.
☎ 07/873-8951

Waitomo Caves
🅰 Map p. 105
Visitor Information
✉ 21 Waitomo Caves Rd., Waitomo
☎ 07/878-7640
waitomocaves.com

The Kiwi

New Zealanders proudly call themselves and all things New Zealand "Kiwi," for this flightless bird has become the national symbol. The shy, nocturnal kiwi, about the size of a large chicken, has been around for 70 million years and is the dwarf cousin of the ratite family, which includes emus and New Zealand's extinct moa, the largest bird to walk the Earth.

The kiwi is difficult to see—most New Zealanders have never spotted one in the wild. Though endangered, and though their habitat is threatened, kiwi populations total about 70,000. The most

common species are the North Island brown kiwi and the great spotted kiwi of the South Island. Other species include the rowi, tokoeka, and little spotted kiwi.

These birds have a highly developed sense of smell and use their long bills to forage in forest undergrowth for worms, insects, and spiders, as well as berries and seeds.

Kiwis lay enormous eggs for their size, about one-fifth of their body weight, and the incubation period is around 80 days. Kiwi pairs are monogamous and the male usually incubates the eggs.

---

proximity to the Waitomo Caves. Kiwi sightings are guaranteed here and a wide selection of New Zealand's native birds is on display throughout the attractive grounds.

Waitomo Caves

Riddled with caves, the limestone wonderland of Waitomo lies in the heart of the King Country, an area named for the Maori King Movement. Forced out of Waikato after the New Zealand Wars, King Tawhiao (1822–1894) retreated

than 300 caves pepper the area, with hundreds of miles of interconnecting passageways, underground springs, and rivers carving great caverns out of the karst.

By the 1890s, tourists began trickling in, and in 1908 the classic Waitomo Caves Hotel (see Travelwise p. 291) was built to cater to the growing crowds. One of New Zealand's premier attractions for a century, Waitomo remains a North Island must-see and a required stop (continued on p. 112)

John Williams's 1845 watercolor, "HMS *North Star*, Destroying Pomare's Pa, Otiuhu, Bay of Islands"

Times of War

With the introduction of muskets, Maori tribal wars quickly escalated, and as European settlement increased in New Zealand from the 1840s, conflict over land was inevitable. A series of land wars, also known as the New Zealand Wars or the Maori Wars, erupted on the North Island.

Musket Wars

Even before the land wars began, Maori chiefs such as Hongi Hika and Te Rauparaha had acquired muskets and used the new technology with devastating effect against their traditional Maori enemies. While a precursor to the Land Wars, the so-called Musket Wars were just as cataclysmic. Lasting from the early 1820s through the 1830s, the wars claimed up to 20,000 lives as the new European weapons of mass destruction turned tribal war into genocide. Hongi Hika, sporting armor given to him by King George IV, led his warriors south against old foes such as the Ngati Paoa around Auckland, wiping out whole villages and taking slaves as he went. Ritual cannibalism to ingest the *mana* (spiritual power) of the conquered was common.

Other tribes, facing extermination, clamored to get their hands on the new weapons. In exchange for muskets, they traded pigs, agricultural produce, and even the smoked heads of slain enemies—macabre trophies for European cabinets.

Wars escalated across the North Island, and the southern warrior Te Rauparaha created havoc along the west coast after being driven out of the Waikato region. From his base on Kapiti Island he then crossed Cook Strait and waged a ferocious campaign against the tribes of the South Island.

By around 1836, the wars began to subside as the balance of muskets, and power, settled.

Missionaries also began to make inroads, but up to a third of the Maori population had been killed by warfare and the growing tide of European-introduced diseases. The battle-hardened warriors that remained then turned their attention to the British, sometimes uniting against the settlers, other times joining colonial troops against traditional enemies. While the Musket Wars resulted in many deaths, the conflicts acclimated Maori to the ways of modern warfare, preparing them in part for sustained fighting against the British colonists. Because of the tactics and weapons acquired during this period, Maori fared much better than other indigenous people in the Empire.

The King Movement

Early skirmishes included the 1843 massacre at Wairau (see sidebar p. 176) in the South Island, when Te Rauparaha slaughtered a British militia sent to arrest him for impeding an illegal land grab. More serious battles broke out in 1845 when Bay of Islands chief Hone Heke, disenchanted with British rule, fought foreign troops for months until a truce was declared.

In the 1850s, as settlers flooded in, the Maori united across tribal boundaries for the first time to form the Maori King Movement (Kingitanga) to put a stop to land sales and elect their own king. The Waikato chief Te Wherowhero became the first king in 1856 and ruled from Ngaruawahia. The King Movement sought to protect Maori land and traditions, but most colonists saw it as treachery and an affront to the rightful monarch, Queen Victoria.

In 1860, a local chief offered to sell land at Waitara, near New Plymouth, to the British, but the supreme chief of the area objected and occupied the area. British troops were sent in, sparking the Taranaki War. A series of bloody battles ensued, with imperial troops suffering heavy losses trying to storm fortified Maori *pa* (villages). Maori forces laid siege to New Plymouth before withdrawing, and the two sides called a truce in 1861.

When fighting broke out again in 1863, Governor George Grey marshaled up to 20,000 men to crush the King Movement. War broke out across the Waikato and Taranaki regions and spread to the Bay of Plenty before the final battles of 1864. Dozens of skirmishes left 1,000 Maori and 700 British troops dead, and huge tracts of Waikato land were seized in retribution.

The Saga of Te Kooti

As the Waikato Wars subsided, the messianic Pai Marire movement rose to prominence in Taranaki. Biblical teachings combined with Maori beliefs gave rise to the Hauhau warriors, who battled to regain Maori land and mana, convinced God had made them invincible. The core of the movement was eventually crushed in 1866 with the aid of opposing Maori tribes, but not before it had spread to the east coast of the North Island. After missionary Carl Volkner was killed at Opotiki in 1865, war escalated until Pai Marire supporters were rounded up and exiled to the Chatham Islands.

One of the exiles, Te Kooti, had fought for the government and protested his innocence, but was refused a trial. In the Chathams he received a series of visions and founded the Ringatu (Upraised Hand) faith. He and his followers staged a dramatic jail break in 1868, seized a boat, and set sail for the North Island.

Te Kooti got his revenge at Matawhero on the outskirts of Gisborne, slaughtering 54 Pakeha (Europeans) and Maori. Chased by colonial and Maori forces, he launched a series of guerrilla raids around Poverty Bay and into the Urewera Mountains before continuing on to Lake Taupo. He built a pa in the desert near the volcanoes, convinced he could defeat troops and tribes alike. His army was crushed, and he finally retreated into the wilds of the King Country in 1872, where he developed his religion; it still survives in New Zealand. Te Kooti, the last warrior of the New Zealand Wars, was eventually pardoned in 1883.

Glowworm Cave

✉ 39 Waitomo
   Caves Rd.,
   Waitomo

☎ 07/878-8228

$ $$$$ (two-cave
   combo)

waitomo.com

for tour buses between Auckland and Rotorua. This being New Zealand, thrill seekers are also indulged with underground adventures.

The big lure is the **Glowworm Cave,** an impressive collection of stalagmites and stalactites illuminated for effect. The cave includes the great Cathedral cavern where New Zealand opera diva Kiri Te Kanawa once performed. A black river flows through the caves, and tour boats glide the glowworm grotto, where the ceiling twinkles with a Milky Way of lights. Reserve guided tours of this and other caves at the huge, impressive Caves Visitor Centre out front.

Glowworms

The New Zealand glowworm (Arachnocampa luminosa) is a different species from the fireflies and glowworms of Europe and the Americas, which are beetles. The glowworms at Waitomo are the larvae of mosquitolike gnats that spin thin, dangling webs to catch insects. The glowworms attract prey with their luminescent green light—the hungrier they are, the brighter they glow. The larvae live for 6 to 12 months before entering the pupa stage, when they hang from the ceiling for one to two weeks. Finally, the gnats hatch, but their lives are short. They exist only to breed, and after the female lays her eggs, she dies.

Two miles (3 km) west on the main road, the **Aranui Cave** was discovered in 1910 by a young Maori, Ruruku Aranui, when his dog disappeared into a hole chasing a wild pig. The high chambers of this riverless cave have stunning stalactite formations of pink, white, and pale brown.

Guided tours of the **Ruakari Cave** (waitomo.com) start at the Legendary Black Water Rafting Co., located 0.6 miles (1 km) before the township on the road coming into Waitomo. The 1-mile-long (1.6 km) path leads to stalactites, stalagmites, underground rivers, and glowworms.

Waitomo is the home of black-water rafting—the sport of riding the underground rapids of the Ruakari Cave in an inner tube. If that fails to excite, rock-climbing, rappelling, and caving adventures are also offered.

Waitomo village (waitomo.org .nz) has a museum/information center, a general store, a tavern, and not much more, though a handful of places to stay are scattered around, including the iconic Waitomo Caves Hotel. The **Waitomo Caves Discovery Centre** in the Information Centre has interesting displays on the caves.

Twelve miles (19 km) south of Waitomo is **Te Kuiti,** where 19th-century Maori guerrilla Te Kooti found refuge. The town also has a "Big Shearer" statue attesting to its sheep-farming credentials, celebrated in lively fashion at the **Great NZ Muster** around April with fairground fun, shearing, and the running of the sheep through the town ∎

Coromandel Peninsula

A popular summer vacation playground for Kiwis, the Coromandel Peninsula has stunning coastal scenery, glorious beaches, rugged mountains, and old gold towns, all less than two hours' drive from Auckland. From the main center of Thames, a scenic road wends along the shoreline of the sheltered west coast to charming Coromandel town, and then over the hills to the surf beaches and resort towns of the east coast. Driving is slow and winding. Allow at least two days to tour the peninsula.

Children sifting through seashells, Whitianga, Coromandel Peninsula

West Coast

European settlement on the Coromandel Peninsula began on the west coast with the discovery of gold near Coromandel in 1852, but the real boom began with the news of a strike at Thames in 1867. Thousands flocked to the goldfields, but in a decade, gold waned and kauri became the main industry. The kauri forests of the mountainous interior were milled almost to extinction by the 20th century, but preservation has made the forests green again.

Today the Coromandel thrives mostly on tourism and real estate. The laid-back lifestyle attracts wealthy retirees and alternative lifestylers alike.

At the bottom of the shallow Firth of Thames, **Thames** is the main town and gateway to the Coromandel Peninsula. Take away the car dealers, real estate agents, and supermarkets, and Thames

Thames

Map p. 105

Visitor Information

✉ 200 Mary St.

☎ 07/868-7284

thecoromandel.com

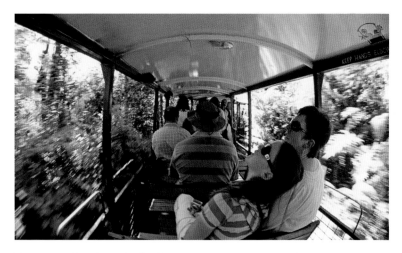

Miniature train from Driving Creek Railway & Potteries

Coromandel

⛰ Map p. 105

Visitor Information

✉ 85 Kapanga Rd.

☎ 07/866-8598

**coromandel
town.co.nz**

looks like a Wild West town, its main street lined with verandahed wooden buildings from the gold rush of the 1860s and '70s.

Housed in some of the oldest buildings, the **Thames School of Mines and Mineralogical Museum** (101 Cochrane St., tel 07/868-6227, $) has an extensive collection of rocks, minerals, and fossils. For a rundown on the town's history, the **Thames Historical Museum** (Pollen & Cochrane Sts., tel 07/868-8509, $) has an interesting photo collection and pioneer relics.

The best thing to do in Thames is the **Goldmine Experience** (tel 07/868-8514, goldmine-experience.co.nz, $) on SH25 just north of town. Informative tours of this former gold mine run every day from late September to the end of April.

Thames is also the start for one of New Zealand's most popular cycling trails, the **Hauraki Rail Trail** (haurakirailtrail.co.nz, see p. 116), running south to Paeroa and then on to Te Aroha or Waihi.

East of Thames, the scenic **Kauaeranga Valley** in **Coromandel Forest Park** has waterfalls, mountain streams, thick forest, and kauri dams accessed by a host of good hikes. These range from 20 minutes to an overnight hike to the craggy outcroppings of The Pinnacles. The **Kauaeranga Visitor Centre** (tel 07/867-9080, doc.govt.nz), 7.5 miles (12 km) from Thames on Kauaeranga Valley Road, has full details.

A twisting, narrow, and impossibly scenic road, SH25 winds right next to the sea for 34 miles (55 km) from Thames north to **Coromandel.** Bohemian Coromandel has long been home to artists, potters, holistic healers, and other rat-race escapees. The town's main drag, **Pollen Street,** is lined with historic buildings–like Thames, the gold rush produced a Victorian building boom, which subsequent decline left intact.

The town and the peninsula were named after the British Royal Navy's H.M.S. *Coromandel,* which called here in 1820 to cut kauri for ships' spars. It was Charles Ring's discovery of gold in 1852, however, that put Coromandel on the map.

The **Coromandel Goldfield Centre & Stamper Battery** (410 Buffalo Rd., tel 0210/232-8262, $), 2 miles (3 km) north of town, is driven by a huge waterwheel to crush rock for gold extraction. Informative tours explain the process, and you can pan for gold.

The town's most notable attraction, **Driving Creek Railway & Potteries** (380 Driving Creek Rd., tel 07/866-8703, $$$) on the northern outskirts, is an eccentric but impressive blend of a pottery factory and a miniature railway that runs through the forest.

The town of Coromandel is a crossroads for travelers. Most visitors head straight across to Whitianga on the east coast via one of two routes—the 309 Road or SH25. You can also leave the beaten path and head north to the remote tip of the peninsula.

The mountainous, unpaved 309 Road to Whitianga goes through some beautiful forest. Recommended stops on the way include excellent short walks to the **Waiau Falls** and a kauri grove. The main highway, SH25, is longer but has fine coastal scenery, and you can detour to isolated beaches such as beautiful **Opito Bay.**

To the north, the scenic, paved Coromandel–Colville road leads to sleepy **Colville,** where a café and general store mark the edge of civilization. The unpaved Port Jackson Road passes **Mount Moehau,** the peninsula's highest peak, and Port Jackson itself before ending at **Fletcher Bay,** a serene inlet with untrammeled beaches. The Port Charles road, the alternate east coast road north of Colville, leads to **Port Charles** and its wonderful beach, then on to **Stony Bay,** where the **Coromandel Walkway** (3 hr. one-way) provides a scenic hike to Fletcher Bay.

The Hairy Moehau

Some stories claim that lurking behind kauri trees in the Coromandel is the fabled Hairy Moehau. Like his elusive American cousin Bigfoot, the Hairy Moehau is described as a cross between a man and an ape. While Maori say he is a descendent of the mythical Maero people, others believe he is merely an escaped gorilla.

East Coast

Like many vacationers, Captain Cook preferred the east coast of the Coromandel and spent most of November 1769 in **Mercury Bay,** where he tracked the transit of Mercury, traded with the Maori, and feasted on seafood. Beautiful Mercury Bay remains the jewel of the Coromandel's east coast.

Over the mountainous spine of the peninsula from Coromandel town, **Whitianga,** Mercury Bay's main resort, boasts curving **Buffalo Beach,** a pretty harbor crammed

(continued on p. 118)

Mercury Bay & Whitianga

Map p. 105

Visitor Information

66 Albert St., Whitianga

07/866-5555

whitianga.co.nz

EXPERIENCE: Great Rides of NZ

Long a world-renowned hiking destination, New Zealand now has a network of mostly off-road trails through countryside and wilderness to get cyclists up close to the country's scenic wonders. Just as the premier backpacking trails are designated Great Walks, the best of the two-wheel tracks are dubbed Great Rides.

Collectively known as the New Zealand Cycle Trail (*nzcycletrail.com*), more than 20 multiday rides cover the varied landscapes of the North and South Islands, from easy rail trails to more demanding mountain bike challenges. Trailheads are near towns, where bike rental, transportation, and tours can be arranged. Most routes have overnight accommodation options, and outfitters can transport your luggage between stops, or you can day-ride shorter sections.

Here are some of the easier and most popular leisure trails for cyclists of all fitness levels.

Hauraki Rail Trail

Grade 1–2, 1–3 days, 51 miles (82 km), haurakirailtrail.co.nz

A popular option close to Auckland and one of the country's easiest rides, this trail starts at the old gold-mining town of Thames (see p. 113) on the Coromandel Peninsula. It crosses the lush farmland of the Hauraki Plains with views of the Kaimai Range and the rural towns of Paeroa and Te Aroha or Waihi. The trail traverses old rail bridges and tunnels and offers scenic side trips and walks. The Karangahake Gorge section is the highlight of the trail and can be done as a day ride from the old Waikino Station, which has a café and bike rentals.

Trails Grades

1 Easy, mostly off-road
2 Slightly more demanding
3 Steeper hills, some on-road or gravel riding
4 Hill climbs and gravel; for experienced riders

Hawke's Bay Trails

Grade 2–3, 1–4 days, 124 miles (200 km), hawkesbaynz.com

This network of trails is mostly flat as it runs along country paths and the quiet back roads of the Hawke's Bay's wine region (see p. 139), with added coastal and rural panoramas. These interconnecting trails include three options: the Wineries Ride, covering the regions around Hastings and Flaxmere, with plenty of cellar door options; the Landscapes Ride, along the coast with views of Cape Kidnappers and inland along the Tukituki River Valley; or the flat and gentle Water Ride near Napier, with Pacific Ocean vistas and the Ahuriri Estuary bird sanctuary. Day-trip options are plentiful.

Tasman's Great Taste Trail

Grade 2–3, 1–4 days, 109 miles (175 km), heartofbiking.org.nz

This ride combines sun, sea, galleries, wineries, craft beer, and seafood in the scenic Nelson region at the top of the South Island. The easy (Grade 2) coastal trail runs on bike paths from Nelson via Richmond and Motueka to Kaiteriteri in Abel Tasman National Park, the country's premier coastal park. Mapua, with cafés, galleries, and a boutique brewery, is a highlight, and from here the trail goes (via a ferry) to the forest trails and beaches of Rabbit Island. Ride the coastal section of this trail one-way, or return via the Motueka Valley inland route (Grade 3), taking in rivers, rural landscapes, wineries, and orchards.

Alps 2 Ocean Trail

Grade 2–3, 1–6 days, 190 miles (306 km), alps2ocean.com

One of the longest Great Rides, encompassing classic South Island vistas, "A2O" takes in views of Aoraki/Mount Cook, the Southern Alps, and glacier-fed lakes before leaving the highlands for the rural plains along the Waitaki River and ending in the historic coastal town of Oamaru. The trail starts in the shadow of New Zealand's highest peak at Aoraki/Mount Cook Village (see p. 211) and descends some 2,000 feet (610 m), mostly off-road, but it includes a climb before Oamarama and some highway riding. Good day-trip options for excellent mountain and lake views include Lake Tekapo to Twizel and Twizel to Lake Ohau Lodge.

Otago Central Rail Trail

Grade 1–2, 1–5 days, 93 miles (150 km), otagocentralrailtrail.co.nz
The mother of all rail trails (see sidebar p. 247), and the original Great Ride, this trail runs through the historic gold country of Central Otago (see p. 246), with its desert landscapes, towns, gorges, viaducts, and tunnels. Well supplied with accommodations and services, it follows the old railway between Clyde and Middlemarch and is most often done as a complete four- to five-day ride, but day sections can be ridden.

with pleasure craft, and a good range of accommodations and restaurants. Whitianga has a small **museum** (11A The Esplanade, $), but the town is all about beaches and water sports, which range from windsurfing and fishing to glass-bottom-boat cruises.

For a cheap cruise, take the ferry across the harbor to **Ferry Landing,** where a pleasant coastal walk leads to the beautiful beach at **Flaxmill Bay,** and then on to the **Shakespeare Cliff lookout** above secluded **Lonely Beach.** The lookout has superb views across the white sands of **Cook's Beach,** where Captain Cook first raised the British flag in 1769.

INSIDER TIP:

Rent a shovel and dig yourself your own oceanside Jacuzzi when the tide goes out on the aptly named Hot Water Beach. The best time to visit is December to March.

—CARRIE MILLER
National Geographic contributor

Cook's Beach is about 2 miles (3 km) on foot from Ferry Landing; it's much longer by car via the circuitous SH25 around Whitianga Harbour. This route will also take you to delightful **Hahei Beach,** 25 miles (40 km) from Whitianga, a must-see on the east coast. As well as a superb beach, Hahei is the starting point for the walk to **Cathedral Cove,** a majestic rock outcropping, a 2.5-hour round-trip hike along the beach (1.5 hours from headland parking lot). This superb walk passes gorgeous bays.

To top off a trip to Mercury Bay, soak in the sands at **Hot Water Beach,** 5.5 miles (9 km) south of Hahei. Two hours either side of low tide, a hot spring percolates up through the sand; you can dig your own spa bath, mingling hot water with seawater.

The SH25 south from Whitianga travels inland until it hits the coast again at **Tairua,** an old milling town and small resort. For some wonderful views, head toward the ocean beach, take Paku Drive off the beach road, and then walk to the **Paku Summit,** a rock mountain that dominates the town.

A short ferry ride across the estuary from Tairua is the town of **Pauanui.** One of the Coromandel's best beaches is only a short walk from the ferry dock, but the town itself is a soulless suburbia.

Whangamata, 25 miles (40 km) south of Tairua, has a large beach resort with plenty of services but not much charm.

To the south, the inland town of **Waihi** boomed in 1878 when gold was discovered. The **Gold Discovery Centre** (tel 07/863-9015, golddiscoverycentre.co.nz, $$) tells the gold story with interactive displays, movies, and more. Arrange tours ($$$) of the still operating **Martha Mine** here.

The **Waihi Arts Centre & Museum** (54 Kenny St., tel 07/863-8386, waihimuseum.co.nz, $) also has good mining exhibits. ∎

Bay of Plenty

The Bay of Plenty is a gently curving coast of sun, beaches, kiwifruit, and real estate booms, for this is one of the country's fastest-growing regions. Farther east, the area's other major attraction is White Island, New Zealand's most active volcano, with tours operating from the pleasant coastal town of Whakatane.

Mount Maunganui waterfront resort

Western Bay of Plenty

Captain Cook named the Bay of Plenty in 1769 for the abundance of food local Maori brought to his ship to trade, a welcome contrast to the hostile reception at his previous stop in Poverty Bay.

The main center of the Bay of Plenty, the city of **Tauranga** (pop. 128,000) is growing rapidly. Its fine harbor (Tauranga means "sheltered anchorage") is New Zealand's busiest port, servicing a major agricultural region.

Abundant sun and fine beaches attract retirees, but Tauranga has not always been so placid. The area has a long Maori history, though by the time Europeans began to settle in the 1830s, the Musket Wars had reduced the population to only 2,000. In the 1860s, the New Zealand Wars spread from the Waikato to the Bay of Plenty, which witnessed fierce fighting that lingered on through messianic movements such as the Hauhau warriors and Te Kooti (see p. 111).

Tauranga
Map p. 105
Visitor Information
95 Willow St.
07/577-6234
bayofplentynz.com

In Tauranga, fierce fighting broke out at Gate Pa. The British established Monmouth Redoubt to cut off Maori reinforcements heading to the Waikato, and in 1864, 1,700 troops launched an assault on 230 Maori at Gate Pa. After artillery bombarded the walls, 300 troops stormed the *pa*, but 100 were slaughtered within ten minutes before the rest retreated. Maori forces evacuated the pa overnight, leaving behind the most devastating British defeat of the New Zealand Wars.

The remains of **Monmouth Redoubt** lie in downtown Robbins Park on Cliff Road, while the impressive Te Awanui war canoe is nearby at the northern end of The Strand, along Tauranga's redeveloped waterfront. **Elms Mission House** *(tel 07/577-9772, theelms.org.nz, $)*, near the Harbour Bridge on Mission Street, is a fine Georgian home built in 1847 by the Reverend A. N. Brown and has original furnishings. Nearby is one of the country's best regional galleries, **Tauranga Art Gallery** *(cnr. Wharf and Willow Sts., tel 07/578-7933, artgallery.org.nz).*

Tauranga may be a popular place to live, but visitors are advised to stay in **Mount Maunganui,** 3 miles (5 km) away across the Harbour Bridge. Dominated by The Mount, a huge

INSIDER TIP:

In town in April, Tauranga's Easter National Jazz Festival features the country's best jazz musicians performing in great venues across the city.

—MARY HERMANSON
Consultant, Whakatane District Council

Surfers prepare to paddle out into the Bay of Plenty.

EXPERIENCE: Into the Volcano

The most accessible volcanoes in New Zealand are in Tongariro National Park near Taupo (see pp. 133–134), but if you want bang for your volcanic sightseeing buck, then Whaakari/White Island has no peer.

Lying 30 miles (48 km) offshore, White Island is expensive to visit, but tours do guarantee an up-close look at an active volcano, where steam and boiling water pour from the youngest crater. Tours land on the island unless the volcano is erupting or seas are too rough (helicopters may be able to land).

Whakatane is the usual place from where to arrange a trip to the island. **White Island Tours** (15 The Strand E., Whakatane, tel 07/308-9588, whiteisland.co.nz, $$$$$) has six-hour boat tours, with a 1.5- to 2-hour tour on the island, visiting the crater and old sulfur mine. From Whakatane airport, **Frontier Helicopters** (tel 07/308-4188, whiteisland.co.nz, $$$$$) spends a little over an hour on the island and does the round-trip in just 2.5 hours, but costs three times as much. Also at Whakatane Airport, **White Island Flights** (tel 07/308-7760, whiteislandflights.co.nz, $$$$$) has much cheaper flight-seeing trips over the island but does not land.

For those in a hurry, **Volcanic Air Safaris** (Rotorua City Lakefront, Memorial Dr., tel 07/348-9984, volcanicair.co.nz, $$$$$) has helicopter flights from the lakefront in Rotorua.

---

volcanic plug rising seemingly out of nowhere, this beach resort with big apartment buildings resembles a mini Waikiki, an almost brash resort in a country that typically likes its beaches back-to-nature.

Mount Maunganui has a sheltered bay beach on one side and, on the other, the wonderful white-sand **Ocean Beach,** stretching 14 miles (22 km) to Papamoa and beyond. You can live it up in a beachfront apartment, but even the campground has a fabulous beach frontage right at the foot of The Mount. The Mount also has good walking tracks and **hot saltwater pools** (tel 07/575-8551) at the base.

Te Puke, 17 miles (28 km) southeast of Tauranga on SH2, is the "kiwifruit capital of the world." In a marvel of marketing, New Zealand horticulturists took the humble Chinese goose-berry, renamed it, and sold it to the world, making even small farmers overnight millionaires in the 1980s. Though now grown everywhere, kiwifruit are still a billion-dollar-a-year industry around here. The latest version, the gold kiwifruit, is a trademark of the local Zespri company.

Te Puke's big attraction is **Kiwi360** (tel 07/573-6340, kiwi360.com, $), an orchard/theme park under the big kiwi on the outskirts of town where "kiwi karts" tour the orchards.

Eastern Bay of Plenty

Viewed from the waterfront, the delightful seaside town of **Whakatane** resembles an archetypal South Pacific port. Yachts shelter in the river harbor, backed by a ring of almost vertical forested hills. But away from this scene, this thriving town is

Whakatane

Map p. 105

Visitor Information

Quay St.

07/306-2030

whakatane.com

attracting increasing numbers, spreading rapidly inland and out 4 miles (6 km) to upscale **Ohope Beach,** a growing resort area with a splendid, long beach backed by Ohiwa Harbour.

Amid the jostle of shops it is easy to miss the drama of the landscape, but look up to see **Pohaturoa** rising from The Strand. This towering rock with a natural archway has long been a landmark for the town, and in 1920 it became a memorial for those who died in World War I.

Just behind, on Canning Place, the **Kohi Point Walkway** leads up to Hillcrest Road, then Seaview Road, where a lookout affords fine views of the harbor. For the

Founding of Whakatane

The hills around Whakatane were once dotted with *pa*, for this area has a rich Maori heritage, beginning with the arrival of the canoe of early explorer Toi. The ancestral Mataatua canoe, voyaging possibly from Poverty Bay, arrived centuries later. Legend tells that on arrival, the men went ashore and the canoe began to drift. In defiance of tradition, the women jumped in the canoe and paddled it back, crying *"Ka whakatane au i ahau"* ("I will be a man"). The settlement henceforth became known as Whakatane ("to be manly").

INSIDER TIP:

Don't miss the scenic Pacific Coast Highway from Manukau to Napier. Highlights include the mural art in Katikati and New Zealand's longest wharf in Tolaga Bay.

—MARY HERMANSON
Consultant, Whakatane District Council

best views of all, take the steps up to the top of **Puketapu,** another huge rock outcropping and the ancient pa site of the Ngati Awa people. Their meetinghouse, the **Mataatua Wharenui** *(105 Muriwai Drive, tel 07/308-4271, $$$$)* can be visited on an excellent cultural tour. Marine activities are popular in Whakatane, including swimming with the dolphins, and it's a base for trips to White Island by sea or air.

New Zealand's only active marine volcano, **White Island,** or Whaakari ("dramatic"), is one of the country's most spectacular sights. Luring scientists and tourists alike, the volcanic island lies 30 miles (48 km) offshore and was so named by Captain Cook because it was shrouded in steam. Various attempts were made over the years to mine sulfur on the island. This had tragic results in 1914 when the crater rim collapsed, burying ten workers under boiling mud. Only the camp cat survived.

The last major eruption, in 2000, covered the island with

mud and scoria and created a new crater, which has a small turquoise lake. This is still a very active volcano, with a minor eruption in 2013, and great jets of steam mixed with hydrochloric acid and sulfur dioxide pour from the fumaroles.

famous mostly for the killing of the Reverend Carl Volkner by Hauhau warriors in 1865. The reverend was thought to be a spy for the British during the New Zealand Wars, and was hanged, beheaded, and his eyes gouged out and eaten.

Opotiki

Map p. 105

Visitor Information

70 Bridge St.

07/315-3031

opotikinz.com

Kiwifruit looms large in Te Puke.

Tours from Whakatane (see sidebar p. 121) land on the island, and you can walk right to the edge of the crater. Boat tours are a full-day trip, and it takes about 1.5 hours to get to the island. Dive tours also run. For those on a tighter schedule, more expensive helicopter tours land on the island and sightseeing planes buzz overhead.

The old-fashioned rural town of **Opotiki** lies in sharp contrast to booming Whakatane, 34 miles (54 km) away via SH2—no condo developments here, despite good beaches just outside town. Opotiki is the gateway to the east coast, a strongly Maori area with a rich history, though it is

Pretty, wooden **St. Stephens Church** *(128 Church St.)* has a headstone inside dedicated to its martyred cleric. Opotiki's **museum** *(tel 07/315-5193, 123 Church St., opotikimuseum.org.nz, $)* details the area's history. Two doors down at No. 129, the old general store is now the **Shalfroon & Francis Museum** *(07/315-5169, $),* filled with memorabilia. Another attraction, **Hukutaia Domain,** about 5 miles (8 km) south of town at the end of Woodlands Road, has scenic walks through native plants from all over New Zealand, some rare or endangered. The Domain includes Taketakerau, a 2,000-year-old tree once used as a Maori burial site. ■

Rotorua

The enduring images of New Zealand—geysers, mud pools, and the fearsome *haka* war dance—are the reality of Rotorua. The biggest tourism destination in the country, Rotorua is where volcanic activity meets Maori culture, all wrapped up in a neat hot springs, haka, and *hangi* (earth oven) package. Water also defines the Rotorua area, which is studded with forested mountain lakes and trout-filled streams.

Rotorua is noted for its intriguing Maori cultural shows.

Rotorua

◮ Map p. 105

Visitor Information

✉ 1167 Fenton St.

☎ 07/348-5179

rotoruanz.com

History

The Rotorua region lies on the volcanic rift that stretches from the White Island to the towering volcanoes of Tongariro National Park. A long history of massive volcanic explosions has rent the countryside, leaving cooled craters filled with lakes, but boiling mud and steam everywhere point to the turmoil still threatening below.

In 1886, nearby Mount Tarawera suddenly blew apart,

showering fire and mud that destroyed whole villages as well as the famous Pink and White Terraces. These spectacular silica terraces, washed by thermal waters, were dubbed a wonder of the natural world and first brought tourism to Rotorua—then, overnight, they were gone.

The local Maori take their name from the ancestral canoe, Te Arawa, which arrived around the 14th century. As the tribe thrived and split into *hapu* (subtribes), conflict was inevitable, but nothing compared to the havoc wreaked by rival Ngapuhi chief Hongi Hika in 1823. Armed with muskets, he slew all before him, and when the Arawa sought refuge on Mokoia Island in Lake Rotorua, he had his men drag canoes over the mountains and onto the lake to finish the job. Hika is still bad news in these parts. When his picture appeared in a Rotorua history exhibition, it caused an outrage and Hika was likened to Adolf Hitler.

More grief later befell the Arawa at the hands of the Waikato Maori, so when war broke out in the 1860s, they aligned with the British against old foes, keeping east coast support from getting through to their enemies.

The end of the war brought peace and tourism to the area. The Tarawera eruption in 1886 slowed the tourist tide, but Rotorua's attractions now lure more than two million visitors a year.

Rotorua City Center

A busy city of 71,000, Rotorua sits on an expansive lake and has a mind-boggling number of attractions. Almost every activity New Zealand has to offer can be found here, including white-water rafting, mountain biking, and a host of other outdoor, adrenaline, and family activities.

Most attractions are on the outskirts or outside the city, but the town center has a few must-sees. One thing you cannot miss is the smell. Sulfur fumes emerge from vents like steam from New

Rotorua's Favorite Lovers

In the middle of Lake Rotorua, Mokoia Island is the setting for Rotorua's favorite love story, that of Hinemoa, who lived on shore, and her lover Tutanekai, who lived on the island. Their union was forbidden by family, but when lovelorn Tutanekai played his flute, the mournful sounds drifted across to Hinemoa. Determined to be with him, Hinemoa braved the freezing water and swam over. She recovered in the island's hot spring, known as Hinemoa's Pool, and was forever united with her love.

York City manholes, giving the city its distinctive rotten-egg odor.

The best place to start a tour is the gracious **Government Gardens,** one block east from the main drag, Fenton Street, and leading down to the lake. In the gardens, the always innovative **Rotorua Museum** is housed in a grand Tudor-style bathhouse built in 1908 for visitors seeking to "take the cure." Tour the old baths and the pumping works. Highlights include the history of tourism, the Pink and White Terraces, Tarawera's eruption, and an impressive new wing devoted to the Te Arawa and their heritage.

Next door, the restored art deco **Blue Baths** *(tel 07/350-2119, bluebaths.co.nz, $)* have a museum highlighting the

Rotorua Museum

✉ Queens Dr.,
  Government
  Gardens

☎ 07/350-1814

💲 $$

**rotorua
museum.co.nz**

salacious joys of mixed swimming in times past, but the thermally heated swimming pool and soak pools are the main attractions.

At the southern end of the gardens, the **Polynesian Spa** (end of Hinemoa St., tel 07/348-1328, polynesianspa.co.nz, $$–$$$$$) has been popular since 1882, when a bathhouse was built over the hot spring. You can swim in private and public pools or indulge in massage and spa treatments.

Along Lakefront Drive, near the end of Fenton Street, the waterfront is a fine spot from which to take in the sunset. Booths sell tickets for jet boating, helicopter flights, and the *Lakeland Queen* (tel 07/348-0265, lakelandqueen.com, $$$–$$$$), an old paddle wheeler that cruises on Lake Rotorua and takes in Mokoia Island in the middle.

Farther west along the lake, the historic Maori village of **Ohinemutu** was once the main

settlement. Communal buildings line the village square, with the traditional **Tamatekapua Meeting House** facing **St. Faith's Anglican Church.** The latter is noted for its fine Maori carvings and a stained-glass window showing Christ in a Maori cloak walking on the water of Lake Rotorua.

While in town, plan to attend a Maori concert and hangi feast, where meat and vegetables are cooked on hot rocks in an underground oven. Concerts feature Maori dance and song, including the inevitable haka and audience participation. A half-dozen operators run tours to the events, which are sometimes cheesy, but often fun and educational.

Whakarewarewa Valley

After Tarawera's eruption, many nearby villagers relocated to the thermal valley 2 miles (3 km) south of town at the end of Fenton Street. Former

Rotorua's Government Gardens

EXPERIENCE: Hot Springs

Hot springs punctuate the land all over New Zealand. In many places their therapeutic waters have been developed into resorts where visitors can soak, swim, or indulge in massage or beauty treatments.

The geothermal activity seething underground rises to the surface most readily in the Central Plateau region of the North Island around Rotorua and Taupo, but keep a towel and swimwear handy everywhere in New Zealand for wonderful hot-springs experiences.

Visitors have flocked to Rotorua for more than a hundred years to "take the cure," particularly at the grand **Government Bath House,** which has become the city museum. Today a host of resorts, motels, and campgrounds have soaking facilities (see opposite page).

In the center of Rotorua, the best known are the **Polynesian Spa,** featuring swimming pools, massage, and spa treatments, and the nearby **Blue Baths,** which have a large heated swimming pool and soak pools. Outside town, the **Hell's Gate** geothermal area has a mud spa and hot pools.

Taupo has a number of hot springs, including the large **DeBretts Spa Resort** (SH5, tel 07/378-8559), a well-kept complex with hot pools, swimming pools, a slide, and spa treatments. In a similar vein, north of Auckland at Waiwera, the **Waiwera Thermal Resort** (see p. 80) has thermal pools, a spa, a sauna, a fitness

Natural hot springs flood Hot Water Beach

center, and water slides for family fun.

Other hot-spring resorts are dotted all around the North Island (nzhotpools .co.nz), as are dozens of natural springs where soaking is free, though the water should always be tested for scalding before entering.

Two well-known natural hot springs can be found at **Hot Water Beach** (see p. 118) on the Coromandel Peninsula, where the spring bubbles up through the sand at low tide, and the **Hot Water Stream** in Taupo, on the Huka Falls walking trail (see p. 133), where the hot stream flows into the Waikato River.

The South Island has less geothermal activity and fewer hot springs, but two excellent sites are at **Hanmer Springs** (see p. 203), a large resort with a variety of pools and a swimming pool, and **Maruia Springs** (see p. 203) at the Lewis Pass. Maruia Springs's Japanese bathhouse and outdoor pools are at their best in winter with snow falling as you soak in steaming hot water. Of the natural springs, hikers rate the **Welcome Flat Hot Pools** on the Copland Track in Westland Tai Poutini National Park as a highlight, but it is a seven-hour walk off the road south of Fox Glacier.

Whakarewarewa

✉ 17 Tryon St.

☎ 07/349-3463

$ $$$

**whakareware
wa.com**

Te Puia

✉ Hemo Rd.

☎ 07/348-9047

$ $$$$$

tepuia.com

guides at the Pink and White Terraces helped build what would become Rotorua's greatest attraction, **Whakarewarewa** *(17 Tryon St., tel 07/349-3463, whakarewarewa.com, $$$).* Called Whaka (pronounced fuk-ka) for short, the village was an enclave of Maori culture in a setting of geysers and boiling mud. In 1997, the village split off from the Maori Arts & Crafts Institute, which became Te Puia, taking up the western half of the valley.

The Fortress of Te Puia

Before Te Puia was a tourist attraction, it was a center of war for hundreds of years. Constructed in 1325, the fortress was one of the most formidable sites of Maori warfare and was passed down to many different *hapu* (subtribes) over the centuries. In battle, the fortress's location couldn't be beaten, protected as it was by an intricate system of terraces and natural obstacles such as geysers and mudpools.

Whakarewarewa doesn't get the same crowds anymore, though the old village with its wooden buildings and superbly carved meetinghouse is the real deal, if somewhat distorted by tourism. The entry fee includes a guided tour, cultural performance, hot-pool cooking class, and a look at the geysers from a viewing platform. Unguided walks lead around the thermal area to mud pools,

INSIDER TIP:

Explore the ruins of Te Wairoa, a village buried when Mount Tarawera erupted in 1886. Frozen in time, it's a South Pacific Pompeii.

—LARRY PORGES
*National Geographic
Travel Books editor*

but the valley is not that active.

Te Puia *(Helmo Rd., tel 07/348-9047, tepula.com, $$$$$, see sidebar left)* offers much the same but is in another league, with a cultural gallery, carving and weaving schools, a re-created Maori village, *marae,* and cultural performances. It also has thermal attractions and good views of the famous **Pohutu** (Big Splash) geyser, which shoots up 70 feet (21 m) or more every hour. The parking lot, gift shop, and café all attest to the popularity of Te Puia.

North Rotorua

A number of themed and other attractions lie north of the city along SH5. Trout teem in the waters of **Rainbow Springs** *(tel 07/350-0440, $$$)*, 3 miles (5 km) from town. The crystal-clear springs swarm with fish, but this mini-zoo has more than just trout ponds. Tuataras and other species are housed in a beautiful setting along with native bird enclosures and kiwi houses.

Nearby, the **Skyline Rotorua** *(tel 07/347-0027, skyline.co.nz, $$)* will whisk you to the top of Mount Ngongotaha for panoramic views. A restaurant, luge, and other amusements are found at the top.

About 6 miles (10 km) north, just off SH5, the **Agrodome** *(Western Rd., tel 07/357-1050, agrodome.co.nz, $$$–$$$$)* provides a look at farming life with a variety of livestock. The star attraction is the sheep show, including shearing and sheepdog displays. Opposite, **Agroventures** *(agroventures.co.nz)* has bungee jumping and other unusual adrenaline rushes such as swooping and shweebing! Nearby, you can **Zorb** *(zorb.com)* downhill in a giant plastic ball, while closer to town **Ogo** *(ogo.co.nz)* is a different franchise of the same thing.

Other nearby attractions on Paradise Valley Road include **Paradise Valley Springs Wildlife Park** *(tel 07/348-9667, paradisev.co.nz, $$$)*, with native and exotic animals, and the **aMAZEme** *(tel 07/357-5759, $)* circular hedge maze.

Visitors watch the erupting Pohutu geyser in Te Puia.

East of Rotorua

Hell's Gate *(tel 07/345-3151, $$$, spa $$$$$)* is a small but action-packed thermal area 10 miles (16 km) northeast of Rotorua on the road to Whakatane (SH30). George Bernard Shaw gave it its name on a visit in 1934. A self-guided walk takes in attractions such as the mud-slapping **Devil's Cauldron** and the steaming hot **Kakahi Falls.** The attached spa (bring swimsuits) is a soothing bonus with mud and hot-water soaking pools. The highway, SH30, continues on to the beguiling, forested Lake Rotoiti and Lake Rotoma. Southeast of Rotorua, take Tarawera Road off SH30 for a scenic drive through attractive lake country. The road passes **Redwoods Whakarewarewa Forest Park** *(redwoods.co.nz)*, planted with California redwoods, with walks, excellent mountain bike trails, visitor center, café, and a suspension walk between the huge trees *($$)* before reaching Blue and Green Lakes. Just off the main road, on the narrow isthmus between the lakes, a fine walking trail goes around the **Blue Lake** *(1.5 hr. round-trip)*, a deep volcanic caldera; **Green Lake** is shallower with a sandy bottom.

About 10 miles (16 km) past the lakes, **Buried Village** *(Tarawera Rd., tel 07/362-8287, buriedvillage.co.nz, $$$)* is the site of Te Wairoa, the tourist village for the Pink and White Terraces before the eruption of Mount Tarawera. The eruption in 1886 killed more than 120 people and buried the village under rocks, ash, and boiling mud. The fascinating museum retells the story of the tragedy, while the grounds have building foundations and a waterfall.

Beyond the Buried Village, serene **Lake Tarawera** is flanked by jagged Mount Tarawera. Boats once took tourists across this lake to walk to the Pink and White Terraces. Cruises today retrace the route from Tarawera Landing, where the Landing Café offers great views.

Lady Knox

In order to erupt, the Lady Knox Geyser must be coaxed with soap. The geyser contains two chambers, one with hotter water than the other. When soap is added to the top chamber, surface tension drops, the two pools mix, and the geyser erupts. This phenomenon was discovered in 1901 by startled convicts trying to do their laundry.

South Thermal Areas

If you want plenty of bang for your thermal buck, then head to the thermal areas south of Rotorua, signposted off the SH5 highway to Taupo. **Waimangu Volcanic Valley** (tel 07/366-6137, waimangu.com, $$$, cruise $$$), 12 miles (19 km) from Rotorua, combines thermal activity with fine walks and a cruise on **Lake Rotomahana,** the site of the legendary Pink and White Terraces. Less touristy than other thermal areas, it has fine panoramas and the best

walks over a large area (allow at least 2 hr. plus 45 min. for cruise; a shuttle bus also operates). Waimangu ("black water") has no geysers, but vents steam and ponds boil throughout. Highlights are the pale blue **Inferno Crater Lake** and the multicolored **Warbrick Terrace.**

The most spectacular and extensive of the thermal areas, **Wai-O-Tapu** (tel 07/366-6333, waiotapu.co.nz, $$$), 17 miles (28 km) from Rotorua, is a most dramatic moonscape of collapsed craters, mud pools, silica terraces, lakes, boiling water, and steam. The prime draw is the regular-as-clockwork **Lady Knox Geyser** (see sidebar left) that blows to 70 feet (21 m) at 10:15 a.m. daily, when the crowds pack in.

Blessed with such suitably demonic names as Devil's Ink Pots and Inferno Crater, the highlights of this feature-packed park also include the **Artist's Palette,** a large pool of changing colors; the adjoining **Champagne Pool,** which bubbles at 165°F (74°C); and the **Devil's Bath,** which can be green or yellow depending on the light. Don't miss the mud pools just off the road five minutes before the main entrance.

Farther south, the scenic **Orakei Korako** thermal area (see pp. 132–133) is 13 miles (21 km) off SH5, a 41-mile (66 km) drive from Rotorua, but closer to Taupo. Along the way, check out a popular stop in Reporoa, between the two resort towns. The **Mihi Café** (4089 SH5, tel 07/333-8909) is a retro-themed Kiwi diner with good local fare and great meat pies, plus a playground for the kids. ∎

Violent Nature

In 2011, the South Island's largest city, Christchurch, was devastated by an earthquake, flattening whole areas of the city and killing 158 people. This was one of the country's biggest disasters, in one of the Earth's most seismically active regions.

As long ago as A.D. 186, Roman historians recorded hazy skies and sunsets that "burst into flame," most likely a result of New Zealand's Taupo eruption, the world's most violent in 5,000 years. The volcano sent great clouds of debris around the world, threw out 70 cubic miles (300 cubic km) of rock, and left a huge crater that formed Lake Taupo. At Rotorua, other great lakes are the product of long-ago explosions, and in 1886, Mount Tarawera unexpectedly blew its top, burying villages and killing about 120 people.

Thermal activity seethes from Rotorua across to Lake Taupo and Tongariro National Park, a volcanic plain known as the Taupo Volcanic Zone. White Island volcano smolders over its northern reaches, 30 miles (48 km) offshore in the Bay of Plenty. At the southern end of the volcanic zone are the most dangerous volcanoes in New Zealand—Tongariro, Ngauruhoe, and Ruapehu, the towering stars of the Tongariro National Park. Mount Ngauruhoe is the youngest vent, erupting more than 40 times in the last century, most recently in 1975. Mount Tongariro had been quiet since 1926, before erupting in 2012.

Ruapehu last erupted in 2008 but remains the most dangerous of this violent, destructive triumvirate. The tallest at 9,173 feet (2,796 m), it has erupted at least 60 times in the past 70 years, with major eruptions in 1895, 1945, and 1995–1996. On Christmas Eve 1953, Ruapehu's crater wall gave way, causing 151 deaths. Water, mud, and boulders swept down into the Whangaehu River, washing away the rail bridge minutes before the Wellington–Auckland express plunged into the swirling waters.

The cause of all this turmoil lies far below, where the Pacific plate is pushing beneath the North Island, pressing against the overriding

Eruption of Mount Ruapehu, Tongariro National Park

Australian–Indian plate on which New Zealand sits. As the plates grind against each other, the massive friction turns rock to magma, which breaks through vents in the weakened crust.

The plates twist farther south around Wellington, and the northern Hikurangi Trench gives way to the Alpine Fault through the South Island. Tectonic plate collision in the South Island pushes up the Southern Alps, but produces no volcanoes. Lying on a fault line, the Wellington area is prone to earthquakes, and in 1855, a powerful quake pushed up great tracts of land along the city's waterfront. In 2016, multistory buildings in Wellington were damaged by a huge earthquake, centered far away on a remote area of the South Island, hitting the town of Kaikoura but sparing the capital from major toll. Hundreds of earthquakes, usually minor, occur throughout New Zealand each year, but the most destructive flattened Napier in 1931, killing 258 people.

Majestic Mount Taranaki in the west of the North Island last erupted in 1755, but scientists have long warned that it is overdue. The densely populated Auckland volcanic field last erupted 600 years ago, but could blow again at any time.

Central Plateau

The volcanic Central Plateau region hosts the volcanoes of Tongariro National Park, a spectacular alpine desert region with fine walks, superb scenery, and skiing in winter. Near the park, expansive Lake Taupo is famed for trout fishing, and on its shores, Taupo town makes a fine base from which to explore the region.

The multihued torrent of Huka Falls, near Taupo

Taupo

Map p. 105

Visitor Information

 Tongariro St.

☎ 07/376-0027

greatlaketaupo.com

Taupo

The resort town of Taupo sprawls around the northeast corner of **Lake Taupo,** New Zealand's largest lake. The product of a massive volcanic eruption (see p. 131), the lake resembles an inland sea, the Tongariro volcanoes making a stunning backdrop.

With magnificent vistas and nearby attractions, Taupo is a thriving resort, with a host of tour operators offering everything from bungee jumping and Maori concerts to some of the world's best trout fishing. It's also near Tongariro National Park and thermal areas.

Not the largest thermal area but crowd-free and in a glorious lake setting, **Orakei Korako** *(tel 07/378-3131, orakeikorako.co.nz, $$$)* is 23 miles (37 km) north of Taupo, off SH1. From the café/gift shop, a launch takes you across Lake Ohakuri to the park's many fine features. A one-hour scenic walk, uphill and down, takes in large silica terraces, the irregular **Diamond Geyser,** mud pools, boiling ponds, and **Ruatapu Cave,** a towering cavern holding an emerald green hot-water pool.

On the outskirts of Taupo, 4 miles (7 km) north of town, **Wairakei** is home to a massive geothermal power station (*SH5, tel 07/378-0913*), open for tours. Wairakei had one of the country's most active thermal areas until the 1958 power station siphoned off most of the action. Among the remaining steam vents and boiling ponds, the man-made **Wairakei Terraces** (*tel 07/378-0913, wairakeiterraces.co.nz, $*) re-create and foster natural silica terraces. A re-created Maori village, spa, and cultural performances add to the scene. A little closer to town on Karapiti Road, steaming **Craters of the Moon Walk** (*cratersofthemoon .co.nz, $*) is a small thermal area with steam vents and boiling ponds.

Taupo is at the source of New Zealand's longest river, the Waikato, which flows out of the lake and surges through the impressive rapids of the **Huka Falls,** on the Huka Falls Road 2.5 miles (4 km) north of town. This road has a number of attractions—a honey center, a prawn farm, jet boating, helicopter flights, and the informative **Volcanic Activity Centre** (*tel 07/374-8375, $*) that monitors the region. **Huka Falls Walkway** is a lovely one-hour trail from the falls along the Waikato River. It comes out at Spa Road, near **Taupo Bungy** (*tel 07/377-1135, $$$$$*), in a superb setting on a cliff over the river.

Tongariro National Park

A highlight of the North Island, Tongariro National Park houses the country's mightiest volcanoes—Mount Tongariro, Mount Ngauruhoe, and Mount Ruapehu. Before a minor eruption in 2012, Tongariro last erupted in 1926, but Ngauruhoe was the most active volcano for much of the 20th century. Ngauruhoe's 1954 lava flows were the largest in recorded history, but its last major show was in 1975.

Taniko Weaving

Taniko **is a special type of Maori** *raranga* **(weaving) that does not require a loom. Also known as finger-weaving or twining, taniko is one of the strongest remaining Maori traditions. The term** *taniko* **also applies to the pattern, a hallmark of New Zealand. The vibrant repetition of triangles can be seen all over the islands.**

In recent times, snowcapped Ruapehu has produced dozens of minor eruptions up to 2008. Major eruptions in 1995–1996 had the region on alert as the volcano belched great clouds of steam, ash, and rock. In 1969, a nighttime lahar (volcanic mudflow) swept an area where 2,000 people had skied that day. In 2007, advance warning systems averted any tragedy from another lahar.

This World Heritage area is a popular playground for visitors year-round. Summer brings day

Tongariro National Park

Map p. 105

Visitor Information

Whakapapa Village, Mt. Ruapehu

07/892-3729

doc.govt.nz/parks-and-recreation/national-parks/tongariro

Turangi

⛰ Map p. 105

Visitor Information

✉ Ngawaka Pl.

☎ 07/386-8999

greatlaketaupo.com

visitors, hikers, and volcano devotees, while the Whakapapa and Turoa ski slopes on Ruapehu come alive in winter.

Whakapapa Village, at the foot of Ruapehu, is the park headquarters where you'll find the historic Chateau Tongariro hotel (see Travelwise p. 296) and the park's visitor center, with excellent displays on the park. Staff can fill you in on the park's many walks, from easy one-hour strolls to the six-day hike around Ruapehu.

Serious hikers favor the three-day **Tongariro Northern Circuit,** but most popular of all is a one-day leg of this walk, the famous **Tongariro Alpine Crossing** (see pp. 136–137) taking in the peaks of Tongariro and Ngauruhoe.

Farther up the mountain, Whakapapa ski village is virtually

deserted in summer. From here, experienced hikers can climb to Ruapehu crater in a day, but, as for all high-altitude hikes, you must be well equipped and prepared for alpine conditions and sudden savage changes in weather.

Around the Park

From Taupo, the highway south (SH1) hugs the lake all the way to **Turangi,** the biggest town near the park. The Turangi visitor center can help with accommodations, the park, activities, and hikers' transportation. The town is also a major trout-fishing destination (see sidebar below) and center for white-water rafting. The **Tongariro National Trout Centre** (tel 07/386-8085, $), 2 miles (3 km) south of town

EXPERIENCE: Trout Fishing

New Zealand has some of the world's best trout fishing, with beautiful lakes and crystal-clear rivers and streams teeming with large fish. Rainbow trout from California were introduced in the 1880s and typically average 3 to 4 pounds (1.5–2 kg), but can grow up to 15 pounds (7 kg) or more. English brown trout arrived 20 years earlier; those in rivers tend to be smaller than their lake cousins.

Good trout fishing can be found throughout the country, with popular destinations including Rotorua and the Lake Brunner region in the South Island. Lake Taupo and rivers that flow into it (especially the Tongariro) are the most famous and have long attracted anglers from around the world.

A license is required to fish inland waters (a separate license is required

for the Taupo area). Fish and Game New Zealand offices (fishandgame.org.nz) issue licenses and provide fishing information, as do local sports shops, where you can rent or buy gear.

Though it is not essential, many visiting anglers hire fishing guides, who are a great source of local information and can also provide lessons. Taupo has the most guides, but they can also be found in tourist centers such as Rotorua, Wanaka, and Queenstown. Tourist offices have details.

If trout fishing begins to pall, chinook salmon were introduced into east coast rivers in the South Island a century ago, and the region has excellent salmon fishing in the Rakaia, Waimakariri, Rangitata, and Waitaki Rivers between November and March.

The National Army Museum in Waiouru

on SH1, is a DOC-run trout hatchery with displays and an underwater viewing area.

SH1 heads south of Turangi to the desert plateau east of the park. Lying in the shadow of the mountains, this is a desolate area of tussock grass and stunted growth. The Desert Road that runs across the plateau is often closed in winter due to snow. This eerie road hits civilization again at **Waiouru,** home to the large **National Army Museum** *(SH1 & Hassett Dr., tel 06/387-6911, armymuseum.co.nz, $$).*

The road from Turangi to Whakapapa (SH47) runs along the eastern side of the park and leads to the town of **National Park** on SH4. This utilitarian grid is scattered with accommodations and is handy for visitors to the park.

Ohakune, on the southern flank of Mount Ruapehu, is the prettiest town near the park and a good base for trips to Whanganui National Park (see pp. 147, 149). A host of chalets cater to the ski crowds at **Turoa ski slope,** 11

INSIDER TIP:

Rent a bach (holiday home) on the lake at Acacia Bay in Taupo. You can roll out of bed, grab your line, and hook a trout for lunch.

—CMDR. MARK WORSFOLD
Asst. Naval Attaché, Embassy of New Zealand, Washington, D.C.

miles (17 km) up the mountain. The main part of town attracts in summer, while the northern edge around the old railway station at the southern entrance to the park buzzes in the ski season. The visitor information center *(54 Clyde St., tel 06/385-8427, visituapehu.com)* has details on good walks and activities. **Mountain Bike Station** *(tel 06/385-8797)* rents bikes for the very scenic, half-day Ohakune Old Coach Road ride. Or try the more frenetic bus-up/bicycle-down service, a great way to see Mount Ruapehu in summer. ■

Walk: Tongariro Alpine Crossing

Dubbed the greatest one-day walk in the world, the spectacular Tongariro Alpine Crossing takes in volcanoes, crater lakes, alpine desert, forest, waterfalls, and hot springs all in seven to eight hours of walking. This glorious 10.6-mile (17 km) walk deserves all the accolades it gets, but appropriate clothing, equipment, fitness, and weather are essential for this demanding high-altitude hike.

The aptly named Emerald Lakes, Mount Tongariro

The walk is usually done in summer, when the trail can sometimes look like a scene from *March of the Penguins*—an endless line of hikers stretching to the horizon. But it can be walked at most times of the year if the weather is good. Buses will drop you at the start of the trail and pick you up at the end. They are easily arranged through visitor centers or through your accommodations.

The walk starts from the **Mangatepopo car park ❶**, crossing a tussock-grass plain to the Mangatepopo Hut. Following the Mangatepopo Stream, the trail climbs gradually through the valley across old lava flows. After an hour or so, you reach the side trail to **Soda Springs ❷** *(10 min. round-trip)*.

From Soda Springs, it is a grinding climb up though volcanic rock, but after an hour you reach the top with fabulous views back down to the valley. From here you can climb towering **Mount Ngauruhoe** *(a demanding 2–3 hr. round-trip)*, but most walkers continue across the flat **South Crater ❸**. This high desert is flanked by the glorious red-tipped cone of Mount Ngauruhoe on the right and the craggy ridge of Mount Tongariro on the left.

After crossing South Crater, the trail climbs up to the ridge and then gets steeper between the two craters. The prevailing westerly is often bitterly cold at this altitude, the ground crunching with ice even in summer. Finally, the track levels out where the trail to **Mount Tongariro** *(1.5–2 hr. round-trip)* leads off to the

NOT TO BE MISSED:

Soda Springs • Red Crater • Emerald Lakes • Blue Lake • Ketetahi Hot Springs

left, and on the right lies the magnificent **Red Crater ❹**. It is indeed red, and black, and is a very menacing presence.

The trail traverses the lip of the Red Crater, the highest point of the walk at 6,188 feet (1,886 m), with views stretching forever. It then plunges down through loose scoria to the superb **Emerald Lakes ❺**, which glisten and steam and make an ideal rest stop for lunch. The hard part of the walk is over, and the end is about 3.5 hours away.

The trail continues across the floor of the desertlike **Central Crater,** then up to the rim and the large **Blue Lake ❻**, another

stunning sight. Past the lake, it is all downhill on the sheltered side of the mountains, where mosses, shrubs, and other stunted plants begin to appear. The trail winds leisurely around the hillside, the panorama of far-off Lake Rotoaira and the lowlands a constant companion. The trail then switchbacks down to **Ketetahi Hut ❼**, now a shelter after being damaged in 2012 by the eruption of the steaming Te Maari crater nearby. After 20 minutes you'll see billowing steam from the Ketetahi Hot Springs, on private Maori land and off limits.

Tussock grass waving in the wind then dominates the slopes, but as the trail continues its inexorable descent, more substantial plants appear until the trail enters forest, a lush surprise after the desert. The trail then hits a gurgling stream and follows it, passing waterfalls, until finally it emerges at the **Ketetahi car park ❽**, where tired but inspired walkers wait for their ride home.

- 🗺 See also area map p. 105
- ► Mangatepopo car park
- ↔ 10.6 miles (17 km)
- 🕐 7–8 hours
- ► Ketetahi car park

47

46

Ketetahi car park ❽

Ketetahi Hut ❼

Central Crater ❻

Blue Lake

Mt. Tongariro 1,967m

Soda Springs ❷

Emerald Lakes ❺

Mangatepopo car park ❶

Red Crater ❹

South Crater ❸

MANGATEPOPO ROAD

Mangatepopo

47

START

0   4 kilometers
0   2 miles

Mt. Ngauruhoe 2,287m

East Coast

The east coast comprises sunny Hawke's Bay—noted for wineries and the art deco city of Napier, and the strongly Maori region of Gisborne and the East Cape. While Napier is the region's premier destination, a drive around the remote East Cape makes a fascinating diversion, and in the hinterland, Te Urewera National Park is a hiker's paradise.

The art deco home of the National Tobacco Company in Napier

Napier
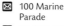 Map p. 105
Visitor Information
✉ 100 Marine Parade
☎ 06/834-1911
hawkesbaynz.com

Napier

Washed by the Pacific, cheery Napier (pop. 61,000) basks in a sunny clime and is noted for its architecture. The central city's art deco streetscapes are a memorial to a disaster.

On February 3, 1931, a magnitude 7.9 earthquake flattened Napier and nearby Hastings, killing 258 people in what remains New Zealand's worst natural disaster. Most of Napier's brick buildings were destroyed and many

wooden ones damaged. Some of the surrounding seabed was lifted more than 6.5 feet (2 m)—today's airport was once land under the Ahuriri Lagoon.

As fires swept the city, Napier had to be evacuated. New Zealand pitched in to rebuild. Remade in the fashion of the time, central Napier is an art deco delight, with almost all of its downtown buildings reflecting the style. Art deco tours and self-guided walks are the highlight of the city, with

Emerson and **Tennyson Streets** holding the pick of the buildings (see sidebar right).

Napier also has seaside holiday attractions and a modern dynamic, with chic cafés, spas, and wineries to tour nearby.

Exploring the city: The delightfully old-fashioned seafront boulevard of **Marine Parade** is lined with majestic pines. It was rebuilt with art deco flourishes such as the **Veronica Sun Bay** near the tourist office, a memorial to a ship that helped survivors after the earthquake. Reminiscent of an English seaside resort, complete with pebble beach, the seafront has a sound shell, sunken gardens, and a host of family attractions. Swimming in the sea, however, is dangerous; head to safer Westshore Beach, north of town.

At the northern end of Marine Parade, the **Ocean Spa** (42 Marine Parade, tel 06/835-8553, oceanspa .co.nz, $), a renovated swimming pool complex, has hot pools, spas, a gym, and massage and spa treatments. A little south, the **statue of Pania of the Reef** is a city icon, illustrating the old Maori legend of how Pania was lured by the siren voices of the sea people and swam out to meet them, only to be turned into the reef.

Across the road, the **MTG Hawke's Bay** (1 Tennyson St., tel 06/835-7781, mgthawkesbay .com, $) is the city's massive new cultural and event center, with theater, art gallery, and museum. Maori artifacts as well as poignant earthquake exhibits are on permanent display.

EXPERIENCE:
Art Deco Napier

To explore Napier's art deco architecture, start on **Emerson Street** at the corner of Marine Parade, where the **T&A Building** with its dome clock tower was built in 1936 to house an insurance company. Farther down Emerson Street, the interior of the **ASB Bank** includes Maori carvings. Next, the **Criterion Hotel** has some wonderful leadlight work, and the **Napier Mall** is lined with art deco masterpieces.

Turn right at the Spanish mission-style **Provincial Hotel** on the corner of Clive Square and head one block to Tennyson Street, where at No. 163 you'll find the art deco former **fire station**. Heading down Tennyson Street to the waterfront, you'll pass the **Municipal Theatre** and the **Daily Telegraph** building, before reaching the **Art Deco Trust** (tel 06/835-0022, artdeco napier.com) at No. 7. All things deco are sold in the center's shop, which also offers guided walks and self-guided brochures.

Heading south on the waterfront, stroll past the visitor center and sunken gardens and you'll see some fine Victorian wooden villas that survived the quake.

Much farther south, the **National Aquarium of New Zealand** (546 Marine Parade, tel 06/834-1404, nationalaquarium .co.nz, $$) has a varied collection of fish and animals, including sharks, turtles, crocodiles, kiwis, and tuataras. Add-ons include an invigorating swim with the sharks or a penguin encounter.

To see some of the city's pre-deco architecture, head up to **Bluff Hill,** which towers over the north of the city. Many of the Victorian wooden villas there

Hastings

▲ Map p. 105

Visitor Information

✉ Russell & Heretaunga St. East

☎ 06/873-0080

visithastings.co.nz

survived, and the lookout on the hill has fantastic views over the bay.

Around Hawke's Bay

Art deco buffs will also appreciate **Hastings** (pop. 78,000), Napier's sister city, but while Napier prospers on tourism, inland Hastings is just a rural service town, 13 miles (21 km) to the south on SH2.

The 1931 earthquake hit Hastings hard and also resulted in an art deco boom. A good place to start a tour is the **Westermans Building** (Heretaunga & Russell Sts.), a former department store that also houses the visitor information

INSIDER TIP:

While traveling on the remote East Cape, stock up on necessities with one-stop shopping at Hicks Bay General Store, post office, and gas station (19 Wharf Rd.).

—BRENT OPELL
National Geographic research grantee

center (tel 06/873-0080). The building has superb bronze-and-leadlight shop windows. The town's Spanish mission masterpiece is the **Hawke's Bay Opera House** (101 Hastings St. S.). Richly ornamented with imposing turrets, it was built in 1915 and repaired after the earthquake.

At the southern tip of Hawke's Bay, **Cape Kidnappers** acquired

its unfortunate name from Captain Cook, after the servant of his Tahitian translator was seized by Maori who had come to trade. "Obliged ... to fire upon them," Cook killed two or three Maori before the servant boy escaped.

Cape Kidnappers is noted for its gannet colony, where clouds of up to 20,000 of these graceful birds come to nest. The birds can be seen from September, when they build their nests, to early May (November to February is best). Seasonal tours *(check with visitor centers in Napier or Hastings)* run along the beach from Clifton to the colony, or it's a five-hour return walk.

The other great attraction of Hawke's Bay is its wineries. The area is noted for its Chardonnay, but red varieties now dominate. Pick up a *Hawke's Bay Winery Guide* brochure for details of local wineries. Highlights include the **Church Road Winery** (150 Church Rd., tel 06/833-8234, churchroad.co.nz) in Taradale, on the outskirts of Napier, with its winery museum tours, and nearby **Mission Estate** (198 Church Rd., tel 06/845-9350) featuring a fine restaurant (see Travelwise p. 297) and imposing cellar door in a former seminary.

Te Urewera National Park

This magnificent park protects the largest untouched native forest on the North Island, but most of the park's woodland, lakes, and mountains are accessible only by walking trails.

The park **visitor center** *(State Hwy 38 RD5, 06/837-3803,*

Apirana Ngata

Born in the East Cape village of Te Araroa, Sir Apirana Turupa Ngata (1874–1950) was one of New Zealand's most able politicians and an inspirational Maori leader. A lawyer and the first Maori university graduate, Ngata entered parliament in 1905 after winning the Eastern Maori seat. He was a skilled orator and political tactician, serving as a cabinet minister until he lost his seat in 1943.

Above all, he is noted for furthering Maori interests in education, health, and land reform, and he worked tirelessly to revive Maori language and traditions.

He was instrumental in setting up Maori arts-and-crafts schools, such as that in Rotorua, and encouraged the building of carved meetinghouses. He collected Maori songs and chants, studied the history of his Ngati Porou tribe, and worked on several Maori dictionaries and translations of the Bible.

Ngata was a pivotal member of the Young Maori Party, which promoted Maori interests by working within Pakeha (European) institutions. Though later criticized by Maori activists, the party was the first effective modern organization run by European-educated Maori.

doc.govt.nz) at Aniwaniwa lies on the shore of the lake, 38 miles (61 km) north of the coastal river town of Wairoa via SH38. The park's crowning jewel is beautiful **Lake Waikaremoana,** ringed by forest except for the cliffs of the spectacular Panekiri Bluff. One of the country's most popular hikes, the **Waikaremoana Track** leaves from the visitor center to circle the lake and can be walked in three to four days; reservations are required. Shorter walks also fan out from the visitor center, including to the nearby **Aniwaniwa** and **Papak-orito Falls,** or to Lake Waikareiti (2 hr. round-trip).

Gisborne

The most easterly city in New Zealand and closest to the inter-national date line, Gisborne (pop. 48,000) is the first city to see in the new year. Gisborne was also the first place Captain Cook set foot in New Zealand in 1769. After killing several Maori, Cook blighted the

area with the name of Poverty Bay.

In a region where 45 percent of the population is Maori, the English explorer is still not very highly regarded, judging by the dreary obelisk that marks **Cook's landing site** behind the docks along The Esplanade. The steep walking trail over the road leads to the **Kaiti Hill lookout,** offering wonderful views across Gisborne and Poverty Bay.

The **Tairawhiti Museum** (18 Stout St., tel 06/867-3832, tairawhitimuseum.org.nz) has a café overlooking the river. Highlights include displays on the messianic guerrilla Te Kooti (see p. 111) and a fine surfboard collection. Gisborne has top surf; **Waikanae Beach** (end of Grey St.) is good for beginners.

Gisborne also has a thriving wine industry. A good first stop is the **Gisborne Wine Centre** (tel 06/867-4085, gisbornewine.co.nz /wine-centre), on The Esplanade, near Cook's landing site. ∎

Gisborne
Map p. 105
Visitor Information
209 Grey St.
06/868-6139
gisbornenz.com

Drive: The East Cape

The East Cape region has remained a remote Maori stronghold, showing the least European influence of any region in the North Island. This lightly populated, rural area is a detour from modern New Zealand along a stunning coastline dotted with Maori towns, churches, and *marae*. It can be driven in one long day or two easy days.

Sunset behind the Ruakokore Anglican church

Begin at **Gisborne** and take SH35 north past fine surf beaches. After 13 miles (21 km), turn off to **Whangara ❶**, a picturesque Maori town with a finely carved meetinghouse on the bay where the film *Whale Rider* was shot.

The main highway again hits the coast at **Tolaga Bay ❷**, on a beautiful sweep of bay embraced by mudstone cliffs. Just before the town, turn off to the long Tolaga Bay Wharf. **Cook's Walkway** *(2.5 hr. round-trip)* starts near the wharf and goes to the top of the cliff, then down to Captain Cook's landing place at Cook's Cove. **Tokomaru Bay** comes next on another beautiful inlet surrounded by mountains. The old wharf and derelict freezing works are relics from better days though a couple of B&Bs have recently hit town.

The East Cape's largest town, **Ruatoria ❸**, lies inland off the main road. A center for the Ngati Porou people, this is also the home of the notorious Ngati Dread, Maori Rastafarians who combined Rasta teachings with the Ringatu faith of guerrilla leader Te Kooti (see p. 111). Back in the 1980s they terrorized the town but few now claim membership of this bizarre sect.

Another 12 miles (20 km) to the north, **Tikitiki ❹** is notable for beautiful **St. Mary's Church,** with its carved Maori entranceway and woven panels and carvings inside. About halfway along the East Cape drive, the small settlement of **Te Araroa ❺** lies on a scenic bay. In the schoolyard, the pohutukawa tree Te-Waha-O-Rerekohu is reputed to be the country's largest at 131 feet (40 m) around.

Te Araroa is also the turnoff to the **East Cape ❻**, 12 miles (20 km) along an unpaved road to the lighthouse, the most easterly such building in the world and the first to see the dawn. The climb to the top of the

See also area map p. 105
► Gisborne
↔ 205 miles (330 km)
🕐 7–8 hours
► Opotiki

N

0 — 40 kilometers
0 — 20 miles

lighthouse is rewarded with expansive views.

Past Te Araroa, **Hicks Bay** ⑦ has a great beach and farther on, **Lottin Point** lies 2.5 miles (4 km) from SH35 along a steep, narrow, and in parts unpaved road—but the views are spectacular. The road hits the coast again just before **Waihau Bay** ⑧; the settlement at **Oriti Point** has historic buildings.

From Waihau Bay, SH35 follows the coast through 65 miles (105 km) of glorious beach and bay scenery, the best of the journey. At **Raukokore** ⑨, the photogenic Anglican church with a carved entry stands out on a lonely promontory. The road then winds and dips through a number of pretty bays, such as

NOT TO BE MISSED:

Tolaga Bay • Tikitiki • East Cape lighthouse • Raukokore

Whanarua Bay, to the town of **Te Kaha** ⑩ with a beautifully carved meetinghouse.

Farther on, the road winds spectacularly along the **Motu River** with awe-inspiring views of mountain, river, and sea. SH35 then passes a number of tiny settlements and lonely beaches before finishing at **Opotiki** (see p. 123).

Taranaki & Whanganui

The adjoining districts of Taranaki and Whanganui lie on the North Island's western bulge, well off the main tourist trail. These rural regions offer a glimpse into old New Zealand and contain two magnificent natural attractions: the towering volcanic cone of Mount Taranaki and the upstream wilderness on the Whanganui River.

A lone camper enjoys the view of Mount Taranaki, Egmont National Park.

New Plymouth
🗺 Map p. 104
Visitor Information
✉ 65 St. Aubyn St.
☎ 06/759-0897
taranaki.info

New Plymouth

New Plymouth (pop. 80,000) is the main city of Taranaki, the district dominated by Fujiesque Mount Taranaki, which looms behind the city. With the only deepwater port on the country's west coast, the city serves the fertile rural interior and the country's offshore oil and gas installations.

The Ati Awa settled the area, but were driven out by musket-wielding Waikato tribesmen in the 1820s and '30s. In 1839, the New Zealand Company bought land

from the few remaining Maori, and the first boatload of settlers from Plymouth, England, landed in 1841.

As the traditional owners drifted back, land disputes were inevitable. In 1860, after Ati Awa chief Wiremu Kingi vetoed a land sale at Waitara, troops were sent in, sparking the Taranaki Wars (see pp. 110–111). Farmhouses burned and settlers fled to the safety of the New Plymouth stockade as Maori forces laid siege to the city. A truce was called in 1861, but conflict flared again

INSIDER TIP:

The King lives on at KD's Elvis Presley Museum *(tel 06/278-7624)* in Hawera, well worth a stop on the way to Whanganui. Phone ahead.

—PETER TURNER
National Geographic author

most renowned modern artists, Len Lye (1901–1980, see sidebar below), are now housed next door in a stunning new building, its pinnacles of stainless steel resembling a giant cookie cutter.

New Plymouth is noted for its beautiful gardens. Don't miss **Pukekura Park,** a ten-minute walk east of downtown, with its lakes, teahouse, fernery, hothouses, zoo, cricket ground, and more within 128 acres (52 ha) of rich greenery.

Egmont National Park

🅰 Map p. 104

Visitor Information

✉ Egmont National Park Visitor Centre, 2879 Egmont Rd.

☎ 06/756-0990

doc.govt.nz/parks-and-recreation/national-parks/egmont

from 1864 to 1866 and continued with Hauhau attacks in South Taranaki until 1869.

In the aftermath, settlers seized Maori land illegally and turned Taranaki into a green dairy farm. Well off the beaten tourist path, Taranaki remains a slice of old-fashioned rural New Zealand. That's where its charm lies, though New Plymouth does its best to put on a bright new face with an artistic bent.

Start a tour of the city at **Puke Ariki,** an impressive modern complex at the visitor information center that includes a library, galleries, cafés, and museum. It also has a fine collection of Maori *taonga* (treasures). In complete contrast at the rear of Puke Ariki, **Richmond Cottage** *(tel 06/759-6060, Sat.–Sun.)* on Ariki Street was built in 1853 and housed prominent early settler families.

The **Govett-Brewster Art Gallery & Len Lye Centre** *(42 Queen St., tel 06/759-6060, govettbrewster .com)* is one of New Zealand's best contemporary art galleries with varied and daring exhibitions. The works of one of New Zealand's

Len Lye

Len Lye (1901–1980), known primarily as a sculptor and filmmaker, was interested in how motion could be incorporated into art. He strove to collapse traditional boundaries between disciplines and cultures, making his films, for instance, by painting and scratching designs directly into the emulsion. His art, which blends Maori and European influences, is best summarized by his theory of life: "Individual Happiness Now."

Egmont National Park

One of New Zealand's most stunning sights, the towering volcano of **Mount Taranaki** is protected by Egmont National Park. Snow-capped for much of the year, Taranaki rises 8,261 feet (2,518 m) from the plains and dominates the horizon for hundreds of miles. A dormant volcano, it last erupted more than 250 years ago. It is an

Tattooing

The Maori traditionally tattooed many parts of their bodies, but the facial tattoos, *moko,* that we are familiar with today were reserved for those of high rank. The painful moko were carved on the face, often over many years, with small bone adzes hit by a mallet and colored with charcoal and other pigments. High-ranking women also had moko, usually just on the chin.

almost perfect cone when viewed from the north, so reminiscent of Japan's Mount Fuji that it was used as a backdrop for the Tom Cruise movie *The Last Samurai.*

Dutch seafarer Abel Tasman was the first European to sight Mount Taranaki in 1642. James

Cook was in awe of it in 1770, naming it Mount Egmont after the Earl of Egmont, and the name stuck for 200 years. But to the Maori it was always Taranaki ("shining mountain"), and the name officially reverted to Mount Taranaki (Egmont) in the 1980s.

The park has three access points: North Egmont on the northern slopes *(take SH3 & turn off at Egmont Village),* East Egmont on the east, and Dawson Falls on the southeast *(both accessed from Stratford on SH3).*

North Egmont is the easiest to reach from New Plymouth. It has a Department of Conservation (DOC) visitor center *(2879 Egmont Rd., tel 06/756-0990)* with good displays, a café, and information on walks, ranging from 20-minute strolls to the three- to five-day **Mountain Circuit.** Be aware that the weather on the mountain is extremely unpredict-

The Watt Fountain stops traffic at the heart of old Whanganui.

EXPERIENCE: Canoeing the Whanganui

Another wonderful New Zealand wilderness experience is canoeing the Whanganui River. The 90-mile (145 km), five-day journey from Taumaranui to Pipiriki through the superb **Whanganui National Park** can also be done in three days (from Whakahoro to Pipiriki) or one day (Taumaranui to Ohinepane or variations). From October 1 to April 30, huts and campsites along the way must be reserved through the Department of Conservation (*doc.govt.nz & search for Whanganui Journey*), which issues a Great Walk Pass for this popular trip.

The river has small rapids, but is easily negotiated; guided trips are also offered. The journey is usually arranged in Tauma-ranui, to the north of the park, where operators provide canoes, as well as all gear, and drop-off and pickup along the river. Operators include **Taumarunui Canoe Hire** (*tel 07/895-7483, taumarunui canoehire.co.nz*) and **Whanganui River Canoes** (*tel 07/385-4176, whanganuiriver canoes.co.nz*) in Raetihi.

In Ohakune, contact **Yeti Tours** (*tel 06/385-8197, whanganui.co.nz*), a group that rents canoes and gear and arranges tours. **Canoe Safaris** (*tel 06/385-9237, canoesafaris.co.nz*) also offers guided trips on the Whanganui as well as a variety of other rivers. Other operators can also be found, check with local tourist offices.

---

able and the highest reaches are suitable only for more experienced climbers.

For an excellent 1.5- to 2-hour walk, the **Veronica Loop Track** climbs steeply for 30 minutes to the junction with the **Holly Track.** Take a ten-minute detour up the mountain on the Holly Hut Track to the lookout for spectacular views. The Veronica Loop Track then gently curls back down the mountain through forest to the park headquarters.

The **East Egmont** access point is at the highest altitude. It leads to the Manganui ski slopes and the popular Stratford Mountain House (*tel 06/765-6100, stratford mountainhouse.co.nz*), which has alpine lodge accommodations and a restaurant. The **East Egmont Lookout** is only a ten-minute walk from the top parking lot and provides panoramic views.

Dawson Falls has an alpine-style tourist lodge and a DOC visitor center (*tel 06/756-0990*). Walks include the one-hour **Kapuni Loop Track** that takes in the cascading Dawson Falls.

Whanganui

The Whanganui River flows from its origins on Mount Tongariro through some of New Zealand's most diverse and beautiful countryside before disgorging its waters into the sea at the city of Whanganui ("expansive river mouth"). A faded river port, the city has enough historical charm to keep the visitor, but the river is the real lure for those with time to explore upstream.

The New Zealand Company settled Whanganui in 1840 based on contentious land sales. Skirmishes blighted the early years of the settlement, which

Whanganui

▲ Map p. 105

Visitor Information

✉ 31 Taupo Quay

☎ 06/349-0508

whanganuinz.com

became a major military base during the New Zealand Wars. Ironically, in 1864 the lower river tribes saved the city against marauding Hauhau warriors coming down the river. In the 1880s, the river

Plague of Rabbits

First brought to New Zealand in the mid-19th century, rabbits provided meat, fur, and a friendly reminder of Britain for homesick colonists. But as the rabbit population skyrocketed, so did damage to the ecosystem. Imported natural enemies such as ferrets and weasels proved just as disastrous to the environment. Finally, in 1947 the government set up the Rabbit Destruction Council, which decommercialized the rabbit meat and fur industries and instituted a "killer policy," advocating the year-round destruction of the animals. Rabbits have since been controlled.

became an artery to the remote interior, and riverboats thrived as much on tourism as on trade.

Today the old heart of the city lies on the corner of the leafy main street, **Victoria Avenue,** and Ridgeway Street, where fine historic buildings surround the **Watt Fountain,** topped by Victorian gas lamps.

Two blocks north in Queens Park, the **Whanganui Regional Museum** (*Watt St., tel 06/349-*

1110, wrm.org.nz) is well worth a visit. Fine Maori artifacts include carvings, war canoes, and greenstone clubs and are regularly featured in rotating exhibits. Next door, the **Sarjeant Gallery** (*tel 06/349-0506, sarjeant.org.nz*) has rotating art exhibits in a fine neoclassical building, but its temporary home is **Sarjeant on the Quay** (*38 Taupo Quay*), while it undergoes redevelopment.

Rejuvenated Taupo Quay is part of the historic riverport district, where the paddle wheeler *Waimarie* provides river cruises re-creating Whanganui's heyday. Cruises depart from the **Waimarie Centre** (*Taupo Quay, tel 06/347-1863, waimarie.co.nz, cruises daily 11 a.m., $$$$*), where a small museum showcases the boat's restoration and the river's history.

Across the river, **Drurie Hill** has panoramic views of the city and Whanganui River. Getting there is half the fun: You proceed along a tiled tunnel into the hillside, then take a 1919 elevator (*$*) that grinds the 216 feet (66 m) to the top. Perched on the hill, the **Memorial Tower,** dedicated to the dead of World War I, has unbeatable views.

A great way to explore the river is in a rented canoe from the **Top 10 Holiday Park** (*460 Somme Parade, tel 06/343-8402, $$$*), located on the river bank 4 miles (7 km) northeast of the town.

Whanganui River

A highlight from Whanganui is the 50-mile (80 km) **Whanganui River Road** drive to Pipiriki. The tiny settlements along the way relied on the river for transportation until the road was built in 1934, and this rugged area is still remote. The road is still not fully paved, but the slow twisting drive is rewarded with superb scenery. Bus tours also operate along this route.

The region's history is one of war and missionaries. The road passes old Maori fortresses high above the river and mission stations with classical names such as Atene (Athens) and Koriniti (Corinth) before reaching picturesque **Jerusalem.** French nun Sister Mary Joseph Aubert established the Catholic mission in 1883 and worked with the sick and poor here until her death in 1926. Jerusalem was also home to poet James K. Baxter, who set up a commune in the 1960s that lasted until his death in 1972.

Pipiriki lies on the southern edge of **Whanganui National Park,** a vast wilderness accessible only by river or on foot. **Bridge to Nowhere Jetboat Tours** *(tel 06/385-4622, $$$$$)* has wonderfully scenic four-hour trips on the river from Pipiriki to the **Bridge to Nowhere,** built for a settlement of returned World War I soldiers and indeed in the middle of nowhere. Pipiriki also hosts a myriad of jet boat, canoe, hiking, and camping tour options.

The park has some wonderful wilderness adventures, ranging from three-day hikes to three- to five-day canoeing trips along the river (see sidebar p. 147), with stays at campsites and huts. From Pipiriki it is 15 miles (24 km) to

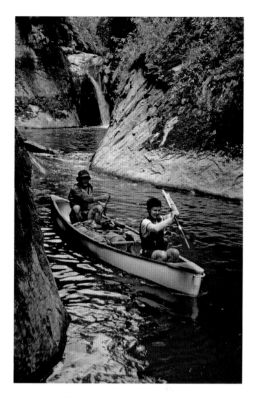

Canoeing the Whanganui River

Raetihi and SH4, if heading north to Tongariro National Park and towns such as Ohakune (see pp. 133–135).

Taumaranui, west of Lake Taupo on SH4, is one of the best places to arrange kayaking trips (guided or independent) on the river. The visitor information center *(116 Hakiaha St., tel 07/895-7494)* is a helpful stop to assess your options.

Railway buffs will appreciate the **Raurimu Spiral,** 23 miles (37 km) south of town. The track negotiates a steep incline with circles, horseshoe curves, and tunnels. ■

The nation's capital and most attractive and cultivated city, blending historical appeal with contemporary élan

Wellington & the South

The Wellington Cable Car transports residents and visitors from Lambton Quay to scenic stops around the city.

Wellington & the South

When the god Maui fished the North Island out of the sea, its tail fell to the north, while the head lay south around Wellington, at the bottom of North Island. Still the country's head, the capital city is a scenic metropolis draped across hills and precipitous gullies around a deep blue harbor.

Many visitors come to Wellington only to catch a ferry to the South Island, but the capital deserves exploration. A compact city easily explored on foot, its streets are a delight to wander. Historic buildings grace the downtown, while the rejuvenated waterfront buzzes with activity. Taking pride of place on the shorefront, the national museum, Te Papa, is not to be missed.

From downtown, take the cable car to the hills and see why Wellington is often compared to San Francisco. The panorama from the top takes in shimmering harbor, city towers, and hills speckled with wooden Victorian villas.

The New Zealand Company's first venture, Wellington was settled in 1840 on land hastily purchased from the Maori by William Wakefield (1801–1848). Land disputes and floods marred the early years of the colony, but Wellington grew and overcame the lack of flat land by reclaiming the shoreline, beginning in 1852.

Lying on a major fault line, the city is often shaken by tremors, none more ferocious than the magnitude 8.2 earthquake that hit the fledgling settlement in 1855. However, the 1855 quake helped the shoreline reclamation process by pushing up large areas of land.

In 1865, the capital shifted from Auckland to Wellington, because of the latter city's central location and proximity to the South Island. Wellington expanded to suburbs such as historic Thorndon, built of earthquake-resistant wood, resulting in impressive structures such as the

Old Government Buildings (1876) in the Parliament District, where the country's lawmakers govern.

Though the population of 208,000 is small for a capital city, greater Wellington, including the adjoining cities of Lower Hutt, Upper Hutt, and Porirua, has a population of 410,000. The city belies its size with a thriving arts scene, lively nightlife, good shopping, and a parade of festivals, concerts, and exhibitions that make it the country's cultural center. The city is also a hub for New Zealand's vibrant film industry, thanks largely to *Lord of the Rings* director and Wellingtonian Peter Jackson.

Visible from the city's hilltops, the South Island lies just across Cook Strait,

NOT TO BE MISSED:

Strolling and eating on Wellington's lively waterfront **155–156**

Te Papa, New Zealand's impressive national museum **156**

Views from the cable car to the Botanic Garden **158**

Historic Parliament District **159–160**

Lively nightlife of Courtenay Place and Cuba Street **160**

A ferry across, or drive around, scenic Wellington Harbour **161**

Tasting the fine wines of romantic Martinborough **162–163**

Fauna of the Pukaha Mount Bruce National Wildlife Centre **163** a swift and sometimes turbulent passage. Windy Wellington is noted for its howling gales, whipping around buildings, buffeting airplanes, and churning seas.

North of Wellington, the Kapiti Coast is something of a resort for the city. Good beaches and points of interest lie just off SH1, the country's main highway heading north. The alternative route, SH2 to Napier, lies over the ranges to the east and goes through the Wairarapa. This district is noted for wineries, historic towns, and the Pukaha Mount Bruce National Wildlife Centre. At the top of the "fish's head," the university city of Palmerston North is a crossroads between the two routes. ■

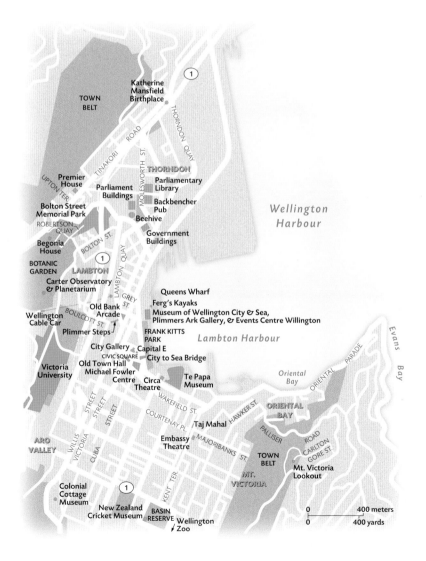

Wellington

Compact and easy to navigate, downtown Wellington is a delight to explore, taking in the city's heritage and the redeveloped waterfront, where the national museum, Te Papa, makes a statement. Riding the cable car to the Botanic Garden provides an overview of the fine harbor and hilly suburbs draped with Victorian villas.

Modern downtown Wellington

Wellington

 Map p. 153

Visitor Information

✉ Civic Square, Victoria & Wakefield Sts.

☎ 04/802-4860

wellingtonnz.com

Civic Square

Often busy with street performers and stalls, Civic Square, behind the visitor information center, lies at the heart of the city's cultural precinct and is a good place to start a tour. Turned into a paved plaza in the 1990s, it is lined with artwork, including stylized nikau palms.

Buildings around the square include the imposing **Town Hall** (1904), saved from demolition in 1983 by a public campaign. The New Zealand Symphony Orchestra

often performs there. The futuristic **Michael Fowler Centre** next door also has a fine auditorium, and is the city's preeminent concert venue. These two are the focus of the biennial **New Zealand Festival** *(festival.co.nz)*, which showcases Wellington as the country's performing-arts capital.

The square is also home to the **Capital E** children's theater and events center, as well as the **City Gallery** *(tel 04/913-9032, citygallery.org.nz)*, in an impressive

INSIDER TIP:

Keep an eye out for the iconic "Ferns" in Civic Square, a giant 385-pound (175 kg) globe suspended midair on wires.

—PETER TURNER
National Geographic author

art deco edifice that hosts rotating exhibitions highlighting New Zealand and international artists.

Waterfront

From Civic Square, take the art-lined City to Sea Bridge to the waterfront. Across the bridge, turn right and go past the **Circa Theatre** *(1 Taranaki St., 04/801-7992),* home to one of the city's liveliest theater companies. Its facade was transplanted from the old Westport Coal Company building, which once stood nearby.

Dominating the waterfront is the pride of the city, **Te Papa,** the Museum of New Zealand (see p. 156). Allow at least a few hours to take in its exhibits.

From Te Papa, walk back north around the waterfront, a lively open space. Dotted everywhere are artworks, such as in **Frank Kitts Park,** built on reclaimed land and one of the few patches of green in the inner city. Past the park, **Queens Wharf** is a dynamic hub of restaurants, bars, museums, and the **TSB Bank Arena,** which hosts concerts and other events. Queens Wharf was built on reclaimed shorefront land after the 1855 quake. Lying on a

fault line, the city is acutely aware of the risk of earthquakes, brought home by the 2016 quake. Though centered on the South Island, it violently shook the downtown high-rise district, causing 16 buildings to close for repair, structural assessment, or strengthening; at least four multistory buildings were demolished after being assessed as beyond repair.

Fascinating facts about the 1855 quake and early settlement can be found at the **Plimmers Ark Gallery** on the south side of Queens Wharf. The gallery houses the remains of the *Inconstant,* an immigrant ship wrecked in 1849 and bought by merchant John Plimmer for use as a bond store

EXPERIENCE:
Lord of the Rings Tours

A number of major operators offer *Lord of the Rings* and *Hobbit* tours:

Hobbiton *(tel 07/888-6838, 501 Buckland Rd., Hinuera, hobbitontours.com),* near Matamata, is the home of the hobbit houses.

From Queenstown, **Pure Glenorchy** *(tel 03/441-1079, pureglenorchy.com)* takes visitors to some of the most spectacular filming sites.

Heliworks *(Queenstown International Airport, Tex Smith Ln., Queenstown, tel 03/441-4011, heliworks.co.nz)* took part in the actual filming and offers aerial Rings tours.

In Wellington, **Wellington Movie Tours** *(tel 027/419-3077, adventuresafari.co.nz)* has location and studio LOTR tours.

Movie fans will get a real thrill by visiting the **Weta Cave** *(1 Weka St., Miramar, tel 04/380-9361, wetanz.com)* at the Weta Workshop studios, with props, displays, and movie insights.

and shop, known as Plimmers Ark. The *Inconstant* was beached in the upheaval of the 1855 earthquake, and some remains of the ship, now just lumps of blackened wood, were discovered in 1997 under the Old Bank Arcade on Lambton Quay.

The gallery forms part of the nearby **Wellington Museum** *(tel 04/472-8904, museumswellington .org.nz)*, housed in the old Harbour Trust and bond store offices (1892), one of the oldest buildings on the waterfront. Crammed with interesting tales of Wellington from its founding to recent times, the museum covers everything from epic rugby games to the *Wahine* ferry disaster, which claimed 51 lives in Cook Strait on April 10, 1968.

Farther north along the waterfront, historic harbor sheds now serve as apartments and restaurants. To see the city from the water, stop at **Ferg's Kayaks** *(tel 04/499-8898, fergskayaks.co.nz)* in Shed 6, owned by Ian Ferguson, winner of four Olympic kayaking gold medals.

Te Papa

The **Museum of New Zealand Te Papa Tongarewa** *(Cable St., tel 04/381-7000, tepapa.govt.nz)*, universally known as Te Papa, houses the most important collection of national artistic treasures in the country. Opened in 1998 after 13 years of planning, the striking modern building on reclaimed waterfront land cost more than NZ$300 million.

Among its impressive architectural motifs, the gray wall that bisects the building symbolizes Wellington's fault lines. The building sits atop the Wellington fault, and its unusual rubber-and-lead foundations are designed to counter the effects of a quake.

Six floors of exhibition space highlight New Zealand's natural environment and Maori heritage, most poignantly at **Te Marae,** the meetinghouse and focal point for the Maori collection. **Toi Te Papa: Art of the Nation** features some of the museum's art collection, once housed in the National Art Gallery.

Perhaps the only criticism of Te Papa is that, with all that space, more of its huge collection could be displayed, but rotating exhibits and innovative displays are designed to keep the masses coming back. More than 1.5 million visitors pour through the doors every year. Te Papa is open every day of the year and admission is free.

Lambton Quay

Now Wellington's premier shopping boulevard, Lambton Quay ran along the shoreline from the time of first European settlement in 1840. Its western flank rises steeply while the east traverses gently to the waterfront on reclaimed land. Lined with arcades and shops, the quay holds many historic buildings, none finer than the 1884 **Old Bank Arcade.** Once headquarters of the Bank of New Zealand, it is now a hub for designer fashion boutiques. Also of interest are the **Plimmer Steps** leading to Boulcott Street, named after prominent early businessman John Plimmer, the "father of Wellington." A statue of Plimmer

TE PAPA

LEVEL 6
SCULPTURE TERRACE

LEVEL 5 ART EXHIBITIONS

LEVEL 4 MAORI WORLD

Te Marae

War canoe

Carved storehouse

Pacific exhibits

Iwi (tribal) exhibition

20th Century
New Zealand

LEVEL 3 HUMAN IMPACT ON
NEW ZEALAND

Bush City Rainforest

LEVEL 2 NATURE &
ENVIRONMENTAL EXHIBITS

Colossal Squid

Soundings Theatre

LEVEL 1 SHOPS AND CAFÉ

Entrance

and his dog Fritz stands at the entrance to the steps.

North on Lambton Quay, opposite Grey Street, lies the entrance to the **Wellington Cable Car** (04/472-2199, wellingtoncable car.co.nz, $), a must on every Wellington itinerary. Completed in 1902, it serviced the new suburb of Kelburn up in the hills as the city expanded beyond the limited flat

EXPERIENCE:
Eco-volunteering

Nature conservation projects across the country are attracting an increasing number of volunteers eager to learn about New Zealand's unique ecology and motivated to get out into the wonderful outdoors and make a difference.

The Conservation Volunteers (conser vationvolunteers.co.nz) has programs from a few days to a few weeks throughout the country for visitors to monitor, preserve, and reestablish the environment. Programs start from around US$300 per week, which includes accommodations and food, with duties such as replanting, wildlife monitoring, park maintenance, etc. **The New Zealand Department of Conservation** (govt.nz/getting-involved) also has several volunteer opportunities, mostly suited to locals, but short-term options also exist.

lands. Cable cars carry residents and tourists daily until 10 p.m., passing Victoria University and terminating at the Wellington Botanic Garden. At the top station, a small museum details the cable car's history. If you want to return to Lambton Quay via cable car, you can head north from the quay to the Parliament District (see opposite page).

Botanic Garden
& Thorndon

At the top of the cable car route, Wellington's premier horticultural spot offers postcard panoramas of the city and harbor in 64 acres (26 ha) of superb gardens, exotic woodlands, and native forest. From the cable car station, walk past Carter Observatory and Planetarium to the garden's **Treehouse Visitor Centre** (tel 04/499-1400) and down to the **Begonia House** and café, with the formal rose gardens at the front.

From the Begonia House, you can continue on back to the city via **Bolton Street Memorial Park,** where many of the city's pioneers are buried. As you walk along Robertson Way through the Jewish section of the cemetery, you'll see the fine villas of Thorndon. Robertson Way comes out at The Terrace and leads back to the Parliament District and the railway station.

Alternatively, north of the Begonia House you can exit the gardens onto Tinakori Road in historic **Thorndon.** Head northeast along this road, which is lined with some of the city's finest houses. In 1865, the area was purchased for the new capital as part of the move from Auckland to Wellington. Behind Thorndon, the precipitous greenery of Tinakori Hill forms part of the Town Belt, a ring of parkland around the city set aside by early planners.

On Tinakori Road just past Upton Terrace, **Premier House** at No. 260 is the prime minister's official residence. The original cottage, built in 1843, underwent substantial additions over the years, but in

Katherine Mansfield

Born Kathleen Mansfield Beauchamp in a small house at 25 Tinakori Road in 1888 (see photo), Katherine Mansfield would go on to become New Zealand's most acclaimed writer. Her father, Harold Beauchamp, was a banker whose career later enabled his family to move to a larger house at 75 Tinakori Road.

Educated at Wellington Girls High School and later at Queens College in London, Mansfield moved permanently to Europe in 1908 and lived a bohemian life there, taking lovers of both sexes before marrying literary critic John Middleton Murry.

Though she published only three volumes of short stories, they garnered high critical acclaim and she mingled with the cream of Britain's literati, including D. H. Lawrence and Bloomsbury group

writers such as T. S. Eliot, Aldous Huxley, and Virginia Woolf. Mansfield died of tuberculosis in 1923 at the age of 34, not long after the publication of *The Garden Party* collection, considered the pinnacle of her short career.

1935 Socialist prime minister Michael Joseph Savage thought it far too grand to live in and it became a children's dental clinic, thereafter dubbed the Murder House. The house was fully restored in 1990, when it once again became the residence of the prime minister.

Number 25 Tinakori Road, the **Katherine Mansfield Birthplace** *(tel 04/473-7268, closed Mon., $)*, was the childhood home of New Zealand's most famous writer (see sidebar above). The beautifully restored house features a video portrait of the author.

Parliament District

At the top end of Lambton Quay, the impressive **Government Buildings** (actually a single edifice) was built in 1876 as offices for public servants and government

ministers. The second largest wooden building in the world (the Todaiji Temple in Japan takes the number one spot), it has a slab-style front designed to look like stone. It now houses Victoria University's law faculty.

Across the road, the distinctive and oft-maligned **Beehive** stands in modern contrast. The circular 1981 building houses the offices of the prime minister, cabinet, and other busy government bees. It is the national symbol of executive power. The parliament meets next door at the neoclassical **Parliament Buildings** *(free tours available)*. Built in 1922, its fine edifice is a bit lopsided, as the southern wing—planned to match the northern wing—was never built. Next along, the delightful **Parliamentary Library** (1899) is

Parliament Buildings

🅰 Map p. 153
✉ For tours, use Molesworth St. entrance
☎ 04/817-9503
parliament.nz

a Gothic fantasy in pink-fringed stone, a survivor of the 1907 fire that destroyed the original wooden Parliament Buildings.

Facing the Parliament Buildings, the famous **Backbencher Pub** *(34 Molesworth St., backbencher.co.nz)* has beckoned politicians for decades and features puppet effigies of the nation's leaders.

Cuba Street: Victorian streetscapes are home to a lively bar and dining district.

Courtenay & Cuba

South of Te Papa and the waterfront, Wellington's liveliest restaurant and nightlife district lies along Courtenay Place and the pedestrian Cuba Street running off it. A great area to dine in, with a host of cuisines catering to all budgets, this buzzing locale really takes off on Friday and Saturday nights, when the bars stay open into the wee hours.

The area is also worth a wander during the day. Cuba Street has fine rows of Victorian merchant buildings and storefronts, as does Courtenay Place with its old theaters and oddities such as the **Taj Mahal** *(cnr. of Cambridge Ter.)*, a baroque public toilet built in 1928 and now a Welsh bar.

From here, head to the waterfront, where Oriental Parade continues around to **Oriental Bay,** a chic area around a fine swimming beach on the edge of the city. Popular with runners, cyclists, and sunbathers, the beach strip has a good selection of dining options.

Wellington Suburbs

Many of Wellington's suburbs are dotted with wooden villas clinging to green hills. The Aro Valley area, south of downtown, has kept many of its fine houses, thanks to resident action against urban renewal in the 1960s and '70s.

Saved from the wrecker's ball, **Narin Street Cottage** *(68 Nairn St., tel 04/384-9122, daily Jan.–Feb., Sat.–Sun. March–Dec., $)* is Aro Valley's oldest building, dating from 1858. The cottage is now a museum furnished in 19th-century style with an attractive garden.

Just over half a mile (1 km) east of the cottage, the **Basin Reserve,** one of the country's prime cricket grounds, was a lake until the 1855 earthquake lifted it. The **New Zealand Cricket Museum** *(tel 04/385-6602, $)* in the Old Grandstand exhibits cricket memorabilia.

For the most stunning panorama of the city, reaching from the Cook Strait and the airport in the south to the full length of the harbor and the Hutt Valley in the north, head to the top of **Mount Victoria.** Though it can be reached on foot from the end of Courtenay Place, it is far easier to drive—take Majoribanks Street next to the Embassy Theatre, turn left at Hawker, then right at Palliser. Or, from Oriental Parade on the other side of the hill, take Carlton Gore Street.

Zealandia (tel 04/920-9200, Waiapu Road, Karori, visitzealandia .com, $) is a unique forest sanctuary just 2 miles (3 km) west of the city. Kiwi, takahe, kaka, other rare birds, and tuatara roam free in a lush valley with miles of walking tracks and an exhibition center. Night tours offer a chance to see birds up close.

INSIDER TIP:

September's World of WearableArt is beyond a fashion show—it's a kaleidoscope performance of color, light, music, and crazy costume constructions.

—CARRIE MILLER
National Geographic contributor

The popular **Wellington Zoo** (200 Daniel St., tel 04/381-6750, wellingtonzoo.com, $$–$$$), 2.5 miles (4 km) south of the city center, has a kiwi house as well as tigers, chimps, and other exotics.

For a wonderful coastal drive around Wellington's eastern suburbs, take Oriental Parade east from downtown and follow the coast for 19 miles (30 km) around a series of pretty coves and beaches including Evans Bay; pine-fringed Mahanga Bay; Breaker Bay, where little blue penguins come to nest;

Out On the Town

Choice Wellington night-spots include:

Goldings Free Dive (14 Leeds St., goldingsfreedive .co.nz) Tucked in an alley, this small craft beer bar has great brews, wine, pizza, and an eclectic crowd.

Library (Level 1, 53 Courtenay Pl., thelibrary .co.nz) Cocktails, sundaes, books, and board games in this intimate, chic favorite.

Matterhorn (106 Cuba St., matterhorn.co.nz) A long-running hip bar, Matterhorn has good food, cocktails, low lighting, and hip sounds till late.

and the surf beaches of Worser Bay and Lyall Bay near the airport. The road changes name many times, but just keep following the coastline until Island Bay, where you head back to Wellington along The Parade/Adelaide Road.

On the way at Miramar, stop at the **Weta Cave** (tel 04/380-9361, 1 Weka St.), a behind-the-scenes mini-museum at Weta Workshop, producers of Lord of the Rings. Entry is free or you can take a studio tour ($$).

For a cheap cruise, take a ferry (tel 04/494-3339, eastbywest.co.nz, $) from Queens Wharf to **Days Bay,** where you can swim, dine at the wharf café opposite the wharf, or walk to the Rimu Street shops in Eastbourne. On weekends, ferries stop at **Matui/Somes Island,** a former POW camp and quarantine station, now a nature reserve open to the public. ∎

The South

The southern "head" of the North Island takes in two regions bordering Wellington: the beach strip of the Kapiti Coast to the north and the farmland, wineries, and remote coastline of the Wairarapa to the east. The university town of Palmerston North is the northern bridge between the two regions.

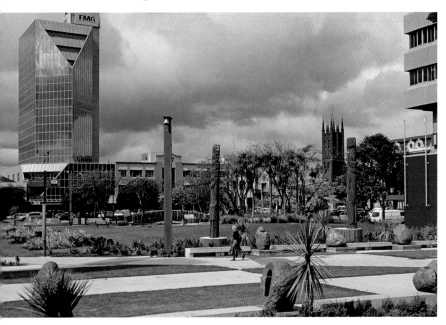

The gardens and main square of Palmerston North, known colloquially as "Palmy."

Martinborough

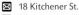 Map: Inside
back cover

Visitor Information

✉ 18 Kitchener St.
☎ 06/306-5010

wairarapanz.com

Wairarapa

The lightly populated Wairarapa District northeast of Wellington lies across the rugged Rimutaka Range. The wilderness of the Tararua Ranges to the north also helps to isolate this undulating farming region of wineries, wildlife, deserted coastlines, and historic towns.

Heading out of the city, take SH2 through the sprawling suburban areas of Lower and Upper Hutt, major population centers of the greater Wellington area.

The Wairarapa takes its name from shallow Lake Wairarapa ("shimmering waters") outside of Featherston, where you turn off SH2 to reach **Martinborough.** Famed for the surrounding wineries, sleepy Martinborough comes alive on weekends when Wellington day visitors and wine sippers on romantic getaways fill the town's cafés and B&Bs. The grand **Martinborough Hotel** (see Travelwise p. 299), built in 1882, is an icon in the center of town, offering fine dining as well as rooms. You can sample local wines and produce at **Martinborough Wine Merchants** (*6 Kitchener St., tel 06/306-9040, martinboroughwinemerchants.com*). The visitor information center has the lowdown on the local wineries, brewery, and tours.

From Martinborough, solitude seekers can head south to the scenic, windswept coast around **Cape Palliser.** Where the road hits the coast, a fine two-hour round-trip walk goes to the spectacular rock formations of the **Putangirua Pinnacles.** Past the isolated fishing village of Ngawi, a large seal colony sprawls on the rocks just before the lighthouse at the end of the road, overlooking the most southerly tip of the North Island.

The Wairarapa's main other tourist town, **Greytown,** farther north on SH2, has historic wooden buildings, including

St. Andrews Church, and a host of antique and craft shops. A pleasing weekend getaway, Greytown has lots of B&Bs and cottages for rent.

Heading north, you come to the Wairarapa's main town of Masterton, but keep going 19 miles (30 km) more on SH2 to the **Pukaha Mount Bruce National Wildlife Centre** (*tel 06/375-8004, pukaha.org.nz, $*), one of the country's most

INSIDER TIP:

Get up close and personal with fur seal pups at the Cape Palliser Seal Colony, then stay after dark to witness the magic of New Zealand's starry skies.

—CHARLOTTE BUEB
National Geographic contributor

important and accessible wildlife centers. This is the place to view New Zealand's fauna—mainly birds, but tuataras and other reptiles are also on view in native surroundings. This important breeding center has many rare species, including the South Island takahe.

Kapiti Coast

A beach retreat and growth corridor for Wellington, the Kapiti Coast runs northwest over the Ohariu fault line from the capital. The rugged Tararua Ranges line SH1 inland, while Kapiti Island dominates coastal views to the west.

Golden Shears

While no country wants to be known just for sheep farming, New Zealand does acknowledge the animal's importance. In celebration, Masterton in Wairarapa hosts the annual Golden Shears Shearing & Wool Handling Championships. Usually held the first week in March, the event has grown in scope and popularity. For tickets and information, contact the Wool Shed (*12 Dixon St., Masterton, goldenshears .nz.com*).

Paekakariki, 25 miles (40 km) north of Wellington, is the first stop of note, a relaxed seaside town stretching back from the main road to a black-sand beach. The vast **Queen Elizabeth Park** located on the northern edge of town includes the last area of natural dunes on the coast

A little spotted kiwi *(Apteryx owenii)* chick with its father at the Karori Sanctuary near Wellington

and offers swimming, fishing, walking, cycling, and horseback riding on the beach. Once home to Maori villages, it housed 20,000 U.S. marines during World War II.

At MacKays Crossing, just off SH1, and 3 miles (5 km) north of Paekakariki, the **Tramway**

Museum *(tel 04/292-8361, wellingtontrams.org.nz, Sat.–Sun., $)* has restored trams that run on a 1.3-mile (2 km) track to the beach.

The coast's largest town, **Paraparaumu,** sprawls down to a fine beach, preferable to the suburban jungle on the highway. The visitor information center *(Coastlands shopping center, tel 04/298-8195)* has details on accommodations and activities. Paraparaumu has one of New Zealand's best golf courses as well as the **Southward Car Museum** *(Otaihanga Rd., tel 04/297-1221, southwardcarmuseum.co.nz, $).*

The main attraction, especially for birders, is **Kapiti Island,** 3 miles (5 km) off the coast from Paraparaumu. Now a nature reserve, the island was once the base of Maori chief Te Rauparaha, whose raiding parties terrorized the west coast down to the South Island. The Department of Conservation has eradicated pests and made the island secure for breeding endangered birds, including a large colony of little spotted kiwis. Access to the island is by tour only, with two operators departing Paraparaumu Beach, and Kapiti Island has a lodge *(tel 03/363-6606, kapitiislandnature tours.co.nz)* for overnight stays. DOC Wellington *(tel 04/384-7770 or doc.govt.nz)* has details.

North of Paraparaumu, Waikanae is a small seaside settlement, and home to **Nga Manu Nature Reserve** *(tel 04/293-4131, 281 Ngarara Rd., ngamanu.co.nz, $),* with tuataras and native bird enclosures, including kiwis. It's a pleasant spot with easy walks for the whole family.

Palmerston North

At the heart of the flat Manawatu farming district, Palmerston North (pop. 86,000) is a very pleasant provincial city on the banks of the Manawatu River. Comedian John Cleese called it the suicide capital of New Zealand, saying if you lacked the courage to take your life then "Palmy" would do the trick. The council renamed its dump Mount Cleese in his honor.

Cleese must have visited when **Massey University** was on vacation, for the country's second largest university drives the city. Palmerston North's nightlife and

INSIDER TIP:

Day trips to Kapiti Island, a birder's paradise, are limited to 50 people, and to only 16 for overnight stays—so book your trip well in advance.

—PETER TURNER
National Geographic author

cultural scene hums during term, but dies over the summer months.

European settlers arrived in 1866 and named the town Palmerston, later adding "North" to distinguish it from Palmerston on the South Island. They laid out the city around **The Square,** an expanse of lawn, gardens, and lakes in the heart of the city.

Just west of The Square, **Te Manawa** *(326 Main St., tel 06/355-5000, temanawa.co.nz)* is a

EXPERIENCE:
Green Hub

As a university town in an environmentally conscious country, Palmerston North has impeccable green credentials. **The Green Hub** *(tel 06/355-8105)* at 235 Main Street recycles computers, cell phones, and all things electronic for free or a small donation. It also offers many recycled bicycles, for this is the incarnation of the Palmerston North Green Bike Trust that has recycled thousands of old bikes since 1998, fixing them up and giving them back to the community. Inquire about bike rentals and bikes to buy from the university workshop.

combined museum/art gallery/hands-on science center in an impressive complex.

In the same building, Palmy's main attraction is the **New Zealand Rugby Museum** *(326 Main St., tel 06/358-6947, rugbymuseum .co.nz, $)*. Crammed with memorabilia, it is a mecca for rugby-mad Kiwis, but the uninitiated will also gain insight.

The much-loved **Victoria Esplanade Gardens,** 1 mile (1.6 km) south of the square on the river, are an oasis of rose gardens, lawns, walks, playgrounds, an aviary, and a miniature railway. The university is just across the river, accessed by the bridge on Fitzherbert Avenue.

Heading east of the city toward Napier and the Wairarapa, SH3 passes through the impressive **Manawatu Gorge.** The popular hike through the gorge takes about three to four hours; you can also take a jet boat tour along the river. ∎

Palmerston North
🅼 Map: Inside back cover
Visitor Information
✉ The Square
☎ 06/358-8414
manawatunz.co.nz

Sun, sea, mountains, wine, and wildlife—delightful introductions to the scenic grandeur of the South Island

Marlborough & Nelson

Sea kayakers explore Arch Point, Abel Tasman National Park

Marlborough & Nelson

The northernmost tip of the South Island encapsulates the country's attractions with craggy coastlines, mountains, beaches, wildlife-watching, and wonderful hiking.

Sheltered by mountains, New Zealand's sunniest region (averaging up to 2,400 hours of sunshine per year) attracts hordes of Kiwi vacationers over the summer, but foreign visitors often miss its delights in the rush to reach the headline attractions farther south.

Marlborough District is the gateway to the South Island for visitors arriving on the ferry from Wellington. After the sometimes choppy voyage across Cook Strait, the Marlborough Sounds are a calmer haven of blue and green.

A glorious landscape of forested coves and islands greets seafarers on their journey

through the convoluted waterways of the sounds. This stretch of coastline, one of New Zealand's finest, makes an ideal retreat. Certainly Captain Cook thought so, for he sheltered here for months on his Pacific voyages.

From the ferry town of Picton, the sounds can be explored or sampled on a wonderful drive to Nelson, the main city of the Nelson District. Those hurrying to the south will press on to the town of Blenheim.

Just a half-hour drive from Picton, Blenheim is the gateway to New Zealand's premier wine district. Vineyards crisscross the sunny Wairau Valley, where many delightful cellar doors offer fine dining and wine sampling. Allow a lazy day for touring the wineries, or two if you are a serious wine buff.

From Blenheim, the road and the rail line hug the rugged coast most of the way to Kaikoura. This fine scenic route combines sea and snow, for the towering Kaikoura Ranges lie just inland and are often snowcapped. The town of Kaikoura is New Zealand's number-one wildlife destination. Whales, dolphins, and seals flock to the nutrient-rich seas off Kaikoura, where a regular schedule of tours all but guarantees wildlife sightings.

Visitors who are not traveling from Picton to Kaikoura often move on to the city of Nelson, a good base for exploring the whole region. One of New Zealand's oldest settlements, and one of its most livable cities, Nelson's warm climate attracts retirees, artists, craftspeople, and others seeking the good life. Victorian villas dot the hilly suburbs nestled around a fine harbor.

Nelson is also the name of the north-western district, and Abel Tasman National Park ranks as its premier attraction. Emerald bays and golden beaches ring the bulbous

peninsula of the park, a glorious meld of forest and sea. Kayaking trips or the park's coastal walking track make the most of nature, boat trips allow more leisurely exploration, and a cruise/walk combination delivers the best of both worlds.

Golden Bay lies barely 124 miles (200 km) from the nation's capital but is far removed from modern hustle. Separated from the rest of Nelson District by the towering Takaka Hill, it requires effort to reach, and once there demands leisurely exploration.

The sleepy town of Takaka moves to an alternative beat and provides access to the less-trammeled northern reaches of Abel Tasman National Park. Farther afield, Farewell Spit and the Kahurangi National Park are off-the-main-tourist-track destinations for those seeking quieter communion with nature.

From Nelson you can also head to the West Coast via Murchison or detour south to Nelson Lakes National Park, a lightly visited gem based on the twin lakes of Rotoiti and Rotoroa. ∎

World War I memorial, Blenheim

Marlborough

Visitors arriving on the ferry from Wellington are treated to some of the world's most picturesque waterways in the superb Marlborough Sounds. The waters can be explored from the pretty port of Picton, while to the south, Blenheim is the Marlborough District's main town, servicing the country's most prolific wine region. Farther south, Kaikoura is a major destination for whale and other marine mammal-watching.

The Havelock Marina, gateway to the Pelorus and Kenepuru Sounds

Picton

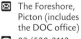 Map p. 168

Visitor Information

✉ The Foreshore, Picton (includes the DOC office)

☎ 03/520-3113

marlboroughnz.com

Picton

The first stop on the South Island for many visitors, Picton is an idyllic introduction to the south's scenic wonders. Ferries from Wellington dock at this town on a reach of Queen Charlotte Sound, one of New Zealand's loveliest bodies of water.

Picton is the gateway to the Marlborough Sounds, which can be explored by cruises from town or with rented kayaks. Picton was

originally the Maori settlement of Waitohi. Little is known of early settlement before Capt. James Cook made Ship Cove, at the head of the sound, his home away from home. Cook spent a total of four months here between 1770 and 1777, trading with local Maori and releasing pigs and goats to breed. From here he claimed New Zealand for King George III and named the sound after George's queen, Charlotte.

This rural idyll was shattered in 1829 when the mighty chief Te Rauparaha crossed Cook Strait and launched a major assault on the Marlborough Sounds, annihilating most of the local tribes. The area was lightly populated when the New Zealand Company came to survey the site for a port in 1849.

After many name changes, in 1859 the town was named for Welsh general Sir Thomas Picton (1758–1815), who fell at the Battle of Waterloo. Picton was declared provincial capital, but soon lost that honor to the burgeoning farming center of Blenheim in 1865. It remains the main port of Marlborough, and though normally sleepy, the town buzzes when ferries arrive.

INSIDER TIP:

In Picton, take a kayaking trip in Kenepuru Sound—you'll share the water with a handful of boats and millions of beautiful jellyfish.

—DAVID LUNDQUIST
*National Geographic
research grantee*

For an insight into Picton's early Maori and European history, the **Picton Museum** *(tel 03/573-8283, pictonmuseum-newzealand .com, $)* on London Quay is staffed by knowledgeable volunteers. Exhibits on whaling and on Cook's visits are highlights.

Pot-Bellied Sea Horse

New Zealand's waters teem with exotic creatures, among them a variety of sea horses. Boasting a (relatively) giant pouch and measuring 13 inches (33 cm) in length, the pot-bellied sea horse is one of the largest in the world. Like other sea horses, it is the males who carry the fertilized eggs. Brood size is normally around 300, although go-getters can hold up to 700 little ponies. While pot-bellied sea horses have few natural predators, they are dwindling in number because they are the principal ingredient in many traditional Chinese and Korean medicines.

The **Edwin Fox Maritime Museum** *(Dunbar Wharf, tel 03/573-6868, edwinfoxsociety.com, $),* near the ferry terminal, houses the *Edwin Fox,* built in Calcutta in 1853 of teak and said to be the ninth oldest ship in the world. It looks it, but the deteriorating hull belies an interesting life that included transporting troops to the Crimean War, convicts to Australia, cargo to Asia, and immigrants to New Zealand.

Next door, the **EcoWorld Aquarium** *(tel 03/573-6030, eco worldnz.co.nz, $$, see sidebar above)* specializes in sea horses and fish but has other species, including tuataras, as well as touch pools to delight children.

Marlborough Sounds

The myriad waterways, coves, bays, and islands of the Marlborough Sounds are the geographical and geological result of the country's two main islands moving toward each other over millions of years.

The South Island, resting on the Pacific plate, is gradually slipping under the Australian

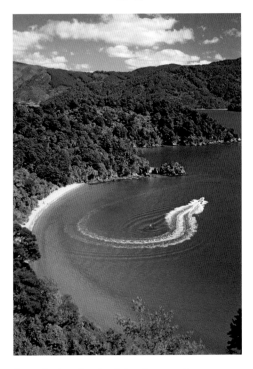

Queen Charlotte Sound curls into Governors Bay

plate holding the North Island, drowning the valleys of the sounds and leaving only the mountaintops and ridges above the sea. The Maori have a mythical yet not dissimilar story about the sounds: When the god Aoraki crashed his canoe

(the South Island) into the North Island, the debris of the shattered prow formed the beautiful sounds.

Whatever the origins, the outcome is divine. Captain Cook thought so, and his descriptions of this refuge acted as a magnet for later seafarers. Whalers followed, hunting in the sounds and founding the first settlements.

Today the sounds are a haven for holiday homes and visitors looking to get away from it all. Peaceful lodgings are scattered throughout the region. A few twisting scenic roads make some of the many coves accessible by car, but boat is the most romantic and far quicker means of transportation. Mail is still delivered by boat in the sounds, and water taxis can drop you off at a B&B or hotel.

Queen Charlotte Drive:

For a drive-through taste of the sounds, try the Queen Charlotte Drive from Picton to Havelock, a dramatic 25-mile (40 km) road winding through native forest. The route hugs the coast of Queen Charlotte Sound before traversing a coastal plain to the lower reaches of Pelorus Sound. Of the many delightful coves on the way, **Governors Bay** is well worth a stop, and the ten-minute walk to **Cullen Point** has fine views across to Havelock. Craft shops and B&Bs are dotted along this road.

Halfway along Queen Charlotte Drive, a turnoff leads to the settlement of Anakiwa and the start of the **Queen Charlotte Track,** a spectacular walk and also a Great Ride through the Marlborough

EXPERIENCE: Visit the Valley's Vineyards

While you can easily put together your own Wairau Valley winery tour, many local tour operators offer informative visits that take away all of your DUI concerns. Most tours are flexible, reasonably priced, and willing to take small numbers. Lunch in a winery restaurant can be included, or even breakfast for early starters.

Bubbly Grape Wine Tours
(Blenheim, tel 0800/228-2253, bubblygrape .co.nz). Small tours typically focus on the region's prized Sauvignon Blanc.

Highlight Wine Tours
(Springlands, Blenheim, tel 03/577-9046, highlightwinetours.co.nz). Personalized tours take in five to seven wineries and last three to five hours.

Marlborough Tours
(Picton, tel 03/573-7122, marlboroughtours .co.nz). Wine, food, craft, and personalized tours, with pickup in Picton or Blenheim.

Molesworth Tours
(Renwick, tel 03/572-8025, molesworth tours.co.nz). A big variety of 4WD and cycling tours as well as wine tours in the Wairau Valley and nearby Awatere Valley.

Sounds Connection
(Picton, tel 03/573-8843, soundsconnection .co.nz). A variety of half- and full-day wine and scenic tours.

Wine Tours by Bike
(Renwick, tel 03/572-7954, winetours bybike.co.nz). Provides pickup, touring bike, and map for self-guided winery tour.

Sounds to historic Ship Cove. The trail goes through lush coastal forest and along ridges offering unsurpassed views of Queen Charlotte and Kenepuru Sounds. The 45-mile (71 km) hike is a three- to five-day walk. It can also be mountain-biked in 13 hours, though two-thirds of the trail is closed to bikes from December through February.

Kenepuru Sound can also be explored by the paved road off Queen Charlotte Drive. The twisting, scenic drive passes farm, forest, and cove to the resort at Portage before reaching Kenepuru Head at the end of the sound. B&Bs can be found throughout. The road is unpaved past the head, but accesses a number of bays across to Pelorus Sound.

The sleepy port of **Havelock** is, along with Picton, a gateway to the sounds, and its harbor is

packed with pleasure craft and fishing boats. The town is the greenshell mussel capital of New Zealand, a status reflected on menus in the town's main-street restaurants, which are a good choice for lunch. Alternatively, dine by the water at the harbor, where cruises and water taxis depart, including the **Pelorus Mailboat,** which takes tourists along with the mail on an all-day trip to the far reaches of Pelorus Sound.

If gravel roads don't deter you, escape the tourist hordes by detouring to the tiny seaside town of **French Pass** and nearby **D'Urville Island.** These communities offer fine scenery, fishing, wildlife-watching, and accommodations. The spectacular road to French Pass begins at Rai Valley,

(continued on p. 176)

Pelorus Mailboat

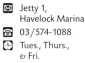
- Jetty 1, Havelock Marina
- 03/574-1088
- Tues., Thurs., & Fri.
- $$$$$, children free

themailboat.co.nz

Marlborough Wine Tour

Marlborough is New Zealand's premier wine-growing district. The sun-drenched, sheltered plains of the Wairau Valley, with its long autumns and crisp winters, produce a unique grape and more than 70 percent of New Zealand's wine. Famous for its crisp Sauvignon Blanc with intense fruit, the area also produces Riesling, Chardonnay, Pinot Noir, and other varieties.

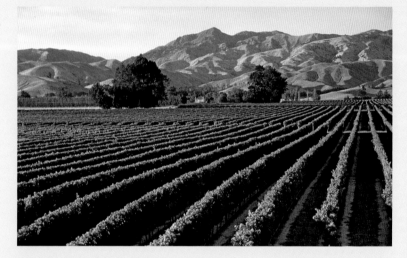

Ripening grapes in a Blenheim vineyard

The small town of Renwick is the center of this prolific wine district, and a few accommodation options have sprung up in the town and among the wineries, but nearby Blenheim is the main base from which to explore the fine wines of Marlborough.

Dozens of wineries are an easy drive from Blenheim or Renwick for a sun-filled day, or two, of tasting. To avoid wining and driving, tours are available by bus or by bicycle (see sidebar p. 173) , but the latter also has its hazards after a few too many drinks.

Wither Hills ❶ *(211 New Renwick Rd., tel 03/520-8284, witherhills.co.nz)* has one of the biggest and most impressive cellars. Sauvignon Blanc, Chardonnay, and Pinot Noir are the focus.

NOT TO BE MISSED:

Wither Hills • Brancott Estate • Allan Scott • Cloudy Bay

Villa Maria ❷ *(Paynters & New Renwick Rds., Fairhall, tel 03/520-8472, villamaria.co.nz)* has a wide selection from budget Sauvignon Blanc to Pinot Noir. **Brancott Estate ❸** *(180 Brancott Rd., tel 03/520-6975, brancottestate.com),* one of the original and biggest names in the valley, has a stunning cellar door/restaurant complex built into a hilltop, and winery tours, tastings, and talks.

Mahi ❹ *(9 Terrace Rd., Renwick, tel 03/572-8859)* specializes in single-vineyard wines, focusing on Sauvignon Blanc, Chardonnay, Gewürztraminer, Pinot Noir, and Pinot Gris. **Wairau River** ❺ *(Rapaura Rd., tel 03/572-9800, wairauriverwines.com)* has a welcoming wine cellar and a fine, reasonably priced restaurant for lunch.

Giesen ❻ *(26 Rapaura Rd., tel 03/572-8500, giesen.co.nz)* is a German winery focusing on white wines—try their Frosé (frozen Rosé) dessert cocktails.

Georges Michel ❼ *(Vintage Ln., tel 03/572-7230, georgesmichel.com)* flies the *tricoleur*, and has dessert wines and cognac in its range; stop at their gift/produce shop. **Herzog** ❽ *(81 Jeffries Rd., tel 03/572-8770, herzog.co.nz)* is a renowned dining spot in the valley with a pretty cottage wine cellar. Dine in the elegant restaurant or the less expensive bistro. The winery produces varieties and wines rarely seen in New Zealand.

Allan Scott ❾ *(Jacksons Rd., tel 03/572-9054, allanscott.com)*, another well-established vintner, also offers winery tours and a good restaurant. **Cloudy Bay** ❿ *(230 Jacksons Rd.,*

tel 03/520-9147, cloudybay.co.nz), more than any other winery, made Marlborough's Sauvignon Blanc famous. The winery has a fine wine cellar, which can be overrun with tipplers, but it remains small.

For a change from wine, **Moa Brewery** ⓫ *(Jacksons Rd., tel 03/572-5146, moabeer.com)*, down a lane off Jacksons Road, is the place for a cleansing pale ale, boutique stout, or cider in a lovely setting.

Hunter's ⓬ *(603 Rapaura Rd., tel 03/572-8489, hunters.co.nz)* with its attractive cellar and garden café is a good choice for lunch in the valley. **Rock Ferry** ⓭ *(80 Hammerichs Rd., tel 03/579-6431, rockferry.co.nz)*, a new kid on the Blenheim block, produces a range of organic wines and has a pleasant, funky café, another good choice for lunch.

🅰	See also area map p. 168
►	Blenheim
↔	26 miles (42 km)
🕐	1–2 days
►	Rock Ferry

Kaikoura

🗺 Map p. 168

Visitor Information

✉ West End, Kaikoura

☎ 03/319-5641

kaikoura.co.nz

Wairau Affray

Colonial settlement around Blenheim was far from easy, and the Wairau Valley, now the country's premier wine district, saw proof of this in the infamous Wairau Affray. With the establishment of the colony at Nelson in 1842, the push was on for more arable land. The New Zealand Company began surveying the Wairau Valley based on its acquisition of a dubious land contract between whaling captain John Blenkinsop and Maori chief Te Rauparaha.

Despite opposition from the local Maori, surveying pushed ahead. When the surveyors' hut was burned down, the government at Nelson decided to step in and exert its authority. An armed party under the colony's leader, Capt. Arthur Wakefield, set out for Wairau in 1843 to arrest Te Rauparaha. Armed with muskets, the Maori had other ideas, and in the resulting battle 22 Europeans, including Wakefield, were killed.

along the road to Nelson about 16 miles (25 km) from Havelock.

Another little-explored but gloriously scenic route is the back road from Picton to Blenheim. Head north over the hill from Picton to its satellite sister Waikawa on a picturesque bay, then follow the **Port Underwood Road.** The road follows Queen Charlotte Sound before heading to the east coast at Port Underwood, where the pavement runs out and the narrow road dips and twists its way to Rarangi on sweeping Cloudy Bay.

Blenheim

Marlborough's largest town, Blenheim (pop. 31,000) sits on the flat, sun-drenched plains of the Wairau Valley. Just another farm town until grapes were introduced in the 1970s, Blenheim is now on the map thanks to the wine industry.

Wineries are the attraction here, but the **Omaka Aviation**

INSIDER TIP:

Don't miss the Marlborough Wine & Food Festival, *(wine-marlborough-festival.co.nz)* in Blenheim in the second week of February.

—JUSTIN KAVANAGH
National Geographic Travel Books editor

Heritage Centre *(79 Aerodrome Rd., tel 03/579-1305, $$$)* with its dioramas is a must for aviation fans. The **Marlborough Museum** *(tel 03/578-1712, marlboroughmuseum .org.nz)* on the southern outskirts of town at Brayshaw Park provides a good insight into colonial life.

The **Awatere Valley** is a wine-growing region south of Blenheim. From here a rugged road heads up to the Inland Kaikoura Range and **Molesworth Station** *(tel 03/575-7043)*, the country's largest farm at

500,000 acres (180,500 ha), now administered by DOC. This cattle station can be visited in summer on 4WD tours from Blenheim or Hanmer Springs, but check if the road is open after extensive damage from the 2016 earthquake.

Kaikoura

Meaning "meal of crayfish," Kaikoura owes its existence to the abundance of the sea. Jutting into the ocean on a peninsula, this is where Maui braced his foot when he fished up the North Island, according to Maori lore. In a stunning setting with the often snowcapped Kaikoura Ranges as a backdrop, Kaikoura today is a thriving tourism center based on wildlife-watching. The 2016 earthquake, however, severely interrupted the flow of visitors, damaged buildings, and closed the main highway (SH1), though the town soon reopened for business (see sidebar, right).

Settled by the Ngati Mamoe and then the Ngai Tahu, the area witnessed fierce battles at fortified hilltop villages around the peninsula. In 1843, Capt. Robert Fyffe (d. 1854) established a whaling station and built **Fyffe House,** now a museum, on whalebone foundations. The whalers did such a good job that whale numbers plummeted in the 19th century.

Ironically, whales are again the town's main industry. Whale-watching and other ecoventures have made Kaikoura a tourist magnet. **Whale Watch Kaikoura** (see sidebar p. 181) has helped rejuvenate the town, and its tours are the town's main attraction.

Other excursions include aerial tours, swimming with dolphins and seals, diving, sea kayaking, and albatross viewing. In summer it is wise to book popular tours in advance, but note that bad weather can cause cancellations.

After all those high-price tours, the **Kaikoura Museum** provides a welcome relief for the purse. It has marine, Maori, and colonial exhibits and the lowdown on the town's whaling industry. For even cheaper thrills, walk south along the shore past Fyffe House to the seal colony. Loop back to town on the peninsula via the clifftop or shoreline tracks, depending on the tide—a fine 2.5-hour walk in all. ∎

Fyffe House
- ✉ 62 Avoca St.
- ☎ 03/319-5835
- 🕐 Closed Tues. & Wed. in winter
- 💲 $

fyffehouse.co.nz

Kaikoura Museum
- ✉ 96 West End
- ☎ 03/319-7440
- 💲 $

Kaikoura Earthquake

In November 2016, a major magnitude 7.8 earthquake hit the South Island, southwest of Kaikoura near the small town of Waiau. Other towns like Hanmer Springs were also hit and the shock waves damaged buildings as far away as Wellington, but Kaikoura, where two people died, became the focus of the quake. A small 8-foot (2 m) tsunami hit the coast, where whole stretches of land lifted out of the sea, while landslides severed the main coastal highway, SH1, cutting off Kaikoura from the outside world. Tourists had to be evacuated by air until the inland road from Waiau reopened a few weeks later. Despite damage to some buildings, Kaikoura was soon welcoming visitors again, but work on SH1 and measures to control landslides continues. Until fully reopened, the main route between Picton and Christchurch is inland via Murchison and Lewis Pass. SH1 has reopened south of Kaikoura, but work on the northern section of the highway and the Coastal Pacific rail line continues. Check the latest conditions.

Nelson

Straddling the northwest tip of the South Island, Nelson District is a sunny, fertile region ringed by mountains and caressed by calm seas. From the pleasant city of Nelson, most visitors make a beeline for Abel Tasman National Park, but fine beaches and laid-back towns can be found right along the coast.

A variety of shops, galleries, and museums tempt visitors to Nelson

Nelson
🅰 Map p. 168
Visitor Information
✉ 77 Trafalgar St.
☎ 03/546-9339
nelsonnz.com

Nelson

Touted as one of the country's most livable cities, Nelson (pop. 51,000) is backed by green hills and lapped by azure seas. It has fine parks, a thriving arts scene, and a sunny disposition.

The New Zealand Company planned the new city in 1839, buying land cheaply from the Maori and selling it at a profit to settlers, who began arriving in 1842. Nelson was declared New Zealand's second city in 1858, despite having only 3,000 inhabitants, and initially the colony struggled. The town has some fine Victorian villas, but workers' cottages from the same era attest to the struggles of the poor. Today Nelson, along with adjoining Richmond, attracts a new wave of sun-seeking migrants, and the district's economy is driven by farming, forestry, fishing, and tourism.

Overlooking Trafalgar Street, the main drag, **Church Hill,** called Pikimai ("climb up here") by the

Maori, once housed a *pa* (fortified village), as well as the New Zealand Company settlement. The ramparts of Fort Arthur, built after the Wairau massacre in 1843 (see sidebar p. 176), can still be seen. From the top of the hill, **Christ Church Cathedral** *(tel 03/548-1008)* and its art deco tower lord it over the town.

Nearby, **Nelson Provincial Museum** *(Hardy & Trafalgar Sts., tel 03/548-9588, nelsonmuseum .co.nz, $)* has a fine modern space with rotating exhibits as well as some detailing the local Maori tribes and European settlers.

INSIDER TIP:

If you're in Nelson on a Wednesday afternoon or Saturday morning, the local markets are a must for tasty treats and handmade gifts (nelsonfarmersmarket .org.nz).

—NICOLAS BARTH
National Geographic research grantee

The **Suter Art Gallery** *(208 Bridge St., tel 03/548-4699, thesuter .org.nz)* in historic Queens Gardens has a significant permanent collection of colonial artists such as John Gully (1819–1888), Gottfried Lindauer, and Petrus Van der Velden, thanks to early collector Andrew Suter, Bishop of Nelson. Contemporary New Zealand art is also well represented, and the gallery has a good café.

Crafts

New Zealand's artisans turn out a wide array of attractive crafts for domestic and tourist consumption. Areas such as Nelson and Waiheke Island are noted for arts and crafts, but studios and galleries stacked with pottery, glassware, and weavings can be found all over the country. Wood turners produce interesting work using native timbers such as kauri and rimu. Glassblowers in Nelson infuse glass with bits of local metal to create handmade beads that reflect both European and native aesthetics. Local tourist offices have brochures detailing regional artists and craft studios.

The **World of WearableArt & Classic Cars Museum** *(95 Quarantine Rd., Annesbrook, tel 03/547-4573, wowcars.co.nz, $),* in the southwest suburbs, features weird and wonderful designs from the annual WOW fashion awards, even though they are now held in Wellington. The exhibition, complete with mechanical catwalk, is small but well done. The adjoining car museum has a fine selection of all-American, Detroit beasts.

Founders Heritage Park *(87 Atawhai Dr., tel 03/548-2649, founderspark.co.nz, $),* 1 mile (1.6 km) northeast of the city center, is a collection of historic *(continued on p. 182)*

Wildlife Wonderland

Despite a lack of land mammals, New Zealand has an abundance of sea life and unique bird species, which can be observed in their natural habitats at a number of locations. Many wildlife-spotting tours operate in the country. The Department of Conservation also oversees designated breeding areas for birds and other wildlife, often with blinds in which you can view animals without disturbing them.

Bottlenose dolphin and diver

Whales

The nutrient-rich waters that surround New Zealand attract 22 species of whale, the most commonly sighted being sperm, humpback, Bryde's, and southern right whales. Maori tradition has it that whales guided the first migrations to Aotearoa. Whalers also tracked the whales, hunting them relentlessly, though now the mammals are primarily sought by tourists. Whale-spotting is a major attraction, notably at Kaikoura on the South Island where sperm whales are often sighted (see sidebar opposite).

Orcas, or killer whales, are also found in New Zealand waters. The small population is most likely to be seen off the east coast of the North Island.

Dolphins

The most numerous of the ten dolphin species in New Zealand are the dusky and the common dolphin. The bottlenose dolphin is also found, while smaller Hector's and Maui dolphins are unique to the country.

Dolphins frolic all around the coasts and often accompany ferry or cruise boats. Swimming with the dolphins is a popular activity, particularly in the Bay of Islands and Kaikoura.

Modern New Zealand folklore has immortalized two dolphins: Opo (see sidebar p. 99), who frequented the resort of Opononi and played in the shallows with children, and Pelorus Jack, a Risso's dolphin who supposedly accompanied ships across the Cook Strait, helping them to avoid rocks and currents.

Seals

After Captain Cook noted the profusion of seals in New Zealand, sealers promptly set up camps on the South Island and hunted the seals for fur to the brink of extinction.

Now protected, fur seals can be seen around the coast at a number of colonies, though again the South Island offers the best viewing opportunities, particularly at Kaikoura, the Otago Peninsula, the Catlins, and Cape Foulwind near Westport.

While fur seals are the most numerous species, other varieties include the much larger Hooker's sea lion and the rarer southern elephant seals and leopard seals. Hooker's sea lions can be seen coming ashore on the Otago Peninsula and in the Catlins.

Birds

Surrounded by ocean, New Zealand has a greater diversity of seabirds than any other

The rare yellow-eyed penguin breeds in New Zealand.

country. Species include penguins, albatrosses, petrels, shags, and terns, though the sooty shearwater is the most numerous.

Of the world's 16 species of penguin, nine are found in New Zealand waters. The three main species are the little blue, yellow-eyed, and Fiordland crested penguin. Others inhabit New Zealand's Antarctic territories and sub-Antarctic islands. Penguins usually nest in sand dunes and are most easily spotted on the South Island.

The Otago Peninsula is also famous for its royal albatross colony, while huge gannet colonies can be seen at Muriwai Beach west of Auckland and Cape Kidnappers close to Hastings.

Many native land birds are threatened, but unique species range from the brilliantly colored takahe to the national symbol, the flightless kiwi. The best place to get an overview of the country's bird species is at the Pukaha Mount Bruce National Wildlife Centre, near Masterton on the North Island. The shy, nocturnal kiwi is easily seen in kiwi houses around the country, but rarely spotted in the wild.

EXPERIENCE: Whale Watch Kaikoura

With sightings of sperm whales all but guaranteed, **Whale Watch Kaikoura** *(tel 03/319-6767, whalewatch.co.nz)* has become the country's foremost wildlife experience, with 100,000 visitors a year taking the company's tours. The organization claims a 95 percent success rate; if you don't spot a whale, you get 80 percent of your money back. Along with sperm whales, dolphins are often sighted, and you may be lucky enough to see humpback whales, orcas, or blue whales. Maori-owned and -operated, Whale Watch Kaikoura was established in 1987 by the Kati Kuri people, a subtribe of the Ngai Tahu, at a time when the town's fishing economy was in decline. From small tours on an inflatable craft, the business has grown to include a catamaran fleet directed to the whales by spotter planes.

EXPERIENCE:
Kayaking Abel Tasman National Park

The stunning coastline of Abel Tasman National Park can be explored on foot or by boat, but nothing compares to gliding through the beautiful coves to remote beaches in a kayak. You can rent a kayak and head off independently, or take a guided tour for a half day or up to as many as three days, staying in huts, campsites, or luxurious lodges along the way. You can also combine kayaking with a hike or water-taxi ride back.

Most operators are based in Marahau on the edge of the park; in Kaiteriteri, 6 miles (10 km) away; and in Motueka. Guided trips are very popular, while independent rentals are generally only for groups of two or more with kayaking and outdoors experience. Camping gear and equipment are provided. In Marahau, companies include **Abel Tasman Kayaks** (*tel 03/527-8022, abeltasmankayaks.co.nz*), **Kahu Kayaks** (*tel 03/527-8300, kahu kayaks.co.nz*), and **Marahau Sea Kayaks** (*tel 03/527-8176, msk.co.nz*). In Kaiteriteri, try **Kaiteriteri Kayaks** (*tel 03/527-8383, seakayak.co.nz*).

Motueka

🗺 Map p. 168

Visitor Information

✉ Wallace St.

☎ 03/528-6543

settler buildings, with a museum, working train, resident artisans, and a craft brewery. On the same street, **Miyazu Japanese Garden** is a small Japanese strolling garden. **Botanic Hill,** above the gardens on the eastern edge of the city along Milton Street, has panoramic views and a marker proclaiming it as the geographical center of New Zealand.

Nelson is also the starting point for one of the country's best Great Rides, the **Tasman's Great Taste Trail** (see p. 116), which directs cyclists along a scenic coastal trail studded with galleries, wineries, cafés, and breweries.

Tasman Bay

Sunny Tasman Bay is dominated by the attractions of Nelson on one side and Abel Tasman National Park on the other, but in between lie a few points of interest. Nelson has a good city beach at Tahunanui, but for a long stretch of uncrowded sand, head to **Rabbit Island.** The island is accessed via a bridge open during the day—the turnoff is halfway between Richmond and the growing seaside town of Mapua.

As in Nelson city, the Tasman Bay region is riddled with artists' studios: potters, jewelers, painters, glassblowers, and wood turners. Pick up a brochure for a countryside art tour. Wineries are also flourishing, particularly in **Richmond** and **Upper Moutere,** once known as Sarau, where the German settlers who founded the town built an impressive Lutheran church.

Lower Moutere, near Motueka, is home to the **Riverside Community,** New Zealand's first commune, set up by pacifists during World War II. The community, which set the scene for the region's alternative lifestyles, can be visited and has an excellent café, well worth a stop.

The center of a fertile orchard region growing apples, pears, berries, hops, and kiwifruit, **Motueka** (pop. 7,000) is well supplied with amenities and provides visitors with a popular base for visiting Abel Tasman National Park nearby. The main town lies a little inland from its muddy port on Tasman Bay. The popular little resort of **Kaiteriteri,** 9 miles (14 km) north, has beautiful golden beaches and also makes a good base for the national park.

Abel Tasman National Park

New Zealand's smallest national park at just 87 square miles (225 sq km), Abel Tasman is nevertheless one of its most famous. Coastal bays, lagoons, golden beaches, and calm, clear waters attract 228,000 visitors per year. Most are day visitors, but longer stays can be spent walking the Abel Tasman Coast Track or kayaking one of the finest coastlines in the country.

The park also contains marble gorges, granite and limestone hills, extensive beech forests, and rain forest growing to the sea's edge. The park is named after Dutch explorer Abel Tasman, who anchored his ships near Wainui Bay in the north of the park on December 18, 1642. Four of his crew died at the hands of the local Maoris, the Ngati Tumatakokiri.

The park's main entrance is the southern gateway of **Marahau,** 12 miles (20 km) from Motueka. Tiny Marahau is well equipped with services to explore the park, including water transportation and kayak rentals. Accommodations are also available, but they are often fully booked in summer.

Reasonably priced cruises, water taxis, and scheduled

launches run into the park from Marahau and farther south from Kaiteriteri. Boats can drop you anywhere along the coast up to Totaranui and pick you up later. A good day-trip option is to take a boat to Torrent Bay or Bark Bay, then walk back to Marahau along the **Abel Tasman Coast Track.** This track, one of New Zealand's Great Walks, runs between Mara-

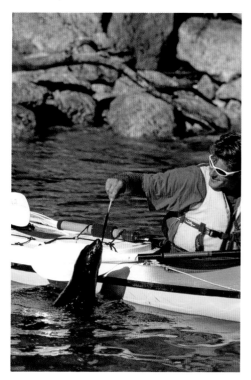

Making friends in Abel Tasman National Park

hau and Wainui Bay in an easy, undulating 37-mile (60 km) trail that can be walked in three to five days. Huts must be booked well in advance in summer, when the trail can resemble a highway—or you can camp. More luxurious private

Abel Tasman National Park

 Map p. 168

Visitor Information

✉ 79 Trafalgar St., Nelson

☎ 03/546-9339

doc.govt.nz/parks -and-recreation /national-parks /abel-tasman

Golden Bay

Map p. 168

Visitor Information

DOC Golden Bay Area Office, 62 Commercial St., Takaka

03/525-8026

goldenbaynz.co.nz

lodgings are also available at Torrent Bay and Awaroa. The estuary at Awaroa Inlet can be crossed only when the tides are low, so tide charts must be consulted.

Caving

The karst landscape around Marlborough and Nelson is characterized by pockmarked cliffs and networks of caves. Once Maori burial sites, many of these caves are now filled with adventurers. The most famous, **Harwoods Hole,** was discovered in 1957. Its 577-foot-deep (176 m) entry shaft was first explored by a harnessed schoolboy lowered down by local townspeople. But while the cave's celebrity brings adventurers from around the world, danger always exists. In 1960, a falling boulder killed the founder of the New Zealand Speleological Society as he explored the hole.

Another three-day trail, the **Inland Track**, loops back from Wainui Bay to Marahau, but this trail is a much more difficult walk through the interior of the park.

The alternative to walking is sea kayaking, a marvelous way to explore coves and remote beaches, while camping overnight or staying in huts or lodges. Kayak companies offer a range of options for both guided and independent rentals.

The northern gateway to the park is **Totaranui,** which has a Department of Conservation office and campground on a long bay with a beautiful beach. Many walkers start or finish the coastal track here and take a boat one-way to Marahau.

The road from Takaka in Golden Bay to Totaranui passes through the sleepy vacation town of **Pohara,** which has a safe beach. Just past Tarakohe harbor, with its cement shipping dock, **Ligar Bay** and **Tata Beach** have fine golden-sand beaches for swimming. The road then soon becomes unpaved but is very scenic. En route to the park, the 45-minute walk to **Wainui Falls** is well worth the effort.

The other entry to the park is a less-used back door. The unpaved Cannan Road leads off Takaka Hill to the park's interior. This area is different from the rest of the national park and comprises intriguing marble gorges, limestone outcrops, sinkholes, and subterranean streams. Most visitors who come this way drive the 7.5 miles (12 km) and then walk some 45 minutes to reach **Harwoods Hole** (see sidebar left), a 577-foot (176 m) marble drop shaft down to the **Starlight Cave.** Great care should be taken around the hole: The cave is suitable only for experienced cavers.

Golden Bay

Takaka Hill, the "marble mountain," shields Golden Bay. From Motueka the road west is a tortuous drive over the hill, but you are rewarded with fine views of the surrounding mountains and valley farmland. Just before the summit of Takaka Hill are the **Ngarua Caves** *(tel 03/528-8093, ngaruacaves.co.nz, $)*, where guided tours leave on the hour from 10 a.m. to 4 p.m. Moa bones can be seen there. North of the Ngarua Caves is

pling is the **Wholemeal Café** *(60 Commercial St., tel 03/525-9426)*, a bustling hippie-style eatery with vegetarian specialties.

Just to the northwest of Takaka, off SH60, don't miss **Te Waikoropupu Springs** (better known as Pupu Springs), which have astonishingly clear waters

Takaka

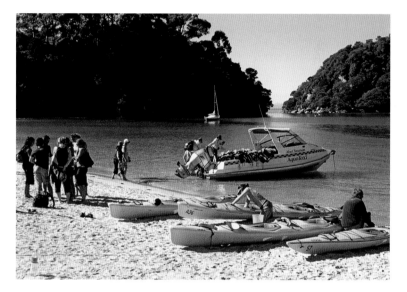 Map p. 168

Visitor Information

✉ Willow St.

☎ 03/525-9136

goldenbaynz.co.nz

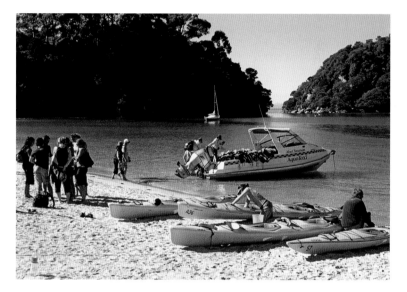

Vibrant kayaks await adventurers at Kaiteriteri Beach in Nelson.

Harwoods Hole (see sidebar opposite).

Laid-back **Takaka,** the main town of Golden Bay, rests at the bottom of the hill and across the fertile Takaka Valley. The rural community is enlivened by murals, craft shops, dreadlocks, and bare feet. **Golden Bay Museum** *(73 Commercial St., tel 03/525-6268, goldenbaymuseum.org.nz)* has historical artifacts, but of most interest is its diorama of Abel Tasman's fateful meeting with Maori in 1642. Another institution worth sam-

with visibility measured to 207 feet (63 m). Water percolates into the springs from underground caves, and walking trails go through forest and past a water race used in old gold workings. The springs are 2.5 miles (4 km) north of town and then 2 miles (3 km) down the turnoff.

From Takaka, the scenic Abel Tasman Road runs to Totaranui (see p. 184) at the northern end of Abel Tasman National Park. Just off the road outside town is **Rawhiti Cave,** studded with

A waterfall pours over a ledge at Cupola Creek, Nelson Lakes National Park.

Nelson Lakes National Park

◭ Map p. 168

Visitor Information

✉ View Rd., St. Arnaud

☎ 03/521-1806

doc.govt.nz/parks -and-recreation /national-parks /nelson-lakes

stalactites. Guided tours are available.

The sleepy little town of Collingwood is the last settlement of any size in Golden Bay. It's a jumping-off point for Farewell Spit, **Kahurangi National Park,** and the renowned **Heaphy Track** (see p. 219), which begins at the Aorere Valley, 17 miles (28 km) from Collingwood.

Farewell Spit is a 22-mile (35 km) arc of sand sheltering Golden Bay and finishing at the Cape Farewell lighthouse, the most northerly tip of the South Island. Access to this important wading-bird habitat is restricted

to tour groups, but the first few miles of walking tracks of this dune-strewn landscape are open to the public. Seals and their pups, basking on the rocks, can be seen from the clifftops.

Nelson Lakes National Park

Sculpted by glaciers during the ice ages, Lakes Rotoiti and Roto-roa anchor the spectacular land-scape of Nelson Lakes National Park. The two lakes reflect alpine peaks—the northern extreme of the Southern Alps—and are a mecca for aficionados of water sports and hiking.

St. Arnaud, the alpine village on the shores of Lake Rotoiti, is popular in summer for boating, trout fishing, and swimming, and in winter it services the nearby **Rainbow Ski Area.** Lying 54 miles (87 km) southwest of Nelson on the SH63 road between Blenheim and the West Coast, St. Arnaud is easily reached, but it is usually skipped by most visitors despite its scenic location on the doorstep of Nelson Lakes National Park.

Lake Rotoiti ("short lake"), serviced by St. Arnaud, attracts the most visitors, many of whom take a picture of the lake and pass on. The lakes and waterways teem with brown trout, particularly **Lake Rotoroa** ("long lake"), a 40-minute drive away. Beyond the lakes, beech-clad mountains harbor alpine valleys strewn with wildflowers and small tarns.

This hidden wonderland can only be reached on foot by walks such as the splendid five-day **Travers–Sabine Circuit,** taking

INSIDER TIP:

If sand flies plague you, try to head for the trees. The pests like open water and clearings, but not the bush. They're also deterred by a diet of Marmite or Vegemite, high in vitamin B.

—KIM FRANCIS
Founder, Black Sheep Touring Co.

you past towering mountains and remote lakes, or the three-day **Lake Angelus Track.**

The easiest way to sample the park's glory is on one of the short lake strolls, embracing water views, birdsong, and beech forest.

Murchison

The last town of note in the Nelson region, mountain-ringed Murchison is found on the dramatic highway through the Buller Gorge (SH6), the gateway to the island's West Coast.

Born a rough-and-ready gold-mining town in the 1860s, Murchison was flattened in 1929 by a nearby earthquake that was powerful enough to shake the whole country. Among the varied items in its rambling collection, the local **Murchison Museum** *(60 Fairfax St., tel 03/523-9392)* has some interesting photographs of the quake's devastation along with vintage machinery.

The **Buller River** provides most of the town's attractions,

including jet boating, white-water rafting, and kayaking. Local outfitters also specialize in fly fishing.

Nine miles (14 km) from Murchison on the way to Westport, the privately run **Buller Gorge Swingbridge** *(tel 03/523-9809, $)* wavers high above the river for breathless views. A zip line, walks, and jet boating are also offered. ■

EXPERIENCE: WWOOFing

In a country dominated by farming, the chance to live and work on a farm delivers unique insights into the New Zealand way of life. WWOOF (Willing Workers On Organic Farms) is a worldwide network offering volunteers (WWOOFers) the opportunity to do just that.

Originating in Britain, WWOOF spread to New Zealand in 1974. The work is unpaid, but farm hosts provide food and accommodations in exchange for help with gardening or other activities. These may include organic farming, weeding and mulching, making wine and cheese, or building straw-bale houses. While popular with students, volunteers of all ages participate.

To become a WWOOFer, you must register and pay a small fee to receive a list of some one thousand participating organic farms. You can join online or by mail (*WWOOF NZ, P.O. Box 1172, Nelson, NZ, tel 03/544-9890, wwoof.co.nz*).

Because food and lodging are provided, New Zealand immigration considers WWOOFing paid work, and a work or student visa is required. One-year to 23-month working holiday visas are readily available for 18- to 30-year-olds (up to 35 for some nationalities) from more than 40 countries, including Canada, the U.K., and the U.S.

From the dynamic city of Christchurch across sheep-strewn plains to the highest peaks of the Southern Alps

Christchurch & Canterbury

The Peacock Fountain graces Christchurch Botanic Gardens at twilight with the Arts Center illuminated in the background

Christchurch & Canterbury

First stop on South Island for many visitors, Christchurch is the south's largest city, traditionally the most English of settlements, and still recovering from the devastating earthquakes of 2010 and 2011.

Christchurch is a city in transition and, years on from the earthquakes, large sections are still a construction zone. Despite these reminders of tragedy, Gothic architecture, punting on the river, and fine gardens survived, and Christchurch still has a number of worthwhile attractions. It remains the cultural, business, and transportation hub of the South Island. It is also the gateway to the surrounding Canterbury region, which includes the highest peaks of the Southern Alps. The city sprawls on the edge of the Canterbury Plains, but is bordered to the east by the Banks Peninsula, a geological oddity rising steeply from the surrounding flatlands. This large volcanic outcrop of pastoral hills and sheltered bays once housed

a French colony, prompting the British to swiftly annex the South Island. The French settlers of Akaroa never lived to see Nouvelle Zéland proclaimed, but they left behind a picturesque town of Gallic influences, one of this area's highlights.

The vast, rich farmland of the Canterbury Plains spreads inland until it hits the foothills of the alps. In the north you'll find pretty Hanmer Springs, the South Island's premier hot springs resort, while beyond lie the northern passes through the alps to the West Coast.

Arthur's Pass is the highest mountain pass and travels through the scenic national park of the same name. This alpine wonderland has a number of snowy peaks, fine hikes, and skiing in the park and at nearby ski slopes.

The most visited part of the alps lies farther south, where Aoraki/Mount Cook, the country's highest peak, towers over the landscape. The trip from Christchurch to Mount Cook via the Inland Scenic Route is one of the most popular and pretty journeys in New Zealand. Heading south across the Canterbury Plains, the route turns inland around Geraldine and travels through undulating farmland before it reaches semidesert plateau landscapes and stunning lakes, such as turquoise Tekapo. Looming behind, the glaciers and peaks of Mount Cook National Park have been the practice ground for many mountaineers, such as Everest conqueror Sir Edmund Hillary.

Aoraki/Mount Cook is the jewel of the alps, but the whole landscape is awe inspiring. For many, the highlight of a park visit is a drink in the Hermitage Hotel lounge, its floor-to-ceiling windows framing the "Cloud Piercer," as the Maori called the mountain.

NOT TO BE MISSED:

The Gothic architecture and gardens of Christchurch 193–195, 197–198

Punting peacefully along Christchurch's Avon River 197

A gondola ride to the top of the Port Hills 198–199

A stroll through the former French colony of Akaroa 200

Soaking in the thermal waters of Hanmer Springs 203

Alpine landscapes in Arthur's Pass National Park 204–205

The turquoise glacial lakes of Tekapo and Pukaki 210

Aoraki/Mount Cook, New Zealand's highest peak 210–212

A walk in the park rewards with wonderful vistas; for the adventurous, scenic flights over the area offer even more stunning views. From Aoraki/Mount Cook, the main tourist route presses on to Queenstown in Otago, the hub of the south for sightseers. The alternative coastal route (SH1) takes you through the ports of Timaru and Oamaru, on the way to Dunedin. ∎

Christchurch

Christchurch (pop. 375,000) is New Zealand's third largest city, slowly regenerating from the earthquakes of 2010 and 2011. Traditionally a clean, green, and very English city, those aspects remain despite the demolition of many heritage buildings. Although in transition, Christchurch remains the welcoming main hub of the South Island. Attractions range from museums and galleries to manicured gardens and punting on the Avon River. Ready to explore beyond the city are the former French town of Akaroa, the Port Hills, and the Canterbury Plains.

Christchurch's Transitional Cathedral, an innovative cardboard construction, was designed to temporarily replace the city's damaged stone cathedral.

Christchurch
🗺 Map p. 191
Visitor Information
✉ Arts Centre,
   Worcester Blvd.
☎ 03/379-9629
christchurchnz.com

History

The expansive Canterbury Plains define the city's geography and history. Flat and grid-based, the city sprawls inland from the Port Hills, which the first European settlers clambered over after arriving at Lyttelton port.

Unlike other rowdy settlements, Christchurch was a planned Church of England venture designed to attract a better class of colonist. In 1848, the Canterbury Association, founded by Edward Gibbon Wakefield and John Robert Godley, set about luring potential land owners to the rich pastures of the plains. The association based its model on England's class society, and laborers and artisans who arrived on the first four ships in 1850 were intended to serve, not become, the landed gentry.

INSIDER TIP:

The world's best street performers descend on Christchurch in January for the World Buskers Festival. The cost is nothing more than the change in your pocket.

—DAVID LUNDQUIST
National Geographic field scientist

A fabulously wealthy elite flourished on the sheep farms of the plains and the scruffy early settlement soon took on a grander air. Wool barons built mansions in the fashionable suburb of Fendalton and helped fund grand private schools for their children. Fine parks of oak and elm as well as neoclassical buildings graced the city as the new aristocrats recreated England in the South Pacific. But the city also acquired a reputation for snobbishness and rigid social structures that long persisted, though recent migration has broadened the city's Anglo-Kiwi population base.

The most dramatic changes to the city, however, have come from the earthquakes of 2010 and 2011 (see p. 196). Though some of its history has been destroyed, the rebuilding city now looks to the future, and visitors are a much-welcome part of that regeneration.

Cathedral Square

Cathedral Square is at the heart of the city's historic district. Once ringed by heritage buildings, much of the surrounding area is now vacant lots littered with weeds, leveled after buildings

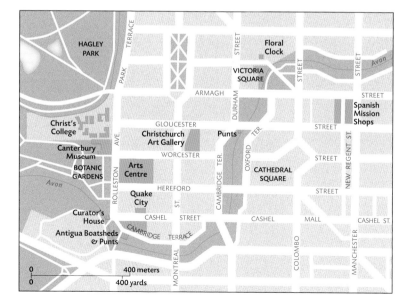

collapsed and suffered irreparable earthquake damage. Construction continues unabated throughout the city center, but it may take a generation to fully rebuild the city.

The icon of the city and symbolic casualty of the quake is **ChristChurch Cathedral,** built between 1864 and 1904. The fine Gothic edifice, named after Oxford University's Christ Church, suffered minor damage in the 2010 earthquake, but the 2011 quake and subsequent tremors

---

Christchurch By Night

Christchurch's weekend nightlife took a massive hit from the earthquake, with suburban bars and pubs taking up much of the slack. But the center is coming back to life.

Christchurch Casino (30 Victoria St., chchcasino.co.nz) is open late every night, with bars featuring 1980s cover bands and quiet conversation nooks.

Dux Central (10 Poplar St., duxcentral .co.nz) Forced into suburban exile by the quake, and happily now back in town, this cool pub offers house brews and good food in a multibar, renovated space.

Pomeroy's Old Brewery Inn (292 Kilmore St., pomspub.co.nz) Boutique beers and live music in a great British pub just northeast of the city center.

---

toppled its spire and then collapsed its west wall. It still lies in ruins, its future clouded by dispute. Faced with massive rebuilding costs, the Anglican Church agreed to a demolition order, but legal battles and negotiations to save the cathedral continue with no resolution in sight. In the interim, a temporary "cardboard cathedral," built by Japanese architect Shigeru Ban,

has been erected at Hereford and Madras Streets, several blocks west. The **Transitional Cathedral** (card boardcathedral.org.nz) is interesting for its modern architecture and as a symbol of resilience and adaptation.

Other heritage buildings in the square were lost, though the stoic **Old Government Building** (1911) survived the wrecker's ball and is now the Heritage Christchurch hotel (see Travelwise p. 301). Facing the cathedral, the **statue of John Robert Godley** (1814–1861) toppled from its pedestal in the earthquake but was reinstated. It honors the city's founding father and first leader of the colony. Irish born but Oxford educated, this Anglican Tory decried the decline of the church's authority and growing egalitarianism in 19th-century England, and saw Christchurch as a chance to preserve British institutions in the Antipodes.

Quake City (tel 03/366-5000, 99 Cashel St., canterburymuseum.com, $$) is a must-see for understanding earthquakes and the devastation in Christchurch. Exhibits, photos, and relics explain the science and local events, but the video stories of residents are the poignant highlight. The "185 Empty Chairs" art installation—rows of white chairs dedicated to the earthquake victims—is another moving memorial on the site of the quake-damaged St. Paul's Trinity Pacific Presbyterian Church, at the corner of Cashel and Madras Streets.

Cultural Precinct

The number of cultural attractions on and around Worcester Boulevard heading west to the Botanic Gardens has led to the area being

Springtime in Hagley Park, Christchurch

Christchurch Art Gallery

 Map p. 193

Worcester Blvd. & Montreal St.

03/941-7300

christchurch
artgallery.org.nz

Canterbury Museum

Map p. 193

Rolleston Ave.

03/366-5000

canterburymuseum
.com

dubbed the Cultural Precinct. Many relatively low-rise buildings survived the earthquakes and this western half of the city holds the most interest for visitors.

The **Avon River** is a green lung, snaking its garden-strewn way through the city. To the north, **Victoria Square** on the corner of Colombo is dissected diagonally by the river. This block—once the commercial heart of the city, known as Market Square—is now a delightful park, with statues of Queen Victoria and Captain Cook, and a pedestrian bridge leading across the river to the floral clock and the modern town hall.

At the heart of the precinct, **Christchurch Art Gallery** is an impressive architectural landmark opened in 2003. Though modern construction methods helped it survive the earthquakes, the glass facade, ceilings, and fittings did sustain damage. Happily, it is back in full operation, with regular rotating exhibitions. Its permanent works include the definitive collection of Canterbury artists, noted

Maori portraits by Bohemian artist Gottfried Lindauer (1839–1926), and "Cass" (1936) by Rita Angus (1908–1970), depicting a lonely Canterbury rail stop, voted one of New Zealand's most loved paintings.

The **Arts Centre** (tel 03/366-0989, artscentre.org.nz) on Worcester Boulevard housed the University of Canterbury until 1974, and the stately stone Gothic buildings (from 1877) are among the city's finest. Once a hive of craft shops, galleries, and artist studios, the Cultural Precinct saw several of its buildings compromised by the earthquakes. Ongoing restorations have revived some buildings, with full restoration due in 2019. For now it houses the city's visitor information center, cafés, a cheesemonger, outdoor cinema, and **Rutherford's Den** ($), a small hands-on science museum dedicated to Kiwi atomic physicist Ernest Rutherford.

Worcester Boulevard ends at Rolleston Avenue, where the **Canterbury Museum** (tel 03/366-5000, canterburymuseum.com) has

The Christchurch Earthquakes

On September 4, 2010, a magnitude 7.1 earthquake, centered 25 miles (40 km) west of the city, struck at 4:35 a.m. It caused widespread damage, cracking buildings and buckling roads, sewers, and water pipes, but no lives were lost, largely because the city slept and the streets were empty. Thousands of aftershocks followed, but they proved to be minor precursors to the destruction of February 22, 2011.

The Cathedral of the Blessed Sacrament after the magnitude 6.3 earthquake of February 2011

The 2011 Earthquake

Centered on the southeastern edge of the city, and only 3 miles (5 km) below the surface, a 6.3 magnitude quake hit the city in the middle of the day and unleashed unforeseen devastation. Already weakened buildings crumbled, houses were ripped apart, people were thrown in the air, and 185 lost their lives, more than half in the six-story Canterbury Television Building, which collapsed floor-upon-floor and caught fire.

In the city center, the area bordered by the "four avenues" (Bealey, Fitzgerald, Moorhouse, and Deans), high-rise buildings were hit hardest and caused the most destruction and loss of life. One quarter of the buildings were damaged beyond repair and face demolition. Many of the significant heritage buildings that defined the city's English character were also lost.

In the eastern suburbs, soil liquefaction produced 440,000 tons (400,000 tonnes) of silt and destroyed many houses. Some areas can never be rebuilt. In all, some 100,000 houses were damaged, 10,000 destroyed. Residents went without power, water, and sewage for weeks as subsequent quakes destroyed infrastructure and roads became unusable. Major aftershocks hit the city again in June and December 2011, and some residents abandoned Christchurch, too traumatized to return.

The majority of Cantabrians, however, marshaled together, along with the rest of the country, to help rebuild the city. Thousands volunteered to help with the cleanup and assist the displaced, and many more made donations.

Rebuilding

The heart of the city, extending many blocks around Cathedral Square, became a "Red Zone" fenced off due to danger from collapsing buildings after the quake. It took months to reopen after the bulldozers moved in, and half-ruined buildings and vacant lots are still scattered around the city. In the eastern suburbs, roads are still buckled and many houses are in various states of disrepair, still waiting for insurance claims to be settled. The large residential red zone along the Avon River to the east was deemed uneconomic to ever rebuild. Despite all the problems, construction is booming and the city is regenerating, with new buildings rising and old ones, such as the Gothic-style Arts Centre, reopening. It has been estimated that half the city has been rebuilt, and while it may take decades to fully recover, a sense of normalcy has returned.

withstood the test of time and earthquake. This delightfully classical museum offers both Kiwi and global exhibits. The moa diorama gives perspective to these giants and the other bird exhibits cover almost all New Zealand species. The Antarctic exploration and Maori exhibits are highlights, and the Paua Shell House is a quirky monument to Kiwi kitsch.

Next to the museum is exclusive **Christ's College.** Established as an Anglican boys' school in 1850, the school is steeped in English tradition, right down to the black and white ties and blazers that the students wear. Its buildings include the Big School, built in 1863, now the library.

The **Christchurch Tramway** (tel 03/366-7830, tram.co.nz, $$) ceased operation in 1954 after 50 years of service, but trams began clacking around a scenic city tourist loop again in 1995. Much of the line buckled in the earthquakes but the tram is back on track, with an extended route and a Tramway Restaurant in the evenings.

Heading south from the Canterbury Museum along Rolleston Avenue, you pass the entrance to the Botanic Gardens before reaching the **Curator's House** (tel 03/379-2252), a charming neo-Tudor cottage built in 1920. Once a fringe benefit of the garden curator's job, it is now a restaurant.

A little farther south on the river, the **Antigua Boatsheds** (2 Cambridge Terr., tel 03/366-6768, boatsheds.co.nz) were built in 1882

of batten and board construction. They're a popular stop for boat (and bike) rentals and afternoon tea in the café. The boatsheds are also home to **Punting on the Avon** (tel 03/366-0337, punting.co.nz, 30 min., $$), Christchurch's most iconic draw. Punters don boaters (straw hats) and stand on platforms at the back of the boats, pushing their poles and taking riders on a delightfully lazy tour at river level. The punts can also be hired farther north at the Gloucester Street Bridge.

From the boatsheds, head over to **Cashel Mall,** a pedestrian

Wizard of New Zealand

A treasured icon of Christchurch, the Wizard appeared at Cathedral Square in summer to mock conventional wisdom and muse on everything from the joys of the English monarchy to globalization and the perils of bureaucracy. Dressed in the traditional black with a conical hat, he is a self-proclaimed "living work of art" who migrated to Christchurch in 1974. The city councilors at first tried to banish him, but he cast a spell on them and soon became one of New Zealand's great eccentrics. In 1990, he was proclaimed Wizard of New Zealand by then prime minister Mike Moore.

Born Ian Brackenbury Channell in England in 1932, the Wizard was a teaching fellow in sociology before embracing cosmology and unorthodoxy. With his usual soapbox, Cathedral Square, in tatters, the Wizard publicly decried the hasty demolition of the city's heritage buildings and announced his retirement. However, he still appears occasionally to cast spells or upbraid civic leaders, and you might spot him, or his apprentices, around New Regent Street. His website is wizard.gen.nz.

Christchurch Gondola

✉ 10 Bridle Path Rd.

☎ 03/384-0310

💲 $$

gondola.co.nz

precinct and the city's main shopping area before the earthquakes. Not to be denied their cherished shopping pleasures, Cantabrians gave the term "pop-up" a whole new meaning with the Re:START Mall retail area, comprising buildings improvised from shipping containers. It is being repurposed as a farmers market near the Quake City museum (see p. 194).

The Curator's House Restaurant at the Royal Botanic Gardens

City Gardens

Early settlers remarked on the drab vegetation of Christchurch's marshy plains and quickly set about transforming their surroundings. Sprawling **Hagley Park,** a green buffer right on the edge of the city center, is a fine city park covering 395 acres (160 ha). The park includes artificial lakes, a golf course, walking and cycling tracks, and the renowned **Botanic Gardens.** These were founded in 1863, with the planting of an English oak to commemorate the marriage of

Queen Victoria's eldest son to Princess Alexandra of Denmark. This delightful expanse of lawn and more than 10,000 exotic and indigenous plants covers 74 acres (30 ha). The gardens also have a café and visitor center.

Just west of Hagley Park, the **Mona Vale** estate *(63 Fendalton Rd., Riccarton)* also straddles the Avon. It once belonged to the Deans, one of Christchurch's first settler families. Dating from 1899, the estate is now used for private functions, but the gardens of European trees, rhododendrons, camellias, and annuals are open to the public.

Christchurch Suburbs

In contrast to the flat Canterbury Plains, the volcanic **Port Hills** provide a dramatic amphitheater for the city. The hills are a favorite retreat of Christchurch residents, who walk, run, bicycle, paraglide, and climb the rugged rock outcrops and tussock-grass slopes. The first settlers crossed over on the Bridle Path, which was the main route between the city and Lyttelton until the rail tunnel was completed in 1867.

A farsighted member of parliament, Harry Ell (1862–1934), successfully lobbied for a network of scenic reserves in the hills along **Summit Road,** which can be explored on a breathtaking drive. In 1918, Ell began building the **Sign of the Takahe,** a rest house for travelers that resembles a medieval castle. This Gothic folly on Dyers Pass Road, halfway to Summit Road from the city center, was reincarnated as a restaurant but is undergoing postquake renovation.

The best way to appreciate the hills is from on high. The **Christchurch Gondola** provides spectacular views of the city, Lyttelton Harbour, and the Southern Alps on a clear day. From the parking lot on Tunnel Road near the Lyttelton tunnel entrance, the gondola shuttles up to the restaurant, summit complex, and museum every day.

Christchurch may look to England, but it also shares an affinity with the South Pole at the other end of the globe. The whizbang **International Antarctic Centre** at the airport has a wealth of displays, interactive exhibits, and movies about the great icy continent. Highlights include the penguins and the Antarctic Storm chamber where you don arctic gear to experience a snowstorm. Hagglund rides and the 4-D theater (3-D with moving seats) are extra.

Northwest of the city, about 5 miles (8 km) behind the airport, **Orana Wildlife Park** *(tel 03/359-7109, oranawildlifepark.co.nz, $$$)* is a sprawling zoo with lions, tigers, giraffes, kiwis, and other native birds. Feeding the big animals is the highlight. Much smaller, but in an attractive garden setting, **Willowbank Wildlife Reserve** *(60 Hussey Rd., tel 03/359-6226, willowbank.co.nz, $$)* houses small animals from around the world, a farm animal enclosure to delight small children, and a good kiwi enclosure, where the elusive birds are easy to see (and to hear). Evening Maori concert performances and *hangi* (earth oven) feast are offered.

Banks Peninsula

On Christchurch's doorstep, the Banks Peninsula was formed by three gigantic volcanic eruptions that pushed the earth upward from the surrounding flatlands. Lava flows cooled and weathered, leaving behind a landscape of steep hills and convoluted harbors and headlands.

Captain Cook named it after his botanist, Joseph Banks, but thought the peninsula was an island, an easy mistake given the dramatically different landscape

Hector's Dolphins

Hector's dolphins are the smallest and rarest of the dolphins. These endangered mammals are found only in New Zealand, primarily around the South Island, with a small number of the very rare Maui dolphin subspecies found in the North Island. They can be easily spotted by their round, black dorsal fins (what locals call "Mickey Mouse ears"). New Zealand has taken protective measures to try to save the dolphins, and it seems to be paying off, with recent aerial surveys suggesting a doubling of the population since the last survey, when they numbered just 7,000.

jutting out into the sea from the flat plains. The Maori preferred the peninsula, with its forest and abundant sea life, to the plains, as did early settlers who sheltered in its harbors.

With its sea aspect and cottages gripping the hillside, **Lyttelton** is a popular satellite of Christchurch, 7 miles (12 km) to the west. Easily reached from the city via a tunnel under the Port Hills, this historic town has a

International Antarctic Centre

- Map p. 191
- 38 Orchard Rd., Christchurch Airport
- 03/357-0519
- $$$

iceberg.co.nz

Akaroa

⚠ Map p. 191

Visitor Information

✉ 74a Rue Lavaud

☎ 03/304-8600

akaroa.com

Akaroa Museum

✉ 71 Rue Lavaud

☎ 03/304-1013

akaroamuseum
.org.nz

The Giant's House

✉ 68 Rue Balguerie

☎ 03/304-7501

$ $

thegiantshouse.co.nz

lively bar/café scene, but it is also Christchurch's port and a harbor with cranes and logs piled high.

Lyttelton was hit badly by the earthquakes and lost several heritage buildings, but it still makes a good escape from the city for a meal, a browse of its farmers market, or a cheap harbour cruise on the ferry to Diamond Harbour (*blackcat.co.nz, $*), from where you can climb Mount Herbert for panoramic views.

The town of **Akaroa** is the jewel of the peninsula, 50 miles (80 km) from Christchurch. French whaling captain Jean Langlois founded Akaroa and in 1840

The *Nimrod* Expedition

On January 1, 1908, Ernest Shackleton and crew set sail aboard the *Nimrod* from Lyttelton en route to the South Pole. Once in Antarctica, they planned to use dogs, ponies, and an automobile to reach the Pole. Due to bad weather and car trouble, they gave up their quest after three months. The trip back to the coast took longer than expected, the party being overcome by hunger and dysentery, and when they arrived they found that their ship had already left for home. In a final effort, Shackleton set fire to their shelter in desperate hopes that the ship would see the smoke. Luckily, it did, and the party was rescued.

---

lured 60 settlers halfway across the world to start a French colony. Langlois had grand visions and urged France to annex the South Island, but by the time the settlers arrived, the Treaty of Waitangi (see pp. 90–91) ensured that the colonists were greeted by a Union Jack flying in Akaroa Harbour.

English and German settlers followed, but those first French families stamped the town with its lingering flavor. French names grace the streets, local cafés serve French food, and pretty cottages provide a French provincial air. Surrounded by scenic hills on a stunning harbor, Akaroa makes a wonderful day or overnight trip. Streets such as Lavaud and Cross were renamed Rue Lavaud and Rue Croix in 1968, with tourists in mind, prompting local wags to erect signs such as Rue Matics, Rue Barb, and Rue de Remarks.

But there's no denying the colonial charm of the town, and its history can be explored at the **Langlois-Eteveneaux House,** one of the original cottages, now part of the **Akaroa Museum,** which also includes the old **Court House** and **Customs House.**

The best thing to do is simply to wander the waterfront and the streets lined with cottages and old churches. **The Giant's House,** the funky gardens/workshop of local artist Josie Martin, makes a colorful stop. You can book activities from kayaking to swimming with dolphins through the information center. Harbor cruises are popular; Hector's dolphins (see sidebar p. 199) and penguins are often seen in these waters. ∎

EXPERIENCE: Surfing Lessons

With all that coastline, New Zealand has an abundance of surf and quality waves. Surfing is a popular pastime for Kiwis and visitors alike, but plenty of uncrowded waves can be found off the beaten path and outside the main summer holiday season.

A surfer rips at popular Wainui Beach, near Gisborne on the North Island.

For beginners, surfing lessons are offered at locations all around the country, and unlike in some surfing classes in places like Hawaii or Australia, class numbers are generally low.

Surf schools provide boards and wet suits, a must in the often chilly waters of New Zealand. A spring suit will suffice up north in summer, but a full wet suit is needed farther south.

The 1966 surfing movie classic *Endless Summer* put the North Island's Raglan on the world surfing map, and it remains the country's most famous break. The Raglan Surfing School has popular 3.5-hour lessons.

The big city, Auckland, has the largest concentration of surfers and surf schools, with good breaks nearby, particularly on the west coast beaches such as Muriwai. The east coast of the North Island also has excellent surf and surf schools, most notably at Gisborne and Mount Maunganui.

Most South Island surf schools are along the east coast at Kaikoura, Christchurch, and Dunedin, which has good surfing at city beaches.

Surfing New Zealand
(surfingnz.co.nz) lists operators, including the following. Check also with local tourist offices.

Aotearoa Surf
11 Te Arai Point Rd.
Te Arai tel 09/431-5760
aotearoasurf.co.nz

Catlins Surf
Curio Bay, Catlins
tel 03/2468-552
catlins-surf.co.nz

Muriwai Surf School
485 Motutara Rd.
Muriwai Beach
tel 021/478-7343
muriwaisurfschool.co.nz

New Zealand Surf School
Marine Parade, Mount Maunganui
tel 021/477-873
nzsurfschool.com

Rapu Adventures
P.O. Box 17509
Greenlane, Auckland
tel 09/828-0426
rapuadventures.com

Raglan Surfing School
5b Whaanga Rd.
Whale Bay, Raglan
tel 07/825-7873
raglansurfing school.co.nz

WOW Surf School
Wainui Beach, Gisborne
tel 022/313-0213
wowsurfschool.com

North Canterbury

North Canterbury is often just a pass-through zone for visitors heading north to Marlborough or to the West Coast over the passes of the Southern Alps. However, Hanmer Springs has the finest hot-springs resort on the South Island, and Arthur's Pass National Park is noted for its superb alpine scenery, with notable ski slopes nearby.

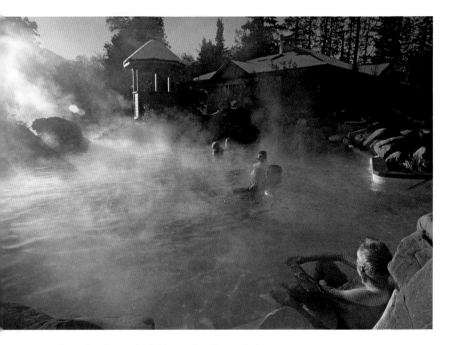

Steam rises from spring-fed hot pools at Hanmer Springs

Hanmer Springs
🅰 Map p. 191

Visitor Information
✉ 40 Amuri Ave.
☎ 03/315-0020

visithurunui.co.nz

Christchurch to Lewis Pass

Lewis Pass is one of three main routes through the Southern Alps to the West Coast. Take SH1 north out of Christchurch and turn off onto SH7 at Waipara. The highway northwest through the alps is a lonely one through farmland and forest, and it passes the hot-springs resort of Hanmer Springs.

Few destinations on SH1 are worth a stop before you reach Hanmer Springs or Kaikoura (see pp. 176–177). Wine buffs will find **Waipara** an exception. This budding wine-growing district, one hour north of Christchurch near the Hanmer Springs turnoff, is a relative newcomer in New Zealand, but has quickly established a reputation for fine wine.

Pegasus Bay *(tel 03/314-6869, pegasusbay.com)* consistently rates as one of the country's top boutique wineries, particularly for its fine Riesling, Chardonnay, and

Pinot Noir. The standout restaurant with its innovative cuisine, chic dining room, and fine views is among the best in the country. **Mud House Winery** (tel 03/314-6900, mudhouse.co.nz) has grown to become one of the region's largest producers, offering a wide variety of wines. **Waipara Springs** (tel 03/314-6777, waiparasprings.co.nz), also on the main highway, has a rustic wine bar and café serving platters stacked with local fare.

Nestled in a high-country basin 50 miles (80 km) north of Waipara, **Hanmer Springs** has long drawn visitors in search of its curative waters. Though rocked by the 2016 earthquake, and close to the epicenter, it escaped major damage. Flanked by a phalanx of shade trees, this pretty town has a fine hot-springs complex right on the main street, with a series of rock pools filled with waters from the springs at around 95°F (35°C). Complete with swimming pools, water slide, café/restaurant, and gift shop, this is the South Island's best-maintained and most extensive springs resort.

The town has a host of good accommodations and a wide range of other activities when soaking in the pools begins to pall. The **Hanmer Forest** has pleasant walks starting from the town. Adventure activities abound, and in winter Hanmer Springs is a ski town, with two small ski areas in the surrounding mountains. The swift Waiau River nearby has jet boating, white-water rafting, and bungee jumping at the scenic bridge outside town.

Once a Maori greenstone

trading route, **Lewis Pass** is the northernmost of the three main passes through the Southern Alps. At 2,835 feet (864 m), it is lower and easier to negotiate than Arthur's Pass (see pp. 204–205) and more lightly traveled, offering a way to avoid the camper-van convoys that block roads all over the South Island in summer.

North of the Pass

Just northwest of Lewis Pass, **Maruia Springs** (tel 03/523-8840, maruiasprings.co.nz, $$) is a small hot-springs resort nestled in the valley next to the highway, surrounded by thickly wooded mountains. The springs were well known to the Maori and a favorite place to camp on the

Japanese Baths

Based more on socializing than scrubbing, the Japanese bath (onsen) is gaining international popularity. The bather washes thoroughly before stepping into the communal bath, which is deeper and hotter than its western counterpart—like a zen hot tub. Traditionally, the onsens were coed, but that is less common now.

journey through Lewis Pass. European settlers were also attracted to the thermal waters and built bathing huts for modesty, followed by a hotel.

Japanese owners brought Japanese bathing traditions (see sidebar above) to this remote part

Hanmer Springs Thermal Pools & Spa

✉ Amuri Ave.

☎ 03/315-0000

$ $$

hanmersprings.co.nz

EXPERIENCE: Climb Every Mountain

The Southern Alps offer demanding, ice-strewn climbing and have long been practice slopes for the world's mountaineers. Sir Edmund Hillary, who conquered Mount Everest with Tenzing Norgay in 1953, cut his climbing teeth in these alps, which include 19 peaks over 10,000 feet (3,000 m), the highest of which is Aoraki/Mount Cook at 12,316 feet (3,754 m).

For budding mountaineers, alpine hikers, or those looking for a one-shot taste of peak bagging, trained guides offer world-class climbing and mountaineering courses. Three of the best-known organizations are **Alpine Guides** (*Mount Cook Village, tel 03/435-1834, alpineguides .co.nz*) based in Aoraki/Mount Cook National Park, **Aspiring Guides** (*Level 1, 99 Ardmore St., Lake Wanaka, tel 03/443-9422, aspiringguides.com*), and **Adventure Consultants** (*20 Brownston St., Wanaka,*

tel 03/443-8711, adventureconsultants.com), which operate mostly in Mount Aspiring National Park.

Courses range from basic mountain skills for hikers and climbers to ice climbing and technical mountaineering. Alpine hikes and climbing expeditions are also arranged. For serious mountaineers, the **New Zealand Alpine Club** (*alpineclub.org.nz*) is an excellent resource and runs most of the alpine huts. The courses don't require prior experience, though a good level of fitness is essential and basic rock-climbing and rope skills are preferred.

Plenty of places offer rock-climbing experience in New Zealand (*climb.co.nz* is a good resource), from indoor venues to cliff faces at noted rock-climbing locations, particularly in Canterbury, Wanaka, Taranaki, and Wellington.

---

of the South Island, with segregated communal bathhouses and individual spas. The outdoor rock pools are at their best on a snowy winter's day, when snow drifts down to refresh steaming bathers.

Arthur's Pass

The most direct way to the West Coast from Christchurch is via Arthur's Pass on SH73. At 3,018 feet (920 m), it is the highest of the main passes over the Southern Alps. For many years it was also the most treacherous—subject to landslides and avalanches—and the most tortuous, with a procession of switchback turns. The impressive Otira Viaduct improved this route immensely.

Flanked by glittering peaks, the road is spectacular. Even better is

the rail link between Greymouth and Christchurch, New Zealand's most scenic train journey. The TranzAlpine runs daily in both directions and passes through the 5-mile-long (8 km) **Otira Tunnel,** one of the longest tunnels in the world when it opened in 1923. The tunnel's length meant this stretch of the line had to be electrified because the buildup of fumes would otherwise be hazardous to passengers.

The tunnel starts at **Arthur's Pass Village,** the main settlement of the area, 3 miles (5 km) south of the pass itself. This tiny alpine hamlet has a population of just 60, but gets more than a quarter of a million visitors a year. It has a busy restaurant where kea (mountain parrots; see sidebar p. 216) enjoy the run of the place, and accommodations cater to the hikers, mountaineers, and skiers who flock to the surrounding **Arthur's Pass National Park.**

The 282,935-acre (114,500 ha) national park straddles the Southern Alps and has 16 peaks over 6,500 feet (2,000 m). Its flora ranges from beech forest in the east to rain forest on the western slopes. The park also has superb hiking, from good short walks to the popular two-day **Goat Pass Track,** the five-day **Harper Pass,** and the even tougher **Harman Pass** route.

For a taste of the park's beauty, the **Devil's Punchbowl Waterfall** is a one-hour round-trip walk from the parking lot on Punchbowl Road, just north of the village. The waterfall can be seen from the highway, but the walk takes in beautiful beech forest. From the same parking lot, another 1.5-hour trail leads to the **Bridal Veil Falls.**

The **Dobson Nature Walk** leads from the top of the pass and is an excellent 15-minute loop through alpine terrain, with wildflowers blooming in summer. The longer one-hour **Bealey Valley Track** to the foot of Mount Rolleston is well worth the effort. The scenic trail starts 1.2 miles (2 km) north of the village and goes through beech forest and tussock clearings after crossing the Bealey River at Bealey Chasm.

The more demanding hike to **Temple Basin,** the nearby ski area, starts at the pass and is a three-hour round-trip. It is rewarded with panoramic mountain views and alpine meadow wildflowers in summer.

Ski Areas

Before Arthur's Pass, the road from Christchurch crosses **Porters Pass,** the highest point on SH73 at 3,103 feet (946 m). Nearby in the Craigieburn Range, Porters ski field is the closest commercial skiing area to Christchurch, just 55 miles (89 km) away. Other ski slopes in the ranges, such as Craigieburn and Mount Cheeseman, also attract day-trippers.

INSIDER TIP:

Even on short walks, in Arthur's Pass National Park be well equipped and prepared for changeable weather. The park gets 177 inches (450 cm) of rain annually, and it can snow at any time.

—PETER TURNER
National Geographic author

Mount Hutt, the most developed ski area near Christchurch, has a long season *(June–Oct.)* and is regarded as one of the best skiing destinations in the country. Nearby **Methven,** a pleasant sleepy town in summer, has accommodations, and in winter it thrives on après-ski. Methven offers a host of other attractions to lure visitors year-round, including fishing, golf, jet boating, hiking, and mountain biking. ∎

Arthur's Pass National Park

Map p. 191

Visitor Information

✉ SH73, Arthur's Pass Village

☎ 03/318-9211

doc.govt.nz/parks -and-recreation /national-parks /arthurs-pass

Ski New Zealand

New Zealand has some of the best skiing in the Southern Hemisphere, with a ski season lasting from June to October. Major ski fields include those on the slopes of the Ruapehu volcano in the North Island, but most skiing takes place on the South Island, particularly near Queenstown and Wanaka, as well as outside Christchurch.

Tourists and Kiwis alike flock to southern slopes like Mount Hutt in Canterbury.

Unlike ski resorts in other countries, New Zealand's tend to have a nature-first policy, with limited development on the mountains and accommodations in surrounding towns. In addition to the main resorts, a host of smaller club areas with limited facilities are scattered around the country.

Mount Ruapehu

Mount Ruapehu offers a unique opportunity to ski down the slopes of a volcano. Though normally quiet, Ruapehu is the most active of three volcanoes in Tongariro

National Park and has a steaming crater lake.

Two areas on the mountain offer the North Island's best skiing. Popular **Whakapapa** (see p. 134) on the northern slopes has panoramic views, 14 lifts, and 30 groomed trails. Smaller **Turoa** (see p. 135) on the southern slopes has the country's longest vertical drop at 2,369 feet (722 m), nine lifts, and more than 20 groomed trails. From the top lift, it is a one-hour walk to the crater lake.

You can stay in Whakapapa Village, 4 miles (6 km) from the ski area, but most accommodations are to be found in the towns of National Park and Ohakune (see p. 135), which has the best après-ski scene.

Canterbury

Arguably the best ski area in New Zealand, **Mount Hutt** (see p. 205) is the highest commercial field, with the longest season. Wide slopes offer first-class powder skiing, boarding, and cross-country skiing. A two-hour drive from Christchurch, the area is serviced by the ski village of Methven.

A number of club ski areas are found in the nearby Arthur's Pass/Craigieburn Range. **Porters Ski Area** is the main commercial field and the closest to Christchurch, 55 miles (89 km) away.

In North Canterbury, the hot-springs resort of **Hanmer Springs** (see p. 203) services two nearby areas: the small club slopes of Hanmer Springs and family-friendly Mount Lyford, with a nearby alpine village offering accommodations.

Mackenzie Country

In the shadow of Aoraki/Mount Cook, more remote Mackenzie Country has uncrowded ski areas with great views of New Zealand's highest mountain.

Near Lake Tekapo, **Roundhill** offers undulating slopes and good snow cover for beginning and intermediate skiing. **Mount Dobson** has the country's largest beginner/intermediate slope and soft powder. And near Twizel, remote **Ohau** (see p. 213) has excellent snow, varied terrain, and less crowded slopes for intermediate and advanced skiers.

Wanaka

On a fine lake, the scenic alpine town of Wanaka, an hour northeast of Queenstown on the South Island, is a popular base for skiing in the surrounding mountains.

With a vertical drop of 2,313 feet (705 m) spread over three basins, **Treble Cone** has exhilarating skiing with a panoramic backdrop of the peaks above Lake Wanaka below.

Advanced and intermediate skiers rate it the best for downhill runs, off-piste powder skiing, and consistently good snow, with wide groomed slopes for all levels.

High-altitude **Cardrona** (see pp. 251 & 253), on the back road to Queenstown, is a family resort with good child-care facilities and gentle rolling slopes suitable for beginners, while more demanding runs cater to all levels.

Across the valley from Cardrona, **Snow Farm New Zealand** is a cross-country terrain park with 32 miles (50 km) of groomed trails and expanses of open country for ski touring, with traditional skiing and snowboarding also available.

Get Into the Action

Some operators and resorts for stellar South Island skiing:

NZSKI
9 Duke St., Queenstown
03/450-1970
94 Main St., Methven
03/302-8811
nzski.com

Lake Wanaka
Four ski resorts
lakewanaka.com

Queenstown

In a superb setting on Lake Wakatipu, Queenstown is the South Island's number one alpine resort, known for its party action.

Less than half an hour from Queenstown, **Coronet Peak** has top-class on-mountain facilities and stunning views of the surrounding ranges and Lake Wakatipu. A wide range of terrain caters to all levels in the South Island's birthplace of skiing.

A spectacular range that defines Queenstown views, **The Remarkables** hosts a popular ski area with three basins that cater to boarders and skiers from beginner to advanced.

South Canterbury

Heading south across the flat-as-a-board farmland of the Canterbury Plains, the main highway (SH1) south to Dunedin reaches the city of Timaru. Most visitors turn off before Canterbury's second city to travel the spectacular inland road to the Southern Alps and mighty Aoraki/ Mount Cook.

A flock of sheep, ubiquitous in New Zealand, enjoy views of the Arrowsmith mountains

Timaru

Timaru

🅜 Map p. 191

Visitor Information

✉ 2 George St. (opposite railway station)

☎ 03/687-9997

Timaru

The largest city in southern Canterbury, Timaru (pop. 30,000) was a whaling station from 1838, but European settlement began in earnest in 1859 when 120 British immigrants disembarked from the *Strathallan*. The city's name is said to derive from Te Maru, or a "place of shelter," where Maori canoes found a haven along the rugged coast, but shipwrecks littered the treacherous bay

until construction began on an artificial harbor in 1877.

Halfway between Christchurch and Dunedin, Timaru is a logical overnight stop on SH1 but tends to lose out to more visited Oamaru to the south. Mindful of Oamaru's regeneration of its historic precinct, Timaru has also undergone a pleasing face-lift in an attempt to shake off its struggling provincial air. Many fine buildings and whole streetscapes survive from the city's heyday, particularly along Beswick, Cain, and Barnard Streets. Among the interesting commercial buildings, the delightfully old-fashioned **Royal Arcade** off Stafford Street has cast-iron columns and ornate Victorian shop fronts. **St. Mary's Anglican Church** (24 Church St.), built in 1880, is pure English Gothic, and the tower can be climbed for views of the city. Built in 1911, **Sacred Heart Basilica** (Craigie Ave.), south of town on the main road, has a large copper dome and is the town's most imposing structure.

The Bay Hill, a renovated street of café-bars and restaurants, is well worth a visit and has striking views over the terraced Piazza above Caroline Bay. This popular, if dated, local beach resort comes alive with fairground attractions over Christmas to New Year.

The **South Canterbury Museum** (tel 03/687-7212, museum.timaru.govt.nz, closed Mon.) on Perth Street houses the usual historical suspects—Maori and settler exhibits—and a replica of the airplane flown in 1902 by locally born Richard Pearse (1877–1953). A quiet dreamer, Pearse constructed his monoplane from bamboo, steel, wire, and canvas. Contrary to world opinion, Kiwis claim Pearse was the first man to fly, a year before the Wright Brothers took off in the Flyer.

Housed in a 1908 homestead, the **Aigantighe Art Gallery** (49 Wai-iti Rd., tel 03/688-4424, closed Mon.) has a fine collection of New Zealand, Pacific, Asian, and European art, particularly British Victorian paintings, a delightful sculpture garden, and Maori

portraits by C. F. Goldie. Content rotates with visiting exhibitions.

Te Ana Maori Rock Art Centre (tel 03/684-9141, 2 George St., teana.co.nz, $$), at the information center, has interesting exhibits on Maori rock art but it's the commentary by Ngai Tahu guides that really bring alive Maori culture and history, and tours also run to rock art sites outside Timura.

EXPERIENCE: Ballooning

The flat Canterbury Plains are ideal for hot-air ballooning. The spreading patchwork of plains farmland stretching to the snow-capped Southern Alps makes for a spectacular panorama. Departure is at dawn for pristine views; celebratory champagne caps off the adventure. **Ballooning Canterbury** (2126 Bealey Rd., Darfield, Christchurch, tel 027/915-4972, ballooningcanterbury.com) has 4- to 5-hour trips from Darfield 30 miles (48 km) west of Christchurch and can provide transfers from the city.

Christchurch to Aoraki/Mount Cook

The most direct route southwest from Christchurch to Queenstown goes via Aoraki/Mount Cook. The inland road has spectacular scenery with rural landscapes giving way to glacial lakes and the drama of the Southern Alps. This is as stunning a drive as any in a country filled with scenic roads.

About an hour's drive south of Christchurch on SH1, the rural town of **Ashburton** makes a

**Aoraki/
Mount Cook
National Park**

Map p. 191

Visitor Information

1 Larch Grove,
Aoraki/Mount
Cook Village

03/435-1186

doc.govt.nz

convenient first stop, but it lacks attractions to keep you long.

Just over the Rangitata River, 22 miles (36 km) south of Ashburton, turn off the main highway onto SH79 and the pretty town of **Geraldine,** at the junction of pasture and foothills. Grab a coffee

Sir Edmund Hillary

Born in Auckland, the world's most famous mountain climber was first a professional bee-keeper. On his days off, however, he got a taste for mountaineering in New Zealand's Southern Alps. After serving in the Royal New Zealand Air Force during World War II, Hillary became intent on scaling Mount Everest. In 1953, he reached the top alongside Sherpa Tenzing Norgay. After spending 15 minutes at the summit resting and eating cake, he descended, quipping, "Well, we knocked the bastard off." In 1958, he led the first vehicle party to reach the South Pole.

or stretch your legs on streets lined with shade trees and historic buildings. The visitor information center *(tel 03/693-1101)* has details on the thriving local craft scene and a number of nearby excursions.

Farther on past Fairlie, the road (SH8) climbs to Burkes Pass and **Mackenzie Country,** named after a sheep rustler turned folk hero caught herding a stolen flock into

the then unexplored Canterbury highlands. The landscape changes dramatically in the shadow of the alps, revealing a harsh but beautiful highland basin of tussock grass and stunning lakes.

The first of the lakes is **Lake Tekapo,** a breathtaking turquoise stretch of water framed by the snowy Southern Alps. The small hamlet of the same name is tour bus heaven, a required stop on the way to Queenstown. Souvenir shops line the main street and tour groups fill the cafés during the day, but few stay on, though the town has a good range of accommodations. The biggest thing in town is **Tekapo Springs** *(tel 03/680-6550, tekaposprings.co.nz),* with hot pools, saunas, and the adjoining ice rink and mini ski slope in winter for snow tubing.

Lake Pukaki, 25 miles (40 km) farther on, is even more stunning with views straight up the lake to towering Aoraki/Mount Cook. Also turquoise, the lake's color is a product of fine powdered rock ground by the glaciers upstream and carried by the meltwater into the lake. Past the dam on SH80 is the turnoff to Aoraki/Mount Cook; the main highway continues on to Twizel (see p. 213). Stop by the visitor center/salmon farm *(SH8, tel 03/435-0427)* at the lake.

Aoraki/Mount Cook National Park

With 19 peaks over 10,000 feet (3,000 m), Aoraki/Mount Cook National Park is the crowning glory of the Southern Alps, which stretch the length of the island. The park is a forbidding

A bronze statue of Sir Edmund Hillary at home among the Southern Alps

INSIDER TIP:

Aoraki/Mount Cook, New Zealand's highest and most sacred peak, lords over the tussock-covered Mackenzie Plains and is as impressive as anything in the Himalaya.

—COLIN MONTEATH
National Geographic photographer

landscape of ice and rock, 40 percent of it covered by glaciers, but access to the park is via an easy drive along the shore of Lake Pukaki up to the Aoraki/ Mount Cook Village.

The village is dominated by **The Hermitage** (see Travelwise pp. 302–303), a grand dame among New Zealand hotels since 1884. Most day visitors don't get beyond the hotel

and its fantastic views of the park, but at the very least, take one of the short walks to better appreciate the grandeur. Also at The Hermitage, the **Sir Edmund Hillary Alpine Centre** has interesting displays on the park and its mountaineering history, while a theater shows Hillary and Mount Cook 3-D films.

Standing tallest among the cluster of peaks is Aoraki, the "Cloud Piercer." Once plain old Mount Cook, it was officially renamed **Aoraki/Mount Cook** in 1998 as part of the government's treaty settlement with the Ngai Tahu people. At 12,316 feet (3,754 m), it is the tallest peak in New Zealand, though it lost 33 feet (10 m) when a large section of rock sheared off in 1991. The mountain is a magnificent sight, but often shrouded in cloud.

Aoraki/Mount Cook has long attracted climbers and is a training ground for New Zealand mountaineers, including Sir Edmund

Hillary, conqueror of Mount Everest (see sidebar p. 210). Though not high by world standards, the climb starts low and the ascent is tough. Since the peak was first scaled on Christmas Day 1894, more than 200 people have died on or around it.

This is by no means a one-peak park, however, and other magnificent mountains such as ones being the Tasman, Hooker, Mueller, Godley, and Murchison. The **Tasman Glacier,** visible from the highway at the entrance to the park, is the largest glacier in New Zealand at 18 miles (29 km) long and up to 2 miles (3 km) wide.

Though increasingly rock-covered in the lower reaches as the glacier retreats, the ice is up to 2,000 feet (600 m) deep in parts.

Lupins enliven the shores of Lake Tekapo.

Tasman, Sefton, Eli de Beaumont, Haast, Dampier, and the Minarets all compete for the attentions of climbers and sightseers. Peaks can also be climbed from the West Coast, for Aoraki/Mount Cook borders Westland Tai Poutini National Park (see pp. 226–227), but for non-mountaineers the two parks are separated by a scenic two-day drive.

Glaciers: The park also has dozens of glaciers, the five major

The Tasman Glacier can be skied in winter, when helicopters drop skiers on the upper reaches, and ski planes also land in summer for up-close viewing. Other sightseeing flights and mountain guides offer a variety of ways to explore the glaciers and the park.

Walks: The easiest way to get out into the park is on one of the many walks from the village. **Governors Bush Walk,** a one-hour loop, goes through stands of silver beech and offers good views of the mountains. The **Kea Point Track,** two hours round-trip, starts from The Hermitage and leads up to the Mueller Glacier moraine wall through subalpine grasslands. The walk ends at a viewing deck with stunning panoramas of the mountains, Hooker Valley, and the Mueller Glacier.

The **Hooker Valley Track** is more demanding, but highly recommended for its views of mountains, glaciers, and lakes. The trail crosses two suspension bridges and passes Mueller Lake before reaching Hooker Lake. The hike takes three hours round-trip from the parking lot at the end of Hooker Valley Road. Be sure to get up-to-date trail and weather information before heading off at the Department of Conservation visitor center.

Twizel

The closest town to the national park, **Twizel** was built in 1968 as a temporary construction village for 6,000 workers employed on the Upper Waitaki hydroelectric power plant. The hydro project was the largest undertaken in New Zealand, and when it was completed 18 years later, the town was due for demolition. The residents successfully fought to retain the town, which lives in large part on tourism, with Aoraki/Mount Cook only 40 miles (65 km) away and a number of scenic lakes with good trout fishing nearby.

Though Twizel lacks old-fashioned charm, the well-stocked town of 1,300 makes a good base and has reasonably priced

A Humbling Rockslide

Around midnight on December 14, 1991, a rockslide started at the peak of Aoraki/Mount Cook. What began as a dull rumble quickly escalated into a massive rock avalanche. Nearby climbers watched as the mountain seemed to collapse upon itself. By the next morning, the mountain had shrunk from a triumphant 12,349 feet (3,764 m) to a slightly more humble 12,316 feet (3,754 m). Yet despite the natural calamity, the mountain is still New Zealand's tallest.

accommodations. The visitor information center *(Market Pl., tel 03/435-0066, twizel.info)* has full details on services and the many activities offered around town. Twizel is a good base to organize a scenic day cycling ride on the **Alps 2 Ocean Trail** (see pp. 116–117), which starts at Aoraki/Mount Cook Village and runs all the way to the coast. Shuttles can drop you at Lake Tekapo or Lake Ohau Lodge for a taste of one of the country's best Great Rides.

Lake Ruataniwha on the southern edge of town is popular for boating, as is **Lake Benmore,** the site of the hydro dam to the east. **Lake Ohau,** 19 miles (30 km) west of Twizel, is popular for boating, swimming, and fishing and as a base for the **Ohau ski field** west of the lake. ■

Stunning scenery, glaciers, old mining towns, and wilderness sandwiched between the Southern Alps and a rugged coastline

West Coast

An adventurer climbs an ice face in a Fox Glacier crevasse, Westland Tai Poutini National Park.

West Coast

**Cut off from the rest of the South Island by the Southern Alps and lashed by drench-
ing rains from the Tasman Sea, the West Coast is a rugged landscape of snow and ice,
dense forest, lakes, and wild beaches.**

The Coast, as it is known for short, stretches
373 miles (600 km) north to south but is
seldom more than 19 miles (30 km) wide. It
is a frontier land, inhospitable but beautiful,
where miners flocked to the goldfields and
hacked settlements out of the thick bush.

Wild West Coast towns peopled by hard-
living, hardworking pioneers sprang up almost
overnight in the 1860s when Westland, as
the area is also known, was briefly the fastest
growing region and biggest exporter in New
Zealand. As gold waned, boomtowns became
ghost towns, but a new breed of miners followed to hack away at coal seams. Coasters are
proud of their working-class roots and still see
themselves as rugged and self-reliant. Today
the Coast is one of the most lightly populated
areas of New Zealand, and the main towns of
Greymouth, Westport, and Hokitika struggle to
keep their youths. Coal mines still operate, but
tourism is now the biggest industry.

The dramatic scenery lures hundreds of
thousands of visitors every year, most on a
beeline for the Fox and Franz Josef Glaciers in
Westland National Park. Near the coast with
no need to drive through snow to reach them,
these great valleys of ice 1,000 feet (300 m)
thick are among the most accessible glaciers in
the world. Even more astonishing, they emerge
in temperate rain forest.

The West Coast is both densely forested and
desolate. When Captain Cook passed in 1770, he
remarked, "No country upon earth can appear
more rugged and barren." Thomas Brunner
(1821–1874), the first European to travel the
length of the Coast in the 1840s, battled the
wilderness on the ground and found it just as
intimidating, saying: "For what reason the
natives choose to live here I cannot imagine."

Few Maori lived on the West Coast,
but it did have one great treasure: *pounamu*
(greenstone or New Zealand jade). For 300
years from around 1400, the Ngati Wairangi
controlled the trade of this precious hard stone,
prized throughout the North Island. The Ngai
Tahu then invaded and took over the resource,
lugging the stone high over passes through the
Southern Alps.

Those passes today provide spectacular
gateways to the West Coast. The northern
routes via Arthur's Pass and Lewis Pass were the
only way to the Coast until the Haast Pass road

Kea

The inquisitive and mischievous kea
(Nestor notabilis) is an alpine parrot
native to the Southern Alps. Unpre-
dictable, noisy, fearless, and easily
accustomed to humans, keas can
sometimes be found at picnic grounds
or outside cafés, such as at Arthur's
Pass Village. These scavengers eat
insects, berries, and other plants and
will dine on carrion such as dead sheep.
This habit earned keas an exaggerated
reputation as sheep killers, resulting in
their widespread shooting by farmers
until they gained protection in 1986.
They have adapted to eating scraps
thrown by visitors who are delighted
at the antics of these cheeky green
parrots, which let out a loud *keeeaaa*
call. But keas also have a destructive
bent, with a penchant for the rubber
around windshields, although tents,
bags, or anything they can get beaks
into may also suffer. Keas can also be
aggressive, so take care.

NOT TO BE MISSED:

Opapara Basin's limestone
   outcrops near Karamea   **219–220**

Punakaiki's "pancake" rock
   formations jutting into
   the sea   **220**

Shantytown, re-creating the old
   West Coast at Greymouth   **223**

The historic mining towns of the
   Grey Valley   **223**

Hokitika for greenstone
   carving and crafts   **223–225**

Isolated Okarito for windswept
   beach walks and kayaking   **225**

Franz Josef and Fox Glaciers,
   blue-tinged rivers of ice   **227–228**

Jackson Bay, the end of the road,
   if not the world   **229**

in the south was opened in 1965. Whichever road you take, stunning mountain scenery is guaranteed.

   On the Coast, historic towns, old mines, and deserted beaches can also be explored. Greenstone is still a precious resource in Hokitika, where renowned workshops carve stone as well as bone, shell, and wood. Stock up on fine crafts and souvenirs here. The main town of Greymouth is the gateway to old mining settlements, and farther north, a stunning coastal drive takes in the strange "pancake" rocks of Punakaiki, another West Coast must-see.

   The very far north around Karamea leads to Kahurangi National Park, a wilderness as remote as any in New Zealand. Here you'll find the Heaphy Track, one of New Zealand's Great Walks. ■

Westport & Beyond

The coal-mining town of Westport is the gateway to western reaches of the diverse Kahurangi National Park, lying at the very north of the West Coast. To the south, the rugged coastline is home to seals and the famed "pancake" rocks of Punakaiki in Paparoa National Park.

A rocky beach near Karamea

Westport

 Map p. 217

Visitor Information

✉ 123 Palmerston St.

☎ 03/789-6658

westport.nz

Westport

Situated where the Buller River meets the sea, Westport is the West Coast's main port and owes its existence to coal. Gold miners first settled Westport in 1861, but the pickings were lean and the coal mines north of the town soon drove development. They still produce most of New Zealand's coal.

Westport is just a small town, but the area has a number of points of interest, most notably Punakaiki

to the south and Kahurangi National Park to the north. In town, the impressive new **Coaltown Museum** (*123 Palmerston St., 03/789-8204, coaltown.co.nz, $*) at the visitor center celebrates Westport's main industry with a re-created mine, interesting displays, and a huge wagon and brake drum from the Denniston Incline.

Westport is a crossroads to the north and east of the South Island. Heading toward Nelson in the north, SH6 follows the Buller River

INSIDER TIP:

Short on time? You can walk just part of the Heaphy Track, or try the Oparara Basin for short forest hikes to spectacular limestone outcrops.

—JORGE I. NÚÑEZ
National Geographic research grantee

through the stunning Buller Gorge. About 12 miles (20 km) from Westport, the twisting road is cut into the mountain and becomes an amazing one-lane drive under a rock roof. SH6 continues up the river to Murchison (see p. 187). Alternatively, turn off SH6 near the small town of Inangahua, 28 miles (45 km) from Westport, to Reefton and the main highway to the east coast via Lewis Pass. On SH6 just past Inangahua is Lyell, starting point for the **Old Ghost Road,** a spectacular 53-mile (85 km) mountain bike track through the wilderness to Seddonville. For well-prepared, experienced riders, this is one of the best Great Rides in the country.

North of Westport

Heading north of Westport, SH67 goes through lightly populated country and ends just past Karamea at the start of the Heaphy Track, the area's main lure (see p. 220). On the way, turn off at Waimangaroa for **Denniston,** 6 miles (9 km) off the highway, high on the

Rochfort Plateau. Once a thriving coal-mining center, Denniston is now almost a ghost town, but its good walks include the very steep **Denniston Walkway** (see sidebar below). This forested bridle trail leads to the Denniston Incline, an impressive cabling feat that transported coal trucks up and down the mountain.

The Denniston Incline

Dubbed the "eighth wonder of the world" by locals, the Denniston Incline was constructed in 1879 to carry coal from the top of the Denniston plateau. Sending wagons filled with 12 tons of coal down the exceptionally steep tracks was a difficult venture and called for a sturdy braking system—which sometimes failed. Many unfortunate souls met their demise at the bottom of the incline after mishaps caused tons of coal to rain down on top of them.

The **Denniston Experience** (*tel 03/789-9021, denniston.co.nz*) guided train tours into the Banbury mine bring coal mining history to life.

The road north then travels through old coal towns, shadows of their former selves, before climbing inland around the scenic, forested **Karamea Bluff** and descending back to the coast and the isolated town of **Karamea,** gateway to **Kahurangi National Park,** a large,

Karamea

Map p. 217

Visitor Information

106 Bridge St., Market Cross

03/782-6652

karameainfo.co.nz

Paparoa
National Park

🄰 Map p. 217

Visitor Information

✉ Main Rd.,
    Punakaiki

☎ 03/731-1895

doc.govt.nz/parks
-and-recreation
/national-parks
/paparoa

Blowholes

Blowholes are formed as a by-product of erosion. Waves beating against the coast will slowly cause the softer rock to crumble, eventually producing underwater caves. In time, bits of the top of the cave wear away, creating small holes—the blowholes. When a wave pours into the mouth of the cave, it is funneled out through these holes. The pressure from the pounding waves results in highly impressive aquatic eruptions.

---

mostly inaccessible wilderness. Here hiking trails explore rushing rivers, alpine fields, and coastal forest. The park's rich vegetation varies markedly from the West Coast's thick podocarp forest and superb tropical-looking nikau palms to beech forests in the east.

The **Heaphy Track** is the most famous of the park's walks, a 49-mile (78 km), five-day hike from the Aorere Valley, near Collingwood in Nelson, to Kohaihai, 10 miles (16 km) north of Karamea. This Great Walk (see p. 19) overnights in huts and must be booked through the Department of Conservation. Or, you can hike just part of the Heaphy, or try the **Oparara Basin**. On the road to the Heaphy Track, turn off at McCallums Mill Road and travel 10 miles (16 km) on gravel road. There you'll find the start of the easy, 20-minute walk to the limestone **Oparara Arch** over the river. The **Moria Arch**

(1 hr. round-trip) is similar, while the **Crazy Paving** and **Box Canyon Caves** are close to the road.

South of Westport

Seven miles (11 km) from Westport, a fine 1.5-hour round-trip walk goes from **Cape Foulwind** along the coast to a populous seal colony. You can also drive to **Tauranga Bay** for a five-minute walk to the seals.

The once-booming town of **Charleston** on the Nile River, 17 miles (27 km) south of Westport, hasn't done much since the gold ran out, but **Underworld Adventures** *(182 Queen St., Westport, tel 03/788-8168, caverafting.com, $$$$$)* runs caverafting trips, glowworm cave tours, and a gentler rainforest train trip up the Nile River from its base here.

Punakaiki *(punakaiki.co.nz)*, about 37 miles (60 km) south of Westport on SH6, is by far the highlight of this part of the West Coast. It is famed for its rock formations, the product of weathered limestone lifted from the seabed by seismic action. An easy 20-minute loop from the village, the walk to **Pancake Rocks and Blowholes** takes in the most spectacular outcrops along this stunning stretch of coast, part of **Paparoa National Park.** Punakaiki has a small selection of accommodations, a tavern, and cafés near the visitor center, which has information on the park and walks. These include the 2.5-hour round-trip **Pororari River Track,** following a spectacular limestone gorge. ∎

Pioneers

European New Zealanders are proud of their pioneering past and often attribute aspects of the national character to the first settlers and their resourcefulness, strength of will, and propensity for hard work.

In the late 18th century, New Zealand was seen as one of the world's last outposts, a remote and hostile land. Though nearby Australia was settled in 1788, few Europeans had ventured farther east.

Sealers established the first settlement in 1792, a rough camp in remote Dusky Sound where they braved the torrential rains. Others followed, attracted by high prices for seal fur and oil. A few took Maori wives and stayed on. One settler, 16-year-old James Caddell, was the only survivor of a Maori attack in 1810 and later married a chief's daughter. He bore facial tattoos and could barely speak English when discovered by Europeans 13 years later.

In the north, whalers had the most significant contact with the Maori from 1792. Mostly English and American, the whalers roamed the South Pacific hunting sperm whales for oil and ambergris, taking shelter in the Bay of Islands. The village of Kororareka traded with the ships and soon acquired a reputation for debauchery. Beginning in 1809, traders settled the port, followed by missionaries in 1814.

Statue to the settlers of 1842, Wakefield Quay, Nelson

British Colonization

Few settlers ventured beyond the Bay of Islands, and by the time Britain annexed New Zealand in 1840, the European population was still only a few hundred. But the New Zealand Company had acquired Maori land and was selling it off to settlers from England and Scotland, many of them first-time farmers. They cleared, plowed, and planted grass to graze sheep. Many lived harsh, isolated lives, but early North Island settlements also ran into problems with local Maori due to suspect land deals.

Mass settlement had to wait for the discovery of gold in Otago in the 1860s. Miners then flocked from the Australian and Californian fields. Towns sprang up overnight as thousands flooded Otago, then the West Coast, then the Coromandel on the North Island. Mostly young and overwhelmingly male, these settlers were mainly English, but Irish, German, and Chinese miners also worked the fields. Their families followed, along with traders and domestics. When the gold ran out, other mines provided some work, and on the West Coast the coal mines attracted many Welsh miners.

In the north of the North Island, the mighty kauri forests attracted settlers in the 1870s. The wealth of this fine timber provided one of New Zealand's main exports, and the rugged workers who felled the logs lived in remote camps. In addition, up to 20,000 gum diggers fossicked in the swamps for kauri gum, the fossilized sap of the trees used in varnish and linoleum.

Greymouth & Hokitika

Most Coasters make their home in the central West Coast, particularly in the main town of Greymouth and nearby Hokitika. Greymouth celebrates its heritage at Shantytown and provides interesting side trips to old mining towns, while Hokitika is the greenstone capital of New Zealand—a great place to stock up on crafts.

A gathering of the Black Powder Musket Club, a shooting group from the Greymouth region

Greymouth

 Map p. 217

Visitor Information

✉ Railway Station, 164 Mackay St.

☎ 03/768-7080

westcoast.co.nz

Greymouth

The largest town (pop. 10,000) and unofficial capital of the Coast, Greymouth was home to the large Maori settlement of Mawhera when the first European, Thomas Brunner, arrived here in 1846. The township was laid out in 1865 at the time of the great gold rush, but in later years coal, forestry, and fishing assumed greater importance.

Set at the mouth of the Grey River, this utilitarian town has just enough interest for an overnight stay and is the western terminus for the famous TranzAlpine, the country's most stunning rail journey over the Southern Alps from Christchurch (see Travelwise p. 279).

In the mornings, keep an eye out for the eerie rolling clouds of The Barber, the icy wind as sharp as a barber's razor that blows in from the Grey Valley.

The **History House Museum** (*27 Gresson St., tel 03/768-4028, closed Sun., $*) has pioneer displays focusing on mining as well as a large collection of historical photos. Family-run **Monteith's Brewing** *(Turamaha & Herbert Sts., tel 03/768-4149, monteiths .co.nz)* was proudly the Coast's own until bought by the large DB Breweries, which tried to close the flagship Greymouth plant. A public outcry forced its reopening, and tours *($$)* run from the impressive brewery.

The big attraction around Greymouth is **Shantytown** *(Rutherglen Rd., Paroa, tel 03/762-6634, shantytown.co.nz, $$$),* located 7 miles (11 km) south of town off SH6. This replica of an 1880s gold town with its Wild West streetscapes and stores does a good job of re-creating the era. Steam-train rides, gold panning, and forest walks are all part of the Shantytown experience.

To the east of Greymouth, **Lake Brunner** is the West Coast's largest and prettiest lake, reached by turning off SH7, which runs northeast through the Grey Valley.

In the valley about 16 miles (25 km) from Greymouth, **Blackball** is an old coal- and gold-mining town, famous for the miners' strike of 1908 that helped form the country's union movement. Wander the old town or have a beer and a sausage in the historic **Formerly the Blackball Hilton** *(26 Hart St., tel 03/732-4705, blackballhilton.co.nz),* which had to amend its name after a run-in with the hotel chain. It is the sole pub left in a town that once had dozens.

Farther north at pretty **Reefton,** the highway heads inland

to Christchurch via Lewis Pass. Named for its gold-bearing quartz reefs, this hamlet has a **museum** on the highway east of town crammed with goldfield relics. Reefton's visitor information center *(tel 03/732-8391)* has details on good short walks and tours to old gold and coal mines.

Greenstone

New Zealand greenstone is a dark green nephrite jade, different from the lighter and rarer jadeite prized in China. Greenstone rocks are usually found in rivers, particularly the Arahura and Taramakau Rivers near Hokitika, but also on West Coast beaches. The hard stone was the major source of trade between the North and South Island Maori, used for adzes, clubs, and ornament. The Maori name for the South Island is Te Wai Pounamu, or "the greenstone water," and under the Treaty of Waitangi the Ngai Tahu tribe was given controlling rights to West Coast *pounamu* in 1997.

Hokitika

The town of Hokitika, 25 miles (40 km) south of Greymouth, boomed in the gold rush of 1864. Thousands flocked from the Australian goldfields and dozens of ships ran aground as they entered the treacherous harbor at the mouth of the Hokitika River. By late 1866,

Hokitika

▲ Map p. 217

Visitor Information

✉ 36 Weld St.

☎ 03/755-6166

hokitika.org

Hokitika Museum

✉ Hamilton & Tancred Sts.

☎ 03/755-6898

💲 $

hokitikamuseum .co.nz

An artisan carves native greenstone in Hokitika.

Hokitika was one of the biggest towns in New Zealand, and in 1873 it became the capital of New Zealand's short-lived Westland province.

Hokitika fell into decline in the 20th century, leaving wide streets lined with grand buildings, detailed in the "Hokitika Heritage Walk" brochure. For another good walk, head south of the town center to the **Gibson Quay** heritage area on the river, along to the **Sunset Point Lookout** at the river mouth, then on to the wild beach.

The town's many fine souvenir, art, and craft stores are the main attraction for visitors, featuring everything from glass-blowing to *paua* (abalone shell) jewelry, to the famed greenstone-carving workshops.

The **Hokitika Museum** is in the neoclassical Carnegie Building that once housed the town library, funded by American philanthropist Andrew Carnegie. The museum has good displays on greenstone (essential viewing

INSIDER TIP:

Hokitika is noted for its greenstone-carving workshops. This is one of the best places in New Zealand to stock up on all kinds of Kiwi souvenirs.

—PETER TURNER
National Geographic author

for those who are looking to buy at the town's workshops), gold, and the pioneering past. It is temporarily closed undergoing seismic assessment but should reopen soon.

Thousands flock to Hokitika's **Wildfoods Festival** (see sidebar opposite, *wildfoods.co.nz, tickets required*) in March for bush food and West Coast specialties, ranging from wild boar to whitebait patties, deep-fried grasshoppers, and *huhu* grubs (a Maori delicacy of roasted larvae).

South of Hokitika, the gold

town of **Ross** produced the Honourable Roddy nugget, the largest gold nugget found in New Zealand at 6.19 pounds (2.81 kg). This was presented to King George V for his 1911

Bush Food

Perhaps eating fried wasp larvae isn't your thing, but what about earthworm truffles? If so, you should head to the Wildfoods Festival, where these tasty items can be had, alongside sautéed lamb's tails. You can also sample bunny burgers, fish eyes, wasp-larva-flavored ice cream, an entire catalog of testicles, deep-fried dolphin, and possum pâté. Expect to line up for these delicacies: Held in March, the festival brings about 20,000 people to the town of 3,000.

coronation, only to be subsequently melted down to make a royal tea set. The information center *(tel 03/755-4077)* has a Roddy replica and several other displays.

About 22 miles (35 km) south of Ross, turn off SH6 to **Okarito** on the coast. This isolated settlement on a wild beach was the setting for Keri Hulme's Booker Prize–winning novel *The Bone People,* about the legacy of violence and mysticism in the lives of the Maori.

The Okarito Lagoon is also known as a major wading-bird sanctuary, home to the rare white heron, or *kotuku*. Nearby rain forests also host the Okarito brown kiwi. Among other outfitters, **Okarito Nature Tours** *(tel 03/753-4014, $$$$$)* has popular eco-kayaking tours and kayak rentals.

For a fine two-hour round-trip walk, head south along the beach until you come to the footbridge and then back via the inland trail, which climbs to **The Trig.** This vantage point affords truly spectacular views of Aoraki/Mount Cook on a clear day. ∎

Maori carving in Hokitika

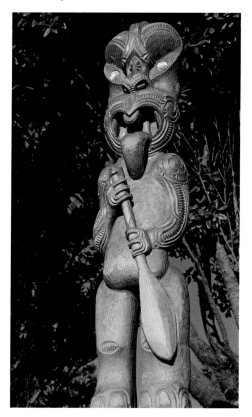

Glaciers & South

Franz Josef and Fox Glaciers are far and away the West Coast's main attractions. Lying in the rugged Westland National Park, these are among the world's most accessible glaciers. The road then follows the coast south to lonely Jackson Bay, passing Haast and the turnoff for the road to Wanaka and Queenstown.

Sunset over Lake Matheson and Mount Tasman

Westland Tai Poutini National Park

🅰 Map p. 217

Visitor Information

✉ 36 Main St., Franz Josef

☎ 03/752-0796

doc.govt.nz/parks -and-recreation /national-parks /westland-tai -poutini

Westland Tai Poutini National Park

The West Coast's biggest attraction, Westland Tai Poutini National Park extends from the highest mountains of the Southern Alps to the beaches of the West Coast, encompassing skyscraping peaks, forests, lakes, and rivers. Above all it is famous for its glaciers—Franz Josef and Fox—which are easily accessible just off the main road and surprisingly close to the sea.

Lying on the western flank of the Southern Alps, the park is split by the Alpine Fault, which pushes up a chain of peaks over 10,000 feet (3,000 m), including Aoraki/ Mount Cook. The West Coast's prolific rainfall dumps huge volumes of snow on the mountains, feeding 140 glaciers in the park, but Franz Josef and Fox Glaciers are by far the biggest and contain two-thirds of the park's glacial ice.

These two colossal brutes of blue-tinged ice push down

through rain forest at the lower reaches, but the glaciers are receding. Over the last one hundred years they have retreated more than 1.5 miles (2.5 km), despite modest advances in the 1990s. In recent years, popular guided walks on the glaciers' lower reaches have been suspended due to rapidly melting ice making them unsafe.

The park centers on the two small villages of Franz Josef and Fox, on the highway close to their respective glaciers. Both have a range of accommodations but can be overrun in peak times, when it pays to book weeks if not months ahead. Walking trails lead close to the glaciers for viewing, but to get onto the ice, you must take a helicopter to land on the glaciers' upper reaches. A host of flight-seeing planes buzz overhead on busy days.

Franz Josef Glacier

This 7.5-mile-long (12 km) glacier was named after the Austro-Hungarian emperor by German geologist Julius von Haast (1822–1887), who explored the area in 1865. The terminal face of this steep, 7,000-year-old glacier lies 12 miles (19 km) from the sea, but originated from an older glacier that did reach the sea.

Glacial melt feeds the Waiho River, and a 45-minute walk along the river from the parking lot leads to within a few hundred feet of the glacier. The area close to the glacier is off limits, with good reason. Tons of ice can crash down from the melting

terminal face without warning. Guided walks booked in the village get up closer to the terminal face, but to get out onto the ice, you will have to take a heli-hike. Outfitters will equip you with ice climbing gear (see sidebar p. 229).

Franz Josef village is 3 miles (5 km) from the glacier parking lot. The **National Park Visitor Centre** offers visitors informative displays on the park and the **West Coast Wildlife Centre** breeds and exhibits the rare rowi and other kiwis.

West Coast Wildlife Centre

✉ Cowan & Cron Sts., Franz Josef
☎ 03/ 752-0600
$ $$$
www.wildkiwi.co.nz

EXPERIENCE:
Heli-skiing

One of the most amazing ways to experience the majesty of the Southern Alps is to ski the remote upper snowfields. If you are an intermediate or advanced skier, a chopper will take you to the top of some amazing slopes, pick you up at the bottom, and then take you to the next pristine slope.

Companies offering this ultimate skiing experience include **Harris Mountains Heli-Ski** (Shotover & Camp Sts., Queenstown, tel 03/442-6722, & 99 Ardmore St., Wanaka, winter only, tel 03/443-7930, heliski.co.nz) and **Mount Cook Heliski** (Alpine Guides, Mount Cook Village, tel 03/435-1834, mtcookheliski.co.nz).

Fox Glacier

Fox Glacier doesn't get the same volume of visitors as Franz Josef, even though the walk is easier and the views good, if not quite as big due to retreat in recent years. This 8-mile-long (13 km) glacier drops some 8,500 feet (2,600 m) on its journey down the Southern Alps and was named after former prime minister William Fox (1812–1893).

From the parking lot, a 40-minute walk leads along the valley to the end of the track near the terminal face of the glacier, about 1,300 feet (400 m) away. Heli-hikes

The lake is 4 miles (6 km) from Fox Glacier, just off the road to **Gillespies Beach,** which presents another side to the national park with its black-sand and quartz-pebble beach. A seal colony is a 1.5-hour walk along the coast.

The rustic Café Nevé at the foot of Fox Glacier

onto the upper ice may be booked in Fox Glacier village, 5 miles (8 km) from the glacier parking lot. The **Doc Area Office** (tel 03/751-0807) in town provides information on the park. Fox Glacier village has a quiet alpine feel and a selection of places to stay.

West of the village, **Lake Matheson** reflects Aoraki/Mount Cook and Mount Tasman in its mirror waters. A lakeside boardwalk leads through forest; allow about an hour for the circuit. In summer, a good café at the parking lot serves meals.

South to Haast

From Fox Glacier, the highway south goes past the **Copland Valley,** where the well-known **Copland Track** heads over an alpine pass through the Southern Alps to Mount Cook Village. This hazardous crossing is only for experienced mountaineers, but hikers can go as far as the **Welcome Flat Hut** and its hot pools, a seven-hour walk.

The road hits the coast again at **Bruce Bay,** where a subtribe of the Ngati Tahu have their marae. Farther south on the Paringa

River, the **Salmon Farm Café** *(tel 03/751-0837)* serves fresh salmon overlooking the fish ponds. Anglers can catch their own Quinnat salmon or trout in **Lake Paringa** a few miles farther on.

After traveling inland, the road heads back to the sea at **Knights Point,** with a fine view from the lookout, and then follows the coast most of the way to Haast.

Haast, 74 miles (118 km) from Fox Glacier, is the southern entry/exit point for the West Coast. Though no destination in itself, Haast has cheaper accommodations than the often full glacier towns. Haast's multiple personalities comprise three towns: Haast Junction, where SH6 meets the

INSIDER TIP:

When traveling between Fox Glacier and Haast, a 40-minute walk through lowland forest just past Lake Moeraki brings you to Munro Beach, one of New Zealand's perfect small beaches.

—BRENT OPELL
National Geographic research grantee

road to Jackson Bay; Haast Beach along that road; and the main Haast Township, 1 mile (2 km) along the SH6 to Wanaka. The **Haast Visitor Centre** *(SH6 & Jackson Bay, tel 03/750-0809)* at the junction has the lowdown on the West Coast if this is the start of your explorations.

The last lonely stretch of the Coast lies along the 31-mile (50 km) dead-end road to **Jackson Bay.** Originally a whaling station, Jackson Bay had plans in 1875 to attract settlers and develop as a port to rival Hokitika, but these

---

EXPERIENCE:
How to Visit the Glaciers

The only way to get on to the glaciers is via a helicopter ride/hike. Guided walks will get you closer to the terminal face than the public trails.

Franz Josef Glacier Guides offers glacier valley walks, ice climbing, and heli-hikes.
  SH6, Main Rd., Franz Josef Glacier
  Tel 03/752-0763
  franzjosefglacier.com
  $$$$$

Fox Glacier Guiding has many tour choices, including hikes to the glacier face, and heli-treks, including to Chancellor Dome.
  SH6, Fox Glacier
  Tel 03/751-0825
  foxguides.co.nz
  $$$$$

---

hopes eventually buckled under the town's geographic isolation and perpetual downpours. Today it is a sleepy fishing village noted for lobsters and whitebait. For lunch on the esplanade, try the **Cray Pot** *(tel 03/750-0035, thecraypotnz.com).*

From Haast, SH6 heads inland up the Haast River and over the **Haast Pass** to Wanaka and Queenstown. This spectacular route has a number of short walks and scenic stops as it makes the journey through Mount Aspiring Park (see p. 254). ■

Glaciers

Like most glaciers around the world, the Fox and Franz Josef Glaciers are retreating, though, strictly speaking, some part of a glacier is always on the move downhill, borne on meltwater. High snowfalls on the Southern Alps in the 1980s actually saw the terminal face of these glaciers advance for a decade, but it was a movement against the long-term trend.

Glaciers are formed by snow that accumulates in a basin, repeatedly freezes and thaws, and becomes compacted—now called névé. As more snow and ice are dumped at the head of the glacier, névé compacts further under pressure, until it becomes blue-tinged glacial ice.

Fox and Franz Josef are temperate glaciers, sitting on ground that is warmer than in most other glacial regions. This results in meltwater at the base of the glacier, which lubricates it and helps it slide down the mountain. Friction further increases melting and basal sliding, and the West Coast glaciers move very rapidly compared to other glaciers—up to 13 feet (4 m) per day.

Composed of layers of ice, glaciers also move internally, some layers moving faster

U-shaped valley

Terminal moraine

Streams

Alluvial plain

Terminal face "snout"

than others, helping the glacier flow slowly like a viscous fluid. The top layer of about 65 feet (20 m) at Fox and Franz Josef moves faster, but is also more brittle and prone to cracking, resulting in deep crevasses, or *bergschrunds*. This makes glaciers dangerous to travel over, for heavy snowfall can cover the crevasses, creating snow bridges that collapse under a climber's weight.

Glaciers gouge out the rock beneath as they travel, collecting large amounts of debris, from huge boulders to fine powder ground out by the constant abrasion. Called "rock flour," this powder is responsible for the milky gray color of glacial rivers. The debris carried by glaciers is deposited at their sides as mounds of rock and gravel called moraines.

Glaciers grind out deep U-shaped valleys over time, as opposed to V-shaped river valleys. Many of the great lakes on the South Island are the product of ancient glaciers that have long since melted.

Arête Cirque Crevasse Snowfield Snowline Medial moraine

FOX GLACIER

Lakes, majestic mountains, and stunning desert landscapes in Otago; stately Victorian cities along the coast; and fascinating wildlife nearby

Otago

Fall paints Arrowtown, Central Otago, in rich autumnal hues.

Otago

Otago encompasses extremes, from historic Dunedin on a fertile coast teeming with sea life, to the interior's surreal, desertlike landscapes stretching out in the shadow of the Southern Alps.

The jewel in Otago's crown is Queenstown, the country's number one resort, located on a glacial lake backed by the majestic alps. In summer, this impossibly pretty alpine town teems with tourists and activities, from the adventurous to the pedestrian, and the international party continues in winter when skiers flock to the surrounding mountains.

Queenstown makes a great base for exploring Central Otago, but for those who like their resorts a little less frenetic, Wanaka also has a glorious lake and snow-tipped-peak views.

Most of the Southern Alps in Otago are encompassed by Mount Aspiring National Park, a scenic wilderness area with the country's best alpine hiking trails, notably the Routeburn Track. The northern part of the park contains the Haast Pass, the gateway through the mountains to the West Coast via a stunning highway drive.

From Queenstown, you can venture into the heart of Central Otago to the plateau desert with its craggy schist landscapes, a favorite backdrop for some iconic Kiwi paintings. Farther from the sea than any other region of the country, it is the hottest in summer and the driest and coldest in winter. The harsh but beautiful landscapes were not immediately amenable to settlement, but old goldfield towns attest to a 19th-century boom.

For it was gold that first brought large numbers of Europeans to New Zealand, and the richest fields were those in Central Otago, discovered in 1860–1861. Miners flocked from all over the world, towns sprang up overnight, and though the rush lasted little more than a decade, in that time New Zealand's population doubled.

Much of the wealth flowed through Dunedin, which became the country's largest and grandest city. Banks, offices, hotels, and

A woodworker shapes a piece in Oamaru, home to many artisans.

imposing churches of stone quickly replaced the dwellings of the early settlers, pious Presbyterians who fled religious persecution in Scotland to build a new world based on farming.

But Dunedin still clings to its Scottish roots, and much of its early legacy remains. The most southerly of New Zealand's main population centers, it is a gracious city strung out on hills around a fine harbor. It makes an interesting stop, though it lies off the Christchurch–Queenstown–Milford tour-bus route—which is part of its appeal.

The biggest attraction for many lies just outside the city on the Otago Peninsula. Combining pastoral views with seascapes, the peninsula is also home to an accessible array of wildlife—giant albatrosses, seals, penguins, and sea lions can be viewed in their natural habitat.

Those journeying along the coastal route can also visit Oamaru, a sleepy town that once had grander dreams and, like Dunedin, boomed during the gold rush. A delightful historic precinct preserves grand Victorian buildings carved of white stone, and penguins also call Oamaru home. ■

NOT TO BE MISSED:

Dunedin's fine museums and Victorian architecture **236–242**

Seeing royal albatrosses, penguins, and other wildlife on the Otago Peninsula **242–243**

Larnach Castle, a testament to the region's past wealth **243**

A visit to the Moeraki Boulders, buried in the beach **245**

Old gold-mining towns and wineries of Central Otago **246–255**

Queenstown, one of the world's great alpine resorts **248–250**

Jet boating, bungee jumping, and other adrenaline activities **252**

Wanaka, adventure and ski resort on a fine lake **253**

Walking in Mount Aspiring National Park **254**

Dunedin & Otago Peninsula

The 1860s gold rush made Dunedin the largest and grandest city in New Zealand, and though long since surpassed, it remains an elegant city with fine Victorian architecture. On the city's doorstep, the Otago Peninsula is one of the best places in the country to see marine wildlife.

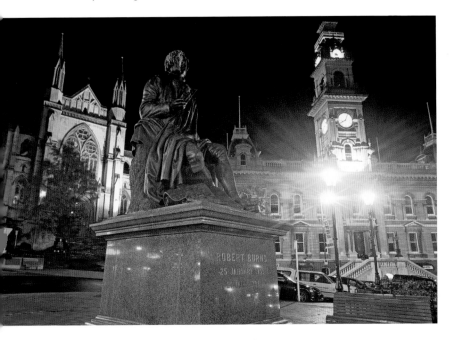

Statue of poet Robert Burns in the Octagon, Dunedin

Dunedin

🄼 Map p. 234

Visitor Information

✉ 50 The Octagon

☎ 03/474-3300

dunedin.govt.nz /isite

Dunedin

Sprawled across steep hills at the end of a long harbor, Dunedin is the South Island's second city, with a population of 127,000. A gracious mix of stately buildings, museums, and art galleries, Dunedin is easy to navigate but large enough to hum with urban life, much of it provided by the University of Otago and its 20,000 students.

Maori settled the coastal areas of Otago from around A.D. 1100, fishing the rich local waters and hunting moa. The first whalers and sealers arrived in the 1820s, but the colony really took off when settlers from the Free Church of Scotland landed in 1848.

Led by Capt. William Cargill (1784–1860) and the Reverend Thomas Burns (1796–1871), they first called the settlement New Edinburgh, but then opted for Dunedin, an old Scots name for Edinburgh. These pious folk set about creating a new vision of their homeland, but were soon engulfed by the gold rush in 1861.

Fortunes were made overnight from the Central Otago goldfields, and the riches flowed through the town. By the 1880s, Dunedin was New Zealand's showpiece. Imposing banks, churches, hotels, and company buildings sprang up in the central city and cable cars plied the hilly streets.

Though the gold eventually ran out and Dunedin was supplanted by upstart northern cities, wealth from farming fed the city right through to the mid-20th century. Today Dunedin is enjoying something of a revival, thanks largely to the university, which has tripled in size since the 1980s and stimulates the city's artistic and nightlife scenes. Tourism is also a growing industry, with visitors attracted by the city's charms and easy access to wildlife on the nearby Otago Peninsula.

The **Otago Museum** (419 Great King St., tel 03/474-7474, otagomuseum.govt.nz) is a great place to spend a rainy day. This fine museum has one of the country's largest collections, spread over three floors. The Tangata Whenua Gallery has impressive Maori artifacts, dominated by an enormous war canoe and superbly carved meetinghouse panels. Other Polynesian and Melanesian cultures are well represented, European settlement and maritime history are covered, and natural history exhibits detail South Island geology and bird life, including the giant moa, penguins, and the nearly extinct takahe.

Just a few blocks away in an impressive modern building is the **Dunedin Public Art Gallery**

World's Steepest Street

It may not be Mount Everest, nor even Aoraki/ Mount Cook, but the climb to the lofty heights of Baldwin Street is one of Dunedin's must-do attractions.

Baldwin Street is the steepest street in the world, according to the *Guinness Book of Records*, with a gradient of 1 in 2.86 (or 19 degrees), which means that for every 2.86 feet (0.87 m) traveled horizontally, it goes up 1 foot (0.3 m). The title is disputed, however, by Canton Avenue in Pittsburgh, among other contenders.

Regardless, this is one mighty steep street, and the climb to the top will get the lungs working overtime, even though it is only a short thoroughfare off North Road. Every summer up to a thousand competitors run up and down it in the Baldwin Street Gutbuster race.

(30 The Octagon, tel 03/474-3240, dunedin.art.museum). Its European art collection is one of the best in New Zealand, featuring many of the great masters, from the Renaissance to impressionism. The gallery also holds extensive early and contemporary New Zealand art. Exhibits are rotated and only a fraction of the collection is displayed at any one time.

(continued on p. 240)

Dunedin Walking Tour

A stroll through Dunedin's inner-city streets reveals grand churches, banks, and office buildings from the 19th-century days when this was the country's biggest city and its financial hub.

Thanks to the fabulous wealth of the 1860s gold rush, Dunedin boasts the largest concentration of Victorian architecture in New Zealand. The heart of the city is the leafy **Octagon ❶**, lined with historic buildings and restaurants spilling onto the sidewalk. Start your walk at the imposing Italianate **Municipal Chambers** (1880), next to the tourist office, and then continue next door to the neo-Gothic **St. Paul's Cathedral ❷**, the city's Anglican cathedral, completed in 1919.

At the front of the church, the **statue of Robert Burns,** dedicated to Scotland's favorite son, is an icon for a city that clings to its Scottish roots. The poet was the uncle of the

Dunedin's neo-Gothic First Church

NOT TO BE MISSED:

The Octagon • First Church • Law Courts • Dunedin Railway Station

---

Reverend Thomas Burns, founding father and religious leader of the early settlement.

From the Octagon, head south past the public art gallery (see p. 237) and on to Princes Street for one block, then turn left on Moray Place. On the next corner, at Burlington Street, the sky-piercing **First Church ❸** was built by the first settlers from the Free Church of Scotland. Completed in 1873, it was designed by Robert Lawson, the architect responsible for much of Dunedin's majestic neo-Gothic architecture.

INSIDER TIP:

Don't miss the small museum at First Church (10 a.m.–4 p.m., Mon.–Sat.), which has interesting pictorial displays and details on the early Scottish settlers.

—PETER TURNER
National Geographic author

From the church, head down Burlington Street and turn right onto Dowling Street with its fine Victorian streetscape. Buildings include the wedge-shaped **Commerce Building** and the **Imperial Buildings** (1906) on opposite corners, **Garrison Hall** (1877) displaying a bulging royal coat of arms carved in stone, and imposing **Milford House ❹** (1883), once the New Zealand Clothing Factory.

At the top of the street, turn left onto

Princes Street, the main thoroughfare and commercial district of the old city. Solid financial houses here include the **National Bank of New Zealand** (rebuilt 1912) and the old headquarters of the **Bank of New Zealand** (1883). Across Rattray Street, the **Cargill Monument** ❺ (1863) is dedicated to Dunedin's founder, Capt. William Cargill, and opposite on Princes Street is the **Grand Hotel** ❻, the city's finest when built in 1883 and still functioning as a hotel and casino.

Walk east along Rattray Street, past historic buildings such as **Consultancy House** ❼ (1908) on Bond Street, built in the American style of the time and hailed as a skyscraper, despite being only seven stories high. The area lies on reclaimed land, much of the fill provided by the 30 feet (9 m) lopped off the top of Bell Hill, on which First Church stands.

Turn left through Queens Gardens and then veer right onto High Street. On the corner of Dunbar Street, the old **Police Station** (1896) and **His Majesty's Prison** (1896) next door

🅰	See also area map p. 234
▶	The Octagon
⬌	1.5 miles (2 km)
🕓	2 hours
▶	Railway Station

carried out colonial justice dispatched by the impressive **Law Courts** ❽ (1899) around the corner on Castle Street.

Past the Law Courts, the magnificent **Dunedin Railway Station** ❾ is the city's most photographed building. Built in Flemish Renaissance style in 1904, its ornate facade of stone and concrete earned New Zealand Railways architect George Troup the nickname "Gingerbread George." Be sure to see the impressive tile-lined booking hall inside, as you consider the scenic rail journeys departing from here. Upstairs in the station, the **New Zealand Sports Hall of Fame** (tel 03/477-7775, nzhall offame.co.nz, $) has well-presented memorabilia devoted to Kiwi sporting heroes.

Yellow-Eyed Penguins

The yellow-eyed penguin is the largest temperate-climate penguin and is unique to New Zealand. So called for the yellow stripe extending back from its eye, the bird also has the descriptive Maori name *hoihoi* (noise shouter). The penguins nest from the Banks Peninsula near Christchurch to Stewart Island. The best chances of seeing them are on the Otago Peninsula and the Catlins in Southland.

Among the rarest penguins, they seek secluded nests in coastal forest, but habitat destruction and introduced animals, such as dogs, threaten their survival. They can live up to 20 years, but after hatching around November, the chicks head north in February or early March for winter feeding, traveling up to 300 miles (500 km) in a dangerous journey that only 15 percent survive.

Olveston
✉ 42 Royal Ter.
☎ 03/477-3320
💲 $

olveston.co.nz

Not art but history is the focus of the **Toitu Otago Settlers Museum** *(31 Queens Gardens, tel 03/477-5052, toitusm .com, $)*, dedicated to Dunedin's founding fathers. With a big new expansion, the museum also covers Maori settlement, but settler and transportation exhibits dominate. It has vintage cars, penny farthings, an early Dunedin cable car, and Josephine the steam engine, but photographs and exhibits covering the Otago goldfields, maritime history, and city development hold most interest. Nearby, the **Dunedin Chinese Garden** *(Moray Place, tel 03/477-3248, dunedinchinese garden.com)* is a tranquil city escape built to recognize the contribution of the Chinese people, dating back to the gold rush.

Also of historic interest is **Olveston,** a grand mansion built between 1904 and 1906 for merchant David Theomin in Jacobean style. Lavishly furnished with a fine art collection, it is a fascinating record of Edwardian privilege and luxury. Note that the one-hour guided

tours of the house must be booked in advance.

More Places to Visit in Dunedin

Dunedin lays claim to the world's steepest street—that's according to the *Guinness Book of Records* (see sidebar p. 237). Baldwin Street was once serviced by a cable car, but the only way up now is to take on the challenging walk. It's about 2 miles (3 km) northeast of the Octagon off North Road.

Tours of the **Cadbury chocolate factory** *(280 Cumberland St., tel 0800/223-2879, cadburyworld .co.nz, $$)* have long attracted chocolate fans to Dunedin. The visits include a look at the factory (but not the manufacturing process), culminating at the chocolate waterfall. Reservations are advisable for the 60-minute tours or you can visit the shop and the small visitor center museum *($).*

Speight's Brewery *(200 Rattray St., 03/477-7697, $$)* also has tours. These 90-minute visits include a sampling of beers from one of the country's oldest breweries. You may notice locals filling containers from the tap outside on Rattray Street; it's not beer, but pure spring water piped from beneath the brewery and used in the brewing process.

The **University of Otago** on Cumberland Street near the Otago Museum comes alive at the end of February during Orientation Week when "scarfies," as students are called because of the scarves they once wore, flood the city. The **Registry Building** (1879) with its distinctive clock tower is one of the city's architectural gems and lies on the banks of the quaintly named Water of Leith.

St. Kilda Beach, 2.5 miles (4 km) south of the Octagon, is as fine a stretch of white-sand surf beach, backed by dunes, as you will find in any city, though a wet suit will come in handy. Adjoining **St. Clair** is one of the city's most popular beaches, with saltwater pools and a café.

Tunnel Beach Walkway, 5 miles (8 km) southwest of the city, is a worthwhile 40-minute round-trip walk along clifftop farmland down to the beach, accessed by a hand-hewn tunnel.

Orokonui Ecosanctuary, 14 miles (22 km) northeast of Dunedin, protects rich birdlife. From the impressive visitor education center, self-guided trails or informative tours explore this nature reserve's extensive forest.

The landmark **Dunedin Railway Station** is the starting point for two quite interesting rail tours with Dunedin Railways *(tel 03/477-4449, dunedinrailways .co.nz).* The **Taieri Gorge Railway** is a spectacular journey along

the Taieri River Gorge through the rugged mountains of Central Otago. A diesel engine pulls 1920s carriages daily to Pukerangi *(4 hr. round-trip)* and to Middlemarch *(6 hr. round-trip)* on Sundays *(also Fridays Oct.–Mar.).* Middlemarch is at the start of the popular **Otago Central Rail Trail** *(otagocentral railtrail.co.nz),* and Dunedin Railways has a connecting bus to Queenstown from either town. The **Seasider** runs along from the coast north of Dunedin to Oamaru *(7 hr. round-trip, with one hour in Oamaru)* with a stop at Moeraki Boulders. Sporadic sea views are spectacular, but the timetable is

Orokonui Ecosanctuary

✉ 600 Blueskin Rd., Waitati

☎ 03/482-1755

💲 $ (tours $$$–$$$$$)

orokonui.org.nz

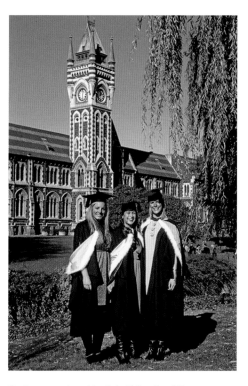

Graduates stand outside of the University of Otago, New Zealand's oldest (1869).

limited, although the train runs most days November to March.

Otago Peninsula

This once volcanic peninsula on Dunedin's doorstep is a crooked claw of inlets and bays, steep sheep-covered hills, and a castle, no less. It has become Dunedin's prime attraction, offering easy access to seaborne wildlife, such as albatrosses, penguins, seals, and sea lions. Apart from seals, wildlife is elusive unless you take tours. But even on your own, the peninsula makes a wonderful day trip with fine scenery.

The trip begins on the outskirts of Dunedin on Portobello Road, which wends around the eastern edge of Otago Harbour just a few feet from the water. The first stop of interest, **Glenfalloch Woodland Gardens** *(430 Portobello Rd., tel 03/476-1775)*, has lovely gardens

surrounding an 1871 homestead. Walks lead through grounds planted with exotic trees, rhodo-dendrons, azaleas, magnolias, and fuchsias. About halfway along Portobello Road, the tiny township of **Portobello** has a few accom-modation and dining options.

At the entrance to Otago Harbour, Taiaroa Head is home to the **Royal Albatross Centre** *(tel 03/478-0499, albatross.org.nz)*, one of the biggest attractions on the peninsula. The world's only mainland breeding colony of the huge royal northern albatross can be visited on walking tours *($$$$$)*, the best way to see these magnificent birds up close. The optimal viewing season, December to February, is also the main tourist season, when reservations are advisable. Tours take in the Taiaroa Head fort *($)*. Alternatively, view displays at the center for free, and

Children enjoy an interactive exhibit at the Royal Albatross Centre.

you might see albatross in flight from the car park walkways, particularly on windy afternoons.

Pilots Beach, just before the center, is a favorite spot for seals to fish and sun themselves on the rocks. After sunset, little blue penguins make their way up the beach here to their nests.

INSIDER TIP:

It's possible to see the royal albatrosses for free if you head toward Taiaroa Head in the early evening, when the adults are returning to their nests.

—MARCUS TURNER
National Geographic contributor

Along the road to Taiaroa Head, tour operators offer more eco-viewing experiences. Monarch Wildlife Cruises (tel 03/477-4276, wildlife.co.nz, $$$$$) has popular one-hour boat tours from a dock at Wellers Rock to see albatrosses, seals, and other species. They also offer half- and full-day cruises from the Dunedin harbor, returning by bus.

Penguin Place (45 Pakihau Rd., tel 03/478-0286, penguinplace.co.nz, $$$$$), off Portobello Road, is a private reserve that protects the endangered yellow-eyed penguin (see sidebar p. 240). Tours must be reserved. Penguin breeding grounds can be viewed at close range via a series of camouflaged tunnels and blinds on farmland leading to the beach.

At Taiaroa Head, Nature's Wonder Naturally (tel 03/478-1150, natureswonders.co.nz, $$$$) are at pains to point out their tours are more natural, with bus and all-terrain vehicles taking in cormorants, seals, and penguins. Seals, penguins, and sea lions also visit ocean beaches such as Allans Beach and Victory Beach on the peninsula's east coast, but access is difficult unless you go by tour.

Heading back to Dunedin from Portobello, take the inland Highcliff Road for fine views of the peninsula. Turn off onto Sandymount Road for an excellent short walk (20 min. one-way) to The Chasm, high above the windswept vertical cliffs with views across the peninsula.

Another very popular walk (40 min. one-way) goes from the end of Seal Point Road to pretty Sandfly Bay, where yellow-eyed penguins nest and can be viewed from blinds. Sea lions also visit.

Farther along Highcliff Road is the turnoff to Larnach Castle (Camp Rd., tel 03/476-1616, larnachcastle.co.nz, $–$$$), once the residence of William Larnach (1833–1898). Typical of the era's entrepreneurs, Larnach amassed a fortune through land deals, farming, and timber and flaunted it at his Gothic "castle." A visit to this impressive mansion is on every itinerary. The grounds have a café, while self-guided tours of the castle cost extra. For overnight stays, a new lodge and converted stables offer well-appointed rooms with breathtaking views (see Travelwise pp. 303–304). ∎

North Otago

On the main highway between Dunedin and Christchurch, Oamaru is the prime attraction, with its colony of nesting penguins and a delightful historic precinct crammed with grand buildings. On the way, don't miss the bizarre Moeraki Boulders, half-buried in the beach.

The Corinthian columns that support the Bank of New South Wales are made from local limestone.

Oamaru

🗺 Map p. 234

Visitor Information

✉ 1 Thames St.

☎ 03/434-1656

waitakinz.com

Oamaru

Oamaru, 71 miles (114 km) north of Dunedin, boomed with the gold rush and then the frozen-meat trade, resulting in a legacy of grand buildings carved from local limestone. Imposing banks, churches, and even an opera house are relics of embarrassing wealth that has long since left this sleepy town of 14,000.

Roughly halfway between Dunedin and Christchurch on SH1, the town's old-time charms, and its waddling penguins, have transformed this rural center into a growing tourist destination.

The heart of the historic town lies around the old waterfront at the southern end of Thames Street, the main road. The Port of Oamaru closed in the 1970s, leaving intact Victorian streetscapes that have been revived as the **Oamaru Historic Precinct.** Cafés, craft and antique stores, markets, and artisans' studios cater to a steady stream of visitors. Brochures from the tourist office outline the many fine buildings. Neoclassical designs and Corinthian columns predominate, and the town's easily worked, creamy white limestone helped create some superbly ornate architecture.

INSIDER TIP:

Oamaru is a hidden gem and well worth a stop. The refurbishment of the historic quarter is fostering a wonderful revival of traditional crafts.

—COLIN MONTEATH
National Geographic photographer

The story of Oamaru stone is told at the **North Otago Museum** (60 Thames St., tel 03/434-0852, northotagomuseum .co.nz), itself housed in a grand stone building that was once a library, the Oamaru Athenaeum. Photographs and artifacts elucidate colonial times and a display on Janet Frame, one of New Zealand's best loved writers, highlights her 14 years in Oamaru, the setting for her early novels.

Housed in a spectacular former bank building, the **Forrester Gallery** has rotating exhibits and a permanent collection of local artists' work. A quirky attraction, **Steampunk HQ** celebrates Victorian sci-fi creations in its small galleries, with a stylized steam engine and zeppelin outside.

Oamaru's little blue penguins prove that tourism can drive conservation. The birds, which used to nest under houses, were once considered a pest. Those pre-ecotourism days have long since passed, and the little blues are now a town icon. They can be seen waddling ashore every evening at the old quarry, now the **Oamaru Blue Penguin Colony** (Waterfront Rd., tel 03/433-1195, penguins.co.nz, $$$–$$$$), where a viewing platform, visitor center, and daytime nest-viewing facility have been erected. Rare yellow-eyed penguins (see sidebar p. 240) also nest at Bushy Beach, on the southern outskirts of town, which has blinds for viewing the shy penguins. ∎

Forrester Gallery
✉ 9 Thames St.
☎ 03/433-0835
forrestergallery.com

Steampunk HQ
✉ 1 Itchen St.
☎ 027/778-6547
💲 $
steampunk
oamaru.co.nz

Moeraki Boulders

One of the more curious geological sights in New Zealand, the Moeraki Boulders are 49 miles (78 km) from Dunedin, just off the highway from Oamaru. Almost perfect spheres of gray rock up to 10 feet (3 m) across lie scattered along the beach, half buried in the sand.

Southern Maori tradition has it that the boulders are food baskets washed overboard from the ancestral canoe, Te Araiteuru, which brought Maori to New Zealand from the homeland, Hawaiki. Geologists say they are concretions, a product of the crystallizing process of mudstone. They usually form before the surrounding sedimentary rock, making them harder and less subject to weathering. You can see boulders still emerging from the cliff as it erodes.

A café above the beach caters to the throngs, and around the bay along the fine beach lies the pretty village of Moeraki, once a whaling station.

Central Otago

In the shadow of the Southern Alps, the schist plateau of Central Otago is a harsh, eerie land-scape of craggy mountains, arid grasslands, and lakes, one of the finest scenes on the glorious New Zealand canvas. At the foot of the alps on a superb lake, Queenstown is the country's number one alpine resort, Wanaka is a smaller version, and other old gold towns and wineries wait to be explored.

Cafés and souvenir shops abound in popular Queenstown.

Cromwell to Alexandra

Most of Central Otago is sparsely populated, but it was not always so, for in the 1860s thousands flocked to the region's goldfields, the richest in the country and the driving force for the early settlement of New Zealand.

The richest fields were around Cromwell, and a number of points of interest lie near Cromwell and Alexandra. Old gold mines and ghost towns dot the hills, lakes nestle in dammed valleys, and wineries now flourish where tent cities once housed miners.

Cromwell is a town with a split personality. Its modern town center is a car-free pedestrian precinct. On its outskirts are the Wild West streetscapes of Old Cromwell Town, a collection of a dozen historic buildings relocated after the town was flooded by the Clyde Dam in 1993. Tourist shops, art galleries, and cafés make this a pleasant stop. Cromwell's newest attraction is the **Highlands Motorsport Park** (*SH6, tel 03/445-4052, highlands.co.nz*), a motor racing circuit, where outside race days you can hit the track in a go-cart or race car, as a driver or passenger. There's also a motorsport museum (*$$*).

Cromwell also has plenty of accommodations when other towns are booked in summer. **Cromwell Visitor Information Centre** (*47 The Mall, tel 03/445-0212*) has a wealth of information on wineries and old mining settlements to explore in the surrounding district.

A five-minute drive south of Cromwell, the hamlet of **Bannockburn** has a clutch of old buildings from its gold-mining past. To the north of town, a road leads past the Mt Difficulty Winery to the old sluices where miners dug in what was Otago's richest alluvial goldfield. A signposted walking trail provides a glimpse of goldfield history.

Seventeen miles (27 km) north of Cromwell off SH8, a steep gravel road leads to the ghost town of **Bendigo** and beyond to the old gold diggings. Bendigo is now nothing more than a couple of old stone cottages, part of a nearby winery, but there is an interesting walk through the old goldfields, 1.8 miles (3 km) farther up a steep road. The desert countryside with its schist rock outcroppings is dramatic.

Just past the Clyde Dam as you head toward Alexandra, the pretty village of **Clyde** is an oasis of greenery in the desert, with European trees and well-watered lawns. Historic stone buildings line the main street, with cafés for a lunchtime stop and a selection of accommodations. A walking trail follows the town's emerald green river; you can also bike along the **Otago Central Rail Trail** (see p. 117 and sidebar below), which ends here.

EXPERIENCE:
Otago Central Rail Trail

Bicycling is a surprisingly popular way to tour New Zealand, given all those mountains, but for the hill shy, the mostly flat Otago Central Rail Trail is an excellent way to explore the goldfields and desert country of Central Otago.

The rail line from Dunedin to Clyde opened up the region, but the trains stopped running in 1963. The track from Middlemarch to Clyde was ripped up in the 1980s, but eventually it became the 95-mile (150 km) Otago Central Rail Trail in 2000. This is the original Great Ride, and still one of the most popular.

A tourist steam train (see p. 241) still runs from Dunedin to Middlemarch, a scenic way to reach the eastern end of this popular bicycling route. Touring bicycles can be rented in Clyde, Alexandra, Middlemarch, and Dunedin, or tour operators run all-inclusive tours. For a comprehensive rundown on the trail and operators, see the excellent *otagocentralrailtrail.co.nz*.

Alexandra is an attractive, well-stocked town and a good base from which to explore the surrounding area, especially for mountain bikers. As well as the Otago Central Rail Trail, other Great Rides include the **Roxburgh**

Queenstown

🏔 Map p. 234

Visitor Information

✉ Shotover &
Camp Sts.

☎ 03/442-4100

**queenstownsite
.co.nz**

**Dept. of
Conservation
Visitor Centre**

✉ 50 Stanley St.

☎ 03/442-7935

Trail from Alexandra to Lake Roxburgh, a scenic one-day ride in two sections connected by a jet boat ride. From Lake Roxburgh, the equally scenic **Clutha Gold Trail** (45 miles/73 km, two days) heads to Lawrence. Wineries abound and Alexandra has an interesting museum at the information center (*21 Centennial Ave., tel 03/448-9515*) highlighting the gold rush.

INSIDER TIP:

Queenstown is *the* place for skydiving. It's the world's adventure capital *and* you get to see the Southern Alps from the sky. Visit *nzonesky dive.co.nz* to get details on jumps.

—CHARLOTTE BUEB
*National Geographic
Intelligent Travel blog contributor*

A pleasant walk along the river leads to historic **Shaky Bridge,** just below the **Alexandra clock,** a town icon set into the rugged hills. You can wander to the clock for fine views or drive to the **Tucker Hill Lookout** for the best overlook of the whole valley.

Queenstown

On the shores of Lake Wakatipu, set against jagged mountains aptly named The Remarkables, Queenstown is the South Island's most famous tourist destination, a well-endowed alpine resort in one of its most stunning settings.

Walk down to the lake through The Mall past just a handful of the town's many restaurants and bars and you'll hear a dozen languages spoken. In summer, tour operators offer every activity and tour imaginable, the restaurants buzz, and the bars hop until the wee hours. With well over a million visitors a year, Queenstown Lakes is one of the fastest-growing regions in New Zealand. This is a resort for all seasons and tastes, from luxury indulgences to backpackers' bars, from summer hiking to winter skiing, from superb scenery to adventure pursuits.

Gold Fever

Queenstown attracted Maori greenstone hunters before William Gilbert Rees established the area's first farm in 1860. But sheep farming was soon forgotten when shearers discovered gold in the Shotover River in 1862. Even Rees's homestead was designated a goldfield, but he did well from the rush, selling meat to miners and shipping supplies and gold across the lake.

Named after Queen Victoria, Queenstown and neighboring Arrowtown were deluged with fortune seekers, but the area went into decline as the gold petered out. By 1900, Queenstown's population had dwindled to 200, and it would have to wait until the 1970s for a new gold rush—tourism.

The best place to start a tour of Queenstown is on the **Skyline Gondola** *(Brecon St., tel 03/441-0101, skyline.co.nz, $$$),* which shuttles up Bob's Peak through a gash in the pine trees to a viewing terminal with a restaurant. Views of The Remarkables and the town are breathtaking year-round. The adventurous can tandem paraglide

TSS *Earnslaw (tel 03/249-6000, realjourneys.co.nz, $$$$$),* the coal-fired Lady of the Lake, departing from the refurbished steamer wharf on Beach Street. Check out the engine rooms and historic displays. Some cruises also take in the **Walter Peak Farm,** a homestead and farm in a beautifully scenic lakeshore setting.

Paragliding high above Queenstown and Lake Wakatipu

back down, the foolhardy can bungee jump, the fun-loving can take a second chairlift at the top and luge back, and the energetic can walk or bike the trails.

The national bird, the kiwi, can be viewed at the small **Kiwi Birdlife Park** *(tel 03/442-8061, kiwibird.co.nz, $$$$),* next to the gondola terminal on Brecon Street. The rare and not-so-rare birds here include the kea, weka, kakariki parrots, and the endangered black stilt. Maori displays and conservation shows round out the tourist experience.

Another impressive way to view Queenstown is aboard the

A short walk from the city center, **Queenstown Gardens** provide a pleasant stroll around flower plantings and pine stands, with fine views of the lake and The Remarkables. A skating rink is open from April to October.

Not much is left of Queenstown's historic buildings, but **William's Cottage,** on the corner of Marine Parade and Earl Street, is Queenstown's oldest building, dating from 1864. Restored to its original condition, it is now a shop.

Underwater Observatory *(tel 03/442-0000, $),* part of the Kawerau jet boat complex on the jetty at the end of The Mall, is a submerged observatory; you can see giant trout through cloudy glass.

For many visitors, Queenstown is about the activities that can be booked at the busy visitor information center or at one of the vendors on Shotover Street. Looking for something to do? How about bungee jumping, jet boating, white-water rafting, river surfing, canyoneering, skydiving, hang gliding, parasailing, kayaking, or horseback riding? Or try a fishing, walking, winery, or mountain-bike tour.

EXPERIENCE:
Routeburn Track

Many rate this Department of Conservation (DOC)–designated Great Walk as the best in the country, but with numbers of hikers rivaling the Milford Track, it must be booked ahead from October to April, preferably online (doc.govt.nz, search for Routeburn) before you come to New Zealand. The track offers a wide variety of terrain and the country's best alpine scenery through Mount Aspiring and Fiordland National Parks. It is normally a three-day walk from Glenorchy, near Queenstown, to The Divide in Fiordland, traversing beech forest and alpine terrain. Transportation to the start can be arranged in Queenstown, as well as from The Divide at the other end. The four DOC huts and two campsites must be prebooked during the peak season.

Scenic flights buzz the heavens for great views of the South Island's mountains, lakes, and fjords. Queenstown is also a good place in which to arrange tours to other parts of the South Island for those short of time, particularly to Milford Sound by bus or air.

For information on walks around town, and some of the world's finest hiking nearby in the Southern Alps, head to the (DOC) office on Stanley Street.

Around Queenstown

Whereas development drives Queenstown, delightful **Arrowtown,** 13 miles (21 km) northeast, clings to its goldfield heritage. In a valley backed by rugged mountains, shade trees line peaceful streets, and many original buildings from the gold rush survive. The picturesque main drag, Buckingham Street, is lined with eateries and tourist stores, and a selection of lodgings offer an alternative retreat from Queenstown.

Gold discovered in the Arrow River in 1862 built the town. Today the **Lakes District Museum & Gallery** (49 Buckingham St., tel 03/442-1824) fields visitor queries, has displays on the town's mining history, and rents out gold pans so you can try your luck in the river.

Off the top end of Buckingham Street, the old gold diggings are worth a look. Here you'll find the **Chinese settlement,** with its original stone buildings and displays on the hardships faced by Chinese miners. Good walking trails lead through the hills around town, and a 4WD track heads into the mountains to remote **Macetown,** with ghost town relics in a scenic gorge.

The quickest route from Queenstown to Arrowtown is the main highway SH6, but take Gorge Road out of Queenstown for the scenic back route with its glorious blend of pastoral and alpine views. It passes Arthur's Point, 3 miles (5 km) north of Queenstown, where jet boats hurtle along the Shotover River. The **Queenstown Trail** *(queens towntrail.co.nz),* a 75-mile (120 km) Great Ride mountain bike loop, also takes in this way to Arrowtown, as well as the Kawerau River and Gibbston Valley.

Another detour off the back road leads to **Coronet Peak** ski area, where lifts operate in summer for sightseers and mountain bikers. Nearby is **Skippers Canyon,** an old gold-mining area and adventure playground for bungee jumping and white-water rafting. Note that most rental car companies forbid travel on the scenic but hair-raising Skippers Road.

Queenstown's and the world's first bungee-jumping site was at the old **Kawarau Bridge,** 14 miles (23 km) northeast of town on SH6. **A. J. Hackett Bungy** (see p. 252; *tel 03/450-1300, $$$$$*) offers the complete bungee experience with a variety of jumps, zipline rides, plus a café and shop in a modern complex. This is the place to jump, and you'll have plenty of onlookers, including clapping tour groups who delight in the bravery, or foolishness, of others.

Two miles (3 km) east on SH6, **Gibbston Valley Winery** *(tel 03/442-6910)* is the best known of the area's many vineyards and one of the pioneers of Central Otago's renowned Pinot Noir. Informative half-hour vineyard and wine cellar tours *($$)* with tastings are held throughout the day. Pick up a local wineries map to put together a tour in the region.

Ski Wonderland

Queenstown is New Zealand's premier ski resort in winter, with four main ski areas nearby. **Coronet Peak** is the closest to Queenstown, 11 miles (18 km) away with runs suitable for all abilities and weekend night skiing. Noted for its views, **The Remarkables** field is 50 minutes away by car or bus and is good for beginner to intermediate skiers. **Cardrona,** on the way to Wanaka, is a high-altitude field noted for dry snow and wide slopes, while **Treble Cone,** close to Wanaka, is the largest and particularly good for advanced skiers and for boarders.

A scenic road heads 25 miles (40 km) west of Queenstown to **Glenorchy,** hugging Lake Wakatipu all the way. In a glorious setting, this tiny outpost is a hive of adventure activity with jet boating, kayaking, and skydiving.

Glenorchy is also the place to arrange a ride to the trailheads of some of New Zealand's finest hikes, including the famed **Routeburn Track** (see sidebar opposite), a three-day hike through the alps to Fiordland. Some walkers choose to return via the **Greenstone** or **Caples Tracks,** or these two can be combined as a four- to five-day loop walk through forested valleys, ending at Lake Wakatipu. The more demanding **Rees-Dart Track** takes in valley and alpine pass terrain.

Adrenaline Rush

Though extreme activities and sport are now found around the globe, New Zealand popularized adventure tourism and still proudly calls itself the "adrenaline capital of the world."

Jet boating on the Shotover River, Queenstown

Bungee jumping, based on Vanuatu land divers who jump off a wooden tower with vines tied to their ankles, originated in New Zealand with A. J. Hackett, a Kiwi daredevil who grabbed headlines by plunging off the Eiffel Tower in 1987. A year later, Hackett founded the world's first commercial bungee operation at the Kawarau Bridge just outside Queenstown (see p. 251). The Kawarau site is still the most popular place to jump, but you can also throw yourself off the Queenstown gondola, 335-foot-deep (102 m) Skippers Canyon (see p. 251), or a host of other places.

Watersports

Jet boating, though relatively sedate by comparison, is another New Zealand invention. Self-taught engineer Bill Hamilton developed a boat that would negotiate the swift, shallow rivers of the South Island. Using a hydro-jet engine, which shoots out water through a steerable nozzle, the jet boat scoots along the water with most of the hull above the surface, reducing drag and allowing for ferocious speeds with high maneuverability. The design has plenty of commercial applications, but in New Zealand the jet boat is best known as a thrill-seeking craft, hurtling passengers along rivers all over the country. Queenstown is known as the home of the jet boat, with rides offered on the Shotover and Kawarau Rivers.

With so many swift-flowing rivers, New Zealand has taken to white-water rafting like a duck to, well, white water. The Shotover and Kawerau Rivers are popular sites, as are the Rangitata and Buller Rivers, also in the South Island. The North Island has plenty of rafting as well, the most exciting being the Kaituna River near Rotorua, which goes over 10-foot (3 m) Okere Falls.

Riding the rapids gave rise to black-water rafting, an inner-tube ride through a cave at Waitomo on the North Island (see p. 112). Operators have since dreamed up a number of other caving adventures, including underground rock climbing and rappelling.

Zorbing & More

Jumping off mountains and out of planes is another New Zealand specialty, usually while strapped to someone who knows what he or she is doing. Parasailing off Bob's Peak in Queenstown (see p. 249) is a spectacular way to see the town, while Wanaka and Taupo are noted tandem skydiving centers.

Variations on a theme include bungee swinging, rap jumping, and river sledging. Inventive New Zealanders have also come up with Zorbing (rolling downhill in a giant plastic ball outside Rotorua; see p. 129) and Shweeb (Rotorua again), a pedal-powered, upside-down-monorail tube that reaches surprisingly high speeds.

Those not walking or flying to Fiordland and Milford Sound will have to take the SH6 south from Queenstown through dramatic desert landscapes. At the bottom of Lake Wakatipu SH6 runs through Kingston, once the railhead and port for the steamers that plied the lake to Queenstown, before you reach the turnoff to SH94, which heads over the Southern Alps to the fjords.

Wanaka

Lying on a superb lake backed by snow-topped mountains, with skiing in winter and a host of activities year-round, Wanaka is inevitably described as a mini-Queenstown. With plenty of accommodations and restaurants but without Queenstown's crowds, Wanaka's setting seems even more spectacular, if only because development doesn't compete so volubly with nature.

Nevertheless Wanaka (pop. 9,700) is growing rapidly, attracting residents as well as visitors to the shores of **Lake Wanaka,** popular for boating, fishing, waterskiing, and swimming from the beach in the town center.

Wanaka is also the gateway to the hiking trails and snowy peaks of Mount Aspiring National Park and to the **Treble Cone** and **Cardrona** ski fields, 12 miles (20 km) and 21 miles (34 km) away, respectively. Cardrona is near the tiny township of the same name, along the high-altitude 73-mile (117 km) Cardrona Road between Wanaka and Queenstown, a scenic alternative to SH6.

Wanaka has myriad activities,

from lake cruises and jet boating to white-water rafting, kayaking, and canyoneering (which involves rappelling down waterfalls, among other thrills). Aerial activities include flight-seeing, skydiving, and paragliding operating out of Wanaka's busy little airport. There you'll also find the **Warbirds & Wheels Museum** (tel 03/443-7010, warbirdsandwheels .co.nz, $). Based around its fine collection of World War II fighter planes, the museum provides fascinating insight into the history of

Cinema Paradiso

For a unique dinner and movie experience, try Wanaka's Cinema Para-diso (Ardmore St., 03/443-1505, paradiso.net.nz). **It has a full menu that can be enjoyed before the film, during intermission, or afterward. Paradiso offers a variety of seating, including vintage couches, an upholstered car, and seats from a Chinese airplane.**

aviation. Its collection features in the **Warbirds Over Wanaka** air show, held every second year, and also includes classic cars.

Also at the airport, the **National Transport & Toy Museum** (tel 03/443-8765, nttmuseumwanaka .co.nz) has a huge, disparate collection, from Barbie dolls to classic cars and aircraft, and if that palls, hit the attached craft brewery.

On the way to the airport toward Cromwell, **Puzzling World** (tel 03/443-7489, puzzlingworld.com, $$) on SH6 is a quirky attraction

Wanaka

Map p. 234

Visitor Information

Lakefront, 103 Ardmore St.

03/443-1233

lakewanaka.co.nz

featuring skewed buildings, optical illusions, and a fun maze.

Mount Aspiring National Park

Straddling the Southern Alps, Mount Aspiring National Park's mix of remote wilderness, alpine meadows, and forested river valleys makes it heaven for hikers and mountaineers.

Part of the Te Wahipounamu South West New Zealand World Heritage site, the park is centered around the jagged peak of Mount Aspiring near Wanaka. To the west and south, the park extends into the dense forest of Fiordland, while its north includes Haast Pass, the gateway to the West Coast.

INSIDER TIP:

The huts in New Zealand's national parks are comfortable and clean and make multiday hikes an absolute must for outdoor enthusiasts.

—CHRISTY RIZZO
Adventure travel expert

The southern reaches closer to Queenstown are the best known to hikers. Here you'll find the famous **Routeburn Track** (see sidebar p. 250) and other popular trails. However, the most visited part of the park is the northern end, where SH6 cuts through from Wanaka to the West Coast.

Glacier-carved valleys punctuate rugged peaks in the park, and **Mount Aspiring,** known as New

Zealand's Matterhorn because of its steep faces, is the only peak over 10,000 feet (3,000 m) outside of Aoraki/Mount Cook National Park. Rugged high-altitude terrain, snow, and ice make much of the park accessible only to experienced mountaineers, but alpine guides in Wanaka offer mountaineering courses for beginners, as well as guided hikes.

Hikes in the Matukituki Valley near Wanaka provide easy access to the central reaches of the park. A one-hour drive from Wanaka, the **West Matukituki Track** goes from the parking lot to the Aspiring Hut *(2 hr. one-way)* for great views of the valley; experienced hikers can climb to the top of the valley *(3.5 hr. more)*.

The more popular **Rob Roy Track** branches off the West Matukituki Track, 15 minutes from the parking lot, and is an easy three- to four-hour walk that crosses the river before climbing through a gorge into beech forest, then into a scenic alpine valley.

For information on the park, contact DOC offices in Wanaka and Queenstown, the Haast Visitor Centre (see p. 229) at Haast township on the West Coast, or the Makarora Tourist Centre *(tel 03/443-8372, makarora .co.nz),* on the edge of the park on SH6 between Wanaka and Haast.

Haast Highway

The road from Wanaka to the West Coast is one of the most spectacular drives in the country, with a number of scenic stops on the way. It crosses the Haast Pass, the most south-

Rippon Vineyard overlooking Lake Wanaka

erly of the three main passes through the Southern Alps.

The main highway, SH6, heads north of Wanaka to **Lake Hawea** and its tiny resort town, then tracks along the lake shore and across The Neck, a narrow strip of land separating Lake Hawea from the northern end of Lake Wanaka. The lake and mountain scenery on this stretch is magnificent, but the real jaw-dropping begins when the road enters the rugged wilderness of Mount Aspiring National Park. The road then leaves Lake Wanaka and follows the Makarora River upstream to the **Makarora Tourist Centre,** a welcome stop with café/bar and accommodations.

Six miles (10 km) from Makarora, an easy 30-minute round-trip walk leads over a river swing bridge and through beech forest to the scenic **Blue Pools,** where trout feed at the mouth of Blue River. A little farther along, at **Cameron Creek,** a

15-minute round-trip walk to a viewing platform is rewarded with spectacular views of the valley and the surrounding mountains.

For the best views, the **Haast Pass** at 1,847 feet (563 m) marks the highest point on the road. A trail leads up above the timberline to a viewpoint with stunning vistas. This more demanding walk takes just over an hour.

Over the pass, the highway follows the Haast River to the coast. Along the way it passes a number of waterfalls, including the high **Thunder Creeks Falls,** an easy five-minute walk from the road through forest. A couple of miles farther, **Pleasant Flat** is indeed a pleasant picnic/camping area next to a mountain stream.

The road continues its descent to the coast, and halfway between Haast Pass and Haast township, the **Roaring Billy Waterfall** can be reached by a fine 25-minute round-trip walk through lush forest and tree ferns. ∎

Stunning fjords, peaks, lakes, and rich farmland ringed by scenic coastline and anchored by Stewart Island

Fiordland & Southland

The renowned Milford Track takes in such spectacles as MacKay Falls.

Fiordland & Southland

Below Dunedin and the 45th parallel, the deep south is as close as most people get to Antarctica, to which New Zealand was once attached. Fjords, lakes, hiking trails, and the surprising fecundity of remote Stewart Island make it worth the trip.

Mount Tutoko, Fiordland's highest peak

Ancient glaciers carved the primordial landscape of Fiordland, leaving behind the famous fjords of the southwest coast, which shelter from the sea behind alpine peaks and dense forest. To the east, on the leeward side of the mountains, the wilderness yields to glacial lakes and the spreading grasslands of Southland sheep farms.

The region's main lure, Milford Sound, draws a road train of tour buses daily from Queenstown, and with good reason. A boat trip through the fjord and its cathedral of peaks is stunning, but getting there is half the reward. The road to Milford travels through the most accessible reach of New Zealand's

most imposing wilderness: Fiordland National Park, the largest in New Zealand and part of Te Wahipounamu South West New Zealand World Heritage site. Thousands of visitors flock to the park each year, most staying overnight in the small resort of Te Anau on the scenic lake of the same name, the last town before Milford Sound.

Much smaller Manapouri township on another fine, eponymous lake is the departure point for Doubtful Sound, the only other fjord to have regular tours. Apart from these two fjords, the rest of the park remains virtually untouched. It has, however, some of the greatest hiking trails in the country, among them the Milford Track and the Kepler Track.

NOT TO BE MISSED:

While Fiordland is wilderness untamed, neighboring Southland has been formed by the human hand. Scottish settlers labored in a harsh domain to create rich sheep farms, and their heritage lives on. The names of towns and rivers mimic Scotland, and the Scottish "burr" lingers on in the voices of Southland.

Southland's prime attraction is the coastal route through the Catlins between Invercargill and Dunedin. Scenery ranges from rugged coastline and sweeping beaches to inland forest and waterfalls. This remote southeast corner of the South Island also teems with sea life, notably seals, sea lions, dolphins, and penguins, including the rare yellow-eyed penguin.

Lying below the South Island, a remote last stop before Antarctica, is one last delightful surprise. Stewart Island, just across the Foveaux Strait, is washed by remarkably warm currents. It has sheltered coves, white-sand bays, and forests with giant ferns: the last jewel in New Zealand's abundant crown. ■

TASMAN SEA

Mt. Pembroke
Milford Sound
Stirling Falls
Mitre Peak
Milford
Homer Tunnel
Lake Ada
94
Lake Marian
The Divide
MILFORD TK.
Murchison Mts.
Lake Te Anau
Knobs Flat
Mirror Lakes
Eglinton / Earl Mts.
Clinton
Hollyford
Eglinton
Cleddau

Doubtful Sound
Lake Orbell
Te Anau
Glowworm Caves
Deep Cove
KEPLER TK.
Te Anau
Wilmot Pass
Manapouri Power Station
West Arm
Manapouri
94
FIORDLAND NATIONAL PARK
Mossburn
6
Lumsden

Dusky Sound
Ohai
94
90
Lake Hauroko
Clifden
96
Gore
1
8
Tuatapere
Te Waewae
6
96
93
Balclutha
Te Waewae Bay
99
Anderson Park & Art Gallery
1
Mataura
CATLINS FOREST PARK
Kaka Point
Monkey Island
Colac Bay/Oraka
Riverton
INVERCARGILL
Owaka
Nugget Point
McLean Falls
Bluff
Fortrose
Waikawa
Cathedral Caves
Bluff Hill
Otara
Curio Bay
Porpoise Bay
NORTHWEST CIRCUIT
Foveaux Strait
Maori Beach
Bluff Ferry
PACIFIC OCEAN
RAKIURA TK.
Ackers Point Lighthouse
Halfmoon Bay (Oban)
Ulva Island
Mason Bay
Paterson Inlet
STEWART ISLAND
RAKIURA NATIONAL PARK

Area of map detail
Auckland
Wellington
Christchurch
New Zealand

0   60 kilometers
0   30 miles

Fiordland

The scenery doesn't get any more spectacular than in remote, brooding Fiordland, with its rugged mountains and stunning fjords. Fiordland National Park encompasses almost the whole region, including famed Milford Sound, one of the country's main tourist attractions, and Doubtful Sound. On the edge of the park, the resort towns of Te Anau and Manapouri accommodate visitors.

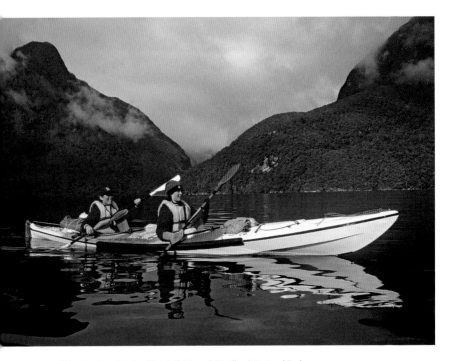

Enjoying the solitude of Doubtful Sound, Fiordland National Park

Fiordland National Park

🏔 Map p. 259

DOC Visitor Centre

✉ Lakefront Dr., Te Anau

☎ 03/249-7924

doc.govt.nz/parks
-and-recreation
/places-to-go
/fiordland/places
/fiordland-national
-park

Fiordland National Park

The wildest, wettest, and most remote part of New Zealand is also its most breathtaking. Drenched by the roaring forties, the winds that blow unimpeded across the Southern Ocean, the park's towering mountains are rent by water—sea, lakes, and rivers.

Most visitors to the park seek the famed beauty of Milford Sound, accessed by road from Te Anau along one of the world's most scenic routes. The other main destination is Doubtful Sound, a quieter introduction to the fjords.

Formed by tectonic folds and faults in the Earth's crust dating back 500 million years, the park is composed mostly of gneiss, schist, and granite rock. Glaciers have gouged the landscape over the last two million years to create deep U-shaped valleys, many of which have filled with water to become fjords and inland lakes.

Forest clings to steep rock faces, growing in only a thin layer of soil, and tree avalanches are common. Beech forest dominates and is often moss draped. Above 3,300 feet (1,000 m), tussock grass and alpine flowers grow.

The park is home to threatened birds, including the colorful, flightless takahe, once thought extinct until discovered in the Murchison Mountains, above the Te Anau Glowworm Caves, in 1948. The last few remaining kakapo, another flightless Fiordland parrot, have been transferred to offshore islands away from predators. Yellow-crowned parakeets, robins, kaka, and long- and short-tailed bats thrive in the Eglinton Valley. Many other species exist throughout the park, including the brown kiwi.

Marine life here is unique. High rainfall creates a layer of freshwater on the sounds. Stained by tannins washed down from the forest, this layer gives the calm waters a black, glassy surface that restricts light to all but the top 130 feet (40 m) of the sounds. Subtropical, cool-water, and deep-water fish all thrive closer to the surface among the sponges and rare black coral trees.

Mountains and water dominate Fiordland. Milford Sound averages 255 inches (650 cm) and more than 180 days of rain a year. Sunshine is a rarity, but the fecund weather is dramatic

when rain pours down and dozens of waterfalls ribbon along sheer mountain sides.

Te Anau & Manapouri

Lying next to Lake Te Anau, the South Island's largest lake, the township of Te Anau is the jumping-off point for Milford Sound in Fiordland National Park. This prosperous, pretty resort is a mini-Queenstown, well supplied with hotels and restaurants, as well as lake and mountain views.

Though a pleasant base, Te Anau has few attractions in itself, but the **Punanga Manu o Te Anau/Te Anau Bird Sanctuary** (tel 03/249-7924) on Manapouri Road, a ten-minute

Te Anau
🅰 Map p. 259
Visitor Information
✉ Lakefront Dr.
☎ 03/249-8900
fiordland.org.nz

EXPERIENCE:
Hiking Fiordland

Fiordland National Park contains three of the country's nine Great Walks (see p. 19) and a number of merely grand ones. The Great Walks are Department of Conservation (DOC)–controlled trails encompassing the best hiking in the country. In summer, they must be booked at DOC offices or, better, online well in advance at doc.govt.nz.

The **Milford Track** is best known (see pp. 264–265) but the **Routeburn Track** (see p. 250) competes as one of the finest walks in New Zealand. It is normally walked from Glenorchy, near Queenstown, to The Divide in the park, but it can also be done in reverse. The other Great Walk is the **Kepler Track** (see p. 262), a three- or four-day strenuous loop walk from Lake Te Anau to Mount Luxmore and Lake Manapouri.

Te Anau Glowworm Caves

 Map p. 259

✉ Real Journeys, Visitor Centre, Lakefront Dr., Te Anau

☎ 03/249-6000

$ $$$$$

realjourneys.co.nz

walk from the DOC visitor center, displays a wide range of native birds, including the rare takahe, and provides an informative introduction to the species found in the national park. The track around the lake makes for a scenic walk, and leads to the start of the **Kepler Track,** one of New Zealand's finest hikes. It's an easy stroll along the

illuminated by hundreds of twinkling, web-spinning glowworms (see sidebar p. 112).

Te Anau's sister town is the small hamlet of Manapouri, just 13 miles (21 km) south in another beautiful location on Lake Manapouri. This resort is the departure point for trips to Doubtful Sound (see p. 267).

Hermit of Milford

One of the highlights of the Milford Track is the high Sutherland Falls, named after Donald Sutherland (1843–1919), the hermit of Milford Sound. An adventurer, the young Scotsman was in turn a fisherman, soldier under Garibaldi in Italy, and merchant seaman before jumping ship in New Zealand. He fought in the Maori wars and was a sealer and gold prospector before setting sail in a small boat from Dunedin with his dog in

1877. He landed in Milford Sound and made it his home for 40 years. Living a hermit's life for many years, he prospected and explored the region, but ended his isolation in 1890 when he married Elizabeth Samuels in Dunedin. They built the Chalet at Milford, catering to summer visitors after the opening of the Milford Track. A taciturn host, Sutherland was a self-proclaimed authority on the region, which he regarded as his own realm.

lake section of the Kepler to Brod Bay, or the superfit can day-hike up to Luxmore Hut and back for expansive views.

The town's top diversion lies across the lake. The **Te Anau Glowworm Caves** are reached by a lake cruise, then a walking tour that follows the pounding water of an underground stream. The stream originates in Lake Orbell high above in the Murchison Mountains before disgorging into Lake Te Anau. Named Te Anau-au, or "cave of swirling waters," by early Maori visitors, the caves were not rediscovered until 1948.

Cave tours end with a boat ride through a darkened grotto

Te Anau to Milford

If the Milford Track is the finest walk in the world, then the 74-mile (119 km) road from Te Anau to Milford Sound must be one of the world's finest drives. As the road approaches the park's great hulking mountains, you'll find yourself craning your neck from your vehicle to take them all in. Chains must be carried in winter.

A number of short walks and viewpoints along the road allow you to fully appreciate the splendor of the terrain. An excellent first stop out of Te Anau, tranquil **Mirror Lakes** at the 36-mile (58 km) mark is easily reached via a boardwalk next to the road. The small lakes reflect the towering Earl Mountains for a postcard photo opportunity.

The Eglinton Valley broadens out at the tiny settlement of **Knobs Flat** (39-mile/63 km mark) and the stretch of road known as the **Avenue of the Disappearing Mountains,** so called because of the optical illusion that seems to make the string of mountains on either side disappear. Farther on, the **Lake Gunn Nature Walk** leads through red beech forest for a pleasant 45-minute round-trip walk.

INSIDER TIP:

One of the best ways to experience Milford Sound is on an overnight cruise. You'll cover the entire sound with enough time to soak up beautiful scenery (realjourneys.co.nz).

—JORGE I. NÚÑEZ
*National Geographic
research grantee*

The Divide (52-mile/85 km mark) is the lowest pass through the Southern Alps at 1,740 feet (531 m) and is a trailhead for one of New Zealand's greatest walks, the **Routeburn Track** (see p. 250). For a taste of the splendor of the Routeburn, you can walk just part of it to **Key Summit** *(2–3 hr. round-trip)* for stunning views.

Just past The Divide is the turnoff to **Hollyford Valley** along a gravel road. One mile (1.6 km) in

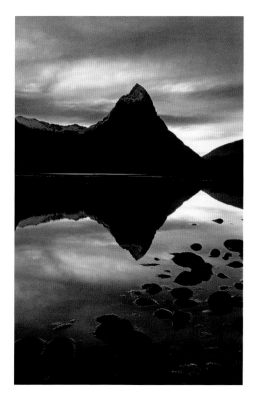

Mitre Peak mirrored in Milford Sound at sunset

is the trail to **Lake Marion Falls.** A lovely 20-minute walk leads from a suspension bridge to the gantry overlooking the falls; another steep one-hour walk leads to alpine **Lake Marion. Gunns Camp,** 11 miles (17 km) from the main road, has a store and small museum crammed with local detritus.

The main road continues to climb to **Homer Tunnel** (63-mile/101 km mark). After nearly 20 years of construction, the 4,170-foot (1,270 m) tunnel opened in 1954 and made Milford Sound accessible to the world. The road then descends sharply through the *(continued on p. 266)*

Walk: Milford Track

Billed in New Zealand as the "finest walk in the world," the Milford Track from Lake Te Anau to Milford Sound takes in all the diverse glory of Fiordland—lakes, alpine meadows, mountains, glaciers, and fjords.

From late October to late April, this popular walk can be done only in one direction as a four-day, three-night hike. Just 40 independent hikers are allowed on the track each day, so reserve months ahead *(starting July 1, doc.govt.nz).*

Bookings are not required in winter, but snow and avalanches make it suitable only for experienced alpine hikers. Be well equipped for all weather (expect plenty of rain) and carry all your own food. You will overnight in basic huts, which have cooking facilities, toilets, and bunks with mattresses. The track can also be done as a pricey guided walk *(ultimatehikes.co.nz)* with food and transportation, staying at more luxurious huts with hot showers.

Start with a cruise on Lake Te Anau from Te Anau Downs to **Glade Wharf ❶**. The track crosses a swing bridge over the Clinton River,

Hikers cross a wire bridge at Giant Gate Falls on the Milford Track.

NOT TO BE MISSED:
Mackinnon Memorial • Sutherland Falls • MacKay Falls • Giant Gate Falls

then follows the river through beech forest for an hour to **Clinton Hut ❷**, the first overnight stop and the end of a short Day One.

The walk begins in earnest on Day Two *(10 miles/16 km, 6 hours)* with a gradual climb following the river to **Clinton Forks** at a confluence with the river's North Branch. The trail follows the West Branch through mostly beech forest for about 40 minutes to a lake. A short side trail leads to **Hirere Falls.**

Back on the track, you enter a narrowing valley between granite walls before coming to grassy flats with glorious views north to Mackinnon Pass. The trail climbs through changing higher altitude flora before reaching **Mintaro Hut ❸** at the end of your second day.

Day Three *(8.7 miles/14 km, 6 hours)* resumes the climb to Mackinnon Pass for two hours to the fine views around **Mackinnon Memorial ❹**, dedicated to Quintin Mackinnon, who explored the area in 1888. It is then 20 minutes to the highest point of the track at the **Pass Day Shelter** (3,786 feet/1,154 m).

The walk then drops 3,280 feet (1,000 m) over 5 miles (8 km) past the Roaring Burn stream, a spectacular stretch of waterfalls and cascades. From the private **Quintin Hut,** a side trip *(1.5 hr. round-trip)* leads to the impressive **Sutherland Falls ❺**, the highest falls in New Zealand, dropping 1,904 feet (580 m) over three leaps. Back at Quintin Hut, it is a one-hour walk to **Dumpling Hut ❻** for a well-earned rest on the third night.

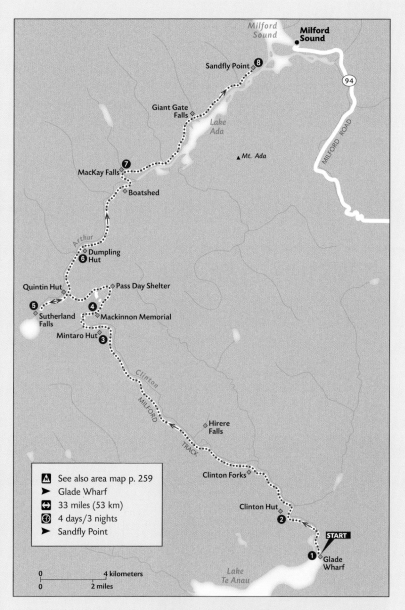

See also area map p. 259
Glade Wharf
33 miles (53 km)
4 days/3 nights
Sandfly Point

0   4 kilometers
0   2 miles

Day Four (*11 miles/18 km, 6 hours*) descends gradually from the hut to the Arthur River and down to the historic **Boatshed,** where a swing bridge crosses the river. You are then just 20 minutes away from **MacKay Falls ⑦** and Bell Rock. The track presses on to Lake Ada and

Giant Gate Falls, where a shelter makes an ideal stopping point for lunch.

About an hour past the lake you reach the flat end of the valley and **Sandfly Point ⑧,** where boats take you on the short last leg to Milford Sound.

M.S. Boat Tours:
Real Journeys
☎ 03/249-7416
$ $$$$$
realjourneys.co.nz

Southern
Discoveries
☎ 03/441-1137
$ $$$$$
southerndiscoveries
.co.nz

Jucy Cruize
☎ 03/442-4196
$ $$$$$
jucycruize.co.nz

Cleddau Valley to the last stop before Milford, **The Chasm.** An excellent 15-minute round-trip walk leads through glorious moss-draped forest to a waterfall and deep gorge carved by the river.

Milford Sound

Milford Sound is Fiordland's most famous attraction. Though not the largest of the fjords, its peaks make it the most spectacular. **Mitre Peak,** named for its resemblance to a bishop's hat, is the standout,

rising 5,551 feet (1,692 m) almost vertically from the sea.

The road from Te Anau ends at the small settlement of Milford, clinging to the end of Milford Sound. Dominated by a large cruise center resembling an international airport, the hamlet has a café/bar, a lodge, and a small airport, but not much else. Most visitors stay in Te Anau, though Milford is serene when tour groups have departed.

INSIDER TIP:

There's a reason it's so green and beautiful in the fjords: It rains. A lot. It may seem basic, but remember to bring a raincoat.

—JANE SUNDERLAND
National Geographic editor

Fjord cruises depart throughout the day, but try to avoid the insane peak time around 1 p.m. when the tour buses roll in. The many tour operators offer similar services of around two hours, which explore the 10-mile (16 km) length of the sound with stops to see plunging waterfalls and wildlife on the rocks.

Cruises turn around at the fjord's concealed entrance to the Tasman Sea, where Captain Cook sailed by thinking Milford was a cove. It took until 1810 for Europeans to discover the majesty that lay behind the bend.

Cruises return via the lovely **Stirling Falls** and **Harrison Cove**

A mossy beech forest along the Milford Track

with the impressive **Mount Pembroke** (6,608 feet/2,014 m) and its glacier looming behind. The **underwater observatory** at Harrison Cove can be visited to view black coral and sea life four stories below the surface (see sidebar right). From the airport, small sightseeing planes buzz Milford Sound throughout the day and provide a close-up view of the mountains, though the grandeur of the peaks mirrored in the glassy water is best appreciated at sea level. Kayak tours offer an adventurous alternative.

Doubtful Sound

Doubtful Sound is less visited than Milford Sound but no less beautiful. Though its peaks are not as immediately impressive, the second largest of the sounds is much more of a wilderness experience. Eight-hour cruises double as nature tours, and the fjord is home to seals, penguins, and bottlenose dolphins, a rarity this far south.

Captain Cook gave the fjord its name in 1770: Doubting that the winds in the sound would carry him back to sea, he sailed on by. A few hardy explorers and sealers visited, but it remained largely isolated until construction began on the Manapouri Power Station in the 1960s.

Trips to Doubtful Sound are very much an all-day (or overnight) experience, starting in Manapouri with a boat tour across **Lake Manapouri** to **West Arm,** where you board buses to spiral underground for 1.3 miles (2 km) to the **Manapouri**

Power Station when open. This hydroelectric station, completed in 1972, has massive turbines driven by lakewater surging down through a 6-mile (10 km) tunnel to Doubtful Sound at sea level.

EXPERIENCE: Beneath the Surface

Milford Sound's unique chemistry limits the amount of sunlight that penetrates the depths of the water. The darkness allows deepwater wildlife to live within 130 feet (40 m) of the surface. The result is a unique, life-filled environment that Jacques Cousteau said was one of his top-ten favorite dives. Creatures include red and black coral, 11-legged sea stars, tube worms, and scarlet wrasses. The **Milford Discovery Centre** (Harrison Cove, tel 03/441-1137, southerndiscoveries.co.nz) allows you to experience the sound from a viewing chamber 34 feet (10 m) down. **Descend Dive** (027/337-2363, descend.co.nz) operates from Milford Sound September–May. Dive cruises go every day at 9 a.m. in summer, otherwise on demand.

A spectacular road built to service the power plant then runs from West Arm to **Deep Cove** on Doubtful Sound, where cruises depart. The road goes through temperate rain forest, past moss gardens and the towering **Cleve Garth Falls,** and then over the 2,200-foot (670 m) **Wilmot Pass.** From the wharf at Deep Cove, cruises take in the length of the sound, similar in many ways to the Milford cruises, but without the distraction of hordes of visitors and the buzzing of overhead flights. ■

Mitre Peak Cruises
☎ 03/249-8110
$ $$$$$
mitrepeak.com

Doubtful Sound Boat Tours:

Real Journeys
✉ Real Journeys, Pearl Harbour, Manapouri
☎ 03/249-6600
🕐 8 hr. & overnight
$ $$$$$
realjourneys.co.nz

Fiordland Cruises
✉ 77 Manapouri-Te Anau Hwy.
☎ 03/249-7777
🕐 Overnight
$ $$$$$
doubtfulsound.com

Southland

The sheep-farming plains of Southland spread out from Invercargill, one of the world's most southerly cities. Southland is primarily a transit zone to Stewart Island or Fiordland, but the Catlins drive takes in wonderful coastal and forest scenery with wildlife-viewing opportunities. The Southern Scenic Route from Invercargill to Fiordland is similarly picturesque.

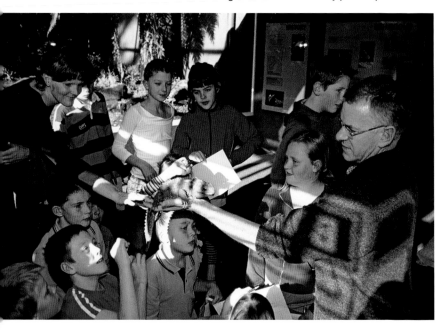

Schoolchildren touch a tuatara at the Southland Museum in Invercargill.

Invercargill

🅜 Map p. 259

Visitor Information

✉ Visitor Centre, Southland Museum & Art Gallery, Queens Park

☎ 03/211-0895

southlandnz.com

Invercargill

Southland's commercial hub and New Zealand's southernmost city, Invercargill (pop. 55,000) was founded in 1856 by Scottish settlers who laid out a well-planned town on a level site. Farming, then lumber and coal, resulted in rapid growth and fine Victorian buildings in the 19th century. The wool boom of the 1950s also brought great wealth, but Invercargill has struggled in recent decades and the tourism boom has largely passed it by.

Invercargill is a city of wide streets dotted with historic buildings and fine gardens, but it is mostly just an overnight stop along the Southern Scenic Route or on the way to Stewart Island.

The city's main focus is **Queens Park,** a 200-acre (81 ha) green lung with botanical gardens, aviary, animal enclosure, golf course, and more. At the park's main entrance, the **Southland Museum & Art Gallery** *(Queens Park, 108 Gala St., tel 03/219-9069, southlandmuseum.com)* has Maori and colonial exhibits, but of most interest are the "Beyond the Roaring 40s" gallery about the sub-Antarctic islands and the prehistoric tuatara reptiles (see sidebar this page), survivors of the dinosaur age.

Bluff

Drab Bluff, Invercargill's port 17 miles (28 km) to the south, is the end of the road. Or at least the end of SH1, which runs the length of the country from Cape Reinga in the north to Stirling Point on the south side of town, where a much photographed signpost points to more exotic worlds.

Southland's main location for exporting frozen meat, fertilizer, and aluminum is primarily a place to catch the ferry to Stewart Island. Points of interest include Bluff Hill for views of the island and the surrounding plains. The **Bluff Maritime Museum** *(241 Foreshore Rd., tel 03/212-7534)* traces the history of the port and local industry, including oyster dredging. Bluff is a mecca for oyster buffs, who eagerly await the opening of the season in March, when New Zealand's plumpest oysters go on sale and are shipped to restaurants all over the country.

Around Invercargill

The diligent Scottish settlers of Southland transformed swampy, tussock-covered plains into rich farmland that once produced more than 20 percent of the country's exports. In the days when the country "rode on the sheep's back," Southland sat tall. Those glory days have receded but sheep farming and dairying are still major industries.

Gore, 41 miles (66 km) north of Invercargill on SH1, is the main inland service town for Southland and also the country-music capital of New Zealand. Every May or

Tuataras

The Southland Museum in Invercargill has long been famous for its tuataras, relics from the age of the dinosaurs. The tuatara is the only surviving member of the Sphenodontidae family, lizardlike reptiles that thrived 220 million years ago. Extinct on the mainland and classified as endangered since 1895, the tuatara is found only on offshore islands and in captivity. The Southland Museum ran the first successful breeding program and exhibits the reptiles in its tuatarium. The star of the show is Henry, reputed to be more than 110 years old, and a grumpy old man by all accounts, with a habit of biting off his girlfriends' tails.

June the town comes alive for the ten-day **New Zealand Gold Guitar Awards.** The rest of the year it's a sleepy place straddling the Mataura River, with trout fishing the major tourist lure. The Gore visitor center *(Hokonui Dr. & Norfolk St., tel 03/203-9288)* has the full lowdown on the town.

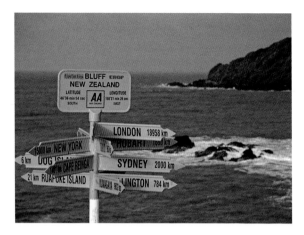

A signpost at Invercargill's Bluff points to distant destinations.

Most visitors bypass Gore and the plains in favor of the less direct but more scenic Catlins road (see Travelwise pp. 272–273) along the east coast or the western Southern Scenic Route to Te Anau.

Southern Scenic Route

The back road from Invercargill to Te Anau is a leisurely drive following SH99 west along the coast before turning inland. First stop of note is **Riverton,** 24 miles (39 km) from Invercargill. This pleasant but chilly seaside resort brashly bills itself as the Riviera of the South, and it does have good sheltered beaches. Farther west, **Colac Bay/Oraka** is a popular surfing spot immortalized by a statue of a surfer riding a wave.

At Te Waewae Bay, a short detour can be made to **Monkey Island,** a whale lookout for local Maori who called it Te Puka O Takatimu ("anchor stone of the Takatimu canoe"). Walk across to the island at low tide and up to the top of the hillock for great coastal and Fiordland views.

Tiny **Tuatapere,** about halfway along the scenic route, is the only town of any note before Manapouri. It has a visitor information office (tel 03/226-6739) with details on local attractions. Here you can book for the **Hump Ridge Track** (humpridgetrack .co.nz), a three-day loop through subalpine wilderness with coastal views and lodge accommodations. Next door, the **Bushman's Museum** (31 Orawia Rd., tel 03/226-6399) has displays on the region's sawmilling history.

Clifden, 8 miles (13 km) from Tuatapere, has a very old suspension bridge as well as caves just north of the town, but they are not developed and care should be taken. Clifden is also the turnoff to scenic **Lake Hauroko,** New Zealand's deepest, 19 miles (30 km) away on a mostly unpaved road. Walks at the lake range from 30 minutes to 3 hours long. ■

EXPERIENCE: Kiwi-Spotting

Few Kiwis (as New Zealanders call themselves) have seen a kiwi (the nocturnal bird and national symbol) in the wild. Though kiwi houses all over the country offer glimpses of these long-beaked, flightless birds, it requires great planning or luck to see them in their natural habitat. Some tour operators can give you a head start with kiwi guides.

One of the biggest concentrations of kiwis can be found on **Stewart Island** at the southernmost point of New Zealand. Populations of the Stewart Island brown kiwi, or tokoeka, number around 20,000. At **Mason Bay,** on the island's remote side, kiwis can even be seen foraging on the beach during the day. Mason Bay can only be reached by an overnight hike or chartered flight. **Ruggedy Range** (tel 03/219-1066, ruggedyrange.com) runs Mason Bay trips and other kiwi and birding adventures.

Alternatively, from the main settlement of Oban, boat tours go to a small offshore island where kiwis nest. **Bravo Adventure Cruises** (tel 03/219-1144, bravoadventurecruises.co.nz) has evening tours, depending on weather and numbers, with a high success rate. If you keep still, the vision-impaired birds often come pecking at your feet searching for food. Tours can be heavily booked and subject to cancellation.

At **Okarito,** near the glaciers on the West Coast of the South Island, **Okarito Kiwi Tours** (The Strand, Okarito, tel 03/753-4330, okaritokiwitours.co.nz) claims a 98 percent success rate in finding kiwis.

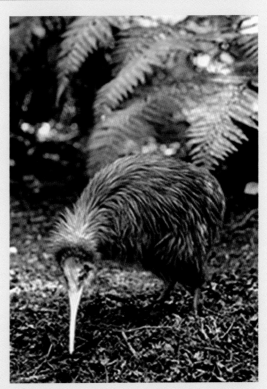

A North Island brown kiwi forages for food.

Trounson Kauri Park (see p. 100) has a DOC program that has helped increase the North Island brown kiwi population.

The **Kauri Coast Top 10 Holiday Park** (Trounson Park Rd., Kaihu, Dargaville, tel 09/439-0621, kauricoast top10.co.nz) runs nightly guided walks through the Kauri forest with about a 50 percent chance of sighting a kiwi.

Other hunting grounds in which to spot the North Island brown kiwi include Aroha Island, Waitangi Forest, and Puketi State Forest. Kapiti Island near Wellington is the best place for kiwi-spotting, but overnight stays require a permit (see p. 164).

Drive Through the Catlins

The winding coastal route from Invercargill to Dunedin runs through the region
known as the Catlins. This fine drive takes in forest and rugged coastline and has a
number of points of interest lying off the road, from beach strolls and waterfalls to
excellent wildlife-spotting.

The lighthouse at Waipapa Point warns ships of a rocky shore.

The scenic stretch from Invercargill to
Balclutha can be driven straight through
in two hours (add another 1.5 hours to
Dunedin on SH1), but allow the better
part of a day to take some side trips and
sample the route's delights.

From **Invercargill** drive 31 miles (50 km)
to **Fortrose** and turn off to **Otara** and the
coastal road to **Waipapa Point ❶**. Take in its
golden beach (with sea lions) and lighthouse,

NOT TO BE MISSED:

**Waipapa Point • Curio Bay
• Cathedral Caves • Matai Falls
• Nugget Point**

---

built after the *Tararua* was wrecked off the
coast here in 1881, killing 131 people. Continue
east to **Slope Point ❷**, the southernmost
point on the South Island. It's a 20-minute
walk across farmland *(access allowed but closed
in lambing season, Sept.–Oct.)* to a sign pointing
to the South Pole.

Next along is **Curio Bay ❸**, where low
tide exposes a 180-million-year-old fossilized
forest with imprints of ferns visible in the
rocks. Yellow-eyed penguins nest here, while
at adjoining Porpoise Bay, Hector's dolphins
can be seen in summer.

The road then passes through **Waikawa**,
which has a small museum and the Niagara

Big-Wave Surfing

Unprotected against the swells of the
Southern Ocean, the Catlins are home
to some of the biggest waves in the
world. Big-wave surfers come from all
over to ride Papas, a wave that reaches
33 feet (10 m). This is tow-in surfing:
Participants rely on jet boats to get to
the waves. Not for amateurs, this type of
surfing is a thrilling and dangerous sport.

See also area map p. 259
► Invercargill
↔ 99 miles (158 km)
⊙ 4–5 hours
► Balclutha

Falls Café, good for a mealtime stop. Back on the main road, it is 12 miles (20 km) to the turnoff to pretty **McLean Falls** ❹, a 45-minute round-trip walk through forest. Just past the falls road, a turnoff leads to **Cathedral Caves** ❺ (cathedralcaves.co.nz, $), an impressive 100-foot-high (30 m) cliff cavern carved out by the sea. Located on Maori land, the caves are reached by a one-hour round-trip walk through forest and along the beach, but they are accessible only at low tide.

Matai Falls ❻ are the easiest falls in the Catlins to reach, lying just off the main road. A 20-minute round-trip walk leads to the waterfall and the **Horseshoe Falls** just above for a wonderfully pretty two-falls-in-one deal. Not far away, **Purakaunui Falls** ❼ are even more scenic and involve a similar walk but a more lengthy drive.

Just past **Owaka** township, take the turnoff to **Cannibal Bay,** where Hooker's sea lions can often be seen. These huge beasts lumber ashore after a feeding foray to roll in the sand and sleep in the sun. Keep your distance— they can charge with remarkable speed.

From Cannibal Bay, gravel roads continue on to **Nugget Point** ❽ lighthouse, perched on top of a cliff and reached by a spectacular track with drop-offs on either side. Seals play on the rocks below, and sea lions and little blue and yellow-eyed penguins also inhabit this natural wonderland. Just before the lighthouse at **Roaring Bay,** yellow-eyed penguins can be viewed from a blind (best before 7 a.m. or after 4 p.m.).

Kaka Point ❾, 6 miles (10 km) away, is a small summer resort with a gentle beach. It is the last town of note before **Balclutha** ❿, where the Catlins drive ends.

Stewart Island

Last but not least of New Zealand's main islands, Stewart Island belies its extreme southerly location. It is rich with forests and wildlife, its white-sand beaches washed by surprisingly warm currents. This remote natural paradise has fine hiking and abundant birdlife, including the kiwi, more easily seen here than anywhere else in New Zealand.

Sunset over Mason Bay, Rakiura National Park, Stewart Island

Stewart Island

🏕 Map p. 259

Visitor Information

✉ 12 Elgin Ter. (near ferry terminal), Oban

☎ 03/219-0056

stewartisland.co.nz

stewartisland
experience.co.nz

Oban & Around

The Maori call the island Rakiura, or "glowing skies," possibly in a reference to aurora australis, the southern lights. About 85 percent of the island, approximately 388,000 acres (157,000 ha), is encompassed by New Zealand's newest national park, **Rakiura National Park.**

For walkers it is an Earthly paradise, with hikes traversing beach and forest, lasting from half an hour to two weeks. Tour operators offer less strenuous glimpses of the island's beauty by boat, bus, or helicopter. The island is also a refuge for native species isolated from the ravages farther north, including the elusive kiwi (see Travelwise p. 271), the flightless, half-blind, nocturnal bird so rarely seen in the wild. Those on a pilgrimage to meet the national symbol in the wild have the best chance here.

Oban, also referred to as Halfmoon Bay, is the island's charming small settlement. It is well supplied

Tui

The tui is one of New Zealand's better known birds and also one of its loudest. With two voice boxes, this large, iridescent honeyeater is capable of singing two different songs at once. As well as producing its song, which is a mixture of melody and atonal coughing, the tui frequently mimics sounds, such as the songs of other birds, human voices, and even the ring of a cell phone. Residents across the country have complained of sleep loss.

with accommodations, a pub, restaurants, and services such as tours, water taxis, car hire, scooters, bicycle, and kayak rentals. The small **Rakiura Museum** *(Ayr St., tel 03/219-1221)* has Maori artifacts, photos, and objects from European settlement. **The Rakiura Environment Centre** on Elgin Terrace near the wharf has displays on the island's wildlife preservation projects.

Offshore **Ulva Island** is a prime attraction, easily reached by the Ulva Island Ferry or water taxi from Golden Bay. Free of predators, the island's regenerating forest teems with birdlife, including weka, kaka, tui (see sidebar above), Stewart Island robin, and the rare saddleback, a member of New Zealand's ancient wattlebird family. Walking trails traverse the island, and informative guided walks can also be arranged.

Nature and walking are what Stewart Island is all about. The **Rakiura Track** is one of New Zealand's Great Walks, a three-day hike from Lee Bay east of Oban. Hikers will see wonderful coastal scenery before heading inland through forest to Paterson Inlet and looping back to Oban.

Another good walk from the town is to **Ackers Point lighthouse** *(3 hr. round-trip)*, a hike that passes historic **Ackers Cottage** and affords fine coastal views. Muttonbirds teem in summer at dusk, when little blue penguins can also be seen.

INSIDER TIP:

For a day-walk taste of the Rakiura Track, Lee Bay to Maori Beach is a three-hour round-trip (six-hour round-trip from Oban) through wonderful coastal and forest terrain.

—PETER TURNER
National Geographic author

Longer hikes include the classic 9- to 11-day **Northwest Circuit** for experienced hikers. The walk takes in **Mason Bay,** backed by impressive sand dunes and noted for kiwis that can often be seen, unusually, during the day. Charter flights also go to Mason Bay, though the best way to see kiwis is on a night tour from Oban, which gives you an excellent chance of seeing the elusive birds up close at a nearby inlet. ∎

Rakiura National Park

🗺 Map p. 259

DOC Visitor Information

✉ 15 Main Rd., Stewart Island

☎ 03/219-0009

doc.govt.nz/parks-and-recreation/national-parks/rakiura

Stewart Island Transportation:

Ferry From Bluff

✉ Stewart Island 21 Foreshore Rd., Bluff

☎ 03/212-7660

🕐 3 times daily (2 per day May–Sept.)

💲 $$$$$

stewartisland experience.co.nz

Stewart Island Flights

✉ Invercargill Airport

☎ 03/218-9129

🕐 3 flights daily

stewartisland flights.co.nz

Rakiura Helicopters

✉ 250 Ocean Beach Rd., Bluff

☎ 03/212-7700

rakiuraheli copters.co.nz

TRAVELWISE

Horse trekking on Lake Tekapo, South Island

PLANNING YOUR TRIP
When to Go

Summer (Dec.–Feb.) is the best season to visit New Zealand. The main tourist season runs from October through May. Outside these months, some attractions, tours, and accommodations close shop, particularly in beach areas. Travel is possible year-round, though, even in midwinter (July/August).

The international tourist season peaks in February/March, when the main tourist towns are overrun and roads are clogged with motor homes. Finding accommodations and rental vehicles can be very difficult, especially on the South Island, so book well in advance. December is a little quieter, but New Zealanders flock to resorts for summer break from around Christmas to the end of January. October/November and April/May are less crowded, cooler, and cheaper, although you miss the summer's charm.

New Zealand has a temperate climate, with regional variations. The Far North of the North Island is subtropical in summer and mild in winter, while the far south of the South Island is mild in summer and cold in winter. Snow tends to be confined to the mountains and rarely falls elsewhere. Average maximum/minimum temperatures for Auckland range from 75/60°F (24/16°C) in January (midsummer) to 59/46°F (15/8°C) in July. In the south, Dunedin ranges from 66/52°F (19/11°C) in January to 50/38°F (10/3°C) in July.

The roaring forties, west winds that blow across the Southern Ocean between latitudes 40° S and 50° S, bring most of the weather. This makes the west coast wetter than the east, particularly on the South Island, where the Southern Alps trap drenching rains. If you hit Milford Sound on a clear day, consider yourself blessed.

Being surrounded by sea, the country's rainfall

is fairly high, with winter slightly wetter than summer. Winds are very changeable, like the weather. It can go from sunshine to showers, from gentle breezes to blustering winds, all in an afternoon.

What to Bring

Given the changeable weather conditions, even summer visitors should bring warmer clothes such as a sweater, anorak, and light rain jacket. Kiwis dress fairly casually, and outdoor fashion is very suited to conditions and activities here. Shorts and T-shirts are fine for beach areas in summer, but bring nicer clothes for good restaurants and nightclubs. In winter, bring sturdy warm clothes.

Good walking shoes are essential. Sport shoes are fine for around cities and short walks, but hiking shoes are recommended for many walks, allowing you to get closer to nature. Serious hikers should be well prepared for all conditions, including freezing temperatures in the mountains, even in summer. Most anything you forget can easily be bought in New Zealand. Accessories for cameras and electronics can be a hassle to find outside main cities, so make sure you bring all cables, chargers, batteries, etc.

Though seldom really hot, New Zealand is noted for fierce sunshine with high UV levels, so good sunglasses and sunscreen are essential. Binoculars are great for wildlife-spotting.

Insurance

Travel insurance is a wise investment. Make sure your big-ticket items—cameras, laptops, etc.—are adequately covered. Travel insurance might save you more than it costs if renting a motor vehicle. Insurance offered by car rental companies comes with large deductibles, but your travel insurance policy may cover the deductible at much more reasonable rates.

Entry Formalities

Visas: Visitors from more than 60 countries—including the U.S., Canada, Mexico, Japan, South Africa, and countries of the European Union—do not need a visa for stays of up to three months. British citizens can visit for up to six months without a visa. Australian citizens and permanent residents do not need visas at all. Those not on the visa-free list must apply for a visitor visa before entering the country. Check at immigration.govt.nz.

Working-holiday visas valid for 12–23 months are available for 18- to 30-year-olds (up to 35 for a few nationalities) from more than 40 countries, including Canada, France, Germany, Japan, the U.K., and the U.S. This visa is for those who intend to supplement their travels with short-term work, primarily agricultural work, and is not valid for permanent work.

Customs: You are allowed to bring in 4.75 quarts (4.5 L) of wine or beer and three 1.18-quart (1.125 L) bottles of spirits, plus 50 cigarettes or 1.7 ounces (50 g) of tobacco or cigars (or a mixture of all three weighing no more than 1.7 ounces/50 g). Customs officials strictly enforce laws designed to protect agricultural industries from imported pests and diseases. Any food and plant items must be declared or you risk fines. Anyone entering or leaving New Zealand with more than NZ$10,000 must declare it to customs.

How to Get to New Zealand

Most international flights go into Auckland, with Air New Zealand (airnewzealand.com) being the major carrier. From North America, Air New Zealand has direct flights between Auckland and Los Angeles, San Francisco, Houston, and Vancouver, with partner airline connections to other U.S. and Canadian cities. American Airlines (aa.com) flies Los Angeles–Auckland direct, United Airlines San Francisco–Auckland, and Hawaiian Airlines flies Honolulu–Auckland.

Pacific stopovers are possible on North American flights. Auckland is a major Pacific hub with flights to and from Hawaii, Tahiti, Fiji, and other Pacific islands. Smaller airlines such as Air Tahiti Nui, Air Pacific, Air Vanuatu, and Virgin Australia also service the Pacific from Auckland, some with connections to the U.S. From South America LAN Chile flies to Auckland, and Air New

Zealand flies to Buenos Aires. More flights go the other direction around the world. Numerous daily flights go to and from Australian cities, particularly Sydney, Brisbane, and Melbourne, with connections to Asia, Europe, and North America. Though Air New Zealand and Qantas/Jetstar are the main operators, Emirates, Virgin Australia, and others fly to and from Australia and beyond.

Some of the cheapest flights from Europe go via Asia. Air New Zealand and Cathay Pacific fly London–Auckland via Hong Kong, while Malaysian Airlines, Singapore Airlines, Thai Airways, and other Asian carriers offer direct flights between their home bases and Auckland with connections to Europe.

New Zealand's other main international airport is Christchurch, but flights are more limited. Most go to Australia's east coast cities, but direct flights also go to and from Singapore, Guangzhou, Dubai, Fiji, and Rarotonga. You can also fly direct from Australia to Wellington, Queenstown, Hamilton, Rotorua, and Dunedin on often discounted flights operated by Air New Zealand, Virgin Australia, and Jetstar.

Most visitors arrive at Auckland airport (auckland-airport.co.nz), 13 miles (21 km) south of the city, reached by bus, taxi, or airport shuttle services. For connecting domestic flights, a free bus operates between the international and domestic terminals, about a half-mile (1 km) apart.

Departure tax is no longer paid at the airport when leaving and is included in the ticket price.

GETTING AROUND
By Air

Air New Zealand (tel 0800/737-000, airnew zealand.com) operates an extensive domestic air network, with daily jet service to Auckland, Hamilton, Wellington, Christchurch, Queenstown, and Dunedin. Air New Zealand Link covers another 21 regional cities with smaller aircraft, from Kaitaia in the north to Invercargill in the south. Air New Zealand offers the New Zealand Explorer Pass to travelers from the U.S. and Canada who fly into the country with the airline. It can be worthwhile if you

will be doing a lot of flying within the country, or to Australia and the Pacific.

Australian airline Jetstar (tel 0800/800-995, jetstar.com) services main cities and tourist centers–Auckland, Dunedin, Wellington, Christchurch, Nelson, Napier, New Plymouth, and Queenstown.

For cheaper flights, purchase discounted tickets through airline websites or travel agents, book well in advance, or travel in off-peak times. Apart from the two majors, a dozen small airlines cover regional routes. These include Sounds Air (tel 0800/505-005, soundsair.co.nz), with scenic flights across the Cook Strait from Wellington to Picton, Nelson, and Blenheim, among others; and Stewart Island Flights (tel 03/218-9129, stewartislandflights.com) between Invercargill and Stewart Island. Sunair (tel 07/575-7799, sunair.co.nz) based at Tauranga has flights to Whitianga, Auckland, Great Barrier, Gisborne, Napier, Rotorua, and Hamilton.

By Car

The most popular way to get around New Zealand is to rent a car or motor home. Public transportation travels to all main destinations but is not always frequent. Often, remote gems can be reached only with your own vehicle. Most New Zealand roads are stunning scenic drives.

Driving is on the left side of the road. Apart from Auckland rush hour, driving is not too fraught, but travel times can be slow. Roads twist, climb, and dip, straight stretches and freeways are rare, and roads are narrow and can suddenly converge on one-lane bridges.

Major international companies and homegrown operators rent cars. Some New Zealand companies do a good job, but others offer worn-out vehicles, iniquitous fine print, and prohibitive cancellation fees. Larger local companies with national networks include Ace Rental Cars, Apex Rentals, Omega Rental Cars, and Pegasus Rental Cars. Hertz (tel 0800/654-321, hertz.co.nz), Thrifty (tel 0800/737-070, 03/359-2720, thrifty .co.nz), Budget (tel 0800/283-438, 09/529-7784, budget.co.nz), and Avis (tel 0800/284-722,

09/526-3256, avis.co.nz) have offices all over the country and at airports.

Book in advance in the peak February/March season, when all rental vehicles are on the road. Insurance deductibles are high (your travel insurance may cover you; see Insurance p. 277) and rates are seasonal—overpriced in summer, dirt cheap in winter.

If traveling between the North and South Islands, some rental companies insist you leave rental cars at the ferry terminal and pick up another across the strait (check when you rent).

Any valid driver's license allows you to drive in New Zealand. Members of AAA and other automobile associations should bring membership proof to receive reciprocal rights with AA New Zealand (tel 0800/500-444, aa.co.nz), including 24-hour roadside assistance and free maps and touring publications.

By Motor Home

The popular motor home or camper van combines vehicle with accommodation in one neat package. This can be a boon in tourist centers in summer, when No Vacancy signs go up, but high-season rates for motor homes can be higher than a car and motel combined. Shoulder and low-season rates are much more reasonable. Smaller vans are easier for driving on New Zealand's narrow, twisting roads.

New Zealand has an excellent network of campgrounds and motor camps. Many cater to families and have good facilities and stunning settings next to a beach, lake, or forest. Free camping in designated sites for fully self-contained motor homes is also popular but sites fill quickly in summer. Some Department of Conservation reserves also have basic sites set aside for motor homes, for a small fee. The Rankers Camping NZ app is excellent for finding campsites and campgrounds, with user ratings.

Major rental agencies operating in New Zealand include Apollo (tel 0800/113-131, 09/889-2976, apollocamper.co.nz), Maui (tel 0800/651-080, 09/225-3983, maui.co.nz), and Britz (tel 0800/831-900, britz.co.nz).

Depots are often outside the airport (some-times quite a long way away), and cancellations incur big penalties. Large deposits are required and insurance premiums are also high.

By Train

The once grand national rail service is now a shadow of its former self since privatization. KiwiRail (tel 04/495-0775, kiwirailscenic.co.nz) operates only four routes, but guarantees comfortable travel with superb scenery.

Among the world's most scenic rail journeys, the TranzAlpine train between Christchurch and Greymouth runs from one side of the South Island to the other over the Southern Alps.

The Coastal Pacific from Christchurch to Picton via Kaikoura is another fine journey, hugging spectacular coast much of the way. This line is still out of operation after the November 2016 earthquake destroyed large sections of the track. Check latest conditions.

The Northern Explorer runs from Auckland to Wellington via Hamilton and skirts the volcanoes of Tongariro National Park. Capital Connection connects Wellington and Palmerston North.

Rail passes are available but don't offer great value. Urban rail services are limited to Auckland and Wellington and are not very extensive.

By Bus

Intercity (tel 09/583-5780, intercity.co.nz), servicing all major cities and towns, offers a variety of bus passes valid for a year with unlimited stops along North and South Island routes. Its Flexipass allows unrestricted travel and is purchased in blocks of travel time from 15 to 60 hours. Passes also include travel on Newmans Coach Lines (tel 09/623-1504, newmanscoach .co.nz), which has sightseeing tours and useful South Island runs.

Nakedbus (tel 0900/625-33, nakedbus.com) also has an extensive all–New Zealand network and discounted online tickets. Its Naked Passport offers blocks of travel at competitive prices.

A number of smaller bus companies run regional routes. One of the most useful, Atomic Shuttles (tel 03/349-0697, atomictravel.co.nz) has services all over the South Island. Tourist offices (or *newzealand.com*) have a full rundown on local bus and coach tour operators, which cover attractions off main bus routes. These include transportation to and from trailheads of the most popular walks.

A number of tour buses for backpackers run set routes, picking up and dropping off at hostels. They include Kiwi Experience *(tel 09/366-4286, kiwiexperience.co.nz)* and Stray Bus *(tel 09/526-2140, straytravel.com)*.

By Ferry

Two companies service the Cook Strait, crossing between Wellington on the North Island and Picton on the South Island: Interislander *(tel 0800/802-802, 04/498-3302, interislander .co.nz)* and Bluebridge *(tel 0800/844-844, 04/471-6188, bluebridge.co.nz)*.

Well-equipped vehicle/passenger ferries cross in a little over three hours, with up to nine daily departures. In Wellington, the Bluebridge terminal is opposite the main railway station. The Interislander terminal is 1.5 miles (2.4 km) north, and a free shuttle runs to and from the train station. In Picton, the ferry terminal is near the town center.

From the ferry terminal in downtown Auckland, Fullers and 360 Discovery *(tel 09/367-9111, fullers.co.nz)* have ferries to Auckland suburbs such as Devonport and to the Hauraki Gulf islands of Rangitoto, Waiheke, Motuihe, Motutapu, Rotoroa, and Tiritiri Matangi, as well as Coromandel town. Sealink *(tel 09/300-5900, sealink.co.nz)* also has ferries to Waiheke and Great Barrier Island.

Other ferries operate in the Bay of Islands and Rawene in Northland, Wellington, and the Marlborough Sounds and between Bluff and Stewart Island (see p. 275).

By Bicycle

Cyclists from all over the world flock to New Zealand in summer. Many bring their own bicycles, but bikes are easily purchased or rented. A host of outfitters renting bicycles and equipment, as well as shuttle services for cyclists, has sprung up in recent years with the building of bicycle paths across the country.

The best trails are known as Great Rides and *nzcycletrail.com* has full details on the rides and outfitters.

PRACTICAL ADVICE
Communications

Internet: Public libraries and many tourist information offices have free Wi-Fi, and the main tourist centers have Internet cafés, though they are becoming harder to find. Almost all accommodations offer Internet access, increasingly free, though data might be limited and speeds glacial. Some big hotels still charge, sometimes exorbitantly, or only offer free Wi-Fi in the lobby. Some offer intranet access in rooms, though wireless services are more common. Cafés often have free wireless access, and free Wi-Fi hot spots can be found in central Auckland, Rotorua, Wellington, and Dunedin. A local SIM card (see Telephone below) is a good investment for data access.

Post Offices: New Zealand Post offers efficient service, with delivery times of four to ten days to most parts of the world. Post offices are open weekdays from around 8:30 a.m. to 5 p.m. and until 1 p.m. on Saturdays. Other retail outlets such as convenience stores also sell stamps and offer basic postal services.

Telephone: New Zealand has good telephone services and an extensive network of public telephones, which use coins, credit cards, or prepaid phone cards. Most hotels and motels have in-room phones but add a surcharge to rates, while even budget hostels will have a phone for guest use.

The cheapest way to call overseas is usually on a landline using an international phone card available from many convenience stores. You dial a toll-free New Zealand number, enter your PIN, then enter the overseas number. Country rates vary between companies—retailers will have details.

Spark (formerly Telecom New Zealand; *spark.co.nz*), Vodafone *(vodafone.co.nz)*, and 2degrees *(2degreesmobile.co.nz)* provide mobile telephone coverage on 3G and 4G (2G is being phased out). A prepaid SIM card is a good investment for data and local calls for bookings from your cell phone. Spark has the best coverage in rural areas, closely followed by Vodafone, while 2degrees has limited coverage in remote areas but roams on Vodafone. Check that your phone has the required bands—850 MHz for rural 3G coverage on Spark (2100 MHz in cities), 900 and 2100 MHz 3G on Vodafone and 2degrees, while LTE 700 and 1800 are the main 4G bands. Resellers like Skinny *(skinny.co.nz)*, operating on the Spark network, and Warehouse Mobile *(warehousemobile.co.nz)*, on the 2degrees network, usually have the cheapest deals. SIM cards and recharges are sold online or at supermarkets, convenience stores, drugstores, and cell phone shops.

The emergency number is 111. The internal access code to dial out of the country is 00 (followed by country code, area code, number). The country code is 64. Area codes in New Zealand are: 09 Auckland and Northland; 07 Coromandel, Bay of Plenty, and Waikato; 06 Hawke's Bay, Gisborne, Palmerston North, and Wairarapa; 04 Wellington; 03 South Island.

Conversions

New Zealand uses the metric system, so road signs are in kilometers, gas is sold in liters, and stores sell in grams and kilos.

1 kilometer = 0.62 miles
1 meter = 3.28 feet or 39.37 inches
1 liter = 0.264 U.S. gallons
1 kilogram = 2.20 pounds

Women's clothing sizes

U.S.	6	8	10	12	14	16
NZ	36	38	40	42	44	46

Men's clothing sizes

U.S.	36	38	40	42	44	46
NZ	46	48	50	52	54	56

Women's shoe sizes

U.S.	6	6.5	7	7.5	8	8.5
NZ	38	38	39	39	40	41

Men's shoe sizes

U.S.	8	8.5	9.5	10.5	11.5	12
NZ		41	42	43	44	45	46

Electricity

The New Zealand electricity supply is 230V AC, 50 Hz. Plugs have three flat pins (one vertical, two angled), as used in Australia. Some hotel and motel bathrooms have two-prong, 110-volt sockets for electric razors, but bring an adapter and dual voltage appliances.

Holidays

January 1 (New Year's Day)
January 2 (Day after New Year's Day)
February 6 (Waitangi Day)
March/April (Good Friday, Easter Monday)
April 25 (Anzac Day)
1st Monday in June (Queen's Birthday)
4th Monday in October (Labor Day)
December 25 (Christmas Day)
December 26 (Boxing Day)
Each NZ province also has its own holidays, called anniversary days, scattered throughout the year.

Liquor Laws

The minimum drinking age is 18 in licensed premises. Children are allowed in pubs with their parents.

Media

Most New Zealand cities have a daily newspaper covering local and international news. The two main newspapers are Auckland's *New Zealand Herald* and Wellington's *Dominion Post.*

Popular local magazines include the *New Zealand Listener* for entertainment and current affairs, *North & South* for current affairs, the Auckland lifestyle magazine *Metro,* and *Cuisine* for all things food and wine.

The publicly owned national broadcaster TVNZ runs the TV1 and TV2 television channels. Maori TV has the most New Zealand content, and Te Reo is broadcast only in Maori. A host of other channels broadcast on digital bands, and Sky TV provides cable services.

Radio New Zealand, the national broadcaster, is supplemented by a host of regional AM and FM stations throughout the country.

Money Matters

The unit of currency is the New Zealand dollar, comprising 100 cents, which replaced pounds, shillings, and pence in 1967, when New Zealand's currency was decimalized. Notes come in $5, $10, $20, $50, and $100 denominations and are made of polymer pro-pylene, a tough, colorful, and difficult-to-forge plastic alternative to the old paper notes. Coins in circulation are the bronze-colored 10c piece, silver-colored 20c and 50c pieces, and gold-colored $1 and $2 coins. Currently one New Zealand dollar is worth about 70 cents, but check the exchange rate before you leave for New Zealand. Traveler's checks are readily exchanged at banks and money changers, but rates are lower than cash, and a cashing fee of at least 1 percent is usually applied to these transactions. Exchanging cash incurs similar fees and rates are normally poor.

Depending on fees charged by your home bank, using credit cards—or better, debit cards—for purchases and cash withdrawals through ATMs is usually cheaper and is certainly more convenient. However, fewer fees usually apply when withdrawing cash from a savings account via ATMs and EFTPOS retail outlets that are connected to international banking networks such as Cirrus, Maestro, and Plus. These are found everywhere throughout New Zealand. Check fees and overseas access with your bank before you leave.

Visa and Mastercard are the most widely accepted credit cards. American Express and Diners Club tend to be limited, and often attract a surcharge. A few hotels even try to charge up to 2 percent extra for Visa/Mastercard transactions, despite insisting you pay with a credit card.

A 15 percent goods-and-services tax applies to all purchases but is always included in quoted prices (be wary of businesses that do not include it). This tax is not refundable for overseas visitors when leaving.

Opening Times

Most shops and businesses are open Monday to Friday from 9 a.m. to 5 p.m., and for late-night shopping until 9 p.m. one or two nights per week (Thurs. and/or Fri.). Large supermarkets usually stay open until 8 or 9 p.m., some until midnight or later in cities, where convenience stores and gas stations are open 24 hours.

Saturday shopping is from around 10 a.m. to 5 p.m., though some shops close at 2 p.m. Most shops close on Sundays, but shopping malls are open from 10 a.m. to 5 p.m. Souvenir shops in main tourist centers are often open late.

Time Differences

New Zealand lies near the International Date Line and is one of the first countries in the world to see the new day. New Zealand is +12 hours GMT, 2 hours ahead of Sydney, and 17 hours ahead of New York standard time. New Zealand daylight saving time is from the last Sunday in September to the first Sunday in April.

Tipping

Tipping is optional in New Zealand. Previously it was considered a foreign custom to tip, but with increasing globalization and a growing tourism trade, the practice is becoming more common among Kiwis. While it is not considered mandatory, a 5 to 10 percent tip is appreciated for good service in the country's better restaurants. (But don't tip if the service is subpar.)

Tip taxi drivers for good service by rounding up the fare, up to 10 percent. In top hotels, it's customary to give porters NZ$1 to $2 for carrying your bags.

Travelers With Disabilities

Accommodations and most public facilities are required to provide wheelchair access and bathrooms for the disabled. Even many short walking trails are wheelchair friendly. Taxis and tour operators with wheelchair access vehicles can be found in major centers. Many car rental companies will fit hand controls to vehicles if contracted well in advance, and motor homes with wheelchair hoists can also be rented. An excellent website for disability services is *weka.net.nz.*

EMERGENCIES
Crime & Police
New Zealand is generally a safe country with low crime rates. Theft from parked cars is a recurrent problem, particularly in remote tourist parking lots such as at trailheads. Avoid leaving valuables in your car or, if you must, lock them out of view in the trunk. Some local police stations have become community police offices tucked away in shopping areas, but they are there if you need to report a crime or obtain a crime report for travel insurance.

Embassies & Consulates
U.S. Embassy, 29 Fitzherbert Ter., Wellington, tel 04/462-6000, fax 04/499-0490, nz.usembassy.gov
U.S. Consulate-General, Level 3, Citigroup Center, 23 Custom St. E, Auckland, tel 09/303-2724, fax 09/303-1069
Canadian High Commission, 125 The Terrace, Wellington, tel 04/473-9577, fax 04/471-2082, canadainternational.gc.ca /new_zealand-nouvelle_zelande
Canadian Consulate, 9th Fl., 48 Emily Pl., Auckland, tel 09/309-3690, fax 09/307-3111
British High Commission, 44 Hill St., Wellington, tel 04/924-2888, fax 04/473-4982, gov.uk/government/world/new-zealand
British Consulate-General, Level 17, 151 Queen St., Auckland, tel 09/303-2973, fax 09/303-1836

Emergency Phone Numbers
The emergency number for police, ambulance, and fire is 111.

What to Do in a Car Accident
In the event of an accident, check all vehicles to see if anyone is injured. Contact emergency services and seek help from bystanders to assist the injured. Failure to stop, check, or assist is a serious offense in New Zealand.

If someone is injured, report the accident to police as soon as possible. If another vehicle or property is damaged, you must notify the owner or report the accident to police within 48 hours. Write down the name, address, registration number, and insurance company of the other driver(s) involved, and the details of witnesses and any police officers in attendance. Give your details, but it is best not to admit liability for any accident.

Report accidents to your rental car or insurance company as soon as possible. If you will be claiming the deductible on your travel insurance, make sure you have a copy of the rental agreement, insurance coverage, repair quotes, police report, and all receipts.

HEALTH
New Zealand has high-quality medical treatment and world-class hospitals. Visitors requiring emergency treatment for a motor vehicle, sport, or recreational accident are covered by New Zealand's accident compensation scheme (ACC). Otherwise, you'll have to pay for medical treatment, and while health care is significantly cheaper than in the U.S. or the U.K., travel insurance is highly recommended.

Healthline is a toll-free, 24-hour telephone medical advice service: tel 0800/611-116.

Tap water is safe to drink in New Zealand, but streams and lakes may contain parasites such as giardia, so water should be boiled or treated before drinking. Amoebic meningitis is very rare but can occur in geothermal waters, such as hot pools in Rotorua. Keep your head above the water to deter infection.

New Zealand has no snakes or dangerous wild animals, though the rare, red-striped katipo spider, found only in coastal sand dunes, is poisonous. The greatest danger in the wild is exposure in alpine areas for ill-equipped hikers and rips and currents at surf beaches.

Hotels & Restaurants

Exclusive country lodges, international chain hotels, delightful B&Bs, roadside motels, and well-equipped backpacker or campground cabins—New Zealand has a big range of accommodations to suit all budgets.

On arrival, pick up a free accommodation guide at the airport or tourist office. Motels, hotels, B&Bs, and backpacker chains all produce their own guides with member listings. The most useful free guides are the comprehensive *Jasons Accommodations Guide* (also online at *jasons.com*) and the guides from the Automobile Association *(aatravel.co.nz),* which provide useful information on sightseeing and/or places to stay.

If you are on a tight schedule and know your itinerary, book all your accommodations before you arrive, especially in the peak summer season when tourist towns fill up. Beware, though, that accommodations in New Zealand often will not refund cancellations. Trying to find same-day accommodation in the high season can be frustrating and time-consuming, though it is less problematic outside tourist areas.

Hotels & Motels

Hotels range from five-star luxury to humble pubs. Big international chains (Hilton, Hyatt, Sheraton, etc.) have hotels in the main cities, but individual hotels and small chains such as Scenic Hotels *(scenichotels.co.nz)* and Millennium *(millenniumhotels.co.nz)* are more common in tourist towns.

Travel agents or online booking services such as *wotif.com* or *agoda.com* offer discount deals that are sometimes cheaper than booking direct, but hotels increasingly offer good online deals direct.

Hotel rates vary considerably with the season. New Zealand has experienced a tourist boom in recent years, with few new hotels built, so prices soar in the main summer tourist season, and Auckland is expensive year-round.

Four-star hotels start at around NZ$150 per room, though more often are around NZ$200 or more. At the very top end, a range of boutique hotels, luxury lodges, and elite resorts—such as the Huka Lodge near Taupo or the Millbrook Resort near Queenstown—offer opulence at extravagant prices.

Mid-range hotels cost from NZ$100 up to NZ$200. These may be pubs but are more likely to be private hotels, with just rooms and maybe a café if you strike it lucky. They compete with motels, or motor lodges as they are called in New Zealand. Many motels in New Zealand have seen better days, but are usually clean, have kitchens, and offer comfort at reasonable prices. Newer motels are usually much better appointed, with rates starting from at least NZ$140.

At the bottom end, pubs in cities and towns often have rooms upstairs, usually basic but sometimes well-appointed motel-style rooms. They start at around NZ$70 for a double without bathroom, but can be noisy if your room is near the bar.

B&Bs

Bed-and-breakfast accommodations are booming, with more homeowners converting rooms or erecting specially designed accommodations. Some are in magnificent heritage buildings, and top-end B&Bs offer some of the finest accommodations in New Zealand. At the bottom end, more basic guesthouse-style places offer budget rooms with shared facilities.

Depending on the room rate, breakfast might be light continental-style or a grand affair. Most B&Bs are convivial places, allowing you to meet Kiwis and fellow travelers in a home atmosphere, or to be completely independent if you choose. Most cost around NZ$120 to NZ$200.

The *New Zealand Bed & Breakfast Book,* available in bookshops, has extensive listings online *(bnb.co.nz).* The *B&B Directory of New Zealand (bed-and-breakfast.co.nz)* is similar.

Budget Accommodations

Campgrounds, known as holiday parks, offer a wide choice of budget accommodations in addition to campsites and powered sites for motor homes. Rooms range from cheap spartan cabins and backpacker rooms to motel units and apartments.

Campgrounds are usually well equipped with communal kitchens, laundries, entertainment areas, playgrounds, and sometimes a pool or even hot-spring baths. Many are on the beach or a lake. For those with a motor home, free camping is available in some designated areas, sometimes even in the middle of cities. Some Department of Conservation parks and reserves also have areas set aside for motor homes, in addition to tent campers, usually for a small fee.

New Zealand is well set up for backpackers, with hostels ranging from big-city hotels to remote farm homesteads. Most independent backpacker hostels belong to one of three hostel networks: Budget Backpacker Hostels (bbh.co.nz), YHA (yha.co.nz), and VIP Backpackers (vipbackpackers.com). Many hostels are well appointed with good-value double rooms that appeal to older couples on a budget. Along with communal cooking facilities and well-appointed common areas, many offer bicycles, tours, free pickup, and a host of extras.

Other

Apartment hotels are springing up everywhere in cities and resorts. Some offer luxury, or they might be minimalist new buildings with modern rooms and fully equipped kitchens. If you don't want all the services of a big hotel, these can offer excellent value.

Holiday homes, or baches as they are called, can also be rented, usually only for longer stays, though sometimes short term (bookabach.co.nz, holidayhouses.co.nz). Real estate agents often handle them, though some tourist offices list them. Tourist offices also handle farm stays and homestays, which can sometimes offer great value. They may just be a room in a family home but are often self-contained units or converted bungalows.

Restaurants

Fine-dining restaurants and more casual cafés are readily available, particularly in big cities, which are also home to numerous Indian, Chinese, Southeast Asian, Middle Eastern, and other restaurants, reflecting New Zealand's broadening immigrant mix and offering some of the best dining value.

Wonderful dining experiences can be found, but a lot of restaurants offer similar variations of lamb/beef/venison/fish on a tower of mashed kumara (sweet potato) at high prices, regardless of quality. Top chefs are limited in resort towns, where chefs come and go. Add inexperienced waitstaff and hordes of diners in the tourist season, and you could be waiting an eon for a very ordinary meal.

That said, New Zealand has wonderful fresh foods—seafood, meat, fruits, and vegetables—and plenty of restaurants and cafés in which to indulge your taste buds. Most eateries are licensed to serve alcohol or you can BYO (Bring Your Own wine or beer bought elsewhere). Smoking is not allowed in New Zealand restaurants, cafés, and bars but may be allowed in some outdoor areas.

Closing hours vary for public holidays, when some restaurants add a surcharge of around 15 percent. Many cafés offering light meals are only open for breakfast and/or lunch. Most restaurants are open for lunch and dinner. Closures are shown in the following listings below using the abbreviations below:

L = Lunch
D = Dinner

Listings: Hotels and restaurants for each destination are listed by price, then in alphabetical order. Note that prices are in New Zealand dollars.

Credit Cards: Abbreviations used are: AE: American Express; MC: Mastercard; V: Visa.

▉ AUCKLAND

⊞ HERITAGE AUCKLAND
$$$$$
35 HOBSON ST., TOWER WING,
22–24 NELSON ST.
TEL 09/379-8553
heritagehotels.co.nz
This luxury hotel in a classic art deco building offers regularly discounted rooms, suites, and apartments, many with kitchens. Rooms in the main building have high ceilings, timber floors, and 1920s élan, while the modern Tower Wing has contemporary decor. The hotel has a heated rooftop swimming pool, indoor pool, sauna, spa, two gymnasiums, and tennis court, right in the city center with harbor views from many rooms.
① 325 🅿 🔄 🛇 🔄 🛥 🍸 🛜 Free
🅰 All major cards

⊞ HILTON AUCKLAND
$$$$$
PRINCES WHARF, 147 QUAY ST.
TEL 09/978-2000
auckland.hilton.com
At the end of Princes Wharf, Hilton Auckland's generous use of glass and open space brings the harbor in. Rooms employ local timber, and ceiling-to-floor windows and balconies in the front apartments deliver wow factor plus.
① 166 🅿 🔄 🛇 🔄 🛥 🍸 🛜 Charge
🅰 All major cards

⊞ SKYCITY GRAND HOTEL
$$$$$
90 FEDERAL ST.
TEL 09/363-7000
skycityauckland.co.nz
You won't get lost if staying underneath the Sky Tower spire, visible all over the city. Superior facilities and service make this five-star hotel popular with business travelers as well as tourists. It is part of the huge SkyCity casino, entertainment, and dining complex, which also includes its sister hotel, the four-star SkyCity Hotel.
① 316 🅿 🔄 🛇 🔄 🛥 🍸 🛜 Free
🅰 All major cards

⊞ SOFITEL AUCKLAND
VIADUCT HARBOUR
$$$$$

PRICES

HOTELS
The cost of a double room in the high season is indicated by **$** signs (NZ dollars).

$$$$$	Over $250
$$$$	200–250
$$$	$150–200
$$	$100–150
$	Under $100

RESTAURANTS
The cost of a three-course meal without drinks is indicated by **$** signs (NZ dollars).

$$$$$	Over $80
$$$$	$60–80
$$$	$40–60
$$	$25–40
$	Under $25

---

21 VIADUCT HARBOUR AVE.
TEL 09/909-9000
accorhotels.com
This bright face on Auckland's hotel scene overlooks Viaduct Harbour, a short stroll from the city's swankest dining/nightlife precinct. Superior service, sleek decor, spa center, and the excellent location put it ahead of most. Expansive windows deliver superb waterfront views in deluxe rooms, though most superior rooms face rows of apartment blocks.
① 173 🅿 🔄 🛇 🔄 🛥 🍸 🛜 Free
🅰 All major cards

⊞ ADINA APARTMENT HOTEL
$$$$–$$$$$
2 TAPORA ST.
TEL 09/393-8200
tfehotels.com
This new, six-story hotel in the Britomart District is a welcome addition to help ease the city's hotel shortage. Construction build looks cheap, and room entry is via open, internal walkways, but excellent rooms with kitchenettes are sparkling new, and rates are reasonable. One- and two-bedroom apartments have full kitchens. A sometimes lively bar/café is located downstairs.
① 140 🅿 🔄 🛇 🔄 🛥 🍸 🛜 Free
🅰 All major cards

PEACE & PLENTY INN
$$$$–$$$$$
6 FLAGSTAFF TER., DEVONPORT
TEL 09/445-2925
peaceandplenty.co.nz
In genteel Devonport, just around the corner from the main street cafés, this delightful B&B makes a wonderful retreat from downtown Auckland, only a ten-minute ferry ride away. Spacious rooms in a meticulously restored Victorian villa are complemented by warm hospitality and sumptuous breakfasts. Homesick pet lovers can take Stanley the Labrador for a stroll around Devonport's streets. Winter rates are more reasonable.

🛈 7 🅿 Ⓢ Ⓔ 📶 Free 🗖 MC, V

THE QUADRANT
$$$$–$$$$$
10 WATERLOO QUADRANT
TEL 09/984-6000
vrhotels.co.nz
This funky apartment hotel near the university on the edge of downtown lacks the extras and service of a big hotel but offers good value for self-caterers. Compact studio, one-, and two-bedroom apartments have fully equipped kitchens and modern furnishings.

🛈 250 🅿 Ⓔ Ⓢ 🗖 📶 Free 🗖 All major cards

AUCKLAND CITY OAKS
$$$–$$$$
188 HOBSON ST.
TEL 09/337-5800
vrhotels.co.nz
Well-appointed apartments with kitchenettes and laundry facilities are a little tired but offer a good deal for couples wanting a small studio. Two-bedroom apartments are good value for families. Centrally located near the casino, and just a short stroll from Queen Street, the location is excellent and prices reasonable for expensive Auckland.

🛈 110 🅿 Ⓔ Ⓢ Ⓔ 📶 Free 🗖 MC, V

PARNELL INN
$$$–$$$$
320 PARNELL RD.
TEL 09/358-0642
parnellinn.co.nz
In the fashionable suburb of Parnell, this welcoming motel/guesthouse makes a good budget choice. The city is a 25-minute walk or a short bus ride away, and the Auckland Museum is nearby. Attractive, well-kept rooms have nice touches, and a small café is on the premises.

🛈 16 🅿 Ⓢ 📶 Free 🗖 MC, V

SHAKESPEARE TAVERN
$–$$
61 ALBERT ST. (AT WYNDHAM ST.)
TEL 09/373-5396
shakespearehotel.co.nz
This classic old pub is in the city center near the casino. Behind the architecturally impressive facade lies good refurbished rooms with private bathrooms, some with balcony, for a budget value with character. The downstairs restaurant and brewery bar are a bonus.

🛈 10 📶 Free 🗖 MC, V

EURO RESTAURANT & BAR
$$$$$
SHED 22, PRINCES WHARF
TEL 09/309-9866
eurobar.co.nz
On Princes Wharf overlooking the harbor, with a new chef and one of the city's most beautiful aspects, Euro is beloved of the glitterati for dinner, late-night barhopping, and expense-account lunches. Dine inside or out on the veranda overlooking luxury yachts. The seasonal menu has a seafood emphasis in summer, but features a wide variety of produce and styles.

🛉 120 Ⓢ Ⓔ 🗖 All major cards

SOMETHING SPECIAL

THE SUGAR CLUB
$$$$–$$$$$
LEVEL 53, SKYCITY GRAND HOTEL,
90 FEDERAL ST.
TEL 09/363-7030
skycitygrand.co.nz
This is not a dessert-only restaurant but a fine-dining tour de force by renowned chef Peter Gordon, who put the *f* in fusion in these parts. Asian, Middle Eastern, and Mediterranean elements combine to make modern New Zealand cuisine in a stunning setting with expansive views across the city from the top of the casino tower. Dining is degustation or fixed price meals—you pay for the number of courses—including vegetarian.

🛉 80 🅿 Ⓛ Ⓢ Ⓔ 🗖 All major cards

CASSIA
$$$$
5 FORT LN.
TEL 09/379-9702
cassiarestaurant.co.nz
Indian food like you've never had it before, Sid Sahrawat's fusion menu combines the best of New Zealand produce with Indian spices and modern flair. Service is impeccable and the space is modern industrial with a long bar and different dining areas.
75 D Sun. & Mon. & L Sat.–Tues. All major cards

DEPOT EATERY & OYSTER BAR
$$$$
86 FEDERAL ST.
TEL 09/363-7048
eatatdepot.co.nz
Federal Street, in the shadow of the casino, has become a fashionable new dining strip, and Depot is the standout. Celebrity chef Al Brown's place is relaxed and hip, with crowds clamoring for oysters and other New Zealand seafood washed down with wines from a well-developed list. Meat-eaters are also well catered to with tasting plates, large and small, from the busy charcoal grill. No reservations—just show up for breakfast, lunch, or dinner, preferably early.
110 All major cards

HARBOURSIDE OCEAN BAR GRILL
$$$$
1ST FL., FERRY BLDG., 99 QUAY ST.
TEL 09/307-0486
harbourside.co
One of Auckland's finest seafood restaurants, Harbourside's emphasis is on fresh fish, but the menu also features meat and game. En-trées often offer the most interesting seafood creations and a chance to sample unique local shellfish. The upstairs deck overlooks the ferry docks below.
200 All major cards

PONSONBY ROAD BISTRO
$$$$
165 PONSONBY RD., PONSONBY
TEL 09/360-1611
ponsonbyroadbistro.co.nz
Sophisticated but casual, this is an Auckland institution. In the busy Ponsonby Road dining strip, dishes range from perfectly cooked fish or chargrilled steak with hand-cut chips to more exotic dishes exhibiting Middle Eastern and Mediterranean influences, with an extensive wine list to match. This is fine dining without the starched table cloths or business account prices.
50 Sun. & L Sat. All major cards

SOUL BAR & BISTRO
$$$$
VIADUCT HARBOUR
TEL 09/356-7249
soulbar.co.nz
This buzzing favorite in the city's liveliest dining precinct packs in a designer casual clientele daily for lunch and dinner, kicks on at the bar until late, then returns for breakfast egg creations to soak up the booze from the night before. The varied fusion menu leans toward seafood and fish, such as whole flounder with capers, lemon, parsley, and marcona almonds. The deck overlook-ing the water is the place to be.
200 P All major cards

FEDERAL DELICATESSAN
$$$
86 FEDERAL ST.
TEL 09/363-7184
thefed.co.nz
Under the Sky Tower, this Kiwi take on a New York deli has good breakfasts, bagels, and house pastrami as well as more substantial strip steak, meatloaf, venison, and spit-roasted chicken. Decor and uniforms are a modern update of a retro diner as is the food, and prices. Open for breakfast, lunch, and din-ner, its bar is well stocked and kicks on late weekends.
100 All major cards

L'ASSIETTE
$$–$$$
9 BRITOMART PLACE
TEL 09/309-0961
lassiette.co.nz
This modern, minimalist café is popular for French-style breakfasts, pastries, and lunch dishes, from salade niçoise to beef bour-guignon. It's in the popular Britomart dining/ drinking district downtown.
40 D All major cards

Hotel   Restaurant   No. of Guest Rooms   No. of Seats   P Parking   Closed   Elevator

🍴 MANUKA
$$–$$$
49 VICTORIA RD., DEVONPORT
TEL 09/445-7732
manukarestaurant.co.nz
A short ferry ride from central Auckland, the seaside village of Devonport makes a pleasant day trip. This airy, casual corner café is popular for its wood-fired pizzas. It has other reasonably priced fare, from seafood entrées to steaks, with a good selection of dishes for vegetarians. Open breakfast, lunch, and dinner.

🔲 100 🔲 🔲 🔲 All major cards

🍴 CAFÉ MIDNIGHT EXPRESS
$$
59 VICTORIA ST. W.
TEL 09/303-0312
cafemidnightexpress.co.nz
With a tent-style roof and Turkish artifacts, this cheerful restaurant near the Sky Tower has been serving reasonably priced food for more than 25 years. Tasty Turkish dishes such as döner kebab and Iskender spit-roasted lamb with hummus and tzatziki are accompanied by rice and salad. Servings are big.

🔲 50 🕐 L Sat. & Sun. 🔲 🔲 AE, MC, V

🍴 SATYA SOUTH INDIAN CAFÉ
$$
271 KARANGAHAPE RD.
TEL 09/377-0007
Queen Street heads up the hill to Karangahape Road, an interesting area with a selection of budget Asian restaurants. Don't be put off by the dated decor; Satya packs them in thanks to consistently good curries and *thali* plate meals appealing to meat-eaters as well as vegetarians. Its popularity has spawned offshoots in Ponsonby and Mount Eden.

🔲 70 🔲 🔲 🔲 MC, V

🍴 TANUKI'S SUSHI & SAKE BAR
$$
319 QUEEN ST.
TEL 09/379-5353
sakebars.co.nz
This urban secret has long been out. At the top end of Queen Street, where cheap Japanese and Korean restaurants abound,

Tanuki's has rustic Japanese decor, a big range of sake, and the usual Japanese specialties and dinner boxes at reasonable prices. Downstairs, the Tanuki Cave is a funky bar for a drink with yakitori or kushiage snacks on skewers.

🔲 106 🕐 L, Fri.–Wed. 🔲 🔲 All major cards

◼ NORTHLAND

WHANGAREI

🏨 LODGE BORDEAUX
$$$$$
361 WESTERN HILLS DR.
TEL 09/438-0404
lodgebordeaux.co.nz
West of the city center on the main highway, this lodge has luxurious studio, one-, and two-bedroom kitchen suites, all with double spa baths. Rated five-star with lots of extras and fine hospitality, this small, family-run boutique lodge is one of the top options in town.

🔲 15 🅿 🔲 🔲 🔲 🔲 Free
🔲 All major cards

🍴 TOPSAIL RESTAURANT
$$$$$
206 BEACH RD., ONERAHI
TEL 09/436-2985
topsail.co.nz
From the fresh seafood, rack of lamb, and venison, to the chocolate mousse and apple and feijoa pie, this fine restaurant does classic dishes with modern flair. At the Onerahi yacht club, about 5 miles (8 km) from town, harbor views and sunsets complement the food.

🔲 40 🕐 L & D Sun.–Tues. 🔲 🔲 MC, V

🍴 KILLER PRAWN
$$$–$$$$
26–28 BANK ST.
TEL 09/430-3333
killerprawn.co.nz
In downtown Whangarei, this cheerful restaurant's signature dish is prawns in a spicy tomato broth with chunky bread for dunking, while other seafood dishes dominate the menu, including tempura fish and green-lipped mussels with the sauce of your choice.

🔲 140 🕐 Sun. 🔲 🔲 All major cards

🔲 Nonsmoking 🔲 Air-Conditioning 🔲 Indoor Pool 🔲 Outdoor Pool 🔲 Health Club 🔲 Wi-Fi 🔲 Credit Cards

BAY OF ISLANDS

Paihia

🏨 **PAIHIA BEACH RESORT & SPA**
$$$$$
116 MARSDEN RD.
TEL 09/402-0111
paihiabeach.co.nz
Around the headland from the main shopping
stretch, this is one of Paihia's top apartment
complexes. Near the beach with great views,
studio, one-, and two-bedroom apartments
are suitably luxurious for the price. The day spa,
sauna, and restaurant top off the indulgence.
ⓘ 21 🅿 🛇 🛇 🏊 📶 Free
🌐 All major cards

🏨 **EDGEWATER PALMS APARTMENTS
(RAMADA SUITES)**
$$$$–$$$$$
8–10 MARSDEN RD.
TEL 09/402-0090
edgewaterapartments.co.nz
One of the multiplying breed of apartment
hotels, this one offers one- and two-bedroom
apartments overlooking the water and one
of New Zealand's most scenic views. An easy
walk into town, it's worth paying extra for the
waterfront rooms.
ⓘ 36 🅿 🛇 🛇 🏊 📶 Free
🌐 All major cards

🏨 **BAYVIEW MOTEL**
$$$–$$$$
MARSDEN RD. & BAYVIEW RD.
TEL 09/402-7338
bayviewmotel.co.nz
Numerous motels provide cheap accommoda-
tions. Many are dowdy, but for a few dollars
more, the Bayview is a cut above most, with
well-kept one-bedroom units, many with sea
views, and a location in the center of Paihia.
ⓘ 11 🅿 🛇 📶 Free 🌐 All major cards

🏨 **COPTHORNE HOTEL & RESORT**
🍴 **$$$–$$$$**
TAU HENARE DR.
TEL 09/402-7411
milleniumhotels.co.nz
Right in the Waitangi Treaty Grounds and only
a mile (1.6 km) from the center of Paihia, this
four-star hotel is a serene retreat with ocean

views, gardens, and a golf course. Rooms have
seen better days, but regular discounts make
this a good buy for the wonderful position
and facilities. The water-view rooms with
balconies are worth the extra cost.
ⓘ 180 🅿 🛇 🛇 🏊 📶 Charge
🌐 All major cards

🍴 **ONLY SEAFOOD**
$$$$
40 MARSDEN RD.
TEL 09/402-6066
onlyseafood.co.nz
Set off the main road upstairs in a two-story
villa overlooking the sea, Only Seafood is a Pai-
hia institution. Only seafood gets the nod with
dishes such as seafood phyllo parcels, game fish
with roasted cashews, smoked salmon with
Brie, and seafood platters with a sashimi bent.
🍴 95 🅿 🕐 L 🛇 🌐 All major cards

🍴 **35° SOUTH RESTAURANT & BAR**
$$$–$$$$
69 MARSDEN RD.
TEL 09/402-6220
35south.co.nz
This aquarium restaurant has pole position
perched over the water in an octagonal
building next to the wharf. The menu strongly
features seafood but also offers steaks, duck,
and lamb. The deck is a sublime spot for a
drink on a sunny day. Open for breakfast,
lunch, and dinner.
🍴 50 🅿 🛇 🌐 All major cards

🍴 **EL CAFÉ**
$–$$
2 KINGS RD.
TEL 09/402-7637
elcafe.co.nz
A great spot for breakfast or lunch, this
small Chilean-run café is just back from the
waterfront near the town center. Excellent
burritos, tacos, quesadillas, huevos, coffee,
and smoothies won't break the bank. Pity it's
not open for dinner.
🍴 20 🅿 🕐 D 🛇 🌐 MC, V

Russell

🏨 **DUKE OF MARLBOROUGH HOTEL**
🍴 **$$$–$$$$**
35 THE STRAND

TEL 09/403-7829

theduke.co.nz

On the waterfront near the Paihia ferry dock, this is one of the country's oldest inns. Though some rooms are a little short on luxury for the price, the waterfront rooms and suites ooze history and charm. The popular restaurant in a beautifully restored dining room offers elegant cuisine.

🚹 24 🅿 🚫 🛜 Free 🗝 All major cards

🏠 HANANUI LODGE & APARTMENTS
$$$–$$$$

4 YORK ST.

TEL 09/403-7875

hananui.co.nz

In the town center, this complex is divided into two sections: well-equipped apartments and units in the lodge on the waterfront. Modern, well-appointed apartments with kitchens range from studio to two-bedroom, while the lodge has older motel-style units with kitchens.

🚹 15 🅿 🚫 🛜 Free 🗝 All major cards

🍴 THE GABLES
$$$$

19 THE STRAND

TEL 09/403-7670

thegablesrestaurant.co.nz

On the waterfront, with dining inside the 1847 building or outside offering panoramic views, this is Russell's pick for creative cuisine. Local beef and lamb stand out on the menu, and of course seafood also features in this waterside restaurant. Prices are reasonable for the high standards. Reserve ahead in summer.

🔲 60 🚫 🅿 🗝 All major cards

MANGONUI

🍴 MANGONUI FISH SHOP
$

BEACH RD.

TEL 09/406-0478

Billing itself as "world famous" may be stretching it, but this renowned fish shop on stilts over the harbor is a de rigueur lunch (or dinner) stop for fish and chips. Oysters, lobster, and other local seafood are also offered, including delicacies like kina (sea urchin); with fishing boats moored alongside, it doesn't get

much fresher. Eat at picnic tables on the covered deck outside.

🔲 60 🗝 MC, V

HOKIANGA

🏠 COPTHORNE HOTEL & RESORT HOKIANGA
$$$$–$$$$$

SH12, OMAPERE

TEL 09/405-8737

millenniumhotels.co.nz

If traveling the Kauri Coast loop, this is the best hotel on Northland's west coast, in the sleepy coastal resort of Opononi/Omapere. The water setting is serene and rooms and apartments are well appointed. The sea-view rooms are best, and the restaurant is surprisingly good.

🚹 33 🅿 🚫 🏊 🛜 Charge 🗝 All major cards

⬛ CENTRAL NORTH ISLAND

WAITOMO

🏠 WAITOMO CAVES HOTEL
$$–$$$$

HOTEL ACCESS RD.

TEL 07/878-8204

waitomocaveshotel.co.nz

Only a five-minute walk to Glowworm Caves, this grand resort hotel built in 1908 is a Waitomo institution, albeit a neglected one. Renovations have been dragging on for years and in the meantime you get what you pay for—cheap rooms are basic, while grander, more expensive suites have real character.

🚹 33 🅿 🚫 🛜 Free 🗝 All major cards

COROMANDEL PENINSULA

Whitianga

🏠 SOVEREIGN PIER ON THE WATERWAYS
$$$$$

73 SOUTH HWY.

TEL 07/867-1236

whitiangaholidays.co.nz

This is the pick of the apartments that have cropped up everywhere in booming Whitianga. About 1.5 miles (2 km) south of the town center,

---

🚫 Nonsmoking 🅒 Air-Conditioning 🏊 Indoor Pool 🏊 Outdoor Pool 🏋 Health Club 🛜 Wi-Fi 🗝 Credit Cards in a gated marina development, spacious, luxury apartments are well appointed with everything laid on, including boat parking.

[i] 48 [P] [≜] [⊗] [▰] [▼] [☎] Free [◈] All major cards

[🏨] **OCEANSIDE MOTEL**
[🍴] **$$$$**

32 BUFFALO BEACH RD.
TEL 07/866-5766
oceansidemotel.co.nz

Less than a mile from town on the best stretch of beach, this well-kept motel with self-contained apartments has a great position and waterfront views.

[i] 9 [P] [⊗] [☎] Free [◈] All major cards

[🍴] **SALT**
$$$$

1 BLACKSMITH LN.
TEL 07/866-5818
salt-whitianga.co.nz

At the front of the Whitianga Hotel, Salt has a great position with a large deck overlooking yachts in the river. Seafood features prominently on a limited but interesting menu that includes steak, lamb, and varied influences.

[▦] 130 [◈] All major cards

[🍴] **SQUIDS BAR & RESTAURANT**
$$$

SHOP 15, 1 BLACKSMITH LN.
TEL 07/867-1710
squids.co.nz

Seafood lovers flock to this reasonably priced restaurant overlooking the yacht harbor, across the street from Salt. Dishes might include a great seafood chowder, seafood pasta, and wonderful Bluff oysters in season. A variety of fish dishes are cooked simply but with flair. Steak lovers are also catered to.

[▦] 40 [⊗] [P] [◈] All major cards

BAY OF PLENTY

Mount Maunganui/Tauranga

[🏨] **THE PAVILIONS**
$$$$$

4 MARINE PARADE, MOUNT MAUNGANUI
TEL 07/572-0001
pavilion.net.nz

PRICES

HOTELS

The cost of a double room in the high season is indicated by **$** signs (NZ dollars).

$$$$$	Over $250
$$$$	200–250
$$$	$150–200
$$	$100–150
$	Under $100

RESTAURANTS

The cost of a three-course meal without drinks is indicated by **$** signs (NZ dollars).

$$$$$	Over $80
$$$$	$60–80
$$$	$40–60
$$	$25–40
$	Under $25

Opposite the beach and near The Mount, the location is unbeatable. Well-appointed unserviced apartments of one to three bedrooms have sea views and balconies in this low-rise development.

[i] 15 [P] [≜] [⊗] [☎] Free [◈] All major cards

[🏨] **OCEANSIDE RESORT & TWIN TOWERS**
$$$–$$$$$

1 MAUNGANUI RD.,
MOUNT MAUNGANUI
TEL 07/575-5371
twintowers.co.nz

Near the town center and the beach, these older tower blocks offer some of the best value accommodations in town, including suites and apartments. The facilities include restaurants, small pool, sauna, and gym.

[i] 40 [P] [≜] [⊗] [▰] [▼] [☎] Free [◈] All major cards

[🏨] **BAY PALM MOTEL**
$$$–$$$$

84 GIRVEN RD., MOUNT MAUNGANUI
TEL 07/574-5971
baypalmmotel.co.nz

This better class of motel has studios and one- or two-bedroom units with kitchens, spa baths, and

---

[🏨] Hotel [🍴] Restaurant [i] No. of Guest Rooms [▦] No. of Seats [P] Parking [◷] Closed [≜] Elevator a heated swimming pool. Outside of Mount Maunganui near the golf course, it is a short walk to Ocean Beach and the Bayfair Mall.

🛈 16 🅿 🆂 🌊 🛜 Free 🆂 All major cards

🍴 MOUNT BISTRO RESTAURANT
$$$$–$$$$$
6 ADAMS AVE., MOUNT MAUNGANUI
TEL 07/575-3872
mountbistro.nz
The decor may not be all glass and chrome, but this is fine dining at its best in The Mount, opposite the hot pools. Dine from the set menu or à la carte, and leave room for the dessert tasting platter.

🍴 70 🕑 L & D Mon. 🆂 🆂 All major cards

🍴 HARBOURSIDE
$$$$
150 THE STRAND, TAURANGA
TEL 07/571-0520
harboursidetauranga.co.nz
The position doesn't get much better than this—perched over Tauranga Harbour in the old yacht club building. Global dishes have flair and service is superior. Try to book a table on the deck.

🍴 90 🆂 🆂 All major cards

🍴 POST BANK
$$$$
82 MAUNGANUI RD., MOUNT MAUNGANUI
TEL 07/575-4782
postbank.co.nz
This heritage building with polished wood and walls lined with books is home to innovative cuisine with international flair. In the main shopping strip, this standout is a deserved local favorite.

🍴 70 🕑 L Sat.–Mon. 🆂 🆂 🆂 All major cards

Whakatane

🏨 TUSCANY VILLAS
$$$–$$$$
57 THE STRAND EAST
TEL 07/308-2244
tuscanyvillas.co.nz
Despite the kitsch architectural homage to Tuscany, and claims to being a boutique hotel, this is one of the best of Whakatane's

numerous motels, right in the town center. Well-appointed studio and one-bedroom suites have kitchenettes, king beds, and spa baths.

🛈 28 🅿 🆂 🛜 Free 🆂 All major cards

🏨 WHITE ISLAND RENDEZVOUS
$$–$$$
15 THE STRAND EAST
TEL 07/308-9588
whiteisland.co.nz
Good motel rooms overlook the waterfront, a short stroll from town. It's run by an island tour operator, with package deals available.

🛈 28 🅿 🆂 🆂 🛜 Free 🆂 All major cards

🍴 ROQUETTE RESTAURANT & BAR
$$$
23–29 QUAY ST.
TEL 07/307-0722
roquette-restaurant.co.nz
Along the river from the tourist office, Roquette offers swank dining. The modern menu features dishes such as a good seafood risotto and Moroccan tagine.

🍴 40 🆂 🆂 All major cards

🍴 SOULSA
$$$
126 THE STRAND
TEL 07/307-8689
soulsa.co.nz
Unpretentious but with a fine-dining bent, the hottest dining spot on Whakatane's main street packs them in (reservations recommended). The twice-cooked duck is a standout on the interesting menu, as is the tasting plate for starters.

🍴 36 🕑 L & D Sun. 🆂 🆂 All major cards

ROTORUA

SOMETHING SPECIAL

🏨 PEPPERS ON THE POINT
$$$$$
214 KAWAHA POINT RD.
TEL 07/5665-4426
peppers.co.nz
This addition to Rotorua's luxury lodge scene is a converted 1930s mansion on a peaceful point on Lake Rotorua, 2 miles (3 km) north of

town. Set on 7 acres (3 ha) of gardens with a private beach and jetty, it has huge luxury suites and cottages decorated with antiques; the four-bedroom villa offers rock-star indulgence.

(i) 13 **P** ⓢ ⓢ 🛇 🛜 Free ⓢ All major cards

🏨 NGONGOTAHA LAKESIDE LODGE
$$$$

41 OPERIANA ST., NGONGOTAHA

TEL 07/357-4020

rotorualakesidelodge.co.nz

This intimate B&B, 6 miles (9 km) north of downtown Rotorua, offers fine hospitality and rooms on the lake. Great views and serenity guaranteed; trout fishing is on your doorstep.

(i) 3 **P** ⓢ 🛜 Free ⓢ MC, V

🏨 MILLENNIUM HOTEL ROTORUA
$$$-$$$$

ERUERA ST. & HINEMARU ST.

TEL 07/347-1234

millenniumhotels.co.nz

A short stroll to the town center, this large hotel encapsulates the Rotorua experience with a day spa, thermally heated swimming pool, gymnasium, saunas, and spa pools. Try to get a lake-view room.

(i) 227 **P** ⓢ ⓢ ⓢ 🛇 🛜 Charge ⓢ All major cards

🏨 PRINCES GATE HOTEL
$$$-$$$$

1057 ARAWA ST.

TEL 07/348-1179

princesgate.co.nz

Built in 1897, this gorgeous two-story wooden hotel lies just outside the entrance to the Government Gardens, right in the middle of town. Rooms can vary, but this boutique hotel offers heritage style and class.

(i) 50 **P** ⓢ ⓢ 🛜 Free ⓢ All major cards

🏨 REGAL PALMS
$$$-$$$$

350 FENTON ST.

TEL 07/350-3232

regalpalms.co.nz

This high-quality motel/resort has a heated pool, children's playground, mini-golf, gym, sauna, and tennis court. Big modern rooms have spa baths. Although more expensive

than most, the facilities and service are excellent in this spacious, well-kept complex.

(i) 50 **P** ⓢ ⓢ ⓢ 🛇 🛜 Free in public areas ⓢ All major cards

🏨 BELLA VISTA MOTEL ROTORUA
$$-$$$

94-98 LAKE RD.

TEL 07/343-6418

bellavistamotelrotorua.co.nz

Away from motel row on Fenton Street but close to the lake north of town, this is one of the better value of Rotorua's dozens of motels. Hospitality and service are first rate. Rooms range from small studios (larger superior rooms are only a few dollars more) to family suites with kitchens.

(i) 18 **P** 🛜 Free ⓢ All major cards

🏨 ROTOVEGAS MOTEL
$$-$$$

249 FENTON ST.

TEL 07/348-5586

rotovegasmotelrotorua.co.nz

Rotorua is overrun with cheap motels, many of them strung out along Fenton Street. This is one of the better appointed motels, and like many, it has hot spa baths, including some in the units, and a heated swimming pool.

(i) 23 **P** ⓢ ⓢ 🛜 Free ⓢ All major cards

🏨 SUDIMA HOTEL
$$-$$$

1000 ERUERA ST.

TEL 07/348-1174

sudimahotels.com

In a fabulous position on the lakefront next to the Polynesian Spa, this large hotel is a favorite with tour groups. Facilities include restaurants, bar, day spa, individual hot pools, and heated swimming pool. Though a little tired in places, online discounts can make it a bargain for the facilities offered.

(i) 250 **P** ⓢ ⓢ ⓢ 🛜 Free ⓢ All major cards

🍴 BISTRO 1284
$$$$

1284 ERUERA ST.

TEL 07/346-1284

bistro1284.co.nz

In a small cottage in central Rotorua, fine dining and good service are assured in what

---

is widely regarded as the city's best restaurant. Noted for beef and lamb dishes, the small dinner-only menu is distinguished by fresh produce and exquisite attention to detail.

🔲 35 🕐 L Sun. 🚭 🏧 All major cards

🍴 ATTICUS FINCH
$$$
1106 TUTANEKAI ST.
TEL 07/460-0400
atticusfinch.co.nz

Since they closed off the lake-end of Tutanekai Street, gave it a covered walkway, and called it Eat Street, everyone flocks here in the evening. Lined with restaurants, this one stands out for its tantalizing shared plates with Mediterranean and Asian influences. Not sure what Harper Lee would make of the *To Kill a Mockingbird* theme, but there's a good craft beer and wine menu, and tables out front for people-watching on a summer night.

🔲 80 🚭 🏧 All major cards

🍴 SABROSO
$$$
1184 HAUPAPA ST.
TEL 07/349-0591
sabroso.co.nz

This pan–Latin American restaurant with a Venezuelan/Mexican focus is a welcome addition to Rotorua's dining scene. Try the superb chimichurri chicken or the Brazilian shrimp stew, washed down with sangria. Small, casual, and homey with great service; reservations are recommended.

🔲 32 🕐 L & D Mon. & Tues.
🚭 🏧 MC,V

🍴 CAPERS EPICUREAN
$$–$$$
1181 ERUERA ST.
TEL 07/348-8818
capers.co.nz

This busy central deli has a good selection from the counter or light meals prepared in the kitchen. Very popular for breakfast and lunch, or coffee and cake anytime, it's also open for more expensive dinner.

🔲 90 🚭 🏧 All major cards

🍴 FAT DOG CAFÉ & BAR
$$–$$$
1161 ARAWA ST.
TEL 07/347-7586
fatdogcafe.co.nz

Fat dog pawprints and murals brighten the funky interior of this popular Rotorua institution. Great for breakfast, while light meals, snacks, and burgers dominate the lunch menu, and dinner offers fancier, more substantial fare.

🔲 100 🚭 🏧 All major cards

TAUPO

SOMETHING SPECIAL

🏨 HUKA LODGE
$$$$$
HUKA FALLS RD.
TEL 07/378-5791
hukalodge.co.nz

The granddaddy of New Zealand's luxury lodges, Huka Lodge has been making the world's great hotel lists for decades. Once a modest fishing lodge, this retreat offers sumptuous rooms and fine dining in the classic main lodge. The exclusive Owner's Cottage can also be rented.

ⓘ 25 🅿 🚭 🛜 Free 🏧 All major cards

🏨 MILLENNIUM MANUELS TAUPO
🍴 $$$$–$$$$$
243 LAKE TER.
TEL 07/378-5110
millenniumhotels.co.nz

Stroll across the grass from one of the few hotels right on New Zealand's largest lake, or take in the view from the rooms, the good bistro, or the restaurant. Well-appointed rooms and good service put it ahead of many hotels in this chain.

ⓘ 51 🅿 🔄 🚭 ♿ 🏊 🏋 🛜 Charge
🏧 All major cards

🏨 ABOVE THE LAKE
$$$$
46 ROKINO RD.
TEL 07/378-8738
taupostay.com

This welcoming B&B is an ideal spot for sightseers and others seeking home-style hospitality. The owners run tours to the thermal areas and other attractions around Taupo, and rooms are spacious and comfortable (upstairs has lake views).

ⓘ 3 🅿 🅂 📶 Free 🗝 MC, V

🏨 SAILS MOTOR LODGE
$$$–$$$$$
138 LAKE TER.
TEL 07/377-0655
sailstaupo.co.nz
At one of the fancier motels strung along the lake, sail-topped balconies finish off modern architectural styling. Lake views and the excellent location within walking distance of downtown make this a standout.

ⓘ 19 🅿 🅂 📶 Free 🗝 All major cards

🏨 TAUPO DEBRETTS THERMAL SPA RESORT
$–$$$$$
76 NAPIER-TAUPO RD.
TEL 07/378-8559
taupodebretts.co.nz
South of the town center, this big resort has something for everyone, from motor home and camping sites, to budget cabins, apartments, and lodge accommodations. Very well run with a café, the big lure is the attached hot springs with outdoor and private pools, waterslides, and day spa. Guests get discounted entry.

ⓘ 42 🅿 🅂 🅂 🏊 📶 Free 🗝 MC, V

🍴 VINE EATERY & BAR
$$$$
37 TUWHARETOA ST.
TEL 07/378-5704
vineeatery.co.nz
On Taupo's unofficial Eat Street lined with restaurants, this former wine shop has undergone a stylish fit-out and offers some of Taupo's best dining. Shared tapas plates feature strongly, but pasta, risotto, salads, and bistro mains with a Mediterranean bent round out the menu. The big wine list acknowledges its former incarnation.

🍴 80 🅂 🅂 🗝 All major cards

🍴 WATERSIDE RESTAURANT & BAR
$$$–$$$$
3 TONGARIRO ST.
TEL 07/378-6894
waterside.co.nz

In the town center overlooking the lake, this delightful restaurant has fires in winter and outdoor tables for balmy summer nights. Steak, lamb, and New Zealand classics feature prominently among well-presented dishes focusing on local produce.

🍴 150 🅂 🗝 All major cards

🍴 THE BRANTRY
$$$
45 RIFLE RANGE RD.
TEL 07/378-0484
thebrantry.co.nz
At the top of the Taupo dining heap, this restaurant tucked away in a 1950s suburban house always has something interesting on the three-course set menu presented with fine-dining flair at exceptional prices. Dine inside or out in the garden. Not to be missed.

🍴 60 🕐 L, D Sun. & Mon. 🅂 🅂 🅿 🗝 All major cards

TONGARIRO NATIONAL PARK

SOMETHING SPECIAL

🏨 CHATEAU TONGARIRO
$$$–$$$$$
SH48, MOUNT RUAPEHU
TEL 07/892-3809
chateau.co.nz
At the base of Mount Ruapehu volcano, this imposing old-money hotel from the 1930s is a New Zealand icon in a stunning setting. A variety of rooms in old and new wings range from tired to superb. It pays to pay extra for a room with a view.

ⓘ 106 🅿 🛗 🅂 🏊 📺 📶 Free 🗝 All major cards

NAPIER

🏨 SCENIC HOTEL TE PANIA
$$$$
45 MARINE PARADE
TEL 06/833-7733
scenichotels.co.nz
This four-star, six-story, horseshoe-shaped hotel is downtown, opposite the beach and the Ocean Spa. All rooms face out to sea with ceiling-to-floor windows for wonderful views.

ⓘ 109 🅿 🛗 🅂 🅂 📺 📶 Free 🗝 All major cards

🏨 SEA BREEZE
$$
281 MARINE PARADE
TEL 06/835-8067
seabreezebnb.co.nz
Napier has many delightful B&Bs strung along the seashore and on Bluff Hill. This downtown Victorian villa survived the earthquakes and has an English seaside boardinghouse charm, themed rooms, and reasonable prices.
🚪 3 🅿 🚭 🛜 Free 🅇 MC, V

🍴 MISSION ESTATE RESTAURANT
$$$$$
198 CHURCH RD., TARADALE
TEL 06/845-9354
missionestate.co.nz
Five miles (8 km) from the town center, but well worth the trip, this winery restaurant offers elegant dining in a former seminary. A contemporary menu with French and other influences highlights the best of local produce and wines. The setting is superb, perched on a hill overlooking the vines and Hawke's Bay—magic on a sunny day or balmy evening.
🔲 180 🚭 🅿 🅇 All major cards

🍴 PACIFICA
$$$
209 MARINE PARADE
TEL 06/833-6335
pacificarestaurant.co.nz
This is an excellent restaurant to try New Zealand's fresh seafood. Fish is the specialty, crusted with herbs or perhaps in coconut taro cream, while oysters and scallops are featured in season. Five-course set tasting menus (seafood or meat) are reasonably priced in this fine restaurant in a breezy casual location opposite the sea.
🔲 40 🕐 D Sun. & Mon. L 🚭 🅇 All major cards

▪ WELLINGTON & THE SOUTH

🏨 BOLTON HOTEL
$$$$–$$$$$
BOLTON ST. & MOWBRAY ST.
TEL 04/472-9966
boltonhotel.co.nz
A favorite with business travelers, this five-star hotel ranks as the city's best. Chic neutral

rooms offer superior facilities and extra touches. Above all, superior service sets it apart.
🚪 142 🅿 🚭 🛜 🅇 All major cards

🏨 MUSEUM ART HOTEL
🍴 **$$$$–$$$$$**
90 CABLE ST.
TEL 04/802-8900
museumhotel.co.nz
Opposite Te Papa Museum and the waterfront, the location doesn't get any better for sightseers. Decked out with art, this popular hotel offers luxury and thoughtful touches in its rooms. Its Hippopotamus restaurant, serving modern French cuisine, is one of the city's top dining venues.
🚪 160 🅿 🚭 🛜 Free 🅇 All major cards

🏨 COPTHORNE HOTEL WELLINGTON
🍴 ORIENTAL BAY
$$$–$$$$$
100 ORIENTAL PARADE
TEL 04/385-0279
millenniumhotels.co.nz
A short stroll from Te Papa Museum, this four-star hotel in chic Oriental Bay is on the edge of downtown but near the beach. Recent renovations have restored this nine-story hotel to high standards, and sleek contemporary rooms have balconies, many with wonderful harbor views.
🚪 117 🅿 🚭 🛜 Charge 🅇 All major cards

🏨 SOUTHERN CROSS SERVICED APARTMENTS
$$–$$$
35 ABEL SMITH ST., TE ARO
TEL 04/802-3441
sxapts.co.nz
Small but value apartments with kitchens on the southern edge of the city center, not far from the Cuba/Courtenay nightlife area.
🚪 118 🚭 🛜 Charge 🅇 All major cards

🏨 HOTEL IBIS WELLINGTON
🍴 $$

153 FEATHERSTON ST.
TEL 04/496-1880
ibis.com

This downtown three-star hotel is very central. Rooms are simple but comfortable with broadband, and the hotel has a bistro and bar. This well-presented budget hotel offers good value.

ⓘ 200 🅿 ⊜ 🚫 ⚙ 🛜 Charge
⬙ All major cards

🍴 ORTEGA FISH SHACK
$$$$

16 MAJORIBANKS ST.,
MOUNT VICTORIA
TEL 04/382-9559
ortega.co.nz

This bright, casual restaurant does wonderful things with fish. Shellfish also features prominently for starters, and desserts match the high dining standards. For a quick bite, you can dine at the bar, which has an extensive beer and wine list.

⬘ 70 🕐 L, D Sun. & Mon. 🚫
⬙ All major cards

🍴 SHED 5
$$$$

QUEENS WHARF
TEL 04/499-9069
shed5.co.nz

Housed in an 1888 wool store overlooking the water on central Queens Wharf, this is one of Wellington's finest restaurants. Seafood is prominent on the menu, from simple fish and chips to fancier creations, and the mains show flair, as do the desserts.

⬘ 180 🚫 ⬙ All major cards

🍴 LOGAN BROWN
$$$–$$$$$

192 CUBA ST.
TEL 04/801-5114
loganbrown.co.nz

The moment you walk into this former bank building with its marble columns and vaulted ceiling with inlay reliefs, you know you are in for something special. This is fine-dining, innovative cuisine at its best, with options from the impressive à la carte and indulgent tasting menus, to the value three-course bistro

menu, or afternoon high tea on Fridays and Saturdays.

⬘ 92 🕐 L, D Sun.–Tues. 🚫 ⚙
⬙ All major cards

🍴 LORETTA
$$–$$$

181 CUBA ST.
TEL 04/384-2213
loretta.net.nz

From a big, leisurely breakfast to a quick lunch or substantial dinner, Loretta does café fare with flair and super service despite the crowds. Pizza, pasta, risotto, steak, lamb, and a whole lot more feature on the menu, and there's a good wine and beer list.

⬘ 120 🚫 ⬙ All major cards

🍴 CAFFE L'AFFARE
$–$$

27 COLLEGE ST.
TEL 04/385-9748
laffare.co.nz

This café made espresso the drink of choice in 1990s Wellington and continues to serve excellent coffee and food. This is the place for a big breakfast, light lunch, or coffee and cake. Popular with inner-city clientele.

⬘ 80 🕐 D 🚫 ⬙ All major cards

PRICES

HOTELS
The cost of a double room in the high season is indicated by **$** signs (NZ dollars).

$$$$$	Over $250
$$$$	200–250
$$$	$150–200
$$	$100–150
$	Under $100

RESTAURANTS
The cost of a three-course meal without drinks is indicated by **$** signs (NZ dollars).

$$$$$	Over $80
$$$$	$60–80
$$$	$40–60
$$	$25–40
$	Under $25

🏨 Hotel 🍴 Restaurant ⓘ No. of Guest Rooms ⬘ No. of Seats 🅿 Parking 🕐 Closed ⊜ Elevator

MARTINBOROUGH

🏨 MARTINBOROUGH HOTEL
🍴 $$$-$$$$
THE SQUARE
TEL 06/306-9350
martinboroughhotel.co.nz
In the center of town, this classic hotel is
an icon of the Wairarapa wine district. The
imposing Victorian hotel with its wooden fret-
work has rooms with French doors opening
onto the wide verandahs upstairs, or equally
delightful rooms open on to the garden. It has
a good restaurant serving bistro fare matched
to the area's superb wines.
🛏 16 🅿 🚭 📶 Free 🏧 All major cards

▦ MARLBOROUGH & NELSON

PICTON/MARLBOROUGH SOUNDS

SOMETHING SPECIAL

🏨 BAY OF MANY COVES RESORT
$$$$$
QUEEN CHARLOTTE SOUND, PICTON
TEL 03/579-9771
bayofmanycoves.co.nz
Perfect for a honeymoon or romantic
getaway, plush apartments with balconies
overlook the water and are nestled into
hillside greenery. Fine-dining restaurant,
waterfront café, and attentive service round
out this special experience. This luxury resort
can be reached only by a 30-minute water-taxi
ride from Picton or by helicopter.
🛏 11 🚭 🏊 📶 Free 🏧 All major cards

🏨 PORTAGE RESORT
🍴 $$$-$$$$$
2923 KENEPURU RD.,
MARLBOROUGH SOUNDS
TEL 03/573-4309
portage.co.nz
On serene Kenepuru Sound, this three-star
resort has a swimming pool, spa, restaurant,
and café. Most rooms and suites have sea
views, and are the place to get away from it
all. Only 15 minutes by water taxi from Picton,
or 1.5 hours by car.
🛏 41 🅿 🚭 🏊 📶 Charge 🏧 All major cards

🏨 HARBOUR VIEW MOTEL
$$$-$$$$
30 WAIKAWA RD., PICTON
TEL 03/573-6259
harbourviewmotel.com.au
Close to the center and built on the hillside,
rooms do indeed have views of Picton's
wonderful harbor. Studios with kitchens have
balconies to take in the vista (top floor is best)
and tariffs are reasonable for expensive Picton.
🛏 18 🚭 🅿 📶 Free 🏧 MC, V

🍴 LE CAFÉ
$$$
12-14 LONDON QUAY, PICTON
TEL 03/573-5588
lecafepicton.co.nz
The waterfront and outside tables make this
great for breakfast through to dinner. Steaks,
rack of lamb, and seafood feature on a well-
presented, straightforward menu. Live music
frequently features in the evening.
🪑 100 🚭 🏧 All major cards

NELSON

🏨 DELORENZOS STUDIO APARTMENTS
$$$$-$$$$$
43-55 TRAFALGAR ST.
TEL 03/548-9774
delorenzos.co.nz
A five-minute walk north of the city center,
these spacious, comfortable apartments are
well equipped with kitchen, dishwasher, washing machine, dryer, large TV, and free Internet.
Very popular, it's often booked in summer, but
more reasonably priced in the off season.
🛏 30 🚭 🅿 ❄ 🏊 📶 Free
🏧 All major cards

🏨 RUTHERFORD HOTEL NELSON
🍴 $$$$-$$$$$
TRAFALGAR SQ.
TEL 03/548-2299
heritagehotels.co.nz
Refurbished rooms are the pick in this older
four-star hotel in an excellent downtown
locale. Try to get a top-floor room for great
views. The facilities include a pool, gym, and
good Japanese restaurant.
🛏 112 🅿 ❄ 🚭 ❄ 🏊 🏋 📶 Free
🏧 All major cards

🚭 Nonsmoking ❄ Air-Conditioning 🏊 Indoor Pool 🏊 Outdoor Pool 🏋 Health Club 📶 Wi-Fi 🏧 Credit Cards

🏨 CEDAR GROVE MOTOR LODGE
$$$
TRAFALGAR ST. & GROVE ST.
TEL 03/545-1133
cedargrove.co.nz
Units, suites, and apartments, some with
air-conditioning and spa bath, and all with full
cooking facilities, are offered in this well-kept
motel. Superior rooms, good service, and a
central position over the river from down-
town make it very popular.
🛈 23 🅿 🚼 🕄 🛜 Free 🅰 All major cards

🏨 NIKAU APARTMENTS
$$–$$$$
79–85 NILE ST.
TEL 03/548-7000
nikauapartments.co.nz
Modern, well-appointed, student-style apartments, from studio to four-bedroom, offer
great value in a downtown location just east
of the cathedral. All apartments have fully
equipped kitchens and free Wi-Fi.
🛈 30 🅿 🚼 🛜 Free 🅰 All major cards

🍴 HOPGOODS RESTAURANT & BAR
$$$$$
284 TRAFALGAR ST.
TEL 03/545-7191
hopgoods.co.nz
The top end of Trafalgar Street, overlooked
by the cathedral, is a fashionable place
for a meal or drink, and Hopgoods serves
consistently good contemporary fare from
an experienced chef/owner, who provides
reliable excellence in a city where chefs come
and go.
🍽 80 🕐 D Sun. 🚼 🅰 All major cards

🍴 BOAT SHED CAFÉ
$$$$
350 WAKEFIELD QUAY
TEL 03/546-9783
boatshedcafe.co.nz
This Nelson institution is perched over the
water on popular Wakefield Quay. The location couldn't get any better for a seafood
restaurant, nor the seafood fresher. From
hearty breakfasts to lighter lunches and
the choice dinner menu, the food and the
views excel.
🍽 60 🅰 All major cards

🍴 MORRI STREET CAFÉ
$$
244 HARDY ST.
TEL 03/548-8110
morrisonstreetcafe.co.nz
In this fashionable café with dining outdoors
and inside, good breakfast and lunch fare
comes with a twist. All locally grown and
supplied fare on a thoughtful menu shows
Mediterranean and Asian influences, and the
service is always first class.
🍽 70 🕐 D 🅰 All major cards

BLENHEIM

🏨🍴 MARLBOROUGH VINTNERS HOTEL
$$$$$
190 RAPAURA RD.
TEL 03/572-5094
marlboroughnz.co.nz
Blenheim town has most of the hotels, but
more are appearing out in the vineyards, like
these designer studios looking out over the
valley. Modern well-appointed rooms, some
with hot tub, are very comfortable and the
vineyard, mountain, and night-sky views are
wonderful. It also has a good restaurant.
🛈 16 🅿 🚼 🕄 🍽 🛜 Free
🅰 All major cards

KAIKOURA

🏨 KAIKOURA GATEWAY MOTOR LODGE
$$$–$$$$
16–18 CHURCHILL ST.
TEL 03/319-6070
kaikouragateway.co.nz
On the highway with a pool and sauna, this
motel is one of the town's newer breed.
Comfortable rooms, including one- and
two-bed units, offer high standards at a
good price.
🛈 20 🅿 🚼 🏊 🛜 Free 🅰 All major cards

🏨 WHITE MORPH
$$$–$$$$$
92–94 THE ESPLANADE
TEL 03/319-5014
whitemorph.co.nz
On the waterfront in town, well-appointed
studio units have small kitchens and offer
some of the best accommodations in town.

🏨 Hotel 🍴 Restaurant 🛈 No. of Guest Rooms 🍽 No. of Seats 🅿 Parking 🕐 Closed 🛗 Elevator

Units range from unexciting standard studios to excellent spa studios with ocean views and a two-bedroom family suite.

ⓘ 31 🄿 🅂 🛜 Free 🄰 All major cards

🍽 GREEN DOLPHIN
$$$$
12 AVOCA ST.
TEL 03/319-6666
greendolphinkaikoura.com
The closest to fine dining this side of the ranges, and beyond, the Green Dolphin does excellent fish and dishes such as pork belly with style. Try to get a window seat with sea glimpses. Kaikoura means "meal of crayfish," and this is the best place in town to sample them in season.

🍴 70 🄻 🅂 🄰 All major cards

◼ CHRISTCHURCH & CANTERBURY

🏢 HERITAGE CHRISTCHURCH
$$$$$
28–30 CATHEDRAL SQ.
TEL 03/983-4800
heritagehotels.co.nz
On Cathedral Square in the heart of the city, this grand hotel in the imposing Old Government Building survived the earthquake and delivers heritage charm. Large one- and two-bedroom apartments have towering ceilings, fully equipped kitchens, and thoughtful touches.

ⓘ 42 🄿 🔄 🅂 🔄 🌊 📺 🛜 Free 🄰 All major cards

🏢 PAVILIONS HOTEL
🍽 **$$$$$**
42 PAPANUI RD.
TEL 03/355-5633
pavilionshotel.co.nz
One mile (1.6 km) northwest of the city past the casino, this hotel has studios, some with spa bath, as well as one- and two-bedroom suites. Well run and comfortable, if lacking in luxury for the price, rooms are well appointed. The restaurant has good food.

ⓘ 88 🄿 🅂 🌊 📺 🛜 Free 🄰 All major cards

SOMETHING SPECIAL

🏢 THE GEORGE CHRISTCHURCH
🍽 **$$$$–$$$$$**
50 PARK TER.
TEL 03/379-4560
thegeorge.com
One of New Zealand's finest boutique hotels, the George boasts luxury in peaceful greenery on the edge of downtown. Generous rooms have indulgent extras and modern-cool opulence. Two fine-dining restaurants and superior service—the hotel boasts a one-to-one staff/guest ratio—round out the George's credentials.

ⓘ 55 🄿 🔄 🅂 🔄 🅂 📺 🛜 Free 🄰 All major cards

🏢 COLOMBO IN THE CITY MOTEL
$$$–$$$$$
863 COLOMBO ST.
TEL 03/366-8775
motelcolombo.co.nz
Top of the line motel, not quite in the city, but close enough, with a number of other motels nearby. Well-appointed units—from studio to two bedroom—are a cut above most, have small kitchens and double-glazed windows.

ⓘ 12 🄿 🅂 🛜 Free 🄰 All major cards

🏢 IBIS HOTEL
🍽 **$$$–$$$$**
107 HEREFORD ST.
TEL 03/367-8666
ibis.com
One of the better hotels in this budget chain, well-appointed refurbished rooms are reasonably priced—a rarity in a city still suffering a chronic room shortage. It has a restaurant and central location, near the Quake City museum.

ⓘ 155 🄿 🔄 🅂 🛜 Charge 🄰 All major cards

🏢 SOUTHWARK APARTMENTS
$$$
25 SOUTHWARK ST.
TEL 03/377-2799
southwarkapartments.co.nz
This new apartment complex has small, student-style studios with kitchenettes and en suites on the southern edge of the city center. Communal areas include fully equipped kitchens and TV lounges. Good value.

ⓘ 56 🄿 🔄 🅂 🛜 Free 🄰 All major cards

🏨 TUSCANA MOTOR LODGE
$$$
74 BEALEY AVE.
TEL 03/377-4485
tuscana.co.nz
One of the best motels on Bealey Avenue, the wide boulevard running along the northern edge of the city center, offering fine hospitality and good rooms, a 15-minute walk from the center.

🛏 12 🅿 🆂 📶 Free 💳 All major cards

🍽 CHRISTCHURCH TRAMWAY RESTAURANT
$$$$$
109 WORCESTER ST. SHOP 13, CATHEDRAL JUNCTION
TEL 03/366 -7830
welcomeaboard.co.nz
Yes, it's very touristy, but what a wonderful way to see the city, on an evening tour in a heritage tram while you dine. Three-course modern New Zealand meals are good, if a tad expensive, as are the drinks, but it's an experience.

🪑 36 🕐 L 🆂 💳 All major cards

🍽 PESCATORE
$$$$$
THE GEORGE, 50 PARK TER.
TEL 03/371-0257
thegeorge.com
Neither a fish nor an Italian restaurant, Pescatore is the city's most innovative fine-dining establishment. Behind a padded door, the dining drama unfolds with unique creations that show artistry and technical muscle in equal portions. Intricate, stylish, and expensive.

🪑 50 🆂 🅿 🆂 💳 All major cards

🍽 SAGGIO DI VINO
$$$$$
179-181 VICTORIA ST.
TEL 03/379-4006
saggiodivino.co.nz
With the country's best wine cellar and a wide range of New Zealand vintages by the glass, *vino* comes to the fore, but this fine restaurant is also *saggio* (wise) when it comes to food. The interior is contemporary chic, the menu European, and the produce fresh local, from New Zealand truffles to venison loin.

🪑 65 🕐 L 🆂 💳 All major cards

🍽 TWENTY SEVEN STEPS
$$$$
16 NEW REGENT ST.
TEL 03/366-2727
twentysevensteps.co.nz
In the lively New Regent Street strip, now the best hunting ground for eats in the city center, this newcomer is wowing the town. Rustic European-inspired cuisine has a decidedly modern twist in a relaxed dining space in an old art deco building.

🪑 80 🕐 L 🆂 💳 All major cards

🍽 RANGOON RUBY
$$$
819 COLOMBO ST.
TEL 022/028-0920
rangoonruby.co.nz
Think Southeast Asian cuisine meets Indian curries with New Zealand ingredients and freshness, and you have this very popular Burmese restaurant, reincarnation in the city center of the ever popular Bodhi Tree. Dining is tapas style—you need to order a number of small plates.

🪑 80 🆂 💳 All major cards

🍽 ARJEE BHAJEE
$$–$$$
13 RICCARTON RD., RICCARTON
TEL 03/365-6633
arjeebhajee.co.nz
This "Indian with attitude" restaurant is as much Nepalese but turns out good regional North Indian dishes from Calcutta fish to Kashmiri chicken. It's in the lively Riccarton shopping strip just west of Hagley Park, one of the main shopping/dining areas relatively unaffected by the earthquake.

🪑 40 🆂 💳 All major cards

MOUNT COOK

SOMETHING SPECIAL

🏨 HERMITAGE HOTEL
🍽 $$$$$
TERRACE RD.
TEL 03/435-1809
hermitage.co.nz
What a setting, what a view! This grande dame of New Zealand hotels (1884) has comfortable rooms in different wings, many with stunning

---

🏨 Hotel 🍽 Restaurant 🛏 No. of Guest Rooms 🪑 No. of Seats 🅿 Parking 🕐 Closed ⬛ Elevator views of the mountain, as well as motel rooms and chalets. Room standards vary and you certainly pay for the location, especially in high season, but low-season discounts are attractive. The fine restaurants and bars look straight up to the "Cloud Piercer."

🛈 214 P 🖨 🚫 🖺 Free 🚫 All major cards

WEST COAST

FRANZ JOSEF

🏨 SCENIC HOTEL FRANZ JOSEF GLACIER
$$$$$
SH6
TEL 03/752-0729
scenic-circle.co.nz

In the center of the township, this older resort hotel has had a face-lift, restoring it to its former grandeur. Big, comfortable motel-style rooms and excellent service make this a good choice, despite painful high-season rates.

🛈 177 P 🚫 🛰 Free 🚫 All major cards

🏨 TE WAONUI FOREST RETREAT
$$$$$
3 WALLACE ST.
TEL 03/752-0555
tewaonui.co.nz

This stylish eco-lodge brings five-star luxury to the wilderness of the West Coast. At the edge of town, wood and glass rooms ring a rain forest compound. Rates include breakfast and a five-course degustation dinner.

🛈 100 P 🖨 🚫 🛰 Free 🚫 All major cards

🏨 ALPINE GLACIER MOTEL
$$$–$$$$
CRON ST. & CONDON ST.
TEL 03/752-0226
alpineglaciermotel.com

This friendly motel in the town center has mountain views. Spotless rooms with kitchen facilities are well appointed and a good value in an expensive part of New Zealand. The hot tub is welcome after a day on the glacier.

🛈 24 P 🚫 🛰 Free 🚫 All major cards

FOX GLACIER

🏨 DISTINCTION FOX GLACIER TE WEHEKA HOTEL
$$$$$
15 MAIN RD., SH6
TEL 03/751-0730
distinctionhotelsfoxglacier.co.nz

This Alpine-style hotel has helped boost room numbers in Fox and offers some of the best accommodation in town. Spacious rooms with small balconies are well appointed and a good value in the off-season, but like everywhere else, much more expensive in summer. Breakfast in the dining room is included in the rates.

🛈 21 P 🚫 🛰 Free 🚫 All major cards

🏨 FOX GLACIER LODGE
$$$$–$$$$$
SULLIVAN RD.
TEL 03/751-0888
foxglacierlodge.com

This cheery alpine lodge, pine lined with a peaked roof, has a cozy feel. Located just behind the main street shops, it has B&B rooms, self-contained units, and a chalet for rent.

🛈 11 P 🚫 🛰 Free 🚫 All major cards

OTAGO

DUNEDIN

🏨 BLUESTONE ON GEORGE
$$$$–$$$$$
571 GEORGE ST.
TEL 03/477-9201
bluestonedunedin.co.nz

Close to the city center, this upmarket motel/hotel has well-appointed, elegant apartment rooms, some of the best in Dunedin. All rooms have kitchenettes and washer/dryers, and many have Jacuzzis. A big hit with corporate as well as leisure travelers.

🛈 15 P 🚫 🖥 🛰 Free 🚫 All major cards

🏨 LARNACH CASTLE
$$$–$$$$$
CAMP RD., OTAGO PENINSULA
TEL 03/476-16164
larnachcastle.co.nz

Larnach Castle, 10 miles (15 km) from Dunedin, provides a range of interesting accommodations. Guests don't stay in the castle building, but can have dinner in the castle dining room. Well-appointed themed rooms in the purpose built lodge have amazing views right across the Otago Peninsula, while the original stables next door have more basic attic rooms (be careful which one you book). The new, luxury Camp Estate outside the grounds offers sumptuous accommodations and superior service.

🛈 21 🅿 🛇 📶 Free 💳 All major cards

🏨 315 EURO
$$$–$$$$

315 GEORGE ST.
TEL 03/477-9929
eurodunedin.co.nz

Modern, stylish apartments range from small studios with kitchenettes to spacious one-bedroom apartments with full kitchens. Just off George Street in the city center, behind the lively retail/restaurant strip, the position is excellent for this motel/apartment complex.

🛈 26 🅿 ⬍ 🛇 📶 Free 💳 All major cards

🏨 THE BROTHERS HOTEL
$$$–$$$$

295 RATTRAY ST.
TEL 03/477-0043
brothershotel.co.nz

The 1920s stately residence of the Christian Brothers has been converted into a boutique hotel, retaining much of its charm. Perched on a hill, the hotel offers stunning views from the balcony and is only a ten-minute walk from The Octagon.

🛈 15 🅿 🛇 📶 Free 💳 All major cards

🏨 🍽 SCENIC HOTEL DUNEDIN CITY
$$$–$$$$

123 PRINCES ST.
TEL 03/470-1470
scenichotels.co.nz

Big, well-furnished rooms and a great location two blocks from The Octagon make this four-star hotel a good choice. Though not brimming with character, it is modern, completely refurbished, and has a good restaurant. Try to get a harbor-view room.

🛈 121 🅿 ⬍ 🛇 📺 📶 Free
💳 All major cards

PRICES

HOTELS

The cost of a double room in the high season is indicated by **$** signs (NZ dollars).

$$$$$	Over $250
$$$$	200–250
$$$	$150–200
$$	$100–150
$	Under $100

RESTAURANTS

The cost of a three-course meal without drinks is indicated by **$** signs (NZ dollars).

$$$$$	Over $80
$$$$	$60–80
$$$	$40–60
$$	$25–40
$	Under $25

🏨 ARDEN STREET HOUSE
$$

36 ARDEN ST., NORTH EAST VALLEY
TEL 03/473-8860
ardenstreethouse.co.nz

A charming 1930s house built by a Scottish sea captain has nautical touches and views from the top of one Dunedin's steepest streets near the Botanic Gardens. Older, quirky rooms, with and without bathrooms, provide good budget accommodations, and the hostess offers warm Kiwi hospitality.

🛈 5 🅿 🛇 📶 Free 💳 MC, V

🍽 PIER 24
$$$$

HOTEL ST. CLAIR, 24 ESPLANADE, ST. CLAIR BEACH
TEL 03/466-3610
hotelstclair.com

Renowned chef Michael Coughlin is back, after renovations to this Dunedin institution, where lamb, beef, seafood, and other selections are served with inventive aplomb. Simpler (and cheaper) lunch and breakfast are offered. Overlooking the beach south of the city, with floor-to-ceiling windows, dramatic Pacific views are assured.

🪑 70 🛇 💳 All major cards

🏨 Hotel 🍽 Restaurant 🛈 No. of Guest Rooms 🪑 No. of Seats 🅿 Parking 🕐 Closed ⬍ Elevator

🍴 TWO CHEFS BISTRO
$$$$

121 STUART ST.

TEL 03/477-7293

twochefsbistro.com

This delightful bistro in the heart of the city does its best to impart a Parisian feel, from the dark wood decor and antique mirrors to the bistro classics, all with an eye to contemporary palates and the best local ingredients. Central Otago Pinot Noir features strongly on an impressive drinks menu.

🔲 50 🕐 L, D Sun. 🚫
🔷 All major cards

🍴 THE REEF
$$$

329–333 GEORGE ST.

TEL 03/471-7185

Three blocks north of The Octagon in the city's busiest restaurant strip, the always popular Reef serves excellent seafood at moderate prices. The seafood platter provides a varied smorgasbord of mostly local seafood.

🔲 75 🚫 🔷 All major cards

🍴 GREAT TASTE
$–$$

12 ST. ANDREW ST.

TEL 03/479-2088

greattaste.co.nz

When in a student town, eat as the students do. The à la carte menu features seafood and steaks with a salad bar, but the very cheap Asian-style buffet is most popular and is even cheaper at lunchtime.

🔲 130 🚫 🔷 All major cards

QUEENSTOWN

SOMETHING SPECIAL

🏨 EICHARDT'S PRIVATE HOTEL
$$$$$

MARINE PARADE

TEL 03/441-0450

eichardts.com

This delightful boutique hotel, a Queenstown original, combines rock-star prices with old-money gentility. In an unbeatable position near the lakefront in the restaurant district, rooms have gigantic beds, fireplaces, dressing rooms, and heated mirrors and floors. New additions include luxury lakefront apartments

and a private residence, a short walk from the original heritage hotel.

🛈 10 🅿 🔁 🚫 📶 Free 🔷 All major cards

🏨 MILLBROOK
$$$$$

MALAGHANS RD.

TEL 03/441-7000

millbrook.co.nz

Nestled in a valley ringed by peaks on the back road to Arrowtown, this luxury resort boasts extensive recreational facilities, including a championship golf course, day spa, tennis courts, gym, and indoor lap pool. Villas and cottages throughout the grounds range from studio units to four-bedroom homes.

🛈 175 🅿 🚫 🔁 🏊 🏋 📶 Free
🔷 All major cards

🏨 NOVOTEL LAKESIDE QUEENSTOWN
$$$$$

EARL ST. & MARINE PARADE

TEL 03/442-7750

novotel.com

In a prime location near the town center on a quiet stretch of lakefront, the Novotel has four-star rooms with a balcony upstairs or opening on to the garden downstairs.

🛈 273 🅿 🔁 🚫 🚫 📶 Free
🔷 All major cards

🏨 SOFITEL QUEENSTOWN HOTEL & SPA
$$$$$

8 DUKE ST.

TEL 03/450-0045

sofitel.com

Elegantly appointed rooms have balconies with mountain or lake views. This luxury hotel heavily promotes its day spa, and all rooms have Jacuzzis and espresso machines.

🛈 82 🅿 🔁 🚫 🚫 🏋 📶 Free
🔷 All major cards

🏨 MERCURE RESORT QUEENSTOWN
$$$$–$$$$$

SAINSBURY RD.

TEL 03/442-6600

mercure.com

Queenstown has plenty of larger four-star hotels offering excellent facilities and rooms for the price, such as the well-maintained

Mercure. About 1.5 miles (2.4 km) from town, it has great views of the lake and The Remarkables, and extensive resort facilities.

🛏 148 🅿 Ⓢ ⛴ 🍸 📶 Free
🏦 All major cards

🏨 SHERWOOD DISCOVERY HOTEL
$$$$–$$$$$

GOLDFIELD HEIGHTS, FRANKTON RD.

TEL 03/442-8032

discoverysherwood.co.nz

Opposite the lake, this eco-friendly apartment-style hotel/motel has wonderful lake and mountain views. Studio, one-, and two-bedroom apartments are comfortable and most have kitchen facilities. It is out of town toward Frankton, where prices are more reasonable, at least in the off season.

🛏 78 🅿 Ⓢ ⛴ 📶 Free 🏦 All major cards

🏨 TURNER HEIGHTS TOWNHOUSES
$$$$–$$$$$

14 TURNER ST.

TEL 03/442-8383

turnerheights.co.nz

On the hill at the end of central Shotover Street, these alpine-style one- and two-bedroom apartments are cute and quiet. Fully equipped and well furnished, some have spa baths and expansive lake views.

🛏 12 🅿 Ⓢ 📶 Free 🏦 All major cards

🏨 BELLA VISTA MOTEL
$$$

36 ROBINS RD.

TEL 03/442-4468

stayqueenstown.com

This chain motel a little north of the town center has modern, clean, well-equipped rooms. Friendly management and reasonable rates in expensive Queenstown make it one of the better motel buys.

🛏 24 🅿 Ⓢ 📶 Free 🏦 All major cards

🍴 RATA
$$$$$

STE NUKU, 43 BALLARAT ST.

TEL 03/442-9393

ratadining.co.nz

Timber, stone, granite, leather, and a giant photo of native rata trees set the eco-scene for one of Queenstown's finest restaurants. Tucked away down a lane, it's worth seeking

out celebrity chef Josh Emett's chic eatery that serves the best of local produce, with an excellent selection of local wines by the glass.

🍴 90 Ⓢ 🏦 All major cards

🍴 FISHBONE BAR & GRILL
$$$$

7 BEACH ST.

TEL 03/442-6768

fishbonequeenstown.co.nz

A cool makeover and affable service in this restaurant covering the seafood spectrum from fish and chips to lobster. The menu focuses on fish but features plenty of local delicacies in season—oysters, mussels, abalone, etc.

🍴 65 🕐 L Ⓢ 🏦 All major cards

🍴 AMISFIELD BISTRO
$$$–$$$$$

10 LAKE HAYES RD.

TEL 03/442-0556

amisfield.co.nz

This superb winery/restaurant between Queenstown and Arrowtown is in a lovely setting with views of Lake Hayes. Well worth the 15-minute drive, the varied menu has mostly Mediterranean-inspired dishes. The "trust the chef" set includes a number of taste treats, such as marinated olives, chorizo, pork with apple and watercress—whatever is available that day. Open for lunch, when you get the best views, and dinner.

🍴 70 Ⓢ 🏦 AE, MC, V

🍴 BATHHOUSE CAFÉ
$$$–$$$$

28 MARINE PARADE

TEL 03/442-5625

bathhouse.co.nz

The perennial favorite packs them in for the unbeatable views, right next to the lake in a heritage bathhouse, as much as the good breakfast, lunch, and dinner fare. Tapas dominates the afternoon and dinner menu, with interesting taste treats to try, but a limited à la carte menu is also available.

🍴 90 🏦 All major cards

🍴 WINNIES GOURMET PIZZA BAR
$$$

7 THE MALL

TEL 03/442-8635

winnies.co.nz

🏨 Hotel 🍴 Restaurant 🛏 No. of Guest Rooms 🍴 No. of Seats 🅿 Parking 🕐 Closed 🛗 Elevator

Upstairs with balcony dining in summer or inside with a roaring log fire in winter, ever-popular Winnies has steak, fish, and pasta on the menu, but most popular are the gourmet pizzas such as the Pescara seafood pizza and the Montonara, with chicken, Brie, sun-dried tomatoes, and sweet chili sauce. Winnies also has pool tables and is open late, or very late.

🚻 90 🚭 🃏 All major cards

🍴 SPEIGHT'S ALE HOUSE
$$–$$$
STANLEY ST. & BALLARAT ST.
TEL 03/441-3065
speightsalehousequeenstown.co.nz
In a restored heritage building, this popular pub does great pub food at reasonable prices. Huge servings focus on traditional fare, such as steak, lamb shanks, and fish and chips, with a Speight's beer recommended for each dish. Boisterous when a rugby match plays on the big screen, this is value Kiwi dining at its best.

🚻 80 🚭 🃏 All major cards

WANAKA

🏨 EDGEWATER RESORT
🍴 $$$$$
SARGOOD DR.
TEL 03/443-0011
edgewater.co.nz
Right on Lake Wanaka just outside town, this is the place for a great recreational vacation, with tennis courts, spa pools, sauna, and bicycle rentals. Studio rooms are well appointed, but the expansive one-bedroom suites, many opening to the lawns and lake, offer kitchens and greater comfort. The resort also has two excellent restaurants.

ℹ️ 104 🅿️ 🚭 🛜 Free 🃏 All major cards

🏨 THE MOORINGS
$$$–$$$$$
17 LAKESIDE RD.
TEL 03/443-8479
themoorings.co.nz
These motel units and apartments in a stylish complex lie just around the corner from the main street. The well-appointed motel units have views of the lake, while the two- and three-bedroom apartments are fully equipped and have decks, many with water views.

ℹ️ 26 🅿️ 🚭 🛜 Free 🃏 All major cards

🏨 WANAKA LUXURY APARTMENTS
$$$–$$$$$
8 STONEBROOK DR.
TEL 03/443-4943
wla.co.nz
In a suburban estate on the town's edge, semi-detached apartments are spacious and wonderfully appointed, with some of the best room standards in Wanaka. One- to three-bedroom apartments have kitchenettes or fully equipped kitchens, and there is a Jacuzzi and small heated swimming pool.

ℹ️ 34 🅿️ 🚭 🏊 🛜 Free 🃏 All major cards

🏨 LAKEVIEW MOTEL
$$$–$$$$
64–68 LISMORE ST.
TEL 03/443-6955
lakeviewmotel.co.nz
One street back from the lake, this motel is one of the better buys in Wanaka, with great views of the water and town. A short walk to the town center, its comfortable studio units have kitchens and cable TV.

ℹ️ 6 🅿️ 🚭 🛜 Free 🃏 All major cards

🍴 BISTRO GENTIL
$$$$$
76A GOLF COURSE RD.
TEL 03/443-2299
bistrogentil.co.nz
New Zealand fresh produce cooked *à la française* with a modern twist is served with fine-dining style. A seven-course tasting menu is offered as well as à la carte dining. The wine list is equally impressive, including a large range of wine by the glass from a self-dispensing wine machine, which preserves the wine's "organoleptic" qualities (alas, no discount if you know what that means).

🚻 100 🕐 L, D Sun. & Mon. 🅿️ 🚭 🃏 All major cards

🍴 RELISHES
$$$–$$$$
1/99 ARDMORE ST.
TEL 03/443-9018
relishescafe.co.nz
Relishes is all things to all diners: generous all-day breakfasts, interesting light café lunches, and in the evenings it turns into a fine-dining restaurant with an innovative contemporary

menu. Central Otago wines feature strongly on an interesting wine list.

🍴 65 🚭 💳 All major cards

🍴 KAI WHAKAPAI
$$–$$$
ARDMORE ST.
TEL 03/443-7795

This Wanaka institution opposite the lake is a bustling place, pumping out breakfast and coffee throughout the day, with a good selection of café fare on the menu through to dinner, and assorted treats in the cabinet. Outdoor tables are always popular in the sun or under the outdoor heaters.

🍴 80 🚭 💳 MC, V

■ FIORDLAND & SOUTHLAND

TE ANAU

SOMETHING SPECIAL

🏨 FIORDLAND LODGE
$$$$$
472 TE ANAU MILFORD HWY.
TEL 03/249-7832
fiordlandlodge.co.nz

Luxury seekers will have to head 3 miles (5 km) north of town to this delightful lodge above Lake Te Anau. The lodge was built of stone and rough-hewn logs, and the lobby has towering ceilings, a huge log fire, and expansive windows. Lodge rooms have wonderful lake and mountain views, and families can rent one of two log cabins. Fine dining and matching wines are offered.

🛏 12 🅿 🚭 🛗 📶 Free 💳 All major cards

🏨 FIORDLAND LAKEVIEW HOTEL & APARTMENTS
$$$$–$$$$$
42 LAKEFRONT DR.
TEL 03/249-7546
fiordlandlakeview.co.nz

The quality chalet-style one- and two-bedroom apartments on the waterfront are a perennial favorite but often full, so book well ahead. Well-kept grounds, good service, and fully equipped rooms make this a better buy than some large hotels that fill up with tour groups.

🛏 13 🅿 🚭 📶 Free 💳 All major cards

🏨 KINGSGATE HOTEL TE ANAU
$$$$
20 LAKEFRONT DR.
TEL 03/249-7421
millenniumhotels.co.nz

One of the largest hotels in town, the Kingsgate gets lots of tour groups but offers good rooms at a reasonable price. Across the road from the lake and a pleasant stroll from town, the location is good, and it compares favorably to Te Anau's other large hotels.

🛏 94 🅿 🚭 📶 Charge 💳 All major cards

🏨 RADFORDS ON THE LAKE
$$$$
56 LAKEFRONT DR.
TEL 03/249-9186
www.radfordslakeviewmotel.co.nz

This well-kept lakeside motel has studio, one-, and two-bedroom units. All units have lake views (best in upstairs rooms), and some have spa baths. Welcoming managers, a central location, and high standards make it very popular.

🛏 14 🅿 🚭 📶 Free 💳 All major cards

🏨 TE ANAU LAKEVIEW HOLIDAY PARK
$–$$$$$
1 TE ANAU-MANAPOURI RD.
TEL 03/249-7457
teanauholidaypark.co.nz

Te Anau accommodations tend to be expensive and full in peak season, so head to this holiday park near the lake for budget options. A huge variety of rooms range from spartan but modern singles in the well-equipped lodge to A-frame cabins, comfortable tourist apartments, and motel units, all at attractive rates.

🛏 200 🅿 🚭 📶 Free 💳 AE, MC, V

🍴 REDCLIFFE RESTAURANT & BAR
$$$
12 MOKONUI ST.
TEL 03/249-7431

In the town center, this charming, relocated wooden cottage has rustic decor but this is as close as you'll find to fine dining and not your ordinary café fare. One of Te Anau's most consistent restaurants, Redcliffe offers fusion flavors and fresh, local produce.

🍴 80 🕒 L 🚭 💳 MC, V

🏨 Hotel 🍴 Restaurant 🛏 No. of Guest Rooms 🍴 No. of Seats 🅿 Parking 🕒 Closed 🛗 Elevator

LA TOSCANA
$$$
108 TOWN CENTER
TEL 03/249-7756
latoscana.co.nz
In a town not renowned for fine dining, you'll get straightforward pasta and pizzas at moderate prices at this ever popular restaurant. It stays open later than most and has an impressive beer list as well as wine.
🍴 42 🕐 L 🚭 🪙 MC, V

INVERCARGILL

ASCOT PARK HOTEL
$$–$$$$
TAY ST. & RACECOURSE RD.
TEL 03/217-6195
ascotparkhotel.co.nz
It's hard to figure out why small Invercargill needs this huge hotel/motel complex spread around acres of garden on the eastern outskirts. Often nearly empty, it has quality hotel rooms, apartments, and motel units at bargain rates. The good facilities include an indoor heated pool, sauna, gym, bar, and restaurant.
🛏 96 🅿 🚭 🏊 🏋 📶 Free 🪙 All major cards

VICTORIA RAILWAY HOTEL
$–$$$
3 LEVEN ST.
TEL 03/218-1281
hotelinvercargill.co.nz
In the center of town, opposite the railway station that closed in 1981, this heritage gem has renovated rooms with lots of character and modern bathrooms. Throw in a cozy bar, restaurant, free parking, and reasonable rates and this hotel is a great option. Cheap old pub rooms with shared facilities are not advertised but available on request.
🛏 22 🅿 🚭 📶 Free 🪙 All major cards

ZOOKEEPERS CAFÉ
$$
50 TAY ST.
TEL 03/218-3373
This fun, funky café—easy to spot by the corrugated elephant atop the verandah—is an Invercargill institution. Open 7 a.m. until late, the café offers big breakfast and soups,

fish, tacos, and steaks done well and at moderate prices.
🍴 120 🚭 🪙 All major cards

STEWART ISLAND

RAKIURA LODGE
$$–$$$
8 MIRO CRESCENT, OBAN
TEL 03/219-1003
rakiuralodge.co.nz
This small, friendly, high-quality lodge has immaculate modern rooms off a well-equipped central sitting/dining/kitchen area, a large self-contained apartment upstairs, and an outside deck for lounging. It is only a five-minute walk to town.
🛏 5 🅿 🚭 📶 Free 🪙 MC, V

SOUTH SEA HOTEL
$–$$$
THE WATERFRONT, OBAN
TEL 03/219-1059
stewart-island.co.nz
This hotel has lots of character. Hotel rooms have shared facilities but, being on the waterfront, some have sea views. The cottage motel units behind have kitchens and bathrooms. The glassed-in restaurant overlooking the harbor serves good food, and the bar is sometimes lively. What better place to hang out and meet locals than the local pub.
🛏 17 🅿 📶 Free 🪙 AE, MC, V

CHURCH HILL RESTAURANT & OYSTER BAR
$$$$
36 KAMAHI RD., OBAN
TEL 03/219-1323
churchhill.co.nz
On the hill above the ferry dock, this excellent restaurant is a surprise find in the island's tiny main settlement. Intimate dining inside, or at tables on the lawn, is accompanied by wonderful harbor views. Seafood (including lobster) features prominently, but lamb, steaks, and other fare are offered, including muttonbird (a somewhat oily local delicacy).
🍴 40 🕐 L 🅿 🚭 🪙 All major cards

Shopping

New Zealand has some distinctive shopping opportunities. A host of art-and-crafts items make interesting gifts, such as Maori greenstone carving, *paua* (abalone) shell jewelry, bone and wood carvings, woolen items, and wines. Galleries and souvenir shops abound in the main cities and tourist towns, and arts and crafts are found around the countryside and in backcountry studios.

For one-stop shopping, the best destination in the country is **Hokitika** on the South Island's West Coast. Famed as the center for Maori greenstone carving, a host of galleries and studios sell a variety of crafts and jewelry.

For last-minute shopping, tourist centers like Queenstown and Rotorua are well supplied with souvenir shops, though prices are often higher than in the countryside.

In **Auckland**, wander **Queen Street** for cheaper souvenirs. Just off Queen Street on Shortland Street, **Aotea Gifts** at No. 3 is one of the biggest souvenir stores, and they also have branches in Queenstown, Rotorua, and Dunedin. The **Britomart** precinct around Quay St./Britomart Place is Auckland's newest and most interesting downtown shopping district. **High Street** in downtown Auckland is the city's premier shopping strip and has chic New Zealand fashion outlets, as does the suburb of **Newmarket.** The city has some good craft galleries, such as **Pauanesia** (*35 High St., tel 09/366-7282*), with handcrafted gifts from the Pacific. The suburb of **Parnell** has more upscale gift shops, including **Elephant House Crafts** (*237 Parnell Rd., tel 09/309-8740*), crammed with New Zealand handicrafts, down an alley off the main road. Of Auckland's many markets, the small **Parnell Farmers Market** (*545 Parnell Rd.*) is close to the center and has a few craft stalls, and well as produce, on Saturday mornings. In the southern suburbs, **Otara Market** (*Newbury St., Otara*) is a large Saturday morning market with a Polynesian flavor selling almost anything.

In **Christchurch,** the Sunday market at **Riccarton House** (*16 Kau Rd., Riccarton*) is good for crafts. Rotorua is overrun with souvenir shops; for something more interesting, **Maori Made** (*1180 Hinemoa St.*) is a collective of local artists and designers producing unique Maori themed art, craft, and clothing. The **Rotorua Night Market** held Thursdays on Tutanekai Street is also well worth a browse for local craft, cheap souvenirs, and food.

Maori Arts: The Maori are known for their craftsmanship, with carving *Pounamu* (greenstone or New Zealand jade), bone, and wood. Intricate work using abalone (*paua*) shell and rolled flax fibers for baskets are traditions carried on today. See pp. 86–87 for more information.

Clothing: New Zealand has a thriving fashion industry, with young and established designers well represented in major city boutiques. The **World of WearableArt Festival,** held annually in Wellington and displayed at the **WOW Museum** in **Nelson,** showcases avant-garde fashion.

Outdoor-loving New Zealanders also produce high-quality outdoor fashion, from hiking gear to rugged, checked Swanndri shirts and jackets beloved by Kiwi farmers. Icebreaker is renowned for outdoor fashion made from high-quality merino wool. Kathmandu, macpac, and Earth Sea Sky also produce quality outdoor fashion and equipment. Rugby fashion has also gravitated to the mainstream with the Canterbury line of rugby jerseys.

Entertainment

New Zealand has a small, thriving arts scene, from theater, ballet, and symphony orchestras to Maori cultural performances, Pacific rap artists, and rock bands. The Tourism New Zealand website *(newzealand.com)* lists up-to-date arts, culture, music, sports, and food and wine events.

Of all performing arts festivals, the **New Zealand International Arts Festival** *(nzfestival .co.nz)* is the country's largest, held every other year in Wellington. Combining the film festivals of the major cities, the **New Zealand International Film Festival** *(nzff.co.nz)* tours the country with a wide selection of non-mainstream films.

Theater: In Auckland the primary professional theater company, **Auckland Theatre Company** *(atc.co.nz)*, performs annually at various venues, including the **Maidment Theatre, Aotea Centre, Town Hall,** and **SkyCity Theatre.** Theater is particularly strong in Wellington, represented by the long-running **Circa** *(circa.co.nz)* and **Bats** *(bats.co.nz)* theater companies. Christchurch has the professional **Court Theatre** *(court theatre.org.nz)*, while Dunedin has **Fortune Theatre** *(fortunetheatre.co.nz)*.

Classical Music, Ballet & Opera: The cultural center of New Zealand, Wellington is home to the **New Zealand Symphony Orchestra** *(nzso.co.nz)*, which performs around the country. The **Royal New Zealand Ballet** *(rnzb.org.nz)* is also based in Wellington and tours regularly, while the **New Zealand Opera** *(nzopera.com)* calls Auckland home.

Maori Performing Arts: Traditional Maori music and dance are a big part of the tourist experience, most often organized through tour operators in Rotorua. Two of the most accessible and professional troupes perform at **Te Puia** in Rotorua and at the **Auckland Museum.**

To see Maori arts at their best, the **Te Matatini Maori Performing Arts Festival** *(tematatini.co.nz)* is held every other year.

Nightlife: Country pubs can be great places to meet locals or hear bands, but the buzzing nightlife is in the main cities, where bars and clubs party late, particularly Friday and Saturday nights.

AUCKLAND (See also p. 60.) The most popular nightlife precincts are by the waterfront on **Viaduct Basin** spilling over to nearby **Princes Wharf** and at **Britomart** on and behind **Quay St.** At night, waterfront restaurants become bars, many featuring DJs and live music. Another good area for bars and clubs is around **Vulcan Lane/High Street** in the city's heart. **Victoria Street** has **SkyCity Casino** and some sophisticated bars. At the top end of Queen Street, **Karangahape Road** has several music venues, from hip-hop clubs to Irish pubs. The inner suburban strips of **Parnell Road** and particularly **Ponsonby Road** have plenty of chic bars that are very lively on weekends.

WELLINGTON (See also pp. 159–160) **Cuba Street/Courtenay Place** and side streets form the heart of Wellington's ebullient nightlife scene. An evening stroll will turn up a host of bars, clubs, and pubs. The waterfront, particularly **Queens Wharf,** also has some good restaurant/bars.

CHRISTCHURCH (See also sidebar p. 194) Christchurch's nightlife took a battering after the earthquake with suburbs such as Addington providing venues, including relocated **Court Theatre,** but new venues are reopening all the time.

Activities

Blessed with so many glorious landscapes, New Zealand's activities focus on getting up close with nature. Every tourist town has a host of activities and tour operators; local tourist offices will connect you with them.

Adrenaline Activities: New Zealand was one of the first countries to popularize adrenaline activities like bungee jumping, white-water rafting, tandem skydiving, etc., and operators all over the country offer myriad ways to scare yourself witless. For an overview, see p. 252.

Cycling: Bicycle touring has always been popular here but it has a hit a new level, with purpose-built bike trails popping up. The best have been designated Great Rides, known collectively as the New Zealand Cycle Trail, and nzcycletrail.com has full details, including outfitters who will rent you a bike and even pick you up (see pp. 116–117). Trails range from flat off-road jaunts to serious gravel adventures for mountain bikers.

Mountain biking has also taken off big time. Some well-known destinations include Rotorua (Whakarewarewa Forest and Skyline Gravity park), Taupo (Great Lake Trail and Timber Trail), Queenstown (Queenstown Bike Park and Rude Rock), Westport (Old Ghost Road), and Christchurch (Christchurch Adventure Park).

Canoeing & Kayaking: Canoeing the Whanganui River through is so popular that it has been designated as a Great Walk and must be booked through the DOC (doc.govt .nz). The three- to five-day journey can be arranged with operators in Taumarunui, Pipiriki, Ohakune, and Whanganui, who provide all gear, pickup, and drop-off.

The most popular sea-kayaking trip, along the coast of Abel Tasman National Park, can be arranged with operators as a guided trip or by experienced kayakers independently. The DOC website has full details on both these journeys.

Sea kayaking is also very popular in the Marlborough Sounds and especially Fiordland, where operators in Te Anau, Manapouri, and Milford offer spectacular trips on Milford and Doubtful Sounds. Outfitters generally only rent to groups of at least two with some experience.

Fishing: Fish are found in abundance. Rainbow and brown trout and Quinnat salmon thrive in New Zealand lakes and rivers. Lake Taupo and the rivers that flow into it (especially the Tongariro) are famous for trout fishing. Rotorua and South Island destinations such as Lake Brunner are also good for trout. Salmon thrive in the east coast rivers of the South Island. A fishing permit from the DOC (doc.govt.nz) is required; the season runs from October to May. The Bay of Islands and Tutukaka in Northland are the main centers for game fishing, for prizes such as marlin, and deep-sea angling for plenty of tasty fish, including snapper, hapuku, tarakihi, mullet, and blue cod. Kiwis love to fish anywhere, from piers to surf casting from beaches. A license is not required.

Golfing: New Zealand has more than 400 golf courses, reputedly the highest per capita in the world. Top courses include Kauri Cliffs in the Bay of Islands, Cape Kidnappers in Hawke's Bay, and Millbrook near Queenstown. While green fees are high at these exclusive resort courses, fees at local links start as low as NZ$20, averaging around NZ$40 for 18 holes. The New Zealand Golf Guide (nzgolfguide.myshopify.com) provides details.

Horseback Riding: Horseback riding is a popular pastime all over the country. Commercial operators offer riding across farms, forests, and beaches, from one hour to many days, and usually have horses for all abilities. The South Island has high-country riding and backcountry expeditions, particularly in Otago and Canterbury. Riding centers can be found on the West Coast, Mount Cook, Tekapo, Queenstown, and Dunedin. On the North Island, Pakiri Beach and Helensville near Auckland have noted riding centers. Horses can also be rented at Raglan, Rotorua, and other destinations. Visitor centers have details on riding operators, or search *truenz .co.nz/horsetrekking* for trekking centers.

Mountaineering & Rock Climbing:

The Southern Alps have been a training ground for many world-class mountaineers, including Sir Edmund Hillary. Mount Cook and Mount Aspiring National Park are major climbing destinations and the preserve of experienced mountaineers, but Alpine Guides *(tel 03/435-1834, alpineguides.co.nz)* at Mount Cook, Aspiring Guides *(tel 03/443-9422, aspiringguides.com),* and Adventure Consultants *(tel 03/443-8711, adventure consultants.com)* in Wanaka have introductory mountaineering courses.

Top rock-climbing destinations include Port Hills and Castle Hill near Christchurch, Wharepapa near Te Awamutu, and Whanganui Bay near Taupo. The Climb New Zealand website *(climb.co.nz)* has intel on many more sites.

Skiing:

Though snowfields are not as extensive as many in Europe and North America, New Zealand offers spectacular backcountry skiing and the best skiing in the Southern Hemisphere when summer hits El Norte. For a rundown on the main snowfields, see pp. 206–207.

Walking & Hiking:

Walking trails are everywhere and provide a delightful way to appreciate the countryside. Many are easy strolls, suitable for families, though serious and not-so-serious hikes can also be found.

National parks have wonderful hiking, known as tramping in New Zealand, from five-day coastal walks to alpine crossings. The most famous and popular trails are designated as Great Walks, and traffic is limited to protect the environment. Overnighting is assigned to desig-

nated campsites or huts, which must be booked in peak summer season, along with the walks. Longer hikes usually require some experience, and hikers should be self-sufficient in food and water and fully equipped for extreme weather conditions. The two most famous walks are the four-day Milford Track (see pp. 264–265) through Fiordland National Park, and the one-day Tongariro Alpine Crossing (see pp. 136–137) between the volcanoes of Tongariro National Park. Department of Conservation offices in national parks and towns have information on more Great Walks and hundreds of others. The DOC website *(doc.govt.nz)* takes reservations for most Great Walks and provides a host of essential information on tramping.

Water Sports:

With such a long coastline, New Zealanders have a variety of ways to enjoy the sea. Sailing is something of a national obsession, and Auckland, City of Sails, is a good place to arrange a sailing adventure. Sailing operators in the Bay of Islands and Nelson will also take you on the water.

Scuba diving is at its best in the upper half of the North Island, with diving at many sites along the east coast, from the White Island volcano to Goat Island near Leigh, and the Poor Knights Island Marine Reserve near Tutukaka, which has good visibility, rich marine life, and the country's best diving. Good diving can also be found farther north around the Bay of Islands, particularly Three Kings Islands. The South Island also has unique diving, most notably in the sounds of Fiordland, where a freshwater layer atop seawater attracts subtropical, deep-, and shallow-water species to the surface. Milford Sound has the world's biggest population of black coral. Two informative diving websites are *divenewzealand.com* and *nzunderwater.org.nz.*

Raglan on the west coast of the North Island is the country's most renowned surfing destination, but there are plenty of others, including Piha and Muriwai near Auckland, Whangamata on the Coromandel Peninsula, and Gisborne. For surf reports and information on the most popular breaks, check *surf.co.nz.*

INDEX

ILLUSTRATIONS CREDITS

All photographs by Colin Monteath unless otherwise indicated below:
Cover, Stephen Matera/TandemStock.com; spine, Eric Sohn Joo Tan/BIA/Minden Pictures; 2–3, Colin Monteath/Hedgehog House/Minden Pictures; 4, SIME/eStock Photo; 12, Markus Kirchgessner; 14–5, Wilfried Krecichwost/Getty Images; 16, powerofforever/Getty Images; 17, Tony Brunt/Hedgehog House New Zealand; 18, RST/Ian Brodie Photo; 20–21, David Wall/Alamy Stock Photo; 22, Andy Reisinger/Hedgehog House New Zealand; 26–7, Alexander Turnbull Library, Wellington, New Zealand; 28–9, Clive Rose/Getty Images; 30, Popperfoto/Getty Images; 36, Markus Kirchgessner; 42, Dave J Hogan/Getty Images; 46, Nick Groves/Hedgehog House New Zealand; 54, Ian Trower/Robert Harding; 58, Chad Ehlers/Getty Images; 63, Kim Christensen/PhotoNewZealand; 65, Tony Brunt/Hedgehog House New Zealand; 69, Rob Brown/Hedgehog House New Zealand; 70, Peter Morath/Hedgehog House New Zealand; 72, Chris Lee—World Rugby/World Rugby via Getty Images; 82, Courtesy SheepWorld; 90, Alexander Turnbull Library, Wellington, New Zealand; 91, Michael Bradley/Getty Images; 106, iStockphoto.com/Focus_on_Nature; 108, David Wall/Alamy Stock Photo; 110, Alexander Turnbull Library, Wellington, New Zealand; 131, Ross Nolly/Hedgehog House New Zealand; 136, Guy Vickers/Hedgehog House New Zealand; 144, Harley Betts/Hedgehog House New Zealand; 149, Andy Reisinger/Hedgehog House New Zealand; 150, Douglas Houghton/Robert Harding; 157, Maltings Partnership, Derby, England; 160, Stephanie Gunther/Alamy Stock Photo; 164, Dave Hansford/Hedgehog House New Zealand; 166, Graham Charles/Hedgehog House New Zealand; 172, Tony Brunt/Hedgehog House New Zealand; 180, Ingrid Visser/Hedgehog House New Zealand; 181, Richard Caswell/Hedgehog House New Zealand; 183, Graham Charles/Hedgehog House New Zealand; 188, travellight/Shutterstock; 192, Mark Eden/Alamy Stock Photo; 196, AP Images/NZPA, David Wethey; 198, Mike Greenslade/Alamy Stock Photo; 201, Logan Murray/Hedgehog House New Zealand; 218, Michael Runkel/Robert Harding; 230–31, Maltings Partnership, Derby, England; 271, Neil Farrin/AWL Images/Getty Images; 272, John Rendle/Hedgehog House New Zealand.

National Geographic
TRAVELER

New Zealand

THIRD EDITION

Since 1888, the National Geographic Society has
funded more than 12,000 research, exploration, and
preservation projects around the world. National
Geographic Partners distributes a portion of the funds
it receives from your purchase to National Geographic
Society to support programs including the conservation of animals and their habitats.

National Geographic Partners
1145 17th Street NW
Washington, DC 20036-4688 USA

Become a member of National Geographic and
activate your benefits today at natgeo.com/jointoday.

For information about special discounts for bulk
purchases, please contact National Geographic Books
Special Sales: specialsales@natgeo.com

For rights or permissions inquiries, please contact
National Geographic Books Subsidiary Rights:
bookrights@natgeo.com

ISBN: 978-1-4262-1883-5

The information in this book has been carefully
checked and to the best of our knowledge is accurate.
However, details are subject to change, and the
National Geographic publisher cannot be responsible
for such changes, or for errors or omissions. Assess-
ments of sites, hotels, and restaurants are based on the
author's subjective opinions, which do not necessarily
reflect the publisher's opinion.

Printed in Hong Kong

17/THK/1